MATTHEW SARDON

# Hidden Fire

*Unfolding the Parables of Jesus*

THEOSIS
HOUSE
PRESS

First published by Theosis House Press 2025

Copyright © 2025 by Matthew Sardon

All rights reserved. No part of this publication may be reproduced, stored or transmitted in any form or by any means, electronic, mechanical, photocopying, recording, scanning, or otherwise without written permission from the publisher. It is illegal to copy this book, post it to a website, or distribute it by any other means without permission.

Matthew Sardon asserts the moral right to be identified as the author of this work.

First edition

This book was professionally typeset on Reedsy.
Find out more at reedsy.com

"He did not speak to them without a parable, but privately to His own disciples He explained everything."
— Mark 4:34

"In every parable Christ hides Himself like fire beneath the husk."
— Origen, Homilies on Luke

# Contents

*Preface*   iii
Prologue   1
Introduction   4

## I   Kingdom Seed

1. The Kingdom in a Handful of Dust   11
2. The Parable Of The Sower (Mk 4:1–20)   15
3. The Parable Of The Mustard Seed & The Leaven (Mt 13:31–33)   58
4. The Parable Of The Growing Seed (Mk 4:26–29)   105

## II   Mercy and Judgment

5. The Fire That Divides and Heals   153
6. The Good Samaritan (Lk 10:25–37)   157
7. The Unforgiving Servant (Mt 18:21–35)   210
8. The Rich Fool (Lk 12:13–21)   256

## III   Banquets and Invitations

9. The Table of the King   305
10. The Great Banquet (Lk 14:15–24)   309
11. The Wedding Feast / Proper Garment (Mt 22:1–14)   359
12. The Ten Virgins (Mt 25:1–13)   420

Epilogue   474

*Appendix A: The Seven-Fold Framework of Interpretation*     477
*Bibliography*     480
*About the Author*     485

# Preface

The words of Jesus have been spoken so often that we risk hearing them no longer. Familiarity dulls fire. The parables, in particular, have suffered this quiet domestication. They once startled a nation; now they decorate homilies and wall art. Yet when they were first uttered along the hills and shorelines of Galilee, they were nothing less than revolutions in story form—seed-sized detonations of the Kingdom.

This book began as an attempt to hear those stories again as if for the first time. I wanted to stand on that shoreline with the crowd, to feel the weight of the silence after He said, "The Kingdom of God is like...," and to watch how ordinary images—soil, yeast, pearl, banquet—became doors into eternity. The more closely I listened, the more I realised that the parables are not explanations of divine things but divine acts themselves. They do what they describe. They sow, they ferment, they search, they summon.

*Hidden Fire: Unfolding the Parables of Jesus* unfolds across two volumes. This first volume, The Kingdom Revealed, gathers the parables in which Christ unveils the mystery of the Kingdom's arrival—its seed hidden in the field of the world, its banquet prepared for those who will receive it, its light waiting to be kindled in vigilant hearts.

The second volume, The Kingdom Fulfilled, will turn to the parables of judgment, mercy, and fulfilment, where the harvest ripens and love's hidden fire becomes glory. Together they trace the arc from revelation to consummation, from the first word sown to the final feast.

The pages that follow are not meant as a technical commentary, though they rest on the foundations of Scripture, tradition, and the Fathers. They are written in the conviction that theology is best learned on one's knees. Each chapter moves through seven stages—hearing, understanding, interpretation, confrontation, revelation, application, and prayer—because revelation itself moves that way. The goal is not analysis alone but transformation: to let the stories burn through the crust of habit until they ignite love.

Many hands and hearts have steadied this work—teachers whose insight opened Scripture anew, friends whose questions refined the language, and readers who reminded me that every commentary is a form of listening together. I thank them quietly here. Above all, I thank the One whose words still search the human heart with undiminished power.

If these pages kindle even a small flame of that light—if one reader finds the familiar strange again, or hears the voice of Christ behind the story—then the labour has been worth it. For the Word still speaks as He once did, in stories that conceal only to reveal, in riddles that heal what they wound, in parables that still burn with hidden fire.

**Matthew Sardon**

# Prologue

The shoreline was thick with people. Fishermen left their nets, mothers held children on their hips, and the old leaned on staves, squinting against the glare that rose from the lake. The water was glass until a breeze rippled across it, carrying the scent of salt and wet cedar from the boats. Out beyond the shallows, a single craft drifted slightly from shore. In it stood a man.

His voice did not thunder, yet it carried farther than the wind. The sound of it bent through the air like light through water—soft, yet impossible to ignore. He did not speak as the scribes, parsing laws and quotations, but as one who seemed to be reading the secret thoughts of the crowd. Every sentence hung in the air like seed released from the hand of a sower, floating, searching for soil.

"The Kingdom of God is like..."

That phrase again and again, as if language itself were being refashioned around a mystery too vast for plain speech. A farmer went out to sow. A woman hid yeast in three measures of flour. A merchant found a pearl of great price. The people nodded, half-comforted by the familiarity of it—soil, seed, labour, bread. But something in His tone unsettled them. The stories were simple; the silence that followed them was not.

Some turned away, shaking their heads. "Parables," they muttered, "pretty riddles."

Others lingered, restless. A few stood very still, as if afraid that even a breath might cause them to miss whatever was being said beneath the words.

On the edge of the crowd a young man—one who had heard rabbis all his life—found himself pierced by a line about a lamp hidden under a basket. It should have been a trivial saying. Yet the image lodged in him like a splinter of light. He felt, without knowing why, that it demanded something of him.

That was the strange power of this Teacher. He spoke in stories, but the stories spoke back.

Later, the disciples would ask Him why. Why not speak plainly, if the message was so urgent?

"Because," He said, "to you it has been given to know the secrets of the Kingdom, but to them it has not been given." Then He quoted Isaiah: *They look but do not see, they listen but do not understand.* His eyes held sorrow, not contempt. The blindness was chosen, not imposed.

He knew what every prophet before Him had known—that truth offered too nakedly is quickly despised. The parable is a veil of mercy. It hides the flame long enough for the eyes to adjust.

So He kept speaking in the language of the everyday: vines, coins, banquets, shepherds. But beneath every familiar shape was a revelation coiled like fire under ash. When He spoke of a vineyard, Isaiah's lament about Israel's unfruitful vines stirred in the listeners' memories. When He told of a wedding feast, they remembered the prophets' promise of the banquet on God's holy mountain. When He described a father running to embrace his lost son, they felt the ache of David's psalms and Hosea's forgiving love. The past was being rewritten in front of them; Scripture was being fulfilled through story.

Night often fell while He taught. The crowds would dwindle, torches appearing one by one along the shore. The lake turned black, and the last sound was His voice echoing across the water. The disciples, exhausted, could not always keep up with the flood of parables. "Explain it to us," they would plead as they pushed away from the crowd. And He would, gently—turning riddles into revelations, making the invisible visible.

They began to realise that each story was more than teaching. It was self-portrait.

He was the Sower whose seed would fall into the ground and die.

He was the Good Samaritan who would cross the road of heaven to bind human wounds.

He was the Bridegroom whose feast would begin with His own blood poured out.

He was the Shepherd who would shoulder the lost until He collapsed beneath their weight.

Every parable was a glimpse of His own heart, spoken before it was pierced.

In time, the stories would become clearer—after the Cross, after the Resurrection. But even now, under the Galilean sun, their meaning pressed close, waiting. The Word was sowing Himself into the world, line by line.

The crowd began to disperse. The man in the boat stood silent, the wind tugging at His robe. Across the water the hills were beginning to burn with evening light. He looked toward them—toward fields, villages, hearts—and for a moment it seemed as though He was listening to something beyond hearing. Then He spoke again, almost as if to the air itself.

"He who has ears to hear, let him hear."

The words drifted across the lake, settling on every heart like a spark. Some would brush it away. Some would cradle it until it burned.

The stories have not stopped. The wind that carried them that day still moves across the world, stirring dust, whispering through pages, calling the deaf to hear and the blind to see.

And still, upon every shore, He stands and speaks again.

# Introduction

The parables of Jesus are among the most familiar words ever spoken—and the least entered. They hang in memory like coloured glass: luminous from a distance, opaque up close. We quote them easily, but to hear them as they were first heard is another matter. When those words first broke the air of Galilee, they did not decorate sermons; they detonated hearts. Some left comforted, some offended, a few converted for life. The same stories that cradle children in Sunday schools once drew swords in synagogues.

Why such power? Because a parable is not ornament but incarnation. It is the Word taking on the form of story so that eternity can touch time without destroying it. In every parable the divine speaks in the dialect of the dust. Jesus does not illustrate theology; He sows Himself. Each tale of seed or lamp or vineyard is grace in narrative motion—a living word cast into the furrows of human hearing, destined to germinate only in soil broken open by faith.

He said it plainly: "To you it has been given to know the mysteries of the Kingdom of Heaven." The distinction between *to you* and *to them* sounds severe until we recognise mercy within it. Revelation withheld is protection; too much light blinds. The parable is God's veil of compassion—concealment that invites pursuit. As in Eden, the flaming sword still guards the Tree of Life; as in Sinai, the glory remains hidden by cloud. The God who hides does so to be sought, and seeking becomes the form of love.

Modern ears, however, have grown impatient with mystery. We prefer morals to mysteries, principles to parables. We flatten them into slogans: *Be kind like the Samaritan. Be ready like the virgins.* Such lessons are true but partial. A parable is not a proverb but a portal. It opens from history into eternity, from the ordinary into the infinite. The Greek *parabolē* and the Hebrew *mashal* both mean more than "story." They name riddles, comparisons, even confrontations—moments when divine wisdom bends down to our level and still leaves us dazzled.

Listen closely and you can hear prophecy echoing behind every line. The prophets spoke in images because Israel had grown deaf to commands. Ezekiel's bones, Hosea's marriage, Isaiah's vineyard—each wrapped judgment and mercy in symbol so that the heart might feel before it understands. Jesus stands in that lineage. He is the final prophet who speaks not about God but as God, continuing the divine habit of hiding glory inside grain and yeast.

## The Rhythm of Unfolding

Revelation always moves in stages—seed to sprout, sprout to flame. Each chapter follows that sacred rhythm.

**The Word Spoken** restores the moment of origin—the sound, setting, and atmosphere in which the parable was first heard. The aim is not retelling but re-hearing.

**The Surface Story** rebuilds the first-century world that made the parable intelligible: its economics, customs, and tensions. Grace begins in realism.

**The Hidden Fire** draws back the veil of Scripture itself. Here the imagery, language, and theology are examined in four movements—textual, theological, typological, and patristic—so that the seed's inner pattern is revealed.

**The Shock and the Turn** exposes the reversal that once startled the crowd—the moral or prophetic sting that makes the parable dangerous.

**The Revelation in the Son** gathers every thread into Christ. Each parable, rightly read, is an icon of Him: the Sower, the Samaritan, the Shepherd, the Judge.

**The Word for Our Age** opens the eternal meaning into the present moment, allowing the ancient light to fall on modern idols.

**Hearing that Becomes Doing** leads the reader into prayer, where exegesis becomes encounter and understanding flowers into obedience.

This sevenfold movement mirrors salvation history itself—creation, covenant, prophecy, incarnation, mission, conversion, and sanctification. The pattern is not mechanical but liturgical. Every parable passes through these stages because revelation always passes through them.

### Four Interpretive Lights

Within that rhythm, four lights guide interpretation.

**Historical realism.** The Word became flesh within a culture—under Roman taxation, among tenant farmers, within Jewish law. Without that world the edge of the parables dulls. A Samaritan helping a Jew, a father granting inheritance early, a landowner paying all workers alike—each carried social scandal. To recover those conditions is to feel the gospel's first shock.

**Scriptural typology.** Jesus never spoke in isolation. Every image He used blooms from Israel's soil. Seeds recall creation's first command, *"Let the earth bring forth."* Vineyards echo Isaiah's song of the beloved but faithless vineyard. Banquets look ahead to the wedding feast of Zion. By tracing these roots we watch the Old Testament come to flower in the New; the parables are the flowering of the whole covenant story.

**Patristic insight.** The early Fathers read these stories with hearts trained by worship. Origen saw the Samaritan as Christ stooping to bind Adam's wounds. Augustine heard in the Prodigal Son the melody of sin and return. Chrysostom turned each image into moral surgery; Ephrem sang them into hymns of light. Their voices remind us that interpretation is an act of communion across centuries.

INTRODUCTION

**Contemporary resonance.** The parables are perennial because the human heart is. Our thorns are distractions, our barns are securities, our far country is the cult of self. Each generation must let these stories read its own idols. The Kingdom they announce still presses against our closed gates.

## The Purpose of Hearing

Beyond structure and method lies encounter. Scripture is not a museum of sacred sayings; it is a living field still trembling with the Sower's footsteps. The reader must therefore approach as hearer, not spectator. The first act of interpretation is attention. Each story is a mirror that refuses to stay flat. You will find yourself inside it before you realise it—sometimes as hero, sometimes as fool, often as both. The parables diagnose the soul by narrative; they teach through recognition.

To stand before them is to stand before fire. Too close, and pride burns; too far, and warmth is lost. The right distance is prayer: humility that lets light reveal and purify. When Jesus says, *"He who has ears to hear, let him hear,"* He is not rewarding intelligence but inviting surrender. Hearing, in Scripture, is covenantal obedience—*Shema Yisrael*—a listening that becomes doing. That is the hearing this book seeks to awaken.

## The Divine Pattern

From the beginning, God has chosen ordinary things as bearers of His glory. He spoke through soil and breath in Genesis, through bush and cloud in Exodus, through bread and wine in the Upper Room. The parables continue that sacramental pattern: heaven translated into the language of earth. They begin in dust and end in glory. Their power lies in proportion—the infinite compressed into the finite until it bursts into flame.

To read them as revelation is to enter that same miracle of compression. The Word that created the world still creates faith; the stories that once tilled Galilean hearts now till ours. Empires have fallen, languages died, but the parables keep working like leaven—silent and unstoppable. They address what never changes: the contest between grace and refusal. They remain young because truth never ages.

In a culture that mistakes information for illumination, these small stories still whisper eternity. They do not shout above the world's noise; they outlast it. One line—*"The Kingdom of God is like a mustard seed"*—contains more theology than volumes of commentary because it is theology spoken by the Theologian Himself. It does not lecture; it reveals.

This, then, is the task of *Hidden Fire*: to listen until the stories live again, to stand within their radiance until they burn away the crust of familiarity. Scholarship serves wonder; exegesis opens to adoration. The destination is not explanation but transfiguration.

So come as listener and as field. Let the Sower speak. The same wind that carried His voice across Galilee still moves across these pages, scattering seed, searching for hearts that will receive it.

Every story begins as sound.

Every sound hides a seed.

Every seed waits to burn.

*He who has ears to hear, let him hear*

# I

# Kingdom Seed

*"The kingdom of God is as if a man should scatter seed upon the ground..." (Mk 4:26)*

# 1

# The Kingdom in a Handful of Dust

Every covenant God makes begins small. The first word of creation—"Let there be light"—was itself a seed, spoken into the soil of chaos. From that single utterance, worlds unfolded. So it is again when the Word walks the fields of Galilee. He stoops, hand open, scattering what looks like nothing: grains that fall, vanish, and wait. Yet within each lies the same divine pattern that shaped the cosmos—life given through surrender, fruit born from hiddenness.

The Kingdom starts where sight ends. No banners, no armies, only seed and soil. But this quiet scene gathers the whole story of salvation: God speaking, creation receiving, history germinating under His breath. What the prophets announced as a new springtime, what Israel longed for in exile, now begins with a peasant's gesture on the hillside.

The first parables of Jesus dwell here, at the threshold of growth. They teach that divine power enters history not by conquest but by cultivation. The Sower's generosity, the seed's mystery, the soil's response—these are the grammar of grace. The Kingdom does not crash into the world; it seeps through it. The Almighty chooses the rhythm of agriculture, not the shock of empire. Heaven's revolution sounds like wind through wheat.

Each image—Sower, Mustard Seed, Leaven, Growing Seed—reveals an aspect of that slow miracle. The Sower discloses the initiative of divine mercy, sowing without calculation. The Mustard Seed shows the disproportion between small beginnings and vast fulfilment. The Leaven unveils transformation from within, holiness fermenting through ordinary life. The Growing Seed reminds us that grace ripens beyond our sight or control. Together they compose the overture of the Gospel: hidden life pressing toward harvest.

In Scripture the language of seed always carries covenant beneath it. To Abraham God promised, "In your seed all nations shall be blessed." Israel herself was called God's vineyard; the Torah was rain that watered her soil. When Isaiah sang that God's word "shall not return empty," he was describing this same divine ecology—speech that becomes substance, promise that becomes people. By the time Jesus speaks, the ground has been prepared for centuries. The Word made flesh is now the Sower sowing Himself.

That is the scandalous beauty of these beginnings. He does not merely teach about the Kingdom; He plants it in His own person. Each syllable He utters carries His life within it. Soon He will enter the earth as seed in a deeper sense—buried in death so that the field of the world might bloom with resurrection. The parables of growth are therefore prophetic: they whisper of Calvary's furrow and Easter's first green shoot.

The soil, too, bears mystery. Divine speech has creative power, yet it consents to need human receptivity. God sows with risk. Perfect seed lands on imperfect ground. Some hearts are path, some rock, some thorn, some good earth. Still, He casts the Word everywhere, for mercy is extravagant. Heaven counts not efficiency but faithfulness. The divine Farmer would rather waste seed on stone than withhold grace from anyone.

Every act of hearing becomes an act of cultivation. To hear is to plough; to believe is to soften; to bear fruit is to let the Word reshape the soil within. Revelation demands cooperation. The Word desires hospitality. Creation's first command—"Let the earth bring forth"—echoes again in every disciple who lets grace take root.

For those who first listened by the lake, this was both familiar and frightening. They knew what it meant to sow into risk: droughts that ruined, birds that stole, weeds that choked. Jesus took their daily vulnerability and made it a theology of trust. The Kingdom, He said, grows of itself—*automatos*—the hidden patience of God bringing harvest in its time. The farmer sleeps and rises; the earth yields silently. So too does the soul in grace. Sanctity is not manufactured; it is received.

The modern ear resists such slowness. We live by speed, proof, and spectacle. We want the Kingdom to appear measurable, immediate, impressive. But God still works by the older rhythm—the humility of process. The seed must die to live. Faith grows downward before it grows upward. What matters most happens beneath the surface: repentance, endurance, prayer in secret. The Church herself lives by that same mystery; she is the field where eternity germinates unseen.

To read these opening parables, then, is to learn again how God acts. His power hides in patience. His glory dwells in the ordinary. He entrusts infinite life to handfuls of dust. The wonder is not that He can make worlds, but that He prefers to begin again in our smallness. The seed that built galaxies now waits for welcome in human hearts.

This first part of *Hidden Fire* follows that path of divine humility. Each chapter will trace how the Word descends into the soil of creation and rises again as faith, hope, and charity. The movement is always the same: sowing, waiting, harvest. The voice that once thundered on Sinai now speaks in parables beside the sea, inviting not fear but fruitfulness. The Kingdom does not demand brilliance; it asks for good earth.

Before you begin, pause as the crowd once did. Feel the afternoon warmth of Galilee, the hush before the Sower's hand moves. Dust hangs in the air, sunlight glints off water, and somewhere a child laughs. Then—sound and silence together—the seed leaves His fingers. The Kingdom begins again in that instant.

It still does. The Word falls whenever Scripture is read, whenever mercy is shown, whenever prayer breaks the crust of habit. It falls into homes, into cities, into hearts that barely know they are listening. Some will receive it, many will not, yet the Sower keeps sowing. His patience is the pulse of history, His generosity its hope.

Kneel beside Him now. Touch the soil of your own heart. Listen for the rustle of grace in the wind. The field is ready; the Sower's hand is lifted.

The Kingdom of God is near—hidden in a handful of earth, alive with eternal spring.

# 2

# The Parable Of The Sower (Mk 4:1–20)

*Again, he began to teach beside the sea. Such a very large crowd gathered around him that he got into a boat on the sea and sat there, while the whole crowd was beside the sea on the land. He began to teach them many things in parables, and in his teaching, he said to them: "Listen! A sower went out to sow. And as he sowed, some seed fell on the path, and the birds came and ate it up. Other seed fell on rocky ground, where it did not have much soil, and it sprang up quickly, since it had no depth of soil. And when the sun rose, it was scorched; and since it had no root, it withered away. Other seed fell among thorns, and the thorns grew up and choked it, and it yielded no grain. Other seed fell into good soil and brought forth grain, growing up and increasing and yielding thirty and sixty and a hundredfold." And he said, "Let anyone with ears to hear listen!"*

*When he was alone, those who were around him along with the twelve asked him about the parables. And he said to them, "To you has been given the secret of the kingdom of God, but for those outside, everything comes in parables; in order that 'They may indeed look, but not perceive, and may indeed listen, but not understand; so that they may not turn again and be forgiven." And he said to them, "Do you not understand this parable? Then how will you understand all the parables? The sower sows the word. These are the ones on the path where the word is sown: when they hear, Satan immediately comes and takes away the word that is sown in them. And these are the ones sown on rocky ground: when they hear the word, they immediately receive it with joy. But they have no root, and endure only for a while; then, when trouble or persecution arises on account of the word, immediately they fall away. And others are those sown among the thorns: these are the ones who hear the word, but the cares of the world, and the lure of wealth, and the desire for other things come in and choke the word, and it yields nothing. And these are the ones sown on the good soil: they hear the word and accept it and bear fruit, thirty and sixty and a hundredfold."*

## The Word Spoken

The morning light over Galilee carries that fine, silver haze that blurs the distance between water and sky. The lake lies still, reflecting the hills that rise like ancient shoulders around it. Fishermen are drawing their boats in after a night's work; ropes creak, nets slap wetly against hulls. The air smells of cedar tar and the faint sweetness of crushed reeds. Along the curve of the shoreline, people begin to gather—first in twos and threes, then by the dozens. A whisper moves through them: *He is here.*

Jesus stands near the edge of the surf, surrounded by His disciples. The crowd is already too dense to move freely. Some climb the slopes for a better view; others sit where they are, the sand spilling over their feet. The variety is astonishing—Galilean farmers with sun-cracked hands, tax collectors in fine cloaks, women with infants wrapped against their chests, and a few Pharisees whose restraint cannot conceal curiosity. The rumours have ripened into expectation. Here is the one who healed the leper, who made the paralytic walk, who forgave sins. But here too is the one who affronted the scribes, who touched the unclean, who spoke of new wine bursting old skins. The atmosphere is charged, like air before rain.

He looks out toward the water, then steps into a small boat moored nearby. A fisherman steadies the bow as Jesus seats Himself—the gesture of a rabbi assuming authority. The crowd hushes. The lake will carry His voice better than any synagogue; the wind off the water makes a perfect amphitheatre. The men in front shade their eyes. Children lean forward on their elbows. The only sound is the rhythmic lick of waves against the pebbles.

Mark's narrative catches this hinge of revelation. Conflict has been mounting—accusations of blasphemy, murmurs of conspiracy. Jesus has withdrawn from the villages not in retreat but in recalibration. The moment demands a new mode of speech. Direct teaching has provoked hostility; now He will speak in parables—truth in story-form, revelation that hides itself in plain sight. It is not evasion but invitation, a sifting of listeners. The same word that enlightens the open will bewilder the closed.

He looks across the multitude—faces turned upward, hands shading brows—and begins with a single command that slices through the morning air: "Listen!" *Akouete*. The imperative rings like a bell over the water. To a Jewish ear it recalls the *Shema*: "Hear, O Israel." The crowd stills further. He waits until the tension tightens to silence. Then He says, "Behold, a sower went out to sow."

The sentence drops like seed into the stillness. The image is instantly familiar. Every farmer there has done the same—walked his furrows with a pouch at his side, casting grain from a practiced swing of the arm. They picture him now: silhouette against the hill, stride steady, dust rising behind. In the folds of the crowd, heads nod. They can almost feel the weight of the seed-bag on their hips, the grit on their palms.

"As he sowed, some seed fell along the path," Jesus says, "and the birds came and devoured it." Even as He speaks, starlings flicker above the waterline, dipping low and vanishing toward the fields. "Other seed fell on rocky ground, where it had not much soil; and immediately it sprang up, since it had no depth of earth. And when the sun rose, it was scorched, and because it had no root, it withered away."

The listeners squint against the actual sun now climbing above the ridge. They know that heat, know the thin crust of soil that hides limestone beneath. They can see the tender green dying before noon. The realism anchors the rhythm of His voice.

"Other seed fell among thorns," He continues, "and the thorns grew up and choked it, and it yielded no grain." At the edge of the crowd, thistles rustle in the breeze. A few men glance toward them, uneasy with how close the picture cuts.

"And other seed fell into good soil and brought forth grain, growing up and increasing and yielding thirtyfold and sixtyfold and a hundredfold."

A murmur spreads. Such yield is beyond their experience. Even the best Galilean field might give tenfold in a good year. Yet the calm certainty in His tone leaves no sense of exaggeration. He speaks of divine arithmetic—excess that only heaven could measure. He pauses, letting the words sink like rain into earth.

Then the closing refrain: "He who has ears to hear, let him hear."

The phrase feels both invitation and verdict. Some smile at the simple wisdom; others frown, waiting for explanation that does not come. He does not elaborate. He lets the silence do the work. It is the first act of discernment—who will ponder, who will forget.

The crowd begins to stir again. A boy throws a pebble into the shallows. A woman wipes her child's brow. The Pharisees whisper among themselves. Jesus rises, motions to the boatman, and they drift closer to shore. He steps onto the wet sand, the hem of His robe darkened by water. The parable is over, yet the meaning has only begun.

The crowd disperses slowly, reluctant to leave. Some discuss yields and soil, convinced He has offered farming advice. Others linger, troubled by a sense that something vast has been spoken in miniature. A few scoff quietly—this, from the miracle worker?—and turn toward the market road. The shoreline empties, leaving only footprints in the wet sand and the hush of retreating water.

Later, as dusk drapes the hills, Jesus walks with the Twelve along the water's edge. The lake has turned to bronze, and the first lamps of Capernaum flicker on the far side. They find a place where reeds whisper, and sit. The disciples are silent for a while, turning over the words they've heard a hundred times before in fields of their own youth. Yet they feel there is more—something hidden beneath the surface of the story, like roots beneath the soil.

Peter breaks the silence. "Rabbi," he says, "why do You speak to them in parables?"

Jesus looks across the darkening water. The reflection of the sky wavers like molten glass. "To you has been given the mystery of the Kingdom of God," He says, "but for those outside, everything comes in parables." His tone is not exclusion but mercy: revelation measured to readiness. He quotes Isaiah—"seeing they may see, and not perceive; hearing they may hear, and not understand"—and the words fall with the quiet authority of ancient truth. The others listen, understanding only that the world has been divided not by creed or class, but by the capacity to hear.

A breeze rises, carrying the scent of damp earth. Jesus crouches, takes a handful of soil, and lets it run through His fingers. "Do you not understand this parable?" He asks softly. "How then will you understand all the parables?" The gesture itself is explanation: seed, earth, hand, word—all one movement.

He speaks then in the slow cadence of evening, explaining what dawn had only hinted: the seed is the Word, the soils are hearts, the growth is grace working in secret. The disciples listen as if the ground itself were opening. The mystery is not about farming; it is about the way God enters the world—quietly, vulnerably, waiting for reception. The Kingdom will not break in like empire but will germinate in obscurity, rising only in those willing to be tilled.

When He finishes, they sit for a long time without speech. The waves lap against the stones; a heron moves through the reeds. Somewhere down the coast, a fisherman's torch wavers over the water like a wandering star. Jesus stands, brushing the dust from His hands. The handful of soil He held moments before now lies scattered at His feet, indistinguishable from the rest.

"Come," He says. They follow Him back toward the village path. Behind them, the lake holds the last light of the day; ahead, the hills deepen into shadow. The parable He spoke that morning is already taking root—in their memory, in their questions, in the soil of time itself.

None of them can yet see how far the harvest will reach. For now, it is enough that the Word has been sown. Somewhere beneath the surface, unseen and unstoppable, the Kingdom has begun to grow.

## The Surface Story

In the hills and plains of Galilee, the rhythm of life was agricultural. The seasons dictated not just work but worship. Rain meant survival, and the drought of one year could shadow the next. The people Jesus spoke to that morning lived close to the earth; their faith was sown and reaped with their fields. They knew the patience of waiting for growth that could not be hurried. The parable of the Sower begins in that world—familiar, hard, and holy.

When Jesus begins, "A sower went out to sow," no one hears allegory. They see a man walking his land with a leather pouch hanging from one shoulder, scattering seed by hand in even sweeps. The movement is deliberate, almost liturgical. Each toss arcs in sunlight, seed catching the air before vanishing into soil. This is the Galilean way: broadcast sowing, seed scattered across unploughed earth before being turned under with a crude wooden plough. It is work done with trust. Once thrown, the seed is beyond retrieval. It must rest in darkness and wait for what the heavens decide.

The land itself was patchwork. No farmer owned broad, enclosed estates; most worked small terraces cut into the slopes. Paths ran through the fields where neighbours walked and animals passed, compacting the soil into hard clay. Beneath the surface lay bands of limestone—too shallow for roots, yet near enough to deceive the eye with quick, green growth. Thorns clustered at the edges of every plot, their roots ancient and stubborn. The Galilean farmer knew all this before he cast a single handful of grain. Still, he sowed. He had to. Without seed, there could be no harvest, and without harvest, no bread.

The listeners that morning understood every detail of this scene. They could feel the tension between generosity and waste. A sower who cast too narrowly risked starvation; one who cast too widely invited loss. The birds would come, quick and clever, following the movement of his arm.

## THE PARABLE OF THE SOWER (MK 4:1-20)

The wind might take the lighter grains. Rocks, weeds, and time would do the rest. Farming in that climate was always a negotiation with failure. When Jesus spoke of seed falling on four kinds of ground, He was not crafting symbolism; He was describing life as they knew it. Every harvest began with faith in what might not survive.

He describes the four outcomes with the precision of someone who has watched them happen. The first seed lands on the path—hard as stone from countless footsteps. It never penetrates. Birds descend immediately. The image is common and pitiless; no one needs explanation. The second falls on rocky soil, where a thin layer of dust covers slabs of limestone. The grain sprouts fast in the warmth, looks promising, then withers under the midday sun. The third finds better soil but shares it with thorns that grow faster and stronger, choking everything else. Only the fourth—somehow, somewhere—finds deep, clean earth. There it grows and multiplies beyond measure.

The realism of the picture holds the crowd. They are not thinking of doctrine but of their own hands and hopes. They know this field. They have walked it, cursed its stones, rejoiced at its fruit. The pattern of the parable mirrors the pattern of their lives—much labour, much loss, occasional abundance. Yet there is something unusual here. No farmer expects one seed to yield thirtyfold, let alone sixty or a hundred. Even tenfold would make a man bless God aloud. But Jesus names a harvest that breaks arithmetic. In their world, such fertility signals divine favour. Isaac once "reaped a hundredfold" and the text adds immediately, "the Lord blessed him" (Gen 26:12). That blessing had marked the continuation of the covenant—the seed of Abraham multiplying as promised. To speak of such a yield is to invoke the language of God's abundance, the measure of His mercy.

The crowd feels it, even if they cannot name it. Jesus has taken the most ordinary act of their day and turned it into a vision of overflowing plenty. They sense that the story is about more than grain, but they stay with what they know. Farming itself had always carried sacred weight in Israel's imagination. The rhythm of sowing and reaping echoed through their

Scriptures. The psalmist sang, "Those who sow in tears shall reap with shouts of joy" (Ps 126:5). Hosea urged, "Sow for yourselves righteousness, reap steadfast love" (Hos 10:12). The prophets spoke of the Lord Himself as the one who plants His people in the land. Even judgment was described as failed harvest. To speak of seed and soil was to speak of covenant—of what God gives and how His people receive it.

At this literal level, the parable would have struck the ears as comfort and challenge in equal measure. There is no trick, no villain, no moral contest. The world of the story is stable, predictable, earthy. Yet it hums with an undercurrent of divine proportion. What farmer does not dream of a harvest beyond his own labour? What hearer, weary of drought and debt, does not long for a word of increase? Jesus gives them that hope, yet cloaked in such simplicity that the proud can dismiss it. He leaves them with the image of a man who keeps casting seed across every kind of ground, indifferent to odds. It is the realism of a farmer and the generosity of something greater.

The structure itself would have felt familiar. Rabbinic teachers often taught through triads and contrasts, but here Jesus expands to four—a completeness that suggests wholeness rather than choice. The sower does not select his ground; he sows across the whole. The sequence—path, rock, thorns, good soil—moves inward, from exposure to depth, from failure to fruit. It is as though the field is not only geography but a mirror of the human condition. Yet that layer of reflection remains beneath the surface. On the plain level, the message is agricultural realism: some seed fails, some thrives, and the harvest belongs to God.

For His listeners, the story also fits the moment. Galilee in that period was under heavy tax pressure. Many small farmers had lost land to debt collectors; Roman estates and Herodian administrators claimed the best fields. The people were tenants and labourers now, sowing for others. The sight of a man scattering seed would have stirred both longing and lament—a memory of independence, an image of hope. The sower's persistence in the face of loss would have sounded almost heroic. In a world governed by scarcity, to keep sowing freely was itself an act of faith.

As the story ends, there is no explanation, no conclusion—just the echo of that final exhortation: "He who has ears to hear, let him hear." It lingers like a refrain from the psalms, demanding not reaction but remembrance. The people turn away with the story lodged in them like seed in soil. Some feel its comfort; others feel its sting. A few understand nothing at all. Yet the simplicity of the image ensures it will stay. They will recall it at the next sowing season, when birds gather and the sun burns their backs. They will remember a teacher by the lake who spoke of their fields and left them wondering whose seed they themselves might be.

At this level—the surface story—everything remains concrete. The sower is a man of the earth; the seed is literal grain; the soils are the stubborn realities of a world where blessing and barrenness coexist. It is a scene of ordinary grace, drawn from life's hardest labour. The story belongs entirely to the world of human effort and natural process, yet within it glimmers the familiar logic of God: life proceeding through loss, abundance rising from what disappears. The farmer does not command the harvest; he trusts it. The earth gives according to its kind, and heaven decides the yield.

For the crowd on that morning, this is the whole meaning. A parable about patience, about labour without guarantee, about faith in what is sown. It honours the dignity of work and the dependence of every creature upon the Creator's seasons. They leave the shore thinking they have heard an agricultural proverb, but the field in their minds has already begun to change. The next rain will remind them. The next sprouting green will look different. The next harvest, however small, will carry the memory of that voice by the lake.

The Kingdom has not yet been named, but its cadence has entered their ears. The Sower has begun His work.

## The Hidden Fire

### a) Text, Translation, and Literary Context
### Greek (Mark 4:3):

Καὶ πάλιν ἤρξατο διδάσκειν παρὰ τὴν θάλασσαν· καὶ συνάγεται πρὸς αὐτὸν ὄχλος πλεῖστος, ὥστε αὐτὸν εἰς πλοῖον ἐμβάντα καθῆσθαι ἐν τῇ θαλάσσῃ, καὶ πᾶς ὁ ὄχλος πρὸς τὴν θάλασσαν ἐπὶ τῆς γῆς ἦσαν. Καὶ ἐδίδασκεν αὐτοὺς ἐν παραβολαῖς πολλά, καὶ ἔλεγεν αὐτοῖς ἐν τῇ διδαχῇ αὐτοῦ·

Ἀκούετε· ἰδοὺ ἐξῆλθεν ὁ σπείρων τοῦ σπεῖραι· καὶ ἐγένετο ἐν τῷ σπείρειν, ὃ μὲν ἔπεσεν παρὰ τὴν ὁδόν, καὶ ἦλθεν τὰ πετεινὰ καὶ κατέφαγεν αὐτό. Ἄλλο δὲ ἔπεσεν ἐπὶ τὸ πετρῶδες, ὅπου οὐκ εἶχεν γῆν πολλήν, καὶ εὐθὺς ἐξανέτειλεν διὰ τὸ μὴ ἔχειν βάθος γῆς· καὶ ὅτε ἀνέτειλεν ὁ ἥλιος ἐκαυματίσθη, καὶ διὰ τὸ μὴ ἔχειν ῥίζαν ἐξηράνθη. Ἄλλο δὲ ἔπεσεν εἰς τὰς ἀκάνθας, καὶ ἀνέβησαν αἱ ἄκανθαι καὶ συνέπνιξαν αὐτό, καὶ καρπὸν οὐκ ἔδωκεν. Καὶ ἄλλα ἔπεσεν εἰς τὴν γῆν τὴν καλήν, καὶ ἐδίδου καρπὸν ἀναβαίνοντα καὶ αὐξανόμενον, καὶ ἔφερεν εἰς τριάκοντα καὶ εἰς ἑξήκοντα καὶ εἰς ἑκατόν. Καὶ ἔλεγεν· Ὃς ἔχει ὦτα ἀκούειν ἀκουέτω.

Καὶ ὅτε ἐγένετο κατὰ μόνας, ἠρώτων αὐτὸν οἱ περὶ αὐτὸν σὺν τοῖς δώδεκα τὰς παραβολάς. Καὶ ἔλεγεν αὐτοῖς· Ὑμῖν τὸ μυστήριον δέδοται τῆς βασιλείας τοῦ Θεοῦ· ἐκείνοις δὲ τοῖς ἔξω ἐν παραβολαῖς τὰ πάντα γίνεται, ἵνα βλέποντες βλέπωσιν καὶ μὴ ἴδωσιν, καὶ ἀκούοντες ἀκούωσιν καὶ μὴ συνιῶσιν, μήποτε ἐπιστρέψωσιν καὶ ἀφεθῇ αὐτοῖς.

Καὶ λέγει αὐτοῖς· Οὐκ οἴδατε τὴν παραβολὴν ταύτην; καὶ πῶς πάσας τὰς παραβολὰς γνώσεσθε;

Ὁ σπείρων τὸν λόγον σπείρει.  Οὗτοι δέ εἰσιν οἱ παρὰ τὴν ὁδὸν ὅπου σπείρεται ὁ λόγος· καὶ ὅταν ἀκούσωσιν, εὐθὺς ἔρχεται ὁ Σατανᾶς καὶ αἴρει τὸν λόγον τὸν ἐσπαρμένον εἰς αὐτούς. Καὶ οὗτοι ὁμοίως εἰσὶν οἱ ἐπὶ τὰ πετρώδη σπειρόμενοι, οἳ ὅταν ἀκούσωσιν τὸν λόγον εὐθὺς μετὰ χαρᾶς λαμβάνουσιν· καὶ οὐκ ἔχουσιν ῥίζαν ἐν ἑαυτοῖς ἀλλὰ πρόσκαιροί εἰσιν· εἶτα γενομένης θλίψεως ἢ διωγμοῦ διὰ τὸν λόγον εὐθὺς σκανδαλίζονται. Καὶ ἄλλοι εἰσὶν οἱ εἰς τὰς ἀκάνθας σπειρόμενοι· οὗτοί εἰσιν οἱ τὸν λόγον ἀκούσαντες, καὶ αἱ μέριμναι τοῦ αἰῶνος καὶ ἡ ἀπάτη τοῦ πλούτου καὶ αἱ περὶ τὰ λοιπὰ ἐπιθυμίαι εἰσπορευόμεναι συμπνίγουσιν τὸν λόγον, καὶ ἄκαρπος γίνεται. Καὶ ἐκεῖνοί εἰσιν οἱ ἐπὶ τὴν καλὴν γῆν σπαρέντες, οἳ ἀκούουσιν τὸν λόγον καὶ παραδέχονται καὶ καρποφοροῦσιν, εἰς τριάκοντα καὶ εἰς ἑξήκοντα καὶ εἰς ἑκατόν.

Mark introduces the Parable of the Sower at a hinge-point in his Gospel.

## THE PARABLE OF THE SOWER (MK 4:1–20)

Jesus has already healed, exorcised, and taught with authority; the crowds are swelling, but understanding is thinning. Chapter 4 opens with a scene that dramatizes this tension. He teaches "again by the sea," sitting in a boat while the multitude lines the shore—a physical image of separation between revelation and response. What follows is the first of several "parables of the kingdom," yet Mark treats it as foundational. When Jesus later asks, "Do you not understand this parable? How then will you understand all the parables?" (v. 13), He makes it clear that this story is the key to decoding every other word He will speak about the Kingdom.

The vocabulary is deceptively simple. The opening imperative, ἀκούετε (akouete)—"listen"—is the same verb that begins Israel's daily confession, the *Shema*: "Hear, O Israel" (Deut 6 : 4). Mark's Greek preserves that covenantal resonance. To hear is to obey; to obey is to enter communion. The Sower's word will test whether Israel still knows how to listen. Immediately Jesus adds ἰδού (idou)—"behold"—marrying ear and eye. Revelation engages both senses: hearing calls to faith, sight to recognition. These twin verbs set the theological rhythm of the parable—faith comes through hearing, but understanding requires seeing with the heart.

The decisive motion that follows—ἐξῆλθεν ὁ σπείρων τοῦ σπεῖραι (exēlthen ho speirōn tou speirai), "the sower went out to sow"—uses the aorist *exēlthen*, a verb Mark often employs to mark divine initiative. The Sower "goes out" as God once went forth to create and to call Abraham. The infinitive *speirai* ("to sow") reveals the purpose of this procession: He goes out in order to give life. In covenant language, God's Word always moves outward before it gathers inward. This is not agricultural routine but the liturgy of divine generosity.

The parable's structure falls into four movements defined by prepositions: *para* tēn hodon ("beside the path"), *epi* ta petrōdē ("upon the rocky places"), *eis* tas akanthas ("into the thorns"), and *epi* tēn kalēn gēn ("upon the good soil"). Mark's sequence is more than geography; it is a moral topography of the heart. Each preposition marks a deeper or shallower level of reception. What lies "beside" the path never truly encounters the Word. What rests "upon" rock receives it briefly but superficially. What falls "into" thorns is trapped within competing loves. Only what lands "upon good soil" finds rest and depth—the restoration of right relationship.

The repetition of *ho men... allon de... allon de... alla de...* ("some... others... others... others") creates a liturgical rhythm of offering. The Sower's act remains constant; variation occurs only in the soil. This is covenant drama in miniature: God's fidelity meets human freedom. The narrative's verb pattern reinforces this theology. The seed *falls (epesen), is devoured (katephagen), springs up (exaneteilen), withers (exēranthē), is choked (synepnixan),* and finally *bears fruit (karpophorei).* Each verb embodies a possible history of the Word in the soul—loss, promise, frustration, fulfilment.

Mark ends the parable proper with a call: Ὃς ἔχει ὦτα ἀκούειν ἀκουέτω (hos echei ōta akouein akouetō), "Whoever has ears to hear, let him hear." It is less exhortation than revelation. Hearing itself is gift; ears that can hear are grace-formed organs. Throughout Scripture, Israel's tragedy is not deafness of body but hardness of heart. The Sower speaks to awaken that inner faculty by which covenant love becomes fruitful.

Verses 10–12 place the parable within Mark's theology of mystery. When the disciples question Him privately, Jesus distinguishes between those to whom "the mystery (*mystērion*) of the kingdom of God has been given" and those "outside" (*tois exō*). The *mystērion* is not a secret code but a divine plan formerly hidden and now revealed—what Paul will later call "the plan for the fullness of time" (Eph 1 : 10). Yet its revelation divides humanity. The same light that illumines some blinds others. Mark quotes Isaiah 6 : 9–10 to show that this concealment is itself part of judgment: the Word respects freedom by letting resistance remain opaque. The parable therefore performs what it proclaims. It is both invitation and sieve.

Jesus' subsequent explanation (vv 13–20) transforms each soil into a human response. The seed is explicitly called "the Word" (*ho logos*), linking the story to the creative speech of Genesis and the personal Word who will become flesh. The four terrains correspond to four spiritual postures.

– The path represents the unguarded heart where evil swiftly seizes what was heard. The verb *airei* ("snatches away") evokes the theft of grace.

– The rocky soil describes impulsive faith that lacks interior root. The phrase *ou ekhousin rhizan en heautois* ("they have no root in themselves") defines immaturity as dependence on surface emotion rather than covenant endurance.

– The thorns recall Genesis 3 : 18, the curse of toil and anxiety. Mark's triad—cares, riches, desires—names the modern pantheon of false gods.

– The good soil receives, retains, and multiplies. Mark's triple yield—thirty, sixty, a hundredfold—is a covenant formula for superabundance, echoing Isaac's harvest in Genesis 26 : 12 and signalling restoration of Edenic fruitfulness.

Literarily, Mark places this parable at the centre of a chiastic sequence of revelation and rejection (4 : 1–34). Around it swirl stories of opposition, misunderstanding, and eventual faith. The Sower's seed is being scattered not only within the narrative but through it—landing on Pharisees, disciples, and crowds alike. The Word He sows will culminate in another field: the hill outside Jerusalem where His body, the true grain, will be buried to bear the hundredfold of resurrection.

In translation, then, the simplicity of Mark's Greek conceals an intricate theology of covenant renewal. The verbs of motion show divine generosity; the prepositions trace human depth; the nouns—*logos*, *gē*, *karpos*—reveal creation's vocation to receive and return love. The parable is not merely instruction about evangelization but a revelation of how God's own Word operates in history: sown freely, resisted often, yet destined to bear fruit through patience.

The literary setting confirms this interpretation. Mark collects parables at the shore precisely because the sea, in biblical imagery, signifies both chaos and the Gentile world. The Sower's boat is a small ark floating upon nations yet to receive the seed. The Kingdom begins from that fragile craft—Church and Christ together—casting Word upon unstable waters until earth becomes fertile again.

Thus, before theology begins in earnest, the text itself already preaches: the Word that created the world now seeks entrance into the human heart. The grammar of sowing is the grammar of grace—an outward act ordered toward inward communion. What unfolds in the next verses is only the fruit of what the text has already planted.

## b) Theological Interpretation

The parable of the Sower opens the inner logic of the Kingdom: it reveals not merely how grace works, but what God Himself is like when He acts. Everything begins with divine initiative. The Sower is not a metaphor for generic human preaching; He is the living image of God's own self-communication. "The sower went out to sow" describes in miniature the entire movement of salvation history—the eternal Word proceeding from the Father, entering the field of creation, scattering Himself across the soil of humanity. Creation, covenant, and Incarnation share this same grammar: God does not remain in the house; He goes out. The verb *exēlthen*, used by Mark, carries the same resonance found in the Exodus when God "brought out" His people, and in the prophets when His word "goes forth" and does not return empty (Isa 55 : 11). The Sower's action is therefore a revelation of divine character—prodigal generosity that expects nothing before giving everything.

To hear this parable as theology rather than farming advice is to recognize that God is not calculating yield before He sows. He casts the seed where success seems impossible—on paths, rocks, and thorns—because His love is reckless by design. This is the mercy that precedes merit. In human economies, investment follows probability; in the divine economy, grace creates possibility. The wastefulness of the Sower is the abundance of the Father. Each handful of seed scattered upon unreceptive ground declares that no human heart is excluded from invitation. Even the hardened path receives its moment of visitation.

Yet the parable also insists that reception matters. Grace is offered universally but bears fruit personally. The Word is constant, but the soil varies; the divine generosity calls forth human freedom. Here we meet the drama of covenant—the meeting of gift and response, promise and fidelity. Scripture never portrays salvation as unilateral. God initiates; humanity answers. When Jesus speaks of seed and soil, He is describing the same covenant rhythm that pulses through the whole Bible: "I will be your God, and you shall be My people." The seed is that promise entering history; the soil is the human heart consenting—or refusing—to host it.

The theology of hearing lies at the centre. The opening command, "Listen," is not incidental. It is the first act of faith, the posture of Adam before he fell and of Abraham when he was called. Sin begins with the refusal to listen; redemption begins with the ear opened. The prophet Isaiah foretold that the Servant of the Lord would awaken morning by morning with an ear trained to hear (Isa 50 : 4–5). Jesus embodies that perfect listening, and now He calls His disciples into the same obedience of hearing. In this light, the parable of the Sower is also a parable of the Incarnation: the Word made flesh now speaks the Word again, inviting His hearers to become what He is—living soil in which divine life can take root.

Mark's sequence of soils describes not types of people fixed by fate but stages of spiritual history. Humanity as a whole has moved through them: the hardened path of Israel's early disobedience, the shallow enthusiasm of transient faith, the choking thorns of worldliness, and finally the cultivated ground of the Church where the Spirit brings forth fruit. Within each believer, these same terrains coexist; conversion is the lifelong labour of allowing the Word to penetrate deeper. The "mystery of the Kingdom" given to the disciples is precisely this interior transformation. The mystery is not information about heaven but participation in divine fertility.

The seed itself—identified by Jesus as "the Word"—is not merely instruction; it is presence. In Scripture, the Word is always performative: what God speaks becomes reality. "Let there be light" was not description but creation. When the Word is sown, the very life of God enters the hearer. Thus, evangelization is never transfer of data but transmission of being. The Gospel does not communicate ideas about God; it communicates God Himself. This is why the seed has inherent vitality even when rejected. It remains potent, waiting for the moment when the soil softens.

The four soils therefore illustrate not simply success or failure but the progressive healing of creation's wound. The first soil, trampled and compacted, recalls the cursed ground of Genesis 3—earth hardened by human rebellion. The birds that snatch the seed evoke the "beasts of the field" that multiplied when dominion was lost; they symbolize the demonic forces that prey on an unguarded heart. The second soil, thin and rocky, mirrors Israel's history in the wilderness—faith that flares up in gratitude for manna yet withers under heat. The third soil, crowded with thorns, reflects the world after Eden, where toil, anxiety, and greed choke communion. Only in the fourth soil is creation restored to its purpose: to receive the Word and bear fruit. The parable thus recapitulates salvation history in miniature, ending where the Bible itself ends—with new earth made fertile by grace.

To say that the Word is "sown" is to confess that God's self-revelation is kenotic—self-emptying. The Sower loses what He gives. Every act of communication entails vulnerability; every word risks rejection. God speaks knowing that His Word will be ignored, twisted, or crucified. Yet He speaks anyway. This is divine patience in narrative form. The seed's slow, hidden growth mirrors the patience of the Creator who waits for the freedom of His creatures. What we call history is, in this parable, the interval between sowing and harvest—the time of divine waiting.

Faith, then, is not an instant response but a cultivation. Grace must break through layers of memory, habit, and fear. The soil must be tilled; the stones of self-reliance must be removed. The Spirit performs this interior agriculture through sacraments, trials, and seasons of pruning. The farmer sleeps and rises while the seed grows; so too the believer does not manufacture sanctity but cooperates with a process already alive within. Sanctification is not self-improvement; it is soil slowly becoming womb.

What begins as agricultural imagery thus opens into a Trinitarian mystery. The Father is the Sower; the Son is the Seed; the Spirit is the rain that causes growth. The fruit that results is participation in divine life—the reproduction of the Word within the Church and within each soul. Every believer becomes, in turn, a small field where the life of God is multiplied. The Kingdom is not built; it grows. Its expansion is organic, not mechanical; relational, not programmatic. The same Spirit who overshadowed Mary now overshadows the soil of the Church, making it fruitful.

In this light, the parable of the Sower is not primarily a moral warning but a revelation of how grace behaves. God is faithful; His Word is fertile. What He asks is cooperation, not competition. The yield—thirty, sixty, a hundredfold—is not measured achievement but overflowing participation in divine abundance. To bear fruit is to become what we were created to be: the image of a generous God whose glory is to give life.

The mystery deepens when we realise that the seed's fruitfulness is not uniform. Jesus' closing words—"some thirty, some sixty, some a hundredfold"—do not describe divine favouritism but the varied capacity of human cooperation. In ancient Judea and Galilee, a tenfold return was excellent; a hundredfold was miraculous. Christ deliberately uses exaggeration to signal the supernaturality of grace. The Kingdom's harvest cannot be explained by soil alone; it is the overflow of God's own life reproducing itself in the creature. This is the logic of covenant fulfilled: what began as promise to Abraham ("I will make your descendants as the stars") now flowers as multiplication of divine life through faith. The fertile soil is the believer who allows the Word to become flesh again within him.

In the theology of Israel, the earth's fertility was always a sign of covenant fidelity. Rain, seedtime, and harvest were sacraments of blessing. When the prophets lamented famine, they meant more than meteorological failure—they meant spiritual barrenness. Hosea warned that idolatry turns the land into thorns; Joel promised that repentance would make the hills drip with wine. Jesus gathers all those oracles into His parable. The good soil is the heart restored to covenant fruitfulness, no longer dry with self-will or crowded with idols. To receive the Word is to be reconciled to creation's original vocation: to bear life from the breath of God.

Yet this fruitfulness does not occur apart from suffering. The seed must die to germinate; the soil must be broken to receive. The mystery of growth is cruciform. When Jesus later explains the parable to the disciples,

He speaks of persecution, tribulation, and worldly cares. These are not accidents but the very furrows through which grace runs. In the Kingdom, fertility and the Cross are inseparable. The Sower Himself will soon be buried like a seed, and the harvest of the Resurrection will prove that apparent failure is the condition of abundance. Every disciple shares that pattern. The plough of providence that cuts our hearts is the same mercy that makes them receptive.

Mark's narrative places this parable at the hinge of his Gospel because it describes how revelation itself must be received. Immediately after speaking, Jesus tells His followers that "to you has been given the mystery of the Kingdom, but to those outside everything is in parables." The contrast between inside and outside is not exclusionary; it is pedagogical. The "inside" is not geography but relationship—those who dwell with Jesus, who ask, who listen again. Hearing alone is not enough; understanding comes through intimacy. The Word cannot be decoded from a distance. It must be lived with, like seed in soil.

This is the difference between curiosity and communion. The crowds hear parables as riddles to be solved; the disciples hear them as invitations to stay. In this sense, the parable of the Sower interprets all parables. It teaches that divine revelation demands proximity, patience, and personal transformation. The mystery of the Kingdom is not secret knowledge but shared life. Only by entering into the rhythm of sowing and growing—of daily hearing and responding—does the disciple come to understand.

Theologically, this moves us from information to participation. God's Word is not primarily propositional but sacramental. It effects what it signifies. When the Sower speaks, creation happens anew; the soil that receives becomes new creation. This is why the Fathers called Scripture "seed of divinity." The same Word that created the world now recreates the believer. Thus the parable is also a map of revelation's movement: from the Father's mouth through the Son's lips into the believer's heart, there to germinate by the Spirit's power. Hearing becomes incarnation; doctrine becomes life.

The four soils also delineate the anatomy of unbelief. The hardened path represents resistance born of pride—the intellect that refuses vulnerability. The rocky ground is the will that begins in enthusiasm but lacks endurance; emotion without rootedness. The thorns are disordered loves, good things grown wild until they strangle the better. These are not psychological categories but theological conditions: ways in which fallen humanity distorts receptivity. Sin, in every form, is refusal to receive. It is soil turned in on itself. Salvation is the slow reopening of the heart to the Word's descent.

Here the theology of grace and freedom intertwines. The Sower's generosity never nullifies human agency. God tills the soil through circumstances, but He does not force fertility. Each hearing of the Word is a moment of decision—whether to cooperate or to resist, to let the seed remain superficial or to allow it to sink into memory and obedience. The parable exposes the tragedy of superficial religion: the heart that receives sermons gladly yet never permits conversion to reach the roots. Jesus' warning is pastoral as well as doctrinal. The seed that springs up too quickly is the life of faith without the cross—emotion without endurance.

For Mark's audience, many of whom faced persecution, this interpretation was painfully concrete. The "sun" that scorches the shallow plant was the heat of opposition from family, synagogue, and empire. The early Church understood that the Word's fruitfulness would always attract resistance. Yet they also knew that endurance under trial became the very condition of maturity. Just as the seed breaks open underground, hidden from sight, so the believer's soul is transformed in the darkness of fidelity. Growth, in this Gospel, is not comfort but communion with the Crucified.

The thorns that choke the Word—"the cares of the world, the deceit of riches, and the desire for other things"—name the perennial temptations of every age. They are not overt evils but legitimate goods grown idolatrous. The heart becomes overplanted; competing loves drain its nutrients. Jesus is not condemning work, wealth, or pleasure, but their usurpation of first place. In the soil of the Kingdom, even good things must be pruned to make room for the best. Detachment is therefore not disdain but reordering— the painful art of giving God back His space in the heart.

When Jesus finally describes the good soil, He does not specify what distinguishes it. He merely says it "hears the word, accepts it, and bears fruit." The verbs are humble and continuous. Hearing is ongoing; accepting is active consent; bearing fruit is the natural outflow of both. The absence of spectacle is deliberate. True holiness, like true fertility, is quiet. The most fruitful souls are often those hidden from the world's notice—the saints who cultivate the soil of daily fidelity. In them, the Kingdom grows as silently as seed sprouting beneath the earth, yet the harvest changes history.

The theological thread running through the entire parable is trust. The Word will do its work if given time and space. The farmer's task is not to manipulate growth but to protect conditions for it. The same holds in the spiritual life. The Church's task is not to force conversions but to preserve receptivity: through teaching, prayer, sacrament, and community. Every liturgy, every confession, every act of charity is the Church tending the field so that grace may breathe.

The parable culminates in this quiet confidence: divine fruitfulness is inevitable when divine patience is met by human perseverance. The seed carries within itself the mystery of God's own fidelity. It may seem buried, delayed, or dormant, yet it will not fail. The same power that raised Christ from the tomb works invisibly in the soil of the heart. This is the eschatological dimension of the parable—the assurance that history itself is a field under cultivation. The apparent delay of the harvest is not divine neglect but divine mercy, allowing every plot of ground to receive its chance. As Peter will later write, "The Lord is not slow as some count slowness, but patient, not wishing that any should perish" (2 Pet 3:9). The Sower's patience is the shape of His love.

Within this framework, "fruit" means more than moral virtue; it means participation in the life of God. In Scripture, fruitfulness is the sign of covenantal union. Adam and Eve were blessed to "be fruitful and multiply." Israel was chosen to bear fruit for the nations. Jesus will later tell His disciples, "By this my Father is glorified, that you bear much fruit and so prove to be my disciples" (John 15:8). The seed's growth, then, is not metaphorical but mystical: the Word reproducing the Word, the Son extending His life in those who hear. The Church herself is the living harvest—the field of redeemed humanity bearing the image of the Sower. Each believer becomes seed again, scattered into the world to begin the process anew.

This ecclesial dimension is crucial. The parable was never meant as private spirituality detached from mission. Just as the seed multiplies beyond itself, so faith cannot remain solitary. The Word that takes root in one heart becomes nourishment for many. In Acts, Luke describes the Gospel's progress with the same agricultural language: "The word of God grew and multiplied." The life of the early Church was itself a visible fulfilment of this parable—simple men and women, rooted in prayer and charity, turning the hard soil of empires into gardens of grace. The Church is not a warehouse for seed but a living field in perpetual spring.

This expansion, however, always meets resistance. Every era repeats the drama of the four soils. Some hearts remain hardened by cynicism; others respond with enthusiasm that evaporates under trial; others allow the Word to be strangled by anxiety and comfort. Yet the good soil still exists—souls who listen, trust, and persevere. The Sower never stops sowing because the field is still the world He loves. Even in apparent decline, the divine logic remains: "The earth produces by itself, first the blade, then the ear, then the full grain in the ear." The mystery of growth is not defeated by the slowness of history.

In personal terms, the fruit of the Word manifests as transformation of desire. The rocky heart becomes capable of endurance; the thorny heart learns simplicity; the hardened heart awakens to compassion. Grace does not bypass nature; it cultivates it. The Spirit respects the contours of each soul's terrain, working uniquely within each to produce a harvest suited to its calling. That is why some yield thirtyfold, some sixty, some a hundred—the diversity of holiness within the unity of grace. In heaven, the differences of yield will not provoke envy but wonder, for all will recognize the same Sower working through different soils.

Theologically, the parable also prefigures the sacramental economy. The

Word that is sown by preaching becomes visible seed in the sacraments. Baptism breaks the fallow ground; Confirmation deepens the roots; the Eucharist feeds the plant with divine life. Penance removes weeds; Anointing strengthens it in weakness; Marriage and Orders scatter new seed into the world. Each sacrament is an act of divine agriculture—God tending His field until the final harvest. The Church's liturgical year itself mirrors the cycle of sowing, growth, and fruition: Advent's preparation, Lent's ploughing, Easter's flowering, Pentecost's abundance. The rhythm of grace is agricultural because grace is organic—it grows in living things, not in abstractions.

This agricultural theology reaches its summit in the mystery of the Cross. The Sower becomes the Seed. He who cast the Word into the world now allows Himself to be buried in it. "Unless a grain of wheat falls into the earth and dies, it remains alone," Jesus will say, "but if it dies, it bears much fruit" (John 12:24). The parable of the Sower thus anticipates the Paschal Mystery: divine life released through death, abundance born from surrender. The entire Gospel can be read as the unfolding of this principle. Christ's descent into death is the supreme act of sowing, and His Resurrection the eternal springtime in which every seed of faith will one day blossom.

At its deepest level, the parable unveils the heart of God's pedagogy. He teaches by giving Himself away, by entering the very soil of human frailty. The Word does not hover above the ground; it mingles with the dust. The Incarnation itself is this sowing—God's self-seed planted in the earth of our nature. In every Eucharist, the same mystery continues: the Sower gives His body as bread, His blood as wine, entering once again the field of the world to make it fruitful. Each Mass is both harvest and new sowing, the perpetual renewal of creation's fertility in grace.

When read through this lens, the parable of the Sower is nothing less than a theology of divine generosity. It portrays a God who never ceases to speak, to give, to trust. His Word is not wasted even when it seems unheard. In every corner of human history, some seed is taking root unseen. The believer's task is not to measure outcomes but to remain receptive, to keep the soil open through prayer, repentance, and charity. To live by faith is to live as soil—dark, hidden, and alive with expectancy.

The section closes where it began: with the Word going forth. The same Sower who began creation continues His work in every generation, scattering truth into the furrows of human hearts until the world itself becomes His garden. The parable does not end with harvest but with hope. The seed still falls; the Word still works; the Kingdom still grows. Its increase is slow but unstoppable, because its life is divine. Every hearing of the Gospel is a moment of new creation—God walking again through the evening of the world, calling to Adam from the furrows, offering life where there was dust.

This is the mystery the disciples were told they had been given: not a code to decipher, but a covenant to dwell within. The Sower sows Himself; the soil becomes the sanctuary; the harvest is communion. In that living cycle—Word proceeding, world receiving, fruit returning—the entire drama of salvation turns like seasons beneath the sun of grace.

### c) Typological and Intertextual Parallels

The imagery of the sower and the seed is not an innovation of Jesus but the culmination of a long biblical genealogy of symbols that trace divine action from creation to covenant, from exile to eschaton. Every term in the parable—seed, soil, thorns, fruit, and harvest—stands within a network of intertextual resonances that Jesus reinterprets through His own person and mission. The parable's true depth lies in how it gathers and transfigures these antecedents, revealing in narrative form the continuity and fulfilment of God's dealings with Israel.

In the beginning, seed is the first sign of life's permanence. Genesis 1:11–12 declares, "Let the earth put forth vegetation, plants yielding seed, each according to its kind." Seed-bearing plants mark the transition from chaos to ordered fecundity; they embody creation's capacity to reproduce what God has spoken into being. When Jesus identifies the Word with seed, He implicitly recalls this primal act. The same creative utterance that called forth life in Genesis now continues as revelatory speech. In both cases, God's Word is productive, not descriptive: it performs what it proclaims. The Sower's gesture in Galilee is thus a reenactment of creation itself—the Word scattering life into the formless soil of human hearts.

The motif reappears in the Abrahamic covenant, where the promise of a "seed" (*zeraʿ*, Gen 12:7; 15:5; 22:18) becomes the axis of Israel's identity. Abraham's descendants are the physical and spiritual fruit of divine speech believed. The Hebrew term *zeraʿ*, like the Greek *sperma*, refers both to seed and to offspring; hence Paul's insistence in Galatians 3:16 that "the seed" is ultimately Christ. The parable of the Sower presupposes that identification. The seed cast into the field is the same promised seed of Abraham, now incarnate and self-distributing. Jesus fulfils the covenant not merely by being its heir but by perpetuating its life in others. The field becomes the world, and Abraham's blessing extends to the nations through the diffusion of the Word.

From creation and covenant, the seed image migrates into the prophetic literature, where agricultural metaphors become instruments of moral and eschatological critique. Isaiah 5's "Song of the Vineyard" portrays God as the planter who expects justice but finds bloodshed; Hosea 10:12 commands Israel to "sow righteousness, reap steadfast love," and to "break up your fallow ground." Jeremiah 4:3 warns, "Do not sow among thorns." Each passage employs cultivation language to articulate the dynamics of sin and repentance. Soil stands for the heart's condition; fruitfulness for righteousness. Jesus inherits this prophetic tradition but reverses its perspective. The prophets urge the people to prepare the soil; Jesus presents God as already sowing despite the soil's resistance. The emphasis shifts from human preparation to divine initiative. Grace precedes repentance.

Isaiah 55:10–11 provides the most direct antecedent. "As the rain and snow come down from heaven… so shall my word be that goes out from my mouth; it shall not return to me empty." The rain-water image describes the cyclical efficacy of divine speech. Jesus converts meteorology into agriculture: what once fell as rain now falls as seed. Both metaphors communicate the same theology of causality—divine utterance enters the earth's processes, disappears within them, and achieves its end through natural mediation. In the parable, this process is personalized: the Word Himself descends into creation's soil. Where Isaiah's rain symbolizes revelation descending upon Israel, Jesus' seed is revelation incarnate, buried within history. The continuity is formal; the difference is ontological.

The Psalter also contributes to the web of associations. Psalm 126:5–6 links sowing with sorrow and redemption: "Those who sow in tears shall reap with shouts of joy." The image here is not merely agricultural but eschatological; it anticipates restoration after exile. Jesus' own ministry recapitulates that pattern. His preaching, often met with rejection, is sowing in tears; His resurrection, the reaping of joy. The psalm's rhythm—loss, waiting, and vindication—becomes the parable's temporal structure. The Sower's patience, seemingly futile, hides the assurance of eventual harvest.

Within the Wisdom literature, particularly Sirach and Proverbs, sowing becomes a metaphor for instruction. "He who sows righteousness gets a sure reward" (Prov 11:18); "Let your heart receive instruction; if you love her, she will guard you" (Prov 4:10). Wisdom is a gardener cultivating the mind. Jesus, who in Matthew 12 is greater than Solomon, assumes this role of divine pedagogue. His parables are acts of sowing wisdom, but wisdom in its ultimate, incarnate form—divine Logos as teacher. Thus, what had been an abstract virtue becomes personal: the Sower is Wisdom Himself, scattering seeds of Himself.

The intertextual threads converge in Jesus' use of the seed as symbol of death and resurrection. John 12:24 offers the hermeneutical key: "Unless a grain of wheat falls into the earth and dies, it remains alone; but if it dies, it bears much fruit." The seed is the Son, whose burial is fecund rather than final. Here the typology reaches its climax. Creation's first seed prefigured life from the earth; Abraham's seed prefigured blessing from promise; Isaiah's rain-seed prefigured word from heaven. In the Incarnation and Passion, these types coalesce: the Creator becomes the creature, the Promised becomes the Promise, the Word becomes the seed that dies to yield eternal life. Jesus' parable, spoken before His death, already intimates this paschal logic. The divine economy unfolds according to agrarian rhythm: sowing, hiddenness, germination, harvest.

Even the "thorns" carry typological freight. Genesis 3:18 marks thorns and thistles as the sign of the curse; they represent creation's resistance to divine intention. When Jesus later bears the crown of thorns, the symbol reaches paradoxical inversion: the curse becomes His crown, sterility becomes fruitfulness. The thorns that once signified futility now proclaim redemption. The soil's hostility is not overcome by avoidance but by assumption; the Sower enters the cursed ground and sanctifies it from within. The parable's imagery thus prefigures the redemptive reversal enacted in the Passion.

Ezekiel's vision of the new heart (Ezek 36:26) deepens this anthropological typology. God promises to replace the heart of stone with a heart of flesh, to make Israel responsive once again to His Spirit. Jesus' differentiation of soils mirrors that promise in experiential form. The "rocky ground" corresponds to the stony heart; the "good soil" to the heart of flesh. Yet the transformation from one to the other can occur only through divine initiative—through the ploughing of grace. The parable therefore implies not only moral exhortation but eschatological renewal. The Sower who scatters seed also recreates the soil.

The typology of harvest culminates in the apocalyptic literature. Joel 3:13 and Revelation 14:15 portray the final judgment as the reaping of the earth's harvest. The same act that gathers the righteous consumes the wicked. By situating His parable within this symbolic field, Jesus places the act of hearing within an eschatological horizon. Every encounter with the Word anticipates the Last Day; every unfruitful soil foreshadows exclusion. The gentle image of growth thus carries the gravity of judgment. The Kingdom's secret growth is preparation for its public consummation.

Finally, the parable draws into itself Israel's liturgical and sacrificial memory. The Feast of First fruits (Lev 23:9–14) and the Feast of Weeks (Deut 16:9–12) sanctified the harvest as offering to God. In Christian reading, these festivals find fulfilment in Easter and Pentecost—the

Resurrection as first fruits of the new creation (1 Cor 15:20), and Pentecost as the Spirit's harvest of souls. The Sower's field ripens into the Church; the Spirit becomes the divine rain that completes the cycle. Thus, the parable is not only prophetic but liturgical, prefiguring the sacramental economy. In the Eucharist, the fruit of the earth and work of human hands becomes the body of the Sower Himself—a perpetual re-sowing of grace.

Taken together, these intertextual correspondences reveal the parable as a microcosm of salvation history. The seed that began as symbol of creation ends as sacrament of redemption. The thorns of curse become crown; the soil of death becomes womb; the harvest of judgment becomes feast. Jesus does not discard Israel's agricultural theology—He fulfils it by embodying its every metaphor. The Sower is Creator, Covenant Lord, Prophet, and Redeemer in one act. His hand scattering seed on Galilean soil is the same hand that shaped Adam from dust and will one day raise the dead from it. Typology here is not literary flourish but ontological truth: the old covenant's imagery has found its living referent.

## d) Patristic and Theological Synthesis

The early Church read the Parable of the Sower not as a moral fable but as a miniature Gospel. Every Father who commented on it recognized in the Sower's hand the same generosity that created the world and redeemed it. For them, this was not a lesson in ancient agriculture; it was the story of salvation condensed into a field.

Origen, writing in the third century, was among the first to see the parable as a map of the soul's journey. In his *Commentary on Matthew*, he taught that the seed is the Word that descends again and again until the heart becomes capable of bearing it. The four soils, he said, are not four classes of people but four stages in each believer. We all begin as the hardened path, needing the plough of repentance to break us open. "Let us," he writes, "become good soil through toil and tears, that the Word might be born in us as Christ was born in Mary." His vision is profoundly incarnational: the Word that became flesh in the Virgin must become fruitful in every Christian. Origen's insight reveals that hearing the Word is not information but conception.

St. John Chrysostom, the golden-mouthed preacher of Antioch, spoke of the Sower's impartial scattering as the sign of divine mercy. In his *Homilies on Matthew* he marvels that the Lord "makes no distinction between the hard and the good ground; He does not desist when the first receives nothing, for He is Lord, not merchant." For Chrysostom, the extravagance of the Sower is a revelation of divine patience—God keeps speaking even to the deaf. Every sermon, every sacrament, every whisper of conscience is another handful of seed flung toward unpromising ground. The preacher's task, he adds, is to imitate that same liberality: to sow even when the audience seems stony. In that pastoral echo, the ancient homily becomes a mirror of the Gospel's generosity.

St. Basil the Great heard in the rocky soil an image of spiritual superficiality. His *Homily on Psalm 1* describes the just man as "a tree planted by streams of water," roots deep in Scripture. Faith without discipline, he warns, is like the seed that sprouts quickly but cannot withstand the sun. Basil's remedy is ascetic realism: the soil of the heart must be softened through fasting, charity, and meditation on the Word. For him, the heat of trial is not punishment but the testing that reveals whether the root is genuine. What the sun scorches, the Spirit purifies.

St. Augustine, writing in North Africa, brought the parable into the great drama of grace and freedom. In his *Sermons on the New Testament*, he insists that God's Word always has power, but its effect depends on the heart's disposition: "The seed is one, the soils are many. The difference is not in the rain but in the ground." He sees in the seed's growth the inner working of prevenient grace—the love of God preceding our response. Yet Augustine also hears a summons to cooperation: "He who made you without you will not justify you without you." The soil must consent to its own cultivation. Here Augustine preserves both the sovereignty of grace and the dignity of human freedom. Salvation is a partnership of patience.

Gregory the Great would later weave these threads into his *Moralia on Job*, seeing in the Sower's patience a figure of divine governance. The Word, he says, "works one way in the heart of the just, another in the heart of the sinner, yet both are tilled by the same hand." God's providence, for Gregory, is continuous cultivation. Even the storms that flatten crops are instruments of renewal. The apparent chaos of history is the slow plough of divine wisdom preparing the final harvest. In his vision, the Sower never leaves the field; He walks among His plants, pruning and supporting until they bear the fruit of glory.

Across the centuries, this patristic harmony forms a single theology: the Word that goes forth from God does not return empty because it carries within itself the energy of the Spirit. The Fathers read Isaiah 55 as commentary on this parable—rain and snow descending, watering the earth, and bringing forth bread for the eater. The seed is Christ Himself; the soil is humanity; the harvest is communion. When Jesus interprets His own story to the disciples, He is already explaining the entire sacramental order. The Word that is heard in preaching becomes visible in the Eucharist, where the same Christ who once sowed now feeds His crop with His own life.

From this patristic reading flows a deeply Trinitarian vision. The Father is the Sower who gives; the Son is the Word that is sown; the Holy Spirit is the hidden power that causes the seed to live. The unity of the divine action mirrors the unity of the Church. Wherever the Word is preached and received, the Trinity is at work. This is why the Church calls Scripture "the soul of theology" and the Eucharist "the source and summit." Both arise from the same divine sowing—the Word spoken, the Word broken, both bearing fruit in the faithful.

Medieval theologians continued this tradition with a more explicit sense of participation. Thomas Aquinas, in his *Catena Aurea*, gathers the voices of the Fathers on this text, but adds a metaphysical note: the seed's power to grow is an image of God's act of creation, in which being itself is given as a gift that participates in divine life. For Thomas, the Word of God is not simply instruction but infusion: the same creative power that called the world into existence now calls the soul into holiness. The parable therefore reveals not moral advice but the structure of reality itself. Everything that exists is, in a sense, seed—called to become more than it is by the energy of divine love.

The Council of Trent, centuries later, would echo that insight in its teaching on justification: the grace of the Holy Spirit is "poured into our hearts" like seed, transforming rather than merely covering the sinner. Modern Catholic theology continues to see this parable as the grammar of sanctification. Grace does not override nature; it heals, elevates, and perfects it. The soil is not replaced but renewed. That is the story of the entire Bible: creation's ground, once cursed, becomes again the garden of God.

In this light, the parable of the Sower becomes a template for the Church's mission. Evangelization is not marketing but agriculture. The Church does not manufacture results; she cultivates conditions for grace. Her preaching is seed-scattering, her sacraments irrigation, her discipline pruning, her charity the warmth that ripens fruit. Every pastor, catechist, and parent participates in the Sower's work. The field of the world belongs to God, yet He entrusts its care to His servants. The patience of divine husbandry becomes the patience of the Church.

For the Fathers, the ultimate horizon of the parable was always eschatological. The harvest is the end of the age when the Sower returns to gather His fruit. Then the Word, having traversed history, will return to the Father not empty but laden with the saints—the living sheaves of His mercy. The soil of creation will finally yield its intended crop: a communion of persons reflecting the triune life. This is the meaning of "a hundredfold": not arithmetic but abundance beyond measure, the superabundance of divine joy shared with the redeemed.

When we stand within this patristic and theological chorus, the parable no longer reads as instruction about faith alone but as revelation of God's own heart. He is the eternal Sower, scattering Himself into the world, risking rejection, rejoicing in every sprout of faith. The Church, nourished by that same Word, becomes both field and farmer, both soil and seed. Every Christian life is a continuation of this parable—Christ sowing Himself anew in each generation until the world becomes Eucharist.

In the end, the Fathers invite us to hear Jesus' closing words not as warning but as invitation: "He who has ears to hear, let him hear." Hearing means conversion; conversion means participation; participation means joy. The mystery of the Kingdom is that God's Word never ceases to become flesh—first in the womb of Mary, then in the heart of every believer. The harvest is already begun, and we live among its growing rows. To believe is to stand in that field, ears open, heart tilled, waiting for the sound of the Sower's steps.

### The Shock and the Turn

The parable ends in peace, yet it is born in provocation. Beneath the calm imagery of seed and soil lies a confrontation as sharp as a prophet's blade. Jesus is not describing how farmers work; He is revealing how God saves—and how Israel has forgotten to listen. When the crowd by the lake heard Him say that the Sower scattered His seed even upon the path, they would have winced. A farmer in Galilee was poor; seed was precious. No one squandered it on hardened ground. But this Sower does. His extravagance is the scandal. Divine wastefulness becomes the first reversal. God is not efficient; He is prodigal. He throws Himself where reason says there is no return.

The shock, then, is double. First, that God would act so recklessly; second, that human beings could respond so carelessly. Jesus' hearers prided themselves on being the covenant people, recipients of the Law and the Prophets. Yet He now tells them that their hearts may be no different from the footpath trampled by traffic. The Word has come to them again—and may find no depth. The parable is less about pagans who ignore God than about believers who assume they already understand Him. It is addressed to the devout, not the indifferent. The hardened path runs through the synagogue.

In this light, the story turns inward. Every heart becomes the field under scrutiny. The line between soil types does not run between "us" and "them" but through every listener. Some parts of us are fertile; others are stony, others tangled. The Sower's generosity exposes this interior geography.

The Word falls where it will, and its failure in us reveals where we have closed ourselves to grace. The parable is therefore judgment disguised as invitation. It leaves no one unexamined.

The priestly teachers of Jesus' day expected the Kingdom to arrive through purity, boundary, and separation. But here comes a Messiah who sows everywhere—on roads, in thorns, across Gentile hillsides. He breaks every agricultural rule, every religious fence. The seed knows no prejudice. That is the true scandal of the Kingdom: mercy that refuses to discriminate. The crowds came seeking confirmation of privilege; they heard instead the democratization of grace. In the Kingdom, chosenness is not inherited but received through hearing. The covenant is renewed not by bloodline but by openness of heart.

The turning point within the parable arrives in the question of **hearing**. "He who has ears to hear, let him hear." The words fall lightly, but they divide the crowd. Some laugh and move on; others linger, uneasy. Hearing becomes judgment. To hear truly means to surrender control, to let another's word rewrite one's life. That is why the Pharisees, for all their learning, could not hear. They guarded revelation as possession; they would not let it possess them. The disciples, by contrast, stay close and ask. Their very confusion becomes openness. Ignorance with humility proves more fertile than knowledge with pride. In this quiet reversal the Kingdom reveals its hidden law: the teachable inherit the mysteries; the self-assured remain blind.

The moral sting extends beyond the first century. The parable unmasks every religious age, ours included. The path hardened by footsteps is the modern heart trampled by noise—newsfeeds, schedules, and self-curated opinions. The rocks are our fleeting enthusiasms, spirituality without discipline. The thorns are our crowded loves: success, comfort, distraction, even ministry when it becomes performance. We still live among these soils. The Word still falls, and its yield still depends on whether we will make space for silence. In an age that measures worth by productivity, the Sower's patience is a rebuke. He works at the speed of growth, not of clicks.

## THE PARABLE OF THE SOWER (MK 4:1–20)

The deeper shock lies in the parable's theology of failure. Three-quarters of the seed produces nothing. By human standards the harvest is disastrous. Yet Jesus calls this the pattern of the Kingdom. In God's arithmetic, apparent loss is the condition of true gain. The Sower accepts rejection because fruitfulness cannot be forced. Grace respects freedom even when freedom wounds it. The cross already casts its shadow across this field: divine love choosing to be ineffective in order to remain love. The listeners who expect triumph receive a story of delay and disappointment. The Kingdom, Jesus says, will come slowly, vulnerably, through failure embraced.

This is why He warns that understanding the parable is the key to all others. Without grasping the logic of the seed, the rest of His teaching will seem incoherent. The Kingdom does not begin in conquest but in concealment. The Son of God comes not with armies but with stories; not with thunder but with whispers. He sows words into hearts and waits. The real battle between good and evil will be fought in the hidden furrows of conscience. That inversion—power through patience, victory through vulnerability—is the divine turn that shatters human expectation.

To the first hearers, this message carried an unmistakable warning. Israel was once the vineyard of the Lord; now she risks becoming the path where birds feed. The prophets had said it long before: "Break up your fallow ground; do not sow among thorns." Jesus repeats their cry but with tenderness. He does not condemn the unfruitful soil; He keeps sowing into it. Even judgment becomes mercy. The hard heart is not abandoned but invited to be ploughed. Every parable, every miracle, every moment of His ministry is another scattering of hope across resistant ground.

For disciples, the shock cuts another way. They must learn to measure success by fidelity, not outcome. The preacher who toils without visible results shares the Sower's mission more perfectly than the one who reaps applause. Evangelization, Jesus implies, will often feel like futility. Yet this is precisely how the Kingdom grows—quietly, imperceptibly, under the soil. The yield is God's to give. Our task is perseverance. What seems waste may, in the hidden logic of grace, already be sprouting.

Silence is part of the sting. After telling the parable, Jesus does not explain it publicly. He lets it linger like seed on the surface, waiting for the rain of contemplation. That restraint is itself pedagogy. Truth that is forced never takes root; only the truth discovered in patience becomes one's own. The crowd leaves with fragments of story; those who desire more will come closer. The parable thus performs its message—it separates without condemning, judges without shouting, invites without coercion.

In the end, the "turn" of the parable is from optimism to trust. The Kingdom's success does not depend on human strategy but on divine fidelity. Our failures are not final because the Sower never ceases to sow. The heart that was once path may tomorrow be garden. The same God who created light from darkness can bring fruit from barrenness. The real miracle of this story is not the hundredfold harvest but the patience that precedes it. The Sower still walks His fields at dusk, scattering grace where we would have given up.

If we listen long enough, the parable ends in silence rather than applause. We are left standing with Him on the shore, watching the breeze ripple across unseen furrows, hearing again the first word He spoke: *Listen*. That command is both judgment and mercy. It exposes how little we hear, yet it opens the door to hearing anew. The path can be softened, the stones removed, the thorns uprooted. The shock of the Kingdom is that God still believes His seed can grow in us.

### The Revelation in the Son

All parables, when followed to their depths, open into the face of Christ. They begin in metaphor and end in revelation, because the Kingdom they describe is not an abstract reign but the presence of the King Himself. In the Parable of the Sower, that disclosure is total. The mystery that shimmered in seed and soil now resolves into a single vision: Jesus is the Sower, the Seed, and the Harvest. The Word He scatters is none other than Himself, given in the extravagance of divine love.

When He steps from the boat to teach by the sea, the eternal Word stands at the edge of creation, speaking once more into the waters from which life first emerged. His voice is the echo of Genesis—"Let there be light"—now personalized, enfleshed, intimate. Each syllable falls like seed into the human heart, and as He speaks, He re-creates the world. The farmer's gesture—flinging seed into earth—becomes the eternal motion of the Incarnation: the Son proceeding from the Father, descending into the furrows of time, to sow Himself within our mortality. Divine generosity becomes flesh.

The image of the Sower going out to sow is therefore a revelation of the divine processions themselves. The Father eternally begets the Son, and the Son, in turn, pours Himself out in creation and redemption. To exist is already to receive this sowing. Every particle of being, every soul, every moment of history is the ground into which the Son casts His light. Yet in Jesus of Nazareth the divine Sower enters His own field. The Word who once spoke the world into existence now walks among its furrows, touching its dust, feeling its resistance. The parable becomes autobiography.

In this light, the seed is not a symbol of wisdom but the Word Himself made small. He falls into the soil of Mary's womb, germinating silently beneath the overshadowing of the Spirit. Bethlehem is the first furrow opened by grace. Nazareth, His hidden life, is the long season of unseen growth. His public ministry is the scattering of His presence through word and miracle. And at Calvary, the Seed completes its descent. "Unless a grain of wheat falls into the earth and dies, it remains alone; but if it dies, it bears much fruit." The Cross is the parable fulfilled—the moment when the Sower becomes the Seed, when the hand that scattered life is itself broken and buried.

This is the luminous paradox at the heart of the Gospel: the fruit of the Kingdom springs from apparent failure. In dying, the Word penetrates the hardest ground—the sealed tomb of sin and death—and from that soil bursts the green shoot of resurrection. The Risen Christ is the hundredfold harvest, the firstfruits of the new creation. Through His wounds the world is irrigated; through His silence in the grave, the world begins again. The farmer sleeping and rising while the seed grows finds its final image in the mystery of Holy Saturday—the divine rest between sowing and harvest, when hidden life is already conquering decay.

Every Eucharist is this parable renewed. The Sower still goes out to sow, but now He sows Himself sacramentally. The seed of the Word becomes the seed of the altar—broken, given, planted in the hearts of those who eat. The Church gathered around the table is the field of redemption, watered by the Spirit, awaiting its fullness. What began on the shore of Galilee continues in every liturgy: the same Lord casting the same life into new hearts, waiting for fruit that will last. The mystery of the Kingdom is therefore Eucharistic at its core. The field becomes a banquet; the harvest becomes communion.

To contemplate this is to see creation transfigured. The soil is no longer mere matter but sacrament, a place where divine and human meet. The rain and the sunlight, the grain and the vine, all become vestiges of the Word's generosity. In Christ, the natural and the supernatural interpenetrate; grace does not abolish nature but fulfills it from within. This is the cosmic scope of the Incarnation: every seed that falls into earth preaches resurrection. Every cycle of growth and decay whispers of a love that will not end in decay. The universe itself is sacramental, a vast field through which the Sower still walks at dawn.

In the person of Jesus, the infinite patience of God receives a human face. His parable about waiting for the harvest is a portrait of His own heart. He endures misunderstanding, rejection, and delay because He knows what time can bring forth. The disciples who fled, the crowds who turned away, the soil that seemed sterile—all are redeemed by His endurance. At Pentecost the scattered seed of His teaching bursts into life: hearts once stony are broken open by fire, and the first fruits of the Church are gathered. The Word that fell upon unpromising ground in Galilee now spreads across the nations. The Sower's hand has reached the ends of the earth.

To read the parable in this light is to encounter not an image but a Person. The Kingdom of God is Jesus Himself—the divine life sown into humanity, growing secretly until all things are drawn into His harvest of light. He is the new Adam tending the renewed Eden, turning the thorns of the curse into crowns of glory. His pierced hands are the true plough that breaks the world open for grace. His Resurrection is the sun that ripens every virtue. And the final judgment, when He returns to gather His crop, will be nothing other than love's recognition of itself in every soul that allowed His life to grow.

The parable thus ends in adoration. The Sower's patience is not strategy but love, and the harvest is not profit but union. In Christ we see what the Father has been doing from the beginning: speaking Himself into the dust until the dust can speak His name in return. Every act of divine sowing, from creation to covenant to cross, culminates in the Word made flesh, who now sows the Spirit into our hearts. The field of history, still scarred and unfinished, already shimmers with hidden light. Beneath its surface, the Kingdom is alive.

The revelation of the Son is therefore the revelation of divine style—humility, generosity, fruitfulness through loss. In Jesus, God shows us not only what He does but how He loves. The same hands that scattered stars now cradle seed; the same Word that upholds galaxies whispers parables by the sea. To believe this is to stand at the meeting point of grandeur and intimacy, where infinity kneels in the dust. The Sower's footsteps echo still, and the earth itself listens for His voice.

## The Word for Our Age

Every generation hears the Parable of the Sower anew, and every generation discovers itself inside it. The details of our landscape have changed—the tractors and screens have replaced oxen and ploughs—but the condition of the heart has not. The Sower still goes out to sow, and the same divine Word still falls upon the ground of human freedom. What has changed is the speed and the noise surrounding that field. The soil of the modern soul is rarely silent long enough to receive seed. We live in an age of constant scattering but little planting, of words without roots.

The hardened path now takes the form of distraction. We hear the Gospel every Sunday, but its syllables bounce off surfaces worn smooth by digital traffic. Screens glow through every waking hour, the mind conditioned to scroll, react, and move on. The soil has been compacted by overuse. Jesus' call, "He who has ears to hear, let him hear," sounds quaint in a culture that measures attention in seconds. Yet the diagnosis remains precise: the Word cannot germinate where noise never stops. To become good soil again, we must reclaim the practice of silence—Sabbath moments carved from the frenzy, spaces where God can speak without competing for bandwidth.

The rocky ground of our time is emotional faith without perseverance. Many begin with enthusiasm—conferences, podcasts, retreats—but the root never reaches depth. When difficulty comes, or when the Church fails to match expectations, the plant withers. We have built a spirituality of experiences rather than endurance. But the Kingdom grows slowly. The saints were not sprinters; they were steady farmers of grace. Endurance in prayer, fidelity in small things, commitment to community—these are the roots that survive heat. The joy of the Gospel must mature into the patience of discipleship.

The thorns are perhaps most subtle. They are not malice but multiplicity. Modern life breeds endless good things that become rivals to the best. Careers, hobbies, relationships, self-improvement—each clamours for the soil's attention. Jesus' triad—"the cares of the world, the deceit of riches, and the desire for other things"—sounds like a summary of the modern calendar. The heart, overplanted with ambition and anxiety, cannot breathe. The thorns of worry choke the air that faith needs to grow. The antidote is simplicity—not deprivation but right order. When God is placed first, everything else finds its proportion. Simplicity clears space for gratitude, and gratitude is the rain that softens soil.

If we read the parable through the lens of today's Church, its realism is bracing. The Sower's harvest still appears small. In many places, faith is fading, parishes shrink, vocations decline. By worldly metrics, the Gospel seems inefficient. Yet this parable reminds us that the Kingdom has always advanced through hidden growth, not spectacle. God does His greatest work beneath the surface—in hearts, in homes, in quiet conversions no statistic can count. The temptation of every age is to measure success by visibility; the call of discipleship is to trust the slow miracle of grace.

For the family trying to live the faith amid exhaustion and noise, the parable offers a map. The dinner table can become the field of sowing, where Scripture is read aloud, gratitude voiced, forgiveness practiced. The Church begins in miniature in that soil. Parents become sowers; children, small furrows of promise. In workplaces, the seed is patience and integrity sown among colleagues. In the loneliness of the digital world, it is the seed of genuine presence, the refusal to treat others as pixels. The parable is not merely ancient instruction—it is the daily rhythm of Christian life: receive, guard, and bear fruit.

For pastors and evangelizers, the message is liberating. Success is not control but cooperation. The preacher is not salesman but servant of the seed. His task is to sow broadly, pray deeply, and trust the Lord of the harvest. This relieves the Church of both pride and despair. Pride imagines results are ours; despair forgets that God still works in hidden soil. The same Spirit who raised Jesus from the dead can raise faith from apparent barrenness. Hope, not strategy, is the Church's engine.

This parable also speaks to our wounded moral imagination. We are tempted to believe that human hearts are fixed—that some are hopelessly hard or perpetually thorny. But the field belongs to God, and He never abandons His land. Soil changes. Seasons change. The hand of the divine farmer never tires. Many who were once rocky ground become saints through suffering. Many who seemed lost among thorns discover, through grace, the joy of pruning. The Gospel does not sort people into categories; it proclaims the possibility of conversion. There is no heart beyond cultivation.

The path to fruitfulness in our age is therefore not innovation but return—to listening, to contemplation, to patience. The Church must rediscover herself as soil before she can act as sower. The Word cannot be reduced to slogans or marketing; it must be planted through witness.

Holiness is the fertility of the field. Every saint is a corner of earth that has yielded a hundredfold because it stayed open to the rain of grace. In a distracted world, sanctity is the last deep silence where the Word can still be heard.

This same parable speaks hope into the cultural weariness that pervades our time. The thorns of anxiety and the heat of conflict may be intense, but the seed has not lost its power. Beneath the headlines, grace is still germinating—young people answering vocations, families rediscovering prayer, parishes feeding the poor, hearts finding reconciliation after years of distance. The Kingdom's rhythm is not linear progress but cyclical renewal: every generation looks barren until spring surprises the earth again. God is patient because He knows what the soil can become.

In personal prayer, the parable becomes a daily examen. Where have I hardened my heart today? What stones of resentment or habit need removing? What thorns of worry have crept back overnight? The Holy Spirit is the gentle gardener of this inner terrain. He does not condemn; He cultivates. When we bring our rough soil to Him in honesty, He breaks it open with mercy. Confession is divine ploughing. Eucharist is divine rain. The spiritual life is not a project to finish but a field to tend with God.

In the end, the Word for our age is the same Word spoken by the lake: *Listen.* Everything begins there. The path can still soften; the rock can still crack; the thorns can still be cleared. The Sower has not stopped walking the world, and His seed has not lost its power. The future of the Church will not be built by strategies but by hearts that hear again. Where the Word is received in faith and lived in love, the Kingdom already grows—quietly, inevitably, and beyond calculation.

The invitation of this parable is as urgent now as it was in Galilee: to become soil that welcomes the Word and to trust that God will do the rest. In a culture that prizes immediacy, we must learn again the divine tempo of growth. The Word does not hurry. It takes root, deepens, and bears fruit in its season. When the world grows restless for results, the disciple remains patient for harvest. Every act of faithfulness, every small prayer whispered in hiddenness, is seed the Sower will one day gather.

In that trust, we find peace. The field may seem ordinary, but the Sower walks it still, His hands full of promise. He bends low, scattering life into the dust of our century, confident that even here, even now, the soil will bloom.

## Hearing that Becomes Doing

The crowd by the lake has drifted away. The waves lap against the shore where the footprints of the Sower have already faded. You remain behind in the silence that follows His words: *"Listen. Behold, a sower went out to sow."* The wind still carries the echo. It is no longer a parable about someone else. It is about you.

Close your eyes and picture the field of your heart. You know its paths, its rocky ridges, its patches of thorns, its corners of soft soil. The Lord has walked through it again and again, scattering His word with a generosity that ignores the odds. Some seeds have taken root; others never sprouted; others bloomed and then withered in heat. Yet He keeps coming. That is the first truth of this parable: the Sower never stops sowing.

Let that comfort you. God has not given up on ground that seems barren. He wastes nothing, not even failure. Every hearing of His word is another handful of seed. You are living proof of His patience—the soil He keeps returning to. Even your weariness is part of the field He loves.

Now begin to walk through it slowly. Where have the birds been feeding lately—the distractions that snatch truth before it can sink in? Perhaps it is the constant noise of your devices, the self-talk of anxiety, the inner critic that mocks every beginning. Name these birds gently, then ask the Lord to guard the field. He does not drive them away with anger but with presence. Attention is the scarecrow of the soul; to notice is already to defend.

Move next to the rocky ground—the places where you receive the word with excitement but without depth. Maybe it is your resolve to pray more, to forgive, to trust. You start strong but tire quickly. Beneath that pattern lies a longing for control. The seed cannot survive there because it is never allowed to sink deep enough to change you. Ask the Spirit to give you courage to stay in silence long enough for roots to form. Depth grows in time, not in emotion.

And what of the thorns? They are not evil; they are simply too many. The cares of this world, Jesus said, and the desire for riches and pleasure. You know them well—the endless planning, the striving to be secure, the quiet addiction to comfort. These are the subtle suffocations of grace. To weed them is not to abandon responsibility but to recover simplicity. Ask God to help you trust that His care is enough, that fruitfulness depends less on your effort than on His rain.

Finally, find the good soil—the small places where grace has already taken hold. A habit of prayer that persists, a wound forgiven, a love that endures. These are holy ground. Kneel there in gratitude. The harvest may look small, but heaven sees the abundance. Every kernel of obedience carries the pattern of a hundredfold return.

This parable is about hearing, but it ends with doing: *"The one who hears the word and accepts it bears fruit."* Hearing, in the biblical sense, means more than sound entering the ear; it means surrender. The Hebrew *shema*—"Hear, O Israel"—is a call to listen with the will. You hear rightly only when you allow the word to reshape you. The fruit is not proof of success but the natural expression of surrender.

Do not be discouraged by how slowly this happens. Growth is measured in seasons, not minutes. The soil cannot rush the seed. You cannot rush grace. Your only task is to stay receptive—to let prayer, Scripture, and the sacraments keep the field open. Every Mass is a sowing; every confession a tilling; every act of love a harvest beginning.

When the word seems buried and lifeless, remember that even Christ became seed. He entered the soil of death, silent, unseen, and from that darkness rose the first fruits of resurrection. The pattern of the Sower is the pattern of the Son. To receive His word is to receive His way: to let yourself be buried in humility, broken in service, and raised in love.

Sit quietly now and listen again: *"He who has ears to hear, let him hear."*

## THE PARABLE OF THE SOWER (MK 4:1–20)

The sentence is not rebuke but invitation. You already have ears; you need only open them. The Spirit speaks through every event, every person, every silence that interrupts you. The word of God is falling constantly—on commute and conversation, on failure and rest. You will begin to recognise it when you start listening not for information but for presence.

This prayer may help you begin that listening:

**Prayer of the Heart's Field**

Sower of all good seed,
turn over the soil of my heart.
Break the hardness that keeps Your word at the surface.
Pull out the thorns of worry and greed.
Water me with Your patience.
Teach me to wait through the nights of unknowing
until Your hidden life rises within me.
Let the harvest You desire ripen in its time—
thirty, sixty, a hundredfold—
all for Your glory.
Amen.

Stay in the silence after the prayer. Listen not for words but for the breath between them. The Kingdom is germinating there, beneath awareness, the same way the seed swells underground. When you rise from prayer, rise gently, as one who has been watered. Go back into your day carrying this certainty: every moment is soil, every encounter a place where the Word can fall anew. The Sower is still walking. His hand is open. The harvest has already begun.

# 3

# The Parable Of The Mustard Seed & The Leaven (Mt 13:31–33)

*He put before them another parable: "The kingdom of heaven is like a mustard seed that someone took and sowed in his field; it is the smallest of all the seeds, but when it has grown it is the greatest of shrubs and becomes a tree, so that the birds of the air come and make nests in its branches."*

*He told them another parable: "The kingdom of heaven is like yeast that a woman took and mixed in with three measures of flour until all of it was leavened."*

### The Word Spoken

The afternoon light over the lake has changed but not yet faded. The boat remains just off the shoreline at Capernaum—a few arm-lengths from the pebbled edge—so Jesus' voice can ride the natural acoustics of water to the "very large crowd" massed on the beach. Fishermen crouch on overturned baskets. Children have fallen asleep in shawls. A ring of Pharisees and scribes—cool-eyed, arms folded—keeps to the back, near the shade of tamarisks. This is the same teaching session that began with the Sower and moved through the field of mixed growth—the Weeds among the

# THE PARABLE OF THE MUSTARD SEED & THE LEAVEN (MT 13:31–33)

Wheat—so the crowd is primed to expect more images of seeds, seasons, and the slow arithmetic of God.

The narrative current is as important as the wind's. Tension with the religious leadership has escalated; recent controversies over Sabbath, exorcisms, and table-fellowship have hardened lines. Open polemic would ignite the conflict too soon. So Jesus persists with parables—speech that disarms even as it divides, that reveals to the hungry and conceals from the hostile. He remains seated, the posture of authority; they remain standing, the posture of learners and litigants. The sea glints like hammered bronze. Quiet. Then He begins again—not with trumpet-blast messianism, but with a speck.

"The kingdom of heaven is like a grain of mustard seed..."

The crowd knows mustard—*Sinapis nigra*, the volunteer of every ditch and field-edge, seed so small it disappears between finger and thumb. No one would choose mustard to symbolize royal dominion, yet that is precisely the shock. Jesus refuses the cedar-of-Lebanon grandeur of imperial propaganda. He starts with the negligible. The line about size is not botanical pedantry but theological provocation: "the smallest of all seeds... and when it has grown it is the greatest of shrubs and becomes a tree." The hyperbole is intentional. He isn't drawing a herbarium plate; He's pressing the paradox that the divine chooses the diminutive as its doorway into history. Smallness is not prelude but strategy.

He adds the birds. To the biblically literate in the crowd, the phrase "the birds of the air come and make nests in its branches" hums with scriptural overtones—Daniel's cosmic tree sheltering the nations; Ezekiel's cedar planted on Zion, branch enough for every wing. Jesus does not quote; He swaps. Not cedar but shrub; not imperial silhouette but invasive hospitality. The Kingdom's reach will be truly universal, but its stature will look like a weed that refuses to stay in neat borders. The irony is gentle and sharp at once. Rome exhibits its dominion in colonnades; Israel remembers hers in temple stones; Jesus proposes neither. A sprawling shrub, alive at ground level, hosting outsiders—that is His emblem.

He pivots without fanfare to a second picture, as if to say: what is true in field is true in home.

"The kingdom of heaven is like leaven which a woman took and hid in three measures of flour, till it was all leavened."

The scene shrinks from hillside to hearth. A woman—no name, no title—kneads a vast quantity of flour (nearly forty litres' worth), enough to feed a village. She takes leaven—a living remnant from yesterday's dough—and *hides* it in the new batch. The verb matters: concealed, buried, worked in until invisible. Hours pass. Nothing to see. Then the quiet swell: the whole lump transformed from within. If the mustard seed is divine disproportion in space (speck to shrub), the leaven is divine transformation in substance (inert to living). Both images insist on hidden beginnings; both end with total change.

Context binds the two. These come after the Sower and the Weeds—after Jesus has taught that the Word meets resistance and that judgment is God's to time. Here He answers the anxious question that hangs in such patience: does the Kingdom actually advance? Yes—but not by spectacle. It advances by smallness and by secrecy, by the stubborn vitality of life itself. He has not abandoned the field to weeds; He has chosen a growth mode the impatient cannot counterfeit.

Between the lines, the movement of the day itself preaches: earlier, He addressed crowds; as evening nears, He will move into a house, turning to the disciples for private explanation. The shift from public shoreline to private interior mirrors the twin images. Mustard is the open-air spread of grace; leaven is the interior ferment of grace. The Kingdom is centrifugal and centripetal at once—pressing outward to birds at the margins, pressing inward until flour itself is changed. The crowd feels the serenity of His cadence and, beneath it, the irony of His claims: a reign without banners, a revolution of yeast.

The mood by the lakeside is serene, yet there is an undertone of divine irony. Every sentence Jesus utters carries both simplicity and subversion. His choice of words—so few, so measured—compresses vast oppositions. In Greek, the phrases are disarmingly plain: *kokkos sinapeōs* ("a grain of mustard"), *mikron* ("small"), *megas* ("great"), *zymē* ("leaven"). These are not random vocabulary. They frame the grammar of divine transformation: *mikron* becoming *megas*, the imperceptible turning world-sized, the hidden (*enekrupsen*) working its way toward universality. In the mouth of Jesus, linguistic proportion itself becomes revelation.

The word *mikron*—small, slight, insignificant—is the beginning. It names what the human eye dismisses. In ordinary Greek usage, it could describe children, coins, or lesser things; in the Septuagint it often shades toward contempt. Jesus seizes that connotation and inverts it. In His Kingdom, *mikron* is not marginal but essential. "Whoever humbles himself like this child is the greatest (*megas*) in the kingdom of heaven" (Mt 18:4). The seed's smallness is not weakness but the chosen vessel of omnipotence.

Then *megas*: "when it has grown it is the greatest of shrubs." The Greek carries not only size but dignity, magnitude of being. Jesus sets the two words side by side—*mikron* to *megas*—to sketch the logic of divine paradox. Greatness, in the Kingdom, is not achieved but generated; not grasped but grown. It is what happens when the infinite compresses itself into the finite and then unfolds. The field becomes a theology of the Incarnation: divinity planted in humility, expanding into hospitality.

The second parable carries the same grammar in a different key. *Zymē*, leaven, was a double-edged term. In common speech it meant fermentation, corruption, the bubbling of what was once pure. In Jewish ritual life it symbolised contamination—the reason for unleavened bread at Passover. Yet *zymē* is also what makes dough rise, what turns dead matter into living. Jesus chooses the ambiguous word deliberately. He names the Kingdom with a term associated with impurity. He thus declares that holiness will henceforth work not by segregation but by permeation. Grace will operate as yeast does—entering, transforming, dissolving boundaries from within.

Notice again the verbs. The woman "took" (*labousa*) and "hid" (*enekrupsen*) the leaven in three measures of flour. The action is quiet, deliberate, maternal. The quantity—three measures—was proverbial for abundance, recalling Sarah's hospitality in Genesis 18:6 when she prepared bread for angelic visitors. The crowd's memory of that scene would not have been accidental. In Abraham's tent, three guests foreshadowed divine visitation; in Jesus' parable, three measures become the site of divine indwelling. The woman's hidden act thus repeats the mystery of visitation in domestic form. The same God who appeared beneath the terebinths now rises invisibly in bread.

As He speaks, the lake mirrors the sky; its surface trembles with light. Fishermen nearby mend nets. Birds cut their arcs over the water. Everything around Him—the wind, the warmth, the murmur of the crowd—embodies what He says: small motions containing vast consequence. The Kingdom is already present in the scene itself.

By now His listeners understand the rhythm of His teaching. He never argues; He images. The logic of His speech is that of creation, not debate. When He says "the kingdom of heaven is like," He does not merely compare—it *becomes* like, in their hearing. Words make worlds. The parables do not illustrate truths; they perform them.

The two stories together trace the movement of the Gospel from invisibility to universality. The mustard seed describes the outward expansion of the Kingdom—its growth through the Church, its gathering of nations, its visible fruit in history. The leaven reveals its inward deepening—the transformation of hearts, cultures, and even matter itself. The first is missionary, the second mystical; one evangelistic, the other eucharistic. Both point toward the same mystery: divine life diffused through creation until all things are made new.

Evening nears. The crowd's faces are lit by the low sun, each expression a different soil. Some smile at the domestic imagery; others stare in silence, sensing that what sounds simple hides something immeasurable. The Pharisees' brows knit. They hear blasphemy in the suggestion that the Kingdom—God's reign of holiness—could be likened to leaven, to corruption redeemed. The fishermen hear hope. The poor hear comfort. The disciples hear invitation.

When Jesus finishes, there is no applause, only the sound of the lake and the faint sigh of wind through reeds. He looks toward the west, where the light over Tiberias turns to copper. The day that began with the Sower now closes with seed and yeast—both destined to vanish before they are seen. Soon He will rise, step from the boat, and walk toward the village. Behind Him, the crowd will disperse, but the parables will stay, lodged like grains beneath the skin of memory.

The Kingdom of heaven, He has told them, is not an event to await but a life already underway. It is mustard beneath the sandals, leaven under the fingernails. It is the divine in miniature, the infinite in embryo. No one applauds, yet the cosmos itself has tilted: *mikron* is now *megas*, and the world's salvation smells faintly of rising bread.

### The Surface Story

The two parables Jesus tells here — of the mustard seed and the leaven — are drawn straight from the daily world of the Galilean poor. They are not lofty metaphors or ornamental symbols; they are kitchen and field, dust and dough. To those who heard Him that afternoon, the imagery was shockingly familiar. It smelled of sweat and yeast. It felt too close to home to be sacred. Which is precisely why it is sacred.

In Galilee, mustard was not a crop. It was a weed. The black mustard (*Sinapis nigra*) sprang up on its own wherever birds or wind had dropped the seed. It grew quickly, its thin stems branching wildly, tangling with whatever tried to share its space. In good soil it could reach three meters tall — large enough for birds to perch, too large to be ignored. No farmer planted it on purpose. Once mustard took root, it claimed the ground. Its roots spread fast; its pods burst, scattering seed across every border. It could invade vineyards and choke barley fields.

The listeners on that lakeshore knew this. They could look around and see its yellow flowers dotting the edges of every field. To them, mustard was both nuisance and necessity — troublesome in the garden, useful in the kitchen. Its oil was used for medicine and cooking; its sharp flavour made bland bread bearable. Yet no sensible man would scatter mustard seed into his own field. Jesus' parable begins, then, with an act of folly: "A man took and sowed it in his field."

The crowd would have murmured. What kind of man sows trouble into his own soil? It was a question as absurd as the image. But Jesus, as always, starts where the mind resists. His farmer acts contrary to wisdom. He plants what cannot be contained. The Kingdom, He implies, spreads like that — unwanted, uncontrollable, resilient.

When Jesus adds that it becomes "the greatest of shrubs," the exaggeration would have drawn a smile. Everyone knew a mustard plant was a spindly, wind-blown bush, not a cedar of Lebanon. The phrasing is intentionally ironic. Greatness here is not elevation but proliferation. The Kingdom's glory lies in its refusal to die. It grows where no one expects, uninvited, unstoppable.

The detail about "the birds of the air" nesting in its branches is what truly startled the crowd. That line echoes the imagery of Daniel 4 and Ezekiel 17, where great trees symbolize empires — Assyria, Babylon, even Israel itself — sheltering the nations. But in Jesus' telling, the imperial cedar is replaced by a peasant's weed. The birds — a Jewish idiom for Gentiles — now find refuge not in an empire or temple, but in a tangle of wild branches. This was subversive. To His Jewish listeners, the Kingdom of God was the restoration of Israel's power and purity, a cosmic cedar towering over the nations. Jesus compares it instead to an invasive plant. The Kingdom will not stand above the world in majesty; it will creep through it in mercy.

They would have understood the realism intimately. The mustard plant was common as dust. It sprouted between the stones of pathways, around ovens, along the borders of every ploughed plot. It grew from nothing. Even children could identify it by sight. And so Jesus anchors divine mystery in something that could be uprooted by hand. The image carries the scent of Galilee — the mix of dry soil, animal dung, and green sap crushed underfoot.

To the local farmers, who lived under crushing taxes and tenancy laws, the mustard plant also carried an ironic symbolism. Like them, it thrived on neglect, clung to poor soil, resisted the plough of empire. In its stubborn vitality, they saw themselves. The Sower who scatters such seed

— wasteful, prodigal, defiant — resembles the God who has not abandoned them. The realism here is more than agricultural; it is social. The parable describes the way divine life takes root among the disregarded.

Jesus' listeners would have recognised this as an implicit challenge to the prevailing vision of holiness. Pharisaic piety sought order, separateness, control — a purity fenced off from contamination. The mustard plant was the opposite: it invaded fences, blurred boundaries, mixed clean and unclean ground. In comparing the Kingdom to such a weed, Jesus overturns the purity codes of His day. Holiness will no longer be about isolation; it will be about expansion. The reign of God will not exclude impurity; it will absorb and transform it.

That tension between nuisance and blessing, chaos and shelter, gives the image its edge. The parable forces the hearer to choose: will you see the mustard as contamination or as miracle? It grows where you wish it wouldn't, but it gives shade to what you never thought worthy of shade. The Kingdom is both disruptive and hospitable.

As He spoke, those gathered could feel the sting of the comparison. Their Scriptures had promised a Messianic reign like a mountain cedar; Jesus offers a weed that grows by trespassing. It was a joke, but also a warning. The Kingdom's arrival would not respect human boundaries. It would break them.

The power of the image lies precisely in its ordinariness. Jesus does not draw on temple ritual or rabbinic learning. He draws on what everyone can see: a field, a weed, a farmer who refuses to act sensibly. The divine revelation hides in plain sight, clothed in the fabric of the everyday. The crowd, whether amused or offended, finds itself disarmed. The story makes them participants: each must decide what kind of ground they are willing to be for this wild seed.

Then, almost without pause, Jesus changes register. The horizon shrinks from field to house, from man to woman, from weed to bread. The mustard seed gives way to the leaven. His listeners would have understood the connection immediately. Both images involve small beginnings, hidden growth, transformation from within. But where the first image moves outward — a field invaded — the second moves inward — dough penetrated.

The woman in His story works in silence. She takes leaven — a lump of sourdough kept from a previous batch — and hides it in "three measures of flour." The act is unremarkable, part of the morning's routine in every household. The realism is domestic and tactile. One can imagine her hands dusted white, the weight of the clay mixing bowl, the warmth of the oven nearby. Nothing divine seems to be happening, and that is the point.

Yet to His audience, this image, too, was strange. In their ritual world, leaven carried a moral charge. During Passover, it was banished from homes as a symbol of corruption. To associate the Kingdom with leaven was to flirt with impurity. Rabbis used leaven as a metaphor for sin, pride, or false teaching. But Jesus reverses the symbol. What the Law once named defilement, He now reveals as renewal. The Kingdom is not the avoidance of fermentation but its sanctification—the hidden transformation of what seemed corrupt into life.

The verb Matthew uses — *enekrupsen*, "she hid" — is precise. The woman conceals the leaven in the flour until it vanishes from sight. The transformation begins invisibly, silently, working through every particle until all is changed. The hiddenness is not incidental; it is essential. The Kingdom does not announce itself. It works in secret, transforming substance from within until the entire world is leavened.

The quantity — "three measures of flour" — would have startled the practical hearer. That much flour, nearly forty litres, could feed a hundred people. This is not ordinary baking; it is abundance. It recalls Genesis 18:6, when Abraham tells Sarah to prepare three measures of flour for the divine visitors at Mamre. Jesus' listeners, well-versed in Scripture, would have recognised the echo. The same God who once visited Abraham's tent now visits the ovens of Galilee. The divine hospitality continues, but now through a woman's hands instead of a patriarch's feast.

The contrast between the two parables is deliberate. In the first, a man plants what he cannot control; in the second, a woman hides what she cannot stop. Both images hinge on surrender. In the field, the seed grows beyond the farmer's reach. In the kitchen, the dough rises beyond the woman's sight. The Kingdom, whether in open field or closed hearth, exceeds human management. God's reign is not manufactured; it happens.

Both would have startled and unsettled their hearers. A weed and leaven — two images of impurity, two metaphors of intrusion. The crowd expected the Kingdom of heaven to resemble temple purity or political power. Instead, Jesus describes something that begins small, works quietly, and refuses to stay contained. His metaphors are not about conquest but about contagion — a holiness that spreads through what is unholy until all is renewed.

By now, the sun is lowering. The crowd's faces are streaked with sweat and light. Some are smiling, intrigued by His homeliness; others are frowning, troubled by the irreverence. The Pharisees whisper among themselves. But a few — fishermen, widows, labourers — are thinking of the mustard sprouting between their fences and the dough fermenting in their homes. Something in those images feels too real to ignore. The Kingdom He describes smells like their own world: earth and bread, sweat and hope.

The realism of these two parables is so exact, so grounded, that the divine meaning seems to vanish inside the details. Yet that is precisely where Jesus intends it to live. He does not preach the Kingdom from the mountain or the synagogue; He locates it in the weed underfoot and the yeast under the fingernail. His audience of farmers, widows, servants, and craftsmen would have understood that both images were daringly irreligious. God, it seems, is now speaking their language.

For centuries, prophets had described God's reign in the vocabulary of grandeur: cedars of Lebanon, mountains exalted, thrones of fire. The Psalms sang of dominion stretching from sea to sea, of Zion as the joy of all the earth. The crowd by the lake had grown up on those images. They longed for a restoration of power, purity, and prestige. But Jesus refuses those symbols. His Kingdom is like a mustard weed and a lump of fermenting dough.

It is difficult to overstate how offensive that would have sounded. The cedar was a national symbol of majesty; the mustard shrub was a joke. The cedar sheltered kings; the mustard tangled around their palaces. Leaven, likewise, belonged not in temple rites but in kitchens, among women and children. To a culture obsessed with ritual cleanness, both images bordered on blasphemy. Yet by choosing them, Jesus redefines holiness itself. He declares that God's glory now hides in the small, the common, the unclean. The sacred will no longer dwell apart from the profane but will dwell *within* it, transforming it from inside.

The realism of the parables forces that truth upon the listener. In the field, the mustard's growth is visible, even aggressive. It invades the ordered rows, reaching upward like green fire. In the dough, the leaven's work is hidden, silent, and slow. Together they describe the two manners of God's presence in the world: the visible and the invisible, the disruptive and the interior. One changes landscapes, the other changes substance.

By pairing a man and a woman in consecutive parables, Jesus also restores a balance long lost in the religious imagination. The farmer and the housewife become co-creators in the Kingdom's unfolding. The masculine world of public labour and the feminine world of domestic care are united in divine purpose. Both act, both wait, both witness transformation that exceeds their control.

The woman's act of hiding the leaven carries particular tenderness. She does not preach or declare; she folds. Her gesture mirrors the humility of the Incarnation itself — God hidden in flesh, divinity folded into humanity. The realism is so quiet that the theological weight could easily go unnoticed, yet that is the brilliance of it. The Kingdom, Jesus insists, does not arrive with fanfare but with hands dusted in flour.

The people who heard these parables were weary of grand promises. Roman soldiers patrolled their roads; tax collectors haunted their doorways. The word "kingdom" in their ears meant power and retaliation. But here, by the lake, that word is reborn. It no longer names an empire but an ecosystem — something living, self-propagating, organic. The "reign" of God is less like an army and more like yeast in dough: invisible, slow, certain.

## THE PARABLE OF THE MUSTARD SEED & THE LEAVEN (MT 13:31–33)

The crowd's minds would have filled with associations as He spoke. They knew what leaven smelled like when left too long — acrid, sour, like rot. They had watched dough rise beside their hearths, watched it swell and breathe. They had seen how one pinch of starter could animate an entire trough of flour. It was ordinary magic. To hear Jesus call that process divine was to feel both scandal and wonder. It meant that the divine work might already be happening in their own kitchens, their own bodies, their own secret struggles.

Likewise, the mustard plant was their neighbour and nuisance. Children played among its stalks; farmers cursed it; birds nested in it. By choosing that image, Jesus was telling them that the Kingdom was already among them, growing untamed in the very fields they walked every day. They didn't need to climb to the temple to find it. It was under their sandals.

Mustard and leaven also carried symbolic edges sharpened by Jewish law. Mustard, with its spreading roots, blurred boundaries between fields — a metaphor for impurity. Leaven, fermenting by decay, symbolised moral corruption. The Torah kept both at a distance from holy things. Yet Jesus binds them to the Kingdom itself. The unclean becomes the medium of the holy. It is not that God ignores the law's distinctions, but that He fulfills their purpose by entering what they excluded.

In doing so, Jesus also critiques a broader cultural obsession with visible strength. His Kingdom will not rival Rome in grandeur or Jerusalem in ceremony. It will begin as what the world overlooks — small communities of faith, poor disciples, hidden virtue — and will grow until it shelters the nations. His parables name a revolution, but not one carried by swords or edicts. The invasion will come through mercy, through witness, through lives transformed.

The listeners, caught between curiosity and disbelief, would have left the shore unsettled. They expected a call to arms; they received a call to patience. The mustard and the leaven do not command; they become. The message was that the reign of God cannot be seized; it must be allowed to happen.

In both parables, Jesus celebrates concealment as divine strategy. The seed vanishes into soil; the leaven vanishes into dough. Growth occurs where eyes cannot see. This hiddenness would become a signature of His Kingdom — a reign born in anonymity, a Messiah revealed in suffering, a glory hidden in the Cross.

To the ordinary Galilean, however, the literal meaning still dominated: a weed and a fermenting dough. These were facts of life. Yet as they walked home that evening, the phrases would have replayed themselves in memory. "The kingdom of heaven is like…" The words would cling like the scent of yeast or the sight of yellow blossoms in the fields. Understanding would come later, slowly, as all living things grow.

By the time the sun set over the Sea of Galilee, those who had truly listened had already begun to change. Something had been hidden in them, something that would rise. The parables themselves were leaven — words buried in the heart, destined to ferment into faith. The realism of the stories, their tactile detail, ensured that they could not be dismissed as abstractions. The listeners would meet them again each morning in the kitchen or the field, and each time, they would hear the echo of His voice: *The kingdom of heaven is like this.*

The parables of the mustard seed and the leaven thus unfold not as allegories to be decoded but as encounters to be lived. Their realism does not explain divinity; it enfolds it. In a world that divided the sacred from the common, Jesus reunites them. He leaves His hearers with the same quiet imperative that still lingers through centuries of commentary: look again at the ordinary. It may already be burning with God.

## The Hidden Fire

### a) Text, Translation, and Literary Context
### Greek (Mt 13:31–33)

Ἄλλην παραβολὴν παρέθηκεν αὐτοῖς λέγων· ὁμοία ἐστὶν ἡ βασιλεία τῶν οὐρανῶν κόκκῳ σινάπεως, ὃν λαβὼν ἄνθρωπος ἔσπειρεν ἐν τῷ ἀγρῷ αὐτοῦ· ὃ μικρότερον μέν ἐστιν πάντων τῶν σπερμάτων, ὅταν δὲ αὐξηθῇ μεῖζον τῶν λαχάνων ἐστὶν καὶ γίνεται δένδρον, ὥστε ἐλθεῖν τὰ πετεινὰ τοῦ οὐρανοῦ καὶ

# THE PARABLE OF THE MUSTARD SEED & THE LEAVEN (MT 13:31-33)

κατασκηνοῦν ἐν τοῖς κλάδοις αὐτοῦ. Ἄλλην παραβολὴν ἐλάλησεν αὐτοῖς· ὁμοία ἐστὶν ἡ βασιλεία τῶν οὐρανῶν ζύμῃ, ἣν λαβοῦσα γυνὴ ἐνέκρυψεν εἰς ἀλεύρου σάτα τρία, ἕως οὗ ἐζυμώθη ὅλον.

Matthew positions the parables of the Mustard Seed and the Leaven at the centre of his great discourse on the Kingdom of Heaven. After the long opening of the Sower and the Wheat and the Tares, the narrative pauses, and Jesus speaks two sentences that hold the entire mystery of divine action within the smallest of images. The simplicity is deliberate. The crowds have heard of sowers, fields, weeds, and harvests; now they are asked to imagine a single grain and a pinch of leaven. The shift in scale marks a shift in focus. What was formerly about reception and judgment becomes about the nature of growth itself—how the Kingdom expands, silently, almost invisibly, from what seems inconsequential.

Matthew's Greek tightens the rhythm. Each parable begins with the identical phrase, *hōmoia estin hē basileia tōn ouranōn*—"the kingdom of heaven is like." The repetition creates a refrain that turns the discourse into liturgy: the Kingdom is described not by definition but by analogy. The noun *basileia* here means not territory but reign—the active exercise of divine sovereignty within human history. The comparison is therefore dynamic. The Kingdom is not static space but motion, an energy entering the world. In the first parable, that movement is outward, from the soil upward; in the second, it is inward, from the dough's centre outward. Together they map the geography of grace.

The first image begins with *kókkon sinápeōs*—"a grain of mustard." The word *kókkos* denotes a small kernel or granule; *sinápi* identifies the mustard plant common on Galilean hillsides. The diminutive construction carries a tone of tenderness: the thing is almost invisible, yet alive. Jesus calls it *mikróteron pantōn spermatōn*, "smaller than all the seeds." The comparison is proverbial, not botanical. Rabbinic literature often used the mustard seed as the emblem of minuteness. The phrasing itself is typical of Semitic exaggeration: what is "smallest" is not literally least but stands as a type for what human sight dismisses. Matthew's sentence is taut, symmetrical, and rhythmic, moving from compression to expansion—smallest of seeds, greatest of shrubs, becoming a tree. The crescendo is grammatical before it is theological.

The verbs carry that movement. The sower *labōn*—"having taken"—and *espeiren*—"sowed"—performs a completed action in the aorist. The result, however, unfolds in the present: it *grows* (*auxanei*) and *becomes* (*ginetai*). The alternation of tenses conveys a hidden timeline: decisive divine initiative, followed by continuous development. The syntax thus mirrors salvation history—the act accomplished once, its effects still expanding. The phrase *en tō agriō autou*—"in his field"—returns the image to the world of the earlier parables. The field is no longer contested ground, as in the story of the weeds, but cultivated soil. Here, growth proceeds without opposition. What astonishes is not conflict but disproportion.

When the mustard plant reaches maturity, Matthew writes, it "becomes a tree, so that the birds of the air come and make nests in its branches." The shift from shrub to tree (*déndron*) stretches the realism. Mustard rarely grew taller than a man; yet the text insists on arboreal scale. This hyperbole is stylistic, not symbolic—at least at this stage. It belongs to the rhetoric of marvel that runs through Jesus' teaching: the ordinary overwhelmed by excess. The phrase *ta peteina tou ouranou*—"the birds of the air"—is a common biblical idiom for creatures of the sky, appearing in the Septuagint of Genesis and the Psalms. In literary context it functions as a measure of abundance: when birds find shelter, fertility is complete. The closing verb *kataskēnoin*—"to dwell" or "make nests"—is rare in Matthew, evoking settled rest. The image of nesting marks the end of the parable's motion: what began as small and buried ends as shelter and repose.

Immediately, Matthew pairs this with the parable of the leaven, introduced by the same formula and nearly identical syntax. The subject changes, as does the setting. A woman replaces the man, and the field becomes dough. The verb *enekrypsen*—"she hid" or "mixed in"—is vivid. It literally means to conceal within, from *enkryptō*. The leaven is not sprinkled but buried. The motion is interior, reversed from the first parable. In both, however, the decisive act is the same: something living is

## THE PARABLE OF THE MUSTARD SEED & THE LEAVEN (MT 13:31-33)

introduced into something inert, and transformation begins.

The measure of flour—*tría sataa aleurou*—has drawn comment since antiquity. One *saton* equalled roughly sixteen liters; three measures would yield enough bread for a household feast. Matthew's audience would have recognized the absurdity of the quantity. Hyperbole again signals the scale of divine work: a tiny portion of yeast animates an impossible mass. The phrase *heōs hou ezymōthē holon*—"until it was all leavened"—is grammatically complete; the participle *ezymōthē* marks the process as accomplished. The leaven's work is quiet, gradual, yet unstoppable. Within the parable discourse, this single clause balances the more visible growth of the mustard shrub. One parable moves through space; the other through substance. The Kingdom expands and permeates.

Taken together, the two sentences form a miniature composition of parallelism and inversion. Each begins with the same verbal frame (*hōmoia estin*), introduces a subject performing an intentional act (*labōn / labousa*), and concludes with a totalizing result (*hoste elthein ta peteina / heōs hou ezymōthē holon*). The symmetry is exact but not redundant: one describes the Kingdom's external spread, the other its interior diffusion. In literary terms, the pair functions as chiasm—outward growth mirrored by inward leavening. Matthew's careful balance of masculine and feminine agents, field and home, visible and hidden, embodies his larger theology of fulfillment: the Kingdom touches every sphere of human life.

The choice of images would have surprised the first hearers. Mustard was a common weed, difficult to control once planted; leaven, in Jewish ritual life, was often a symbol of impurity. Both therefore carried ambiguous overtones. By using them as analogies for the Kingdom, Jesus shocks expectations. Yet Matthew's text itself remains neutral; it records no explanation, no moral. The emphasis lies not in the moral reversal but in the linguistic pattern: small element, large result. At the textual level, this proportion is what unites the parables of chapter 13. The grammar of the Kingdom is the grammar of growth from the least.

Within the broader narrative, Matthew situates these sayings between public and private teaching. The audience still consists of the crowd, yet the tone is quieter. The evangelist's connective phrase *Allēn parabolēn paretheken autois*—"He put another parable before them"—appears twice, marking formal unity. The doubling of *another* (*allēn... allēn*) signals progression: the same truth refracted in new imagery. The compositional device allows the two parables to operate as one unit, a single poem with two stanzas. Later, in verse 34, Matthew notes that Jesus "spoke all these things to the crowds in parables." The phrase closes the series like a refrain, confirming that these short images complete the pattern of revelation begun with the Sower.

In translation, the texture of Matthew's Greek is deceptively plain. Its vocabulary belongs to the speech of home and field; its structure is balanced, almost architectural. Each clause rests upon another with measured symmetry, revealing a writer who crafts theology through syntax. The alternation of active and passive, completed and continuing tenses, creates a sense of steady movement without haste. The parables do not dramatize action; they describe inevitability. The Kingdom's presence is organic, not imposed.

Before theology begins in earnest, the text itself has already preached. The rhythm of smallness leading to fullness, the pattern of concealment preceding revelation, the pairing of outward and inward—all these are inscribed in the grammar. Matthew's literary precision turns ordinary words into vessels of mystery. Without stating what the Kingdom is, the text lets its motion be felt in language. The smallest seed grows; the hidden leaven works; and even on the level of syntax, the field and the dough are already alive with quiet expansion.

### b) Theological Interpretation

The two parables are joined not only by structure but by spirit. Both expose the logic of divine power: the paradox that God's might reveals itself through what appears insignificant. They are small windows into the great economy of grace—the way God acts in creation, in Israel, and in the Church. The theology that arises from them is therefore a theology of *hiddenness and transformation*, of patience and promise. Through the mustard seed and the leaven, Jesus teaches that the Kingdom of Heaven operates by the same principle as the Incarnation itself: the infinite entering the finite without fanfare, the Creator redeeming His world from within.

In the first image, the grain of mustard represents divine initiative in its most distilled form. It is not a metaphor for potential alone but for God's deliberate self-limitation. The smallest of seeds becomes a symbol of how the Almighty chooses to work within the bounds of the small. Throughout salvation history, this has been His signature. He does not summon empires; He calls Abraham. He does not raise an army; He forms a family. Israel's vocation was never to dominate by number but to bear witness by faith. "The Lord set His heart on you," says Deuteronomy, "not because you were more numerous than others, but because He loved you" (Deut 7:7–8). The mustard seed is that covenant logic expressed in creation. It reminds Israel that greatness in God's plan always begins in littleness.

Jesus' contemporaries expected the Kingdom to erupt with spectacle. They longed for political liberation, for the messianic reign to overthrow Rome and restore David's throne. Instead, He offers a parable of almost comic humility: a farmer sowing an unremarkable plant. The contrast is deliberate. God's reign enters history not with trumpet but with whisper. It grows quietly, according to an inner vitality that cannot be forced. The seed carries within itself the mystery of divine life—the Logos, the Word through whom all things were made. Just as creation unfolded from a single divine utterance, so the new creation begins from a single Word spoken into the soil of the world. The seed's power is not in its appearance but in its nature.

When that seed "becomes a tree," the transformation is not mere growth but transfiguration. A shrub becoming a tree is the language of miracle; it signifies nature lifted beyond itself. The Kingdom does not simply evolve from human effort; it surpasses the limits of what humanity can achieve. Grace perfects nature; it does not replace it, but it draws it upward. This is the hidden theology of the parable: that divine life, once planted in the human field, expands until it fulfills creation's original destiny—to be the dwelling place of God. What began in Genesis as a garden ends in Revelation as a city where God "makes His home among men." The mustard seed's improbable growth is the story of that journey.

The birds that find rest in its branches introduce another layer of meaning. They evoke the ancient imagery of the Gentile nations gathering under the shelter of God's people. In Ezekiel and Daniel, the "tree with branches" was the symbol of empire. But where Babylon's cedar towered in pride, the mustard tree grows in humility. Jesus reverses the metaphor: the Kingdom that truly endures will not oppress but give refuge. The inclusion of the nations in salvation history—the great mystery that Paul will later call the "ingrafting" of the Gentiles—is prefigured here. The tree that grows from the smallest seed becomes the Church herself: universal, sheltering, a place where the weary of every race can find rest. The parable's logic thus moves from creation to covenant to Church. Divine generosity expands outward until it embraces all humanity.

The second parable continues the same theology from another direction. If the seed reveals God's action in history, the leaven unveils His action in the soul. The woman who hides yeast in flour performs a domestic act that becomes the sign of divine sanctification. The verb "hid" (*enekrypsen*) implies intimacy. The Kingdom does not impose itself from without; it works from within. Grace is not an external pressure but an interior ferment. Once the leaven is mixed in, separation is impossible—the dough has been changed in its very being. This is how the Spirit transforms the human heart. Conversion is not surface reform but inward participation in divine life. What was once inert begins to rise.

Theologically, the leaven parable describes the sanctifying power of grace as it spreads through the human community and through each person's inner life. The whole lump of dough—the *holon*—symbolizes the totality of creation. "Till it was all leavened" marks the divine goal: nothing in human life is to remain untouched by grace. Just as the Spirit brooded over the waters in Genesis to bring forth life, so now the Spirit works within the human world, raising it toward communion. The three measures of flour recall the language of offering in Genesis 18, where Sarah prepares "three measures of fine flour" to serve the mysterious visitors at Mamre. Matthew's readers, steeped in Scripture, would have recognized the echo. The woman's act becomes priestly. The ordinary task of kneading bread becomes an image of hospitality to the divine.

Together, the two parables describe both the external and internal dimensions of redemption. The mustard seed speaks of mission—the outward spread of the Gospel across time and space. The leaven speaks of sanctification—the inner conversion that makes that mission credible. The Kingdom grows in the world and in the soul, by the same hidden grace. Both depend on patience, because divine life respects the rhythm of creation. A seed cannot be forced to grow; dough cannot be hurried to rise. The Kingdom's power is not control but vitality. It works in its own time, because it is alive.

This theology of patience runs through all of Jesus' teaching. God is not slow, but He is never rushed. The delay between sowing and harvest, between mixing and rising, is the time of faith. In that interval, the world sees only smallness, but heaven sees certainty. The seed may be unseen beneath the soil, but it is alive with the energy of resurrection. The dough may appear unchanged, but within it the process has begun. The Church lives in that tension. Her task is not to force the outcome but to remain faithful to the process—to protect the conditions where grace can work. Every sacrament, every prayer, every hidden act of charity is the leavening of the world in miniature. The same divine energy that raised Christ from the tomb now rises through history, one heart at a time.

The theology of the seed and the leaven reveals not only *how* the Kingdom grows, but *who* God shows Himself to be in its growth. He is not a monarch commanding obedience from a distance but a Father who entrusts His life to fragile vessels. The act of sowing a seed or hiding leaven is an act of vulnerability. In both images, something precious is risked—cast into soil, buried in dough, surrendered to process. That surrender is the signature of divine love. The Kingdom's advance is not triumphal but sacrificial. Every movement of grace mirrors the kenosis of the Incarnation, where the Word of God empties Himself into creation, content to work unseen until the appointed hour of revelation.

At the heart of both parables stands a theology of participation. The seed does not grow apart from the soil, nor the leaven apart from the dough. Each depends upon contact. Grace, in the same way, does not bypass the created order but enters it. The Creator works through His creation, redeeming it from within. This has always been the pattern of salvation: God does not destroy what He sanctifies; He transforms it. Israel was not replaced by the Church but fulfilled in her; the Old Covenant was not abolished but completed in the New. The mustard seed and the leaven reveal this divine method—continuity without confusion, change without loss. The Kingdom's power is integrative, not competitive; it assumes what it perfects.

This pattern also describes the moral life. Grace does not erase human effort; it animates it. Just as the leaven works by permeating the dough, so the Spirit works by penetrating our habits, desires, and intentions. Holiness is not flight from humanity but the full flourishing of humanity under grace. When Jesus says that the whole was leavened, He implies that sanctity reaches the edges of ordinary life. The Christian does not live two lives—one spiritual, one secular—but one life transformed from within. The home, the workshop, the classroom, the kitchen—all become fields of grace. The parables thus redefine holiness not as separation from the world but as its transfiguration. The Kingdom's yeast is meant to rise through the whole loaf of creation.

The logic of the mustard seed also discloses the Church's missionary identity. The Sower of the seed is not only Christ but all who bear His Word. The Kingdom's growth in history follows the same organic pattern as its origin in Galilee: it begins small, often despised, yet carries divine inevitability. The Church's expansion across centuries—from hidden catacombs to the ends of the earth—is the living proof that the seed is alive. What sustains her is not strategy but vitality, the indwelling Spirit. As long as the seed of faith remains, the tree cannot die. The parable therefore calls believers to humility in mission. Evangelization is not conquest but cultivation. The sower's task is patience, not control. The growth belongs to God.

There is also an ecclesial theology hidden in the yeast. Just as the leaven disappears into the dough, the Church must be immersed in the world to sanctify it. Withdrawal cannot save; only presence can. Yet the presence must be interior, transformative, not assimilated. The distinction between the dough and the leaven remains, even as their union brings life. This is the balance of Christian engagement: in the world but not of it, shaping culture from within by the quiet pressure of holiness. The leaven does not shout; it changes substance by contact. The world is converted not by argument alone but by participation in a life that cannot be explained apart from grace.

In both images, time becomes the medium of divine fidelity. The process of germination and fermentation cannot be hurried; they require the patience of God and the cooperation of man. The parables thus teach the virtue of hope—not wishful thinking but steadfast confidence in divine timing. God's promises unfold according to the rhythm of love, which always gives space for response. The waiting is not wasted; it is the form that grace takes in history. Israel waited through centuries for the Messiah; the Church waits still for His return. Between those two advents stretches the long growing season of the Kingdom, where faith must persevere and trust must mature.

At a deeper level, the two parables disclose the inner unity of Christ's redemptive work and the Spirit's sanctifying work. The seed, once planted, becomes the tree that shelters life—that is Christ's Paschal mystery, the Cross and Resurrection. The leaven that works through the dough is the ongoing presence of the Spirit who applies that redemption to souls. What Christ accomplishes historically, the Spirit accomplishes sacramentally. The Church, like the woman in the parable, hides the leaven of grace in the matter of human life: water, oil, bread, words, gestures. Through those humble means, divinity enters history again and again. The yeast of the sacraments ensures that the world is never without fermentation.

If the mustard seed teaches us how God acts, the leaven teaches us how we must respond. Faith begins as small as a seed, yet its potential is divine. Jesus will later tell His disciples that "faith as a mustard seed" can move mountains. That is not hyperbole but metaphysical realism: faith participates in the omnipotence of God because it is union with His will. To believe is to allow the Word to take root in us, to surrender control of growth to the God who alone gives increase. In the same way, the life of prayer resembles yeast working unseen; its fruit appears slowly, almost imperceptibly, until the whole person is changed. Grace matures in secret. The Christian who expects instant transformation misunderstands the nature of divine life. The Kingdom grows according to God's rhythm, not ours.

The convergence of the two parables—the seed that grows outward and the leaven that transforms inward—reveals the fullness of God's plan for creation. The Kingdom is not an intrusion from above but a renewal from within. What sin fractured, grace repairs by entering it. Both images affirm that God trusts His creation. He does not abandon it as corrupt beyond redemption; He believes it capable of bearing His life again. This is the deepest meaning of the Incarnation and of the parables that mirror it: divine confidence in the material world as the chosen instrument of salvation. Matter becomes the medium of mystery, soil the cradle of glory, dough the substance of communion. The theology is profoundly incarnational—spirit and flesh, heaven and earth, bound together by a love that refuses separation.

Such confidence transforms the way we view the Church and her mission. The seed's growth into a tree portrays not institutional expansion for its own sake but the natural expression of divine life. The Church is not merely an organization that manages belief; she is the organic continuation of the Incarnation, the visible growth of the invisible Word. Her sacraments, disciplines, and teachings are the living branches through which the Spirit breathes. When the nations find rest in her shade, the prophecy of the mustard tree is fulfilled: the covenant of Israel has become catholic, embracing all peoples. The unity of humanity under one faith is not the erasure of difference but the flowering of communion. The birds that nest in her branches are the multitudes of history taking shelter in mercy.

The leaven extends this ecclesial vision into the moral and spiritual life. The Church is leaven within the world, not an enclave apart from it. She sanctifies culture from within, not by domination but by diffusion. The great conversions of history—the abolition of slavery, the defence of life, the dignity of the poor—have followed the same pattern: silent yeast, patient influence, invisible grace changing the texture of civilization. Every Christian vocation participates in that same leavening. The believer who forgives an enemy, the family who welcomes life, the worker who labours with integrity—all are the yeast of the Kingdom. The transformation of the world begins not in legislatures or courts but in the heart that has been kneaded by the Spirit.

Both parables therefore disclose the mystery of divine humility. God is omnipotent, yet He prefers the power of patience. The world measures success by speed and size; the Kingdom measures by fidelity and fruit. The Sower does not shout; the Woman does not hurry. The Word works while hidden, and in that concealment it manifests God's gentleness. The Almighty stoops to the pace of growth. This humility of method reveals His nature: He is not content with domination; He desires communion. Love, by its essence, persuades rather than coerces. The Kingdom advances by attraction—the quiet magnetism of holiness drawing all things back to their source.

The smallness of the seed and the invisibility of the leaven also define the spirituality of discipleship. Jesus is teaching His followers to trust divine disproportion. We are called to sow without seeing results, to mix grace into the world without proof of its effect. Every act of faith, however small, carries eternity within it. The smile offered, the prayer whispered, the hidden sacrifice—these are mustard seeds whose fruit will appear only in the light of the final harvest. In God's economy, nothing sown in love is wasted. The field of history is filled with seeds that await resurrection. Faith is therefore patience in action, the confidence that what seems lost will one day shade the weary.

Inwardly, the leaven teaches that holiness is the slow conversion of the whole person. The dough must rest; it must be stretched, folded, left alone. So too must the soul. The process is not failure but formation. The Spirit works beneath the surface of consciousness, transforming motives and desires long before results are visible. The saints are those who allow the yeast of grace to complete its work. Their apparent ordinariness is the true sign of the Kingdom's presence. God delights to hide His greatest works in the texture of daily life. In this way, every kitchen becomes a sanctuary, every field an altar.

The culmination of both images is Eucharistic. The seed that becomes a tree and the leaven that makes bread both point to the same mystery: the transformation of creation into communion. The grain ground and baked, the dough risen and broken, find their fulfillment in the bread that becomes the Body of Christ. What was symbol becomes sacrament; what was parable becomes presence. The Kingdom of Heaven is not only like these things—it continues through them. In every Mass, the seed is sown again, the leaven works anew, until the whole world is transfigured into thanksgiving.

Ultimately, the theology of the mustard seed and the leaven is a theology of divine fidelity. God is never in a hurry because He is never uncertain. The end is as sure as the beginning. What He plants will grow; what He mixes will rise. The Kingdom's progress through time mirrors the patience of its King, who still sows in the fields of human freedom and still believes the soil will yield. The parables invite us into that same trust. They ask us to live with the confidence of the Sower and the quiet perseverance of the Woman—to work, to wait, and to believe that grace is already at work beneath the surface.

In this way, the twin parables become more than instruction; they are revelation. They disclose the very heart of God: love that hides itself to heal, power that stoops to raise, life that multiplies through surrender. The Kingdom of Heaven grows not by storm but by seed, not by command but by communion. Its leaven is already within us, and its harvest has already begun. The only question is whether we will let it rise.

## THE PARABLE OF THE MUSTARD SEED & THE LEAVEN (MT 13:31-33)

### c) Typological and Intertextual Parallels

The images of the mustard seed and the leaven do not appear in a vacuum. Jesus' words, brief as they are, draw on centuries of biblical memory. Every detail—the seed, the tree, the birds, the woman, the flour, the hidden leaven—echoes Israel's Scriptures and distils their hope. When He spoke these parables, He was not inventing new metaphors; He was revealing their fulfillment. The God who once sowed a garden in Genesis is now sowing His Kingdom in the world.

From the beginning, the seed has been the sign of promise. The first covenantal word spoken to fallen humanity was a seed-promise: "I will put enmity between you and the woman, and between your seed and her seed" (Gen 3:15). From that moment, salvation history became a story of seed and soil, of blessing handed down through generations. God's covenant with Abraham was sealed with the same word: "To your seed I will give this land" (Gen 12:7). Paul will later call that singular "seed" Christ Himself (Gal 3:16). The mustard seed, then, is not simply an agricultural image; it is the distilled symbol of divine fidelity. Every time Israel sowed grain, she was rehearsing the hope of that first promise—that life would spring from barrenness, that blessing would emerge from exile, that God's Word would not return void.

The prophets continued that pattern. Isaiah compared God's word to rain that waters the earth and "gives seed to the sower and bread to the eater" (Isa 55:10). Hosea spoke of God "sowing Israel for Himself in the land" (Hos 2:23). In both, sowing becomes an image of recreation—God replanting His people after judgment. Jesus stands in that line but turns it inward: the field is not merely the land of Israel but the human heart, the whole world as God's garden. When He speaks of a man taking a mustard seed and sowing it, He is acting out the divine role of the Sower who began creation and continues it through grace.

The growth of the seed into a tree recalls one of Scripture's most striking images: the great tree of Daniel and Ezekiel. In Ezekiel 17, the Lord promises to take a tender sprig from the cedar of Lebanon, plant it on a high mountain, and make it "a noble cedar, and under it shall dwell every kind of bird; in the shade of its branches birds of every sort will nest." The image symbolized Israel restored under the rule of God. Yet by Jesus' day, that restoration had not come as expected. The cedar of empire had fallen; Rome's shadow covered the land. Into that context, Jesus speaks of a seed becoming a tree where birds find rest—a deliberate echo of Ezekiel's prophecy. But instead of a cedar on a mountain, He names a mustard shrub in a field. The contrast is pointed: the Kingdom's glory will not resemble worldly grandeur. The cedar's height becomes the mustard's humility; the mountain becomes the soil of everyday life. Yet the promise is the same—the nations (the "birds of the air") will find shelter in its branches.

Daniel 4 employs the same image when Nebuchadnezzar dreams of a great tree reaching to heaven, with birds nesting in its branches. The tree in Daniel's vision represents the pride of empire, and its fall marks divine judgment. By adopting the same imagery, Jesus reverses its meaning: the Kingdom of God will be the true empire, the tree that endures when Babylon and Rome crumble. It will not rise by conquest but by life. The nations will not be subdued by force but gathered by grace. The mustard tree becomes the living antithesis of Babel—the unification of humanity not through human ambition but through divine mercy.

The leaven, too, is steeped in the story of Israel. Its first biblical appearance is in the Exodus. On the night of liberation, the Israelites were commanded to eat unleavened bread, for there was no time for the dough to rise. Leaven therefore became a symbol of corruption and haste—a trace of Egypt to be purged before the feast. For centuries, Jews removed every crumb of leaven before Passover as a sign of purification. Yet the same substance that once signified impurity becomes, in Jesus' parable, the sign of sanctification. The reversal is striking. The Kingdom will not avoid contact with the world's ferment; it will transform it. What was once excluded becomes the agent of renewal. Grace takes what sin distorted and redeems it from within.

The woman who hides the leaven into the dough recalls another matriarchal scene—the story of Abraham and Sarah in Genesis 18. When

## THE PARABLE OF THE MUSTARD SEED & THE LEAVEN (MT 13:31-33)

three mysterious visitors arrive at their tent, Abraham asks Sarah to prepare "three measures of fine flour" and bake cakes. That detail is unusual enough to be remembered; nowhere else in Scripture is that quantity used in domestic cooking. Early Jewish tradition regarded it as the origin of the covenant meal, the prefiguration of Israel's worship. When Jesus speaks of a woman hiding leaven in "three measures of flour," His audience would have heard the echo immediately. Sarah's hospitality to the divine guests prefigured the Incarnation—the moment when God would dwell among His people. Now, in the parable, the woman becomes an image of the Church, mixing the leaven of divine life into the world's substance. What was once a meal of promise becomes a mystery of fulfillment.

Another echo lies in the Wisdom literature, where the imagery of bread and leaven merges with that of divine teaching. "Come, eat of my bread," cries Wisdom in Proverbs 9:5. In Sirach, Wisdom plants herself "like a vine" and fills her children with fruit. Bread and seed, vine and grain—these symbols of nourishment and growth all converge in the Word of God. When Jesus uses them, He is identifying Himself as that Wisdom made flesh. The parables, then, are not merely about the Kingdom but about the King—the divine Wisdom who now teaches in human voice what He once spoke through Israel's poets and prophets.

The transformation of seed to tree and dough to bread also anticipates the Eucharistic mystery. In Israel's sacrificial worship, grain and bread symbolized thanksgiving for creation. The offering of the first fruits was both acknowledgment and communion: the creature returning to the Creator what the Creator had first given. In the Eucharist, that rhythm reaches perfection. The grain that was sown and the dough that was leavened become the Body of Christ—the Kingdom in sacramental form. The parables thus foreshadow the liturgical life of the Church. The field becomes the altar, the leavened bread becomes the sign of redeemed creation. Every Mass is a replay of these parables: small gifts offered, hidden grace at work, until the whole is transformed.

Paul extends the same typology when he describes the Church as God's field and building (1 Cor 3:9). The seed of the Word planted by the apostles continues to grow; the Spirit is the leaven that gives life to the body. In Ephesians 2, Paul speaks of Gentiles who were once far off now being brought near—echoing the birds who come to nest in the tree's branches. The unity of the Church across nations fulfills the prophetic vision of Ezekiel's sheltering tree. In Colossians, he describes the Gospel "bearing fruit and growing throughout the whole world" (Col 1:6)—a direct continuation of the mustard seed's image. For Paul, the parable is not only an agricultural analogy; it is the story of salvation history summarized in one sentence: what began in Israel now fills the earth.

The Book of Revelation closes the arc. The seed sown in Galilee becomes the Tree of Life standing at the centre of the New Jerusalem, whose leaves are "for the healing of the nations." The leaven that worked through the dough becomes the Marriage Supper of the Lamb, where the bread of earth and the wine of toil are transfigured into eternal communion. The movement that began in hiddenness ends in glory, but the substance remains the same. God's Kingdom is not a different world but this world fulfilled, creation restored to harmony with its Creator. The tree that shelters the birds of heaven is the Cross; the bread that feeds creation is the Eucharist; the leaven that transforms the world is the Spirit poured into human hearts.

When Jesus spoke of a mustard seed and a handful of leaven, He was telling Israel that her Scriptures had come true. The promise to Abraham had sprouted; the cedar of Ezekiel had begun to grow; the bread of Genesis had begun to rise. The Kingdom of Heaven was not an idea but a Person standing before them, fulfilling every figure and type. What had been symbol in the past was now substance. The covenant history that stretched from Eden to exile to expectation found its centre in this single revelation: God Himself has entered the field and the dough of creation. Nothing small will stay small, and nothing hidden will stay hidden. The Word that was sown in Scripture has become flesh and will not cease to grow until all things are leavened in love.

## d) Patristic and Theological Synthesis

The early Fathers read the twin parables of the Mustard Seed and the Leaven as small doors opening onto the vast mystery of how God works. Beneath their simplicity they discerned an entire theology of divine action—power hidden in humility, wisdom advancing not by invasion but by indwelling. For them, these were not illustrations for moral comfort but sacramental sayings, words that carried within themselves the very energy of the grace they described.

Origen was among the first to hear that depth. In his *Homilies on Matthew* he calls the mustard seed "the smallest of all teachings, yet filled with the fire of God." The seed, he says, is the Word sown in the soul. At first it seems insignificant—a command, a verse remembered in prayer—but once watered by contemplation it grows into a great tree of virtue, its branches wide enough for the powers of the soul to rest. The birds are the thoughts that once fluttered restlessly but now find shelter in divine understanding. The leaven, for Origen, is the secret wisdom of Christ working within the mind until the whole person is raised into truth. The Incarnation itself is repeated in miniature within each believer: the Logos takes root in human thought and, by quiet expansion, turns intellect into temple.

John Chrysostom saw the parables through the lens of history. Preaching in Antioch, he marvelled that a message born among fishermen in Galilee should soon "fill the whole world." For him, that improbable triumph proved the Gospel's divine origin. "The doctrine of the cross," he said, "has outlived the palaces of kings." The sting of mustard—its sharp taste and burning after it is crushed—became for him the fire of the Spirit. The Word may wound before it heals, but the pain is cleansing. On the leaven, Chrysostom sees the same rhythm: the hidden ferment of love changing the human mass from the inside. "Let us not be ashamed of small beginnings," he writes, "for it is God's way to begin with little and end with much."

Augustine carries the meditation inward. In *Sermon 101* he turns the field into the human heart and the leaven into faith that "inflames love."

"When the Word enters," he says, "it does not transform at once; but as the leaven works, the heart expands with charity until all is sweet." For him, leaven is *caritas*—the divine love that stretches the soul beyond itself into communion. The "three measures of flour" signify either the theological virtues of faith, hope, and love, or the tripartite powers of memory, understanding, and will. In either sense, grace must work through every faculty before holiness is complete. The parables, in Augustine's reading, reveal not merely the spread of the Church but the gradual divinisation of the human—the slow conversion of dust into participation in God.

Gregory the Great gathers these insights into a single vision. "Christ was a grain when seen, a tree when believed," he writes. The Incarnation is the seed planted in the soil of the world; the Resurrection, the moment that seed becomes the tree of life in whose branches the nations find rest. The woman who hides the leaven, he says, is the Church herself, kneading faith into the hearts of humanity until all creation is raised. Gregory's synthesis completes the Trinitarian pattern: the Father plants, the Son becomes seed, the Spirit ferments the world from within.

In the East, Ephrem the Syrian turns the same symbols into poetry. He calls the mustard seed an image of the Eucharist—tiny, ordinary, yet containing the infinite Christ. "In the little bread," he sings, "burns the fire that blazed in the bush." The leaven, for him, is the Spirit's life that animates creation, ensuring that what is blessed will one day rise. When the faithful eat the Eucharistic bread, they receive that divine ferment destined to raise them on the last day. The Cappadocian Fathers extend the same mystery into metaphysics. Gregory of Nyssa writes that "the good which is mingled with us increases until it makes us what it is." The leaven signifies participation; the mustard seed, divine expansiveness. God is never contained; He contains. Grace enlarges the soul until it becomes capable of infinity.

Medieval commentators continued this harmony. Bede called the mustard tree "the Church whose branches are the ranks of believers," while Aquinas, compiling the Fathers in his *Catena Aurea*, defined the seed as "the fervour of faith" and the leaven as "the operation of charity." The

Kingdom's spread through history and the soul's growth in grace are, for them, the same mystery seen from different vantage points—the outward and inward flowering of one life.

Modern theologians have returned to these small parables as keys to the Incarnation's logic. Hans Urs von Balthasar called them "icons of kenosis," in which divine glory hides in smallness so it may be diffused universally. Joseph Ratzinger, later Benedict XVI, wrote that "the grandeur of the Kingdom is the grandeur of the Cross." The mustard seed and the leaven, he said, disclose the pattern by which God rules: descent before exaltation, weakness as strength, surrender as victory.

Across the centuries, the Fathers' collective voice forms a single confession. The mustard seed unveils the Christological mystery—the Son descending into littleness to embrace the world. The leaven unveils the mystery of the Spirit—divine life working silently within creation to bring all things to their proper form. Together they describe the Church herself: vast yet hidden, universal yet domestic, mighty yet meek. Her true growth is not measured by numbers or influence but by how deeply divine charity transforms her members and, through them, the world.

In these parables, the Fathers recognised the heartbeat of salvation history. The seed is Christ sown into the earth; the leaven is the Spirit breathing through humanity; the field and the dough are creation itself, waiting to be transfigured. What begins as insignificance ends in universality. What is hidden becomes the substance of all things. The Kingdom of God is not a distant realm but a process already underway—grace fermenting beneath history, preparing it for glory.

When Jesus speaks of a grain and a handful of yeast, He is not merely consoling the small or counselling patience. He is unveiling the very architecture of divine action. God conquers by humility, works by secrecy, and triumphs by love that disappears in order to renew. The cedar yields to the shrub, the temple to the table, power to presence—and in that surrender, the world is saved.

## The Shock and the Turn

The crowd that heard these parables expected power. They lived under empire, prayed for deliverance, and longed for a Messiah who would seize history by force. Their Scriptures spoke of cedars of Lebanon, of kings whose rule would reach "from sea to sea." Into that longing, Jesus offered two sentences about a weed and a woman kneading dough. It was not only anticlimactic; it was scandalous. The Kingdom of Heaven, for which Israel had waited centuries, was being compared to the smallest seed and the most common household task. No one listening could have missed the provocation. It was as though He had said, "What you call insignificant is what God calls holy." The shock of the parables lies not in mystery but in simplicity. They overturn the scale by which the human heart measures greatness.

For those who craved spectacle, the mustard seed was an insult. It grew wild, unruly, and was banned by rabbinic gardeners for invading fields. A proper kingdom, they thought, should be planted in cedar, not mustard. Yet Jesus deliberately chooses this nuisance shrub as His emblem of divine reign. The choice unmasks a deeper idolatry—the belief that God's Kingdom must resemble human strength. Every empire in history has shared that delusion: to equate visibility with victory, speed with success. The mustard seed reveals another order entirely. The Almighty enters history not as Caesar but as seed, taking root in the margins. What offends the proud is not that God reigns, but that He reigns in humility.

The leaven deepens the scandal. To a Jewish listener, leaven was the residue of corruption, purged from homes before Passover. It symbolized what must be cleansed before worship. Yet Jesus likens God's Kingdom to this contaminant. He dares to call holy what religion had learned to fear. The image would have landed like a quiet thunderclap: holiness is no longer fragile. In the new covenant, purity spreads by contact rather than withdrawal. The woman who hides yeast in flour performs a revolutionary act. She hides grace in the world's ordinary matter; she makes sanctity infectious. The parable overturns the boundary between sacred and profane. The Kingdom's power is not defensive but diffusive. It sanctifies by touching.

# THE PARABLE OF THE MUSTARD SEED & THE LEAVEN (MT 13:31–33)

The turn of the parables comes here, in this reversal of expectation. God will not build His Kingdom through conquest but through communion. The divine strategy is concealment. Hiddenness becomes the form of victory. That is what no one in the crowd could have anticipated—that the King would conquer by being unnoticed. The seed must disappear before it bears fruit; the leaven must vanish into the dough before it transforms it. What looks like loss is actually the beginning of life. Every miracle of growth begins with burial. In the grammar of God, descent precedes ascent, and weakness conceals strength.

To hear that truth is to stand before judgment. The Kingdom is not delayed; it is already here, hidden in the ordinary. The question is not when it will arrive but whether we can perceive it. These parables expose the poverty of our attention. We crave signs, and God gives seeds. We ask for proofs, and He gives process. We want to manage the harvest, and He invites us to trust the soil. The spiritual shock is that the Kingdom demands patience instead of control. Faith must learn to wait in darkness, believing that divine life works beneath the surface. That patience is not passivity but participation in God's own rhythm. The waiting is itself a form of imitation.

The listeners who imagined that God's reign would erupt with violence now faced a decision. Would they accept a Messiah who worked like yeast—silently, invisibly, from within? Or would they cling to their dream of spectacle? The same question confronts every generation of believers. We would rather see God act than trust that He already is. We seek progress that can be measured, success that can be counted, holiness that can be displayed. Yet the mustard seed remains God's only method: growth through surrender, power through littleness. The leaven continues to work only where it disappears. The Kingdom's greatest victories are often those we will not notice until the last day.

This is the reversal that pierces pride. The divine Kingdom is not an empire rising over the earth but grace at work within it. It will not crush opponents; it will convert them. It will not separate the pure from the impure; it will transfigure both. The rule of God is not a regime but a relationship—the quiet reign of mercy spreading from heart to heart. The greatness of this reign lies precisely in its refusal to dominate. The Kingdom grows by love, and love by definition cannot be imposed. The smallness of the seed, the hiddenness of the leaven—these are not metaphors of delay but revelations of the very nature of divine power.

What would have stunned the crowd most, perhaps, is the way Jesus places the divine work in human hands. "A man took… a woman hid." The initiative is shared. God entrusts His reign to our cooperation. The mystery of grace unfolds through human freedom. That, too, would have startled the listeners. The Kingdom is not something descending fully formed from heaven; it is something planted, tended, mixed, and nurtured through our yes. The great divine surprise is not that heaven invades earth, but that it does so through the humble fidelity of human lives.

The final turn of the parable is quiet but absolute. "Until the whole was leavened." That sentence contains the scandal and the promise of Christianity. Nothing will remain untouched. The world will not be discarded but redeemed; the human heart will not be condemned but converted. The Kingdom's horizon is totality—*holon*, the whole. What began as a handful of faith will one day fill creation. The shock is that the process will look nothing like power and everything like patience. It will unfold through forgiveness, anonymity, and sacrifice. God's reign will not arrive in thunder but in bread.

This is the turning point for the listener and for the disciple. The parables expose the choice between admiration and conversion. We can admire the image of divine gentleness, or we can let it redefine our lives. To follow the Sower and the Woman is to accept obscurity, to believe that what is hidden is not lost. The scandal of the Kingdom is that it begins beneath notice and will end beyond measure. Its growth is as slow as mercy and as certain as dawn.

The shock has not faded. We still look for grandeur, and God still chooses seeds. We still flee contamination, and He still hides Himself in the dough of the world. The cross will be the final parable, where the seed falls into the earth and the leaven of love is buried in death. The grain will die; the bread will rise. Only then will the secret of these parables be understood—that the Kingdom of Heaven is nothing less than the humility of God transforming the world from within.

**The Revelation in the Son**

Every parable of the Kingdom is, at its core, a veiled Christology. Beneath the images of field and dough, of seed and leaven, lies the mystery of the Son Himself. He is the hidden power at work in creation, the divine life entering matter to transform it from within. The mustard seed and the leaven do not merely describe how God acts—they describe who God is in Jesus Christ. Their quiet energy is the pulse of the Incarnation, the Word made flesh, divine glory compressed into the smallest form so that it might grow in the soil of the world.

Christ is the true mustard seed: the smallest in appearance, yet containing in Himself the infinite. In Him the majesty of God becomes measurable, the Eternal enters time. The mystery of divine condescension is not an episode but the very structure of salvation. "Though He was in the form of God," writes Paul, "He emptied Himself" (Phil 2:6–7). That self-emptying—kenosis—is the sowing of the Seed into the field of humanity. The infinite God allows Himself to be contained within the womb of a woman, within the limits of human weakness, within a single life subject to growth and death. In Bethlehem, the Kingdom began as invisibly as a seed beneath soil. The world saw an infant; heaven saw the Tree already taking root.

The life of Christ follows the rhythm of the seed's growth. Hidden in Nazareth, He lives thirty years of silence, unseen by empire or temple. Like the grain germinating underground, His divinity works in obscurity. The public ministry that follows is the sprouting—words and wonders breaking the surface of the world. Yet even at its most visible, His glory remains veiled, offered only to those with eyes to see. And then, at Calvary, the Seed falls again into the earth. "Unless a grain of wheat falls into the ground and dies, it remains alone," He says, "but if it dies, it bears much fruit" (John 12:24). The Cross is the burial of the Seed; the Resurrection is its bursting forth into the Tree of Life. From that tree the nations find shelter, and from its fruit the world is fed. What began in parable is completed in Paschal mystery.

In that light, the parable's birds—those who nest in the branches—become the image of all who draw life from Christ. The Church herself is that tree, born from the pierced side of the crucified Seed. Her branches extend across centuries and continents; her shade is the mercy of God. Every sacrament, every act of grace, is a branch growing from that trunk. The universality that the parable foresaw—the gathering of all nations—unfolds through her. The "birds of the air" that once symbolized Gentile peoples now represent every soul who finds rest in Christ's mercy. The Church is not parallel to the Tree; she is its extension, its visible growth in time.

The leaven deepens this revelation still further. If the mustard seed shows the Word entering the world, the leaven shows the Spirit entering the human heart. The same Word who was sown in flesh is now mixed into the substance of humanity through the gift of the Spirit. Just as yeast cannot be separated from dough once kneaded, so divinity and humanity are now inseparable in the one Person of Christ. The Incarnation is the cosmic kneading of God and man. In Him, heaven and earth are mixed—without confusion, without division—so that creation itself begins to rise toward communion. The leaven works silently, yet inexorably, just as the Spirit works in souls to make them "partakers of the divine nature" (2 Pet 1:4).

Christ's hidden years anticipate this mystery. The child in Nazareth is the divine leaven quietly working through human history. Every gesture of that ordinary life—obedience, labour, love—was a fermenting of creation from within. What appeared insignificant was already transforming the dough of the world. When He entered His Passion, that interior work reached its climax. The Cross was the kneading of love and suffering, humanity and divinity pressed together in perfect obedience. His burial was not the end of fermentation but its moment of culmination: the leaven had filled the whole. The Resurrection, then, is the proof that the world has begun to rise. The unleavened bread of the old covenant—symbol of haste and incompletion—has become the risen bread of the new: Christ Himself, the living Bread come down from heaven.

The Eucharist reveals this parable in sacramental form. On the altar, the grain and the leaven, the seed and the dough, converge in mystery. Bread—human labour and divine gift—is taken, blessed, broken, and given. In that moment the Kingdom is no longer a future hope but a present reality. The leavened bread of the altar is the visible sign that creation has been transformed. What the parable promised—"until it was all leavened"—the Eucharist begins to fulfill. Every Mass is a continuation of that hidden working: Christ, the Leaven of God, entering the matter of the world and raising it toward glory.

The Incarnation, the Cross, and the Eucharist are not separate acts but one movement—the self-giving of God that transforms what it enters. In Christ, the infinite mingles with the finite, the holy with the ordinary, until the whole is sanctified. He is both the Seed sown into the soil of history and the Leaven concealed in the dough of creation. His humility is not a phase of His mission but its revelation: the Eternal Word chooses littleness as His form. The mystery of the Kingdom, therefore, is not simply that God reigns but that He reigns through self-emptying love.

To see Christ as the mustard seed and the leaven is to recognize the pattern of divine life itself: expansion through surrender, victory through vulnerability, glory through giving. The universe was created by that logic and redeemed by it. Every particle of creation now bears the imprint of the Word who entered it. The mustard seed fallen into the soil of Mary's womb has become the living order of grace. In the Incarnation, the Creator and creation were joined so intimately that the history of the world became the growth of a single Seed. The Gospel is not the story of humanity reaching for God, but of God's life diffusing through humanity until nothing remains untouched.

This is why the Kingdom cannot be localized or confined. Wherever Christ is present, the leaven is at work. Wherever His Body is offered, the seed bears fruit. The Church's mission flows from this reality. She is not an organization spreading an idea; she is the continuing expansion of the divine life that began in Nazareth and burst from the tomb. Her holiness is not moral superiority but participation in the life of the Leaven Himself. When she preaches, forgives, feeds, and heals, the same energy that moved within Jesus moves through her. The field of the world becomes Eucharistic: creation lifted toward its Creator through the offering of love.

The Paschal mystery is therefore the interpretive key to both parables. The seed must die before it can grow; the leaven must disappear before the dough can rise. These are not agricultural observations but revelations of the Cross. Christ's descent into death is the ultimate concealment—divinity hidden in dereliction. Yet in that very hiding, grace works most powerfully. The tomb becomes the oven where the bread of new creation is baked. Resurrection is not God's escape from suffering but the transformation of suffering into glory. What was sown in weakness is raised in power, and the whole of humanity begins to rise with Him.

From that point forward, the story of salvation unfolds as the slow expansion of Easter. The Spirit, poured out at Pentecost, is the breath that causes the dough to lift. The apostolic mission, moving from Jerusalem to the ends of the earth, is the visible growth of the mustard tree. Every soul baptized, every Eucharist celebrated, is another measure of flour being leavened, another branch stretching outward. History itself becomes sacramental—the gradual revelation of what was already accomplished in Christ. Time is the medium through which the hidden work of grace becomes visible.

In this way, the parables do not simply teach theology; they teach the very *method* of God. The Kingdom's logic is the logic of the Trinity: self-gift, communion, indwelling. The Father sows, the Son descends, the Spirit animates; the field and the dough become creation itself, alive with divine movement. What began as symbol resolves into a living Person. The Kingdom is not an abstraction but the radiance of Christ's presence filling all things. He is the axis around which the cosmos turns, the Word in whom the seed and the leaven, matter and spirit, find their unity.

To confess that truth is to see everything anew. The smallest gesture of love, the quietest act of faith, participates in cosmic renewal. Every believer becomes a mustard seed of grace, a fragment of leaven placed by God in the world. The Church's saints are the visible fruit of that process—the branches heavy with life, the bread risen and fragrant with holiness. Yet even their glory points beyond itself. The final goal is not the flourishing of the Church but the transfiguration of creation. The end of the story is the beginning restored: a garden that has become a city, a field that has become a feast. The Tree of Life, whose leaves heal the nations, is the Cross transformed; the bread of angels is the fruit of the earth made divine. In that consummation, the parables reach their fulfillment: the whole is leavened, the Kingdom complete.

Until then, the mystery continues in every Eucharist, in every hidden act of charity, in every heart where faith takes root. The Son remains the Seed working through history, the Leaven permeating the world. The Incarnation is not a past event but a living process: God's life continually entering ours until all creation becomes transparent to His glory. The silence of Nazareth, the stillness of the tomb, the hush before the words of consecration—all bear the same truth: the Kingdom of Heaven advances in stillness.

In Christ, the small has become infinite. The seed has become a tree whose roots reach into eternity and whose branches shelter the cosmos. The leaven has filled the whole loaf of creation with divine breath. To see Him is to see what the world is destined to become: God dwelling in all, and all dwelling in God. The parables of the Kingdom end where the Gospel of John begins—"And the Word became flesh." That Word, once sown in secrecy, now fills heaven and earth. The reign of God is nothing less than the radiance of the Son expanding until love is all in all.

### The Word for Our Age

We live in an age that mistrusts smallness. Our world worships the visible—

the post that goes viral, the campaign that trends, the achievement that can be measured in metrics. We are taught from youth that meaning must be noticed to be real. Yet the parables of the Mustard Seed and the Leaven speak a word directly against this modern creed. They remind us that the Kingdom of God advances not through spectacle but through substance; not by being seen, but by being *sown*. The divine method remains the same in every century: God enters the world quietly, through hearts converted and homes sanctified. What He began in Galilee continues in every act of hidden fidelity.

For the modern disciple, this is both a challenge and a liberation. It is a challenge because we are addicted to immediacy. We expect visible results from every effort—proof that prayer "works," evidence that faith "matters." The silence of the seed unnerves us; the slowness of leaven offends our efficiency. We want God to operate at the speed of technology. But the Kingdom still grows at the pace of love, and love cannot be rushed. To live as a Christian today is to learn again the patience of the sower and the trust of the baker. The soil may look barren, the dough unchanged, yet the divine life is already at work beneath the surface. Fidelity, not visibility, is the measure of fruitfulness.

At the same time, these parables liberate us from the tyranny of comparison. In a world driven by performance, Jesus redefines greatness. The seed is smallest; the leaven is hidden; yet both hold the power to change everything. The mother raising children in faith, the teacher who prays for her students, the young man who resists temptation, the elderly woman who offers her loneliness for others—all are mustard seeds of the Kingdom. Their lives may never trend, but heaven watches their growth with delight. The Gospel's comfort is that nothing surrendered in love is wasted. The most ordinary moments of fidelity become instruments of eternal transformation.

The Church herself must also hear this word afresh. In an era of shrinking numbers and waning influence, it is easy to grow anxious or nostalgic for power. Yet the parable warns against equating the Kingdom with visibility or control. The Church began as a handful of believers, a mustard seed in an indifferent empire. Her vitality did not depend on approval but on grace. When she forgets this—when she seeks prominence instead of purity—she ceases to be leaven and becomes lump. The future of evangelization will not come from strategies of influence but from communities of holiness: families who pray, parishes that serve, friendships formed in truth. The renewal of the Church will begin again where it always has—among the hidden faithful whose faith works like yeast in the dough of the world.

The parables also speak powerfully to the despair of our age. Many people, even within the Church, feel overwhelmed by the magnitude of evil, the collapse of faith, the seeming futility of goodness. They see culture turning away from God and conclude that the battle is lost. But the Kingdom was never a contest of numbers. A single seed in the soil contains more hope than all the weeds in the field. Grace does not require majority opinion; it requires cooperation. Every act of conversion, every confession, every Eucharist is the quiet advance of God's reign. Evil makes headlines; holiness rarely does. Yet history belongs to the holy. The parables call us to recover that supernatural optimism—the conviction that hidden grace is stronger than visible sin.

At the personal level, the lesson of the leaven is one of interior renewal. Too often we look for holiness outside ourselves: in causes, movements, or new techniques. Yet Christ teaches that transformation begins within. The Kingdom must first rise in the soul before it can rise in the world. The leaven is the Holy Spirit, and the dough is the human heart. Prayer, confession, and the sacraments are the kneading that make our hearts malleable. When we allow the Spirit to work in our weakness, the texture of our lives changes. We begin to think with mercy, to speak with patience, to love with endurance. This is how grace becomes visible—not by display, but by diffusion. The world does not need louder Christians; it needs holier ones.

The same principle applies to evangelization in the digital age. Social media tempts believers to measure influence by visibility, to confuse witness with branding. But the Gospel spreads by presence, not performance.

A simple conversation, a quiet prayer, a small act of forgiveness may carry more weight than any public argument. The leaven of truth rises through relationships. We are not called to conquer the internet but to sanctify the human heart. In the online noise of outrage and division, the calm consistency of a life shaped by the Beatitudes is itself a form of evangelization. The algorithm cannot predict grace.

For those discouraged by the hiddenness of their vocation—the parents who feel unseen, the priests labouring in obscurity, the single believers wondering if their faith matters—the mustard seed offers reassurance. God's arithmetic is not ours. He measures time by eternity, and fruitfulness by fidelity. The field may not show results today, but the roots are already spreading. A lifetime of quiet love will yield more than a decade of applause. Heaven's harvest is prepared in hidden seasons. What matters is not how visible our work is, but how fully we let the Word take root. The only failure in the Kingdom is to stop sowing.

The call of these parables, then, is profoundly hopeful. They assure us that the Kingdom is not in decline; it is in process. Its growth is not arrested but ongoing, often in places unseen: in the conversion of a single soul, in a child's first prayer, in a reconciliation long delayed. The Spirit has not ceased to act; the leaven is still rising. Our task is to cooperate with that quiet work, to plant and to wait, to knead and to trust. Every generation must learn again that God writes history with invisible ink. The Church may seem small, but she carries within her the fullness of divinity. The world may appear hardened, but it is still dough in the hands of the Creator.

If we could see the world as God sees it, we would never despair of small beginnings. The field of human history is already alive with seeds sown by saints and martyrs. The dough of creation is already warm with divine ferment. The Kingdom is not a project to build but a reality to trust. It advances wherever love takes root and wherever grace is allowed to work unhindered. In our families, our workplaces, our communities, we are called to be that mustard seed, that leaven—content to disappear if only the world may rise.

# THE PARABLE OF THE MUSTARD SEED & THE LEAVEN (MT 13:31–33)

The Word for our age is therefore a word of courage and quiet perseverance. The Kingdom does not compete with the world's empires; it outlasts them. The empires of noise will crumble, but the whisper of grace will remain. Every small act of faith, every hidden sacrifice, every sincere prayer is the Kingdom advancing. The only thing small about the mustard seed is its beginning. The end is a tree that fills the earth. Our task is to keep sowing and to believe that, in God's time, the harvest will come—and that when it does, it will be greater than we could ever imagine.

## Hearing that Becomes Doing

The crowd has gone home, but the words remain: *"The kingdom of heaven is like a mustard seed... like leaven hidden in three measures of flour."*

Two images—tiny, invisible in the hand, yet restless with power. The Lord has spoken not of empires but of yeast; not of armies but of seeds. When the noise fades, these small things keep working. They are still working now, inside you.

Let the images meet in silence. The seed and the leaven are different in form but the same in mystery. Both disappear to become fruitful. Both live by dying. You cannot watch their progress, only trust it. This is how the Kingdom grows: quietly, insistently, beyond measurement or applause.

Begin by remembering the smallest act of faith in your own life—a prayer whispered when you felt nothing, a gesture of kindness nobody saw, a single honest confession. Those moments were mustard seeds. You may have forgotten them, but grace has not. What vanishes into God never stops living.

The mustard seed begins almost weightless. It is thrown into the ground, lost among stones and dust. You could mistake it for nothing. Yet within it lies a tree large enough for birds to rest in its shade. This is how sanctity begins. A single surrender, a hidden "yes," becomes shelter for many. You do not need to plan greatness; you need only to plant fidelity. The soul that gives itself to the ordinary becomes extraordinary in time.

Look around your life. Most of what God asks of you is small: to listen when tired, to forgive again, to hold your tongue, to show up. Each act may seem microscopic, but holiness accumulates the way daylight does—quietly, until suddenly everything is bright. The saints did not start as giants; they began as seeds consenting to obscurity.

Now turn to the leaven. It works by disappearance. Once kneaded into the dough, it can no longer be separated, yet it transforms everything from within. This is the pattern of divine grace in a believer's life. The Spirit does not shout; He mingles. His presence is hidden but pervasive. To live by faith is to let Him penetrate every corner of your thought, word, and action—until nothing remains untouched by His fermenting love.

Consider where the leaven is still absent in you. Perhaps in your patience, your trust, your generosity. The unconverted parts of the heart are simply dough waiting for the yeast of grace. Ask the Lord to knead His mercy there. Transformation begins not by self-perfection but by yielding to His touch.

Modern life resists such smallness. We live amid noise and spectacle, drawn to the visible and immediate. Yet the Gospel insists that what endures is almost invisible. The mustard seed will outlast the palace; the leaven will outlive the empire. The Church herself began as a handful of frightened disciples in an upper room, and today she stretches across centuries. That is the same mystery still at work in you. Heaven's mathematics begins with almost nothing.

When you pray, do not despise what feels insignificant. One Hail Mary whispered with love has more weight than hours of distracted labour. One act of charity done for Christ outweighs a thousand done for recognition. God counts differently. He delights in what the world ignores. Each hidden act becomes a pulse in the heart of the Kingdom.

Let the parable invite you into simplicity. You are not asked to produce greatness but to allow growth. The seed's task is not strategy but surrender. The leaven's power is not dominance but diffusion. So it is with the soul: holiness is not achieved; it happens where humility meets grace.

Spend time each day noticing the mustard seeds around you—the small, steady goodness that keeps the world alive. A teacher patient with a difficult child. A nurse praying over a sleeping patient. A neighbour checking in. These are branches of the tree Jesus foresaw. You are surrounded by the Kingdom's quiet architecture. Seeing it will teach you to trust it.

If you wish to cooperate with that Kingdom, begin at the smallest level: guard your thoughts, speak blessing instead of complaint, choose gratitude over resentment. Every time you resist cynicism, you add one more grain of heaven to the earth. Every time you refuse to despair, you become leaven in the dough of your generation. Grace multiplies through faithfulness.

You might feel, at times, that your efforts vanish into nothing. They do—but that is how they work. Seeds die before they grow; yeast disappears before it feeds. The measure of success in the Kingdom is not visibility but transformation. You will know grace is ripening in you when peace becomes more natural than panic, when hope outlasts fear, when love keeps acting even when unreturned.

At the end of your day, pray this slowly:

### Prayer of the Hidden Kingdom

Lord of the small and unseen,
plant in me the seed of Your patience.
Let my ordinary hours become Your field.
Mix Your Spirit into my worries
until they rise with the warmth of Your peace.
Teach me to trust the power of little things—
a kind word, a silent prayer, a small mercy.
May I live as leaven in the world,
unnoticed yet indispensable,
until all is raised in the light of Your coming.
Amen.

Stay in that stillness. The Kingdom is already working. Its roots are threading through your heart; its fragrance is rising in the world. You cannot hear it, but heaven is spreading through the dough of time. The only task left is to believe it, to keep your hands open, and to let the smallness of God grow great within you.

# 4

# The Parable Of The Growing Seed (Mk 4:26–29)

*He also said, "The kingdom of God is as if someone would scatter seed on the ground, and would sleep and rise night and day, and the seed would sprout and grow, he does not know how. The earth produces of itself, first the stalk, then the head, then the full grain in the head. But when the grain is ripe, at once he goes in with his sickle, because the harvest has come."*

### The Word Spoken

The day was long, and the sun hung low above the Sea of Galilee. The crowd still pressed close to the shore—fishermen, farmers, women with children on their hips—drawn by the strange authority of the man teaching from the boat. Behind them, the hills shimmered with ripening grain; the smell of wet earth and crushed stalks filled the air. It was sowing season again, the most ordinary rhythm of their lives. Jesus spoke into that rhythm.

This short parable came near the end of a long afternoon of teaching. The Sower had already been spoken, the Lamp, the Measure, and the growing tension with the Pharisees was still in the air. Jesus had begun to describe the Kingdom not in decrees but in mysteries—images that forced the crowd to listen twice. He wasn't giving them new rules; He was giving them a new way to see. The Kingdom, He said, was not coming with armies or decrees but like seed falling into soil—quiet, invisible, unstoppable.

He turns again to the same image: *"The kingdom of God is as if a man should scatter seed upon the ground."* Everyone there had seen it. Sowing was daily work. It meant bending your back to the earth, trusting clouds, rain, and time. To the people of Galilee—tenant farmers under Roman taxation—seed was precious. It was a wager against drought, blight, and debt. And yet Jesus used that fragile act as the doorway to divine revelation.

The story is simple: a farmer scatters, then goes about his days. He "sleeps and rises night and day," Mark says, and in that quiet cycle, the mystery happens: *"the seed should sprout and grow, he knows not how."* The phrase *ouk oiden autos*—"he himself does not know how"—would have caught their attention. Most rabbis used nature to illustrate divine law; Jesus uses it to illustrate divine mystery. Growth happens beyond the reach of explanation. It is not the farmer's toil that brings life, but the secret energy of the earth.

Mark's Greek preserves that wonder with one crucial word: *automatos*—"of itself." The earth bears fruit *automatically*, without visible cause. The farmers listening would have nodded. They knew how little control they had once the seed disappeared beneath the soil. They could guard, weed, pray—but they could not make a seed split or roots emerge. The process belonged to the mystery of creation. Jesus lifts that helpless knowing into hope: the Kingdom grows the same way.

The rhythm of the parable—"sow... sleep and rise... sprout and grow... first the blade, then the ear, then the full grain"—matches the heartbeat of rural life. It sounds like ordinary time passing. Yet within that ordinariness, Jesus reveals divine activity. The Kingdom's growth is not a miracle that breaks the natural order but a miracle that lives within it. The listeners, many of them poor labourers and anxious parents, would have understood immediately: God's work was already unfolding in their waiting, in their sowing, in their unseen days.

The crowd listening that day was made up of ordinary people—villagers

## THE PARABLE OF THE GROWING SEED (MK 4:26–29)

who knew what it meant to work hard and wait long. Some were fishermen with nets drying on the shore; others, farmers who knew the ache of hope as they watched the sky for rain. Among them were Pharisees too, listening with folded arms, uneasy with His refusal to speak in the language of command. They wanted clear moral law, not stories about soil. Yet Jesus spoke to both the weary and the proud with the same quiet insistence: the Kingdom is growing, even when you cannot see it.

The setting matters. Mark places this parable in a moment of transition. The crowds have begun to divide—some hearts open, others harden. Jesus has just finished explaining the Parable of the Sower to His disciples in private, saying, "To you has been given the mystery of the kingdom of God" (Mk 4:11). Now He gives them this new image: the mystery at work. It is as if He were saying, "You have received the seed; now watch what happens when you let it grow."

The language He uses is spare, even conversational. There are no thunderous commands, no moral lectures. He simply describes a farmer who trusts the hidden process of life. "The earth produces of itself," He says—*automatos*. That one word, more than any other, opens the meaning of the scene. It means "spontaneously," "without human intervention." In Greek thought, *automatos* could describe a spring that bubbles up on its own, or a vine that bears fruit unpruned. Jesus applies it to God's reign. The Kingdom, He says, is not the product of force, persuasion, or human cleverness. It unfolds because it is alive.

To a world accustomed to control—then as now—this was disorienting. Israel longed for a Messiah of action, one who would drive out oppressors, purify worship, and make God's sovereignty unmistakable. Yet the Teacher who sat in the boat spoke instead of sowing and sleeping, of time passing and harvests ripening. He described divine power not in thunder or conquest but in patience—in the slow faithfulness of growth. The reign of God, He implied, would come not as spectacle but as season: quiet, hidden, certain.

The final image—"when the grain is ripe, at once he puts in the sickle, because the harvest has come"—would have stirred both familiarity and awe. The farmers heard their own work in it: the feel of the sickle's handle, the weight of the sheaves, the scent of ripe grain. But they also heard echoes of Scripture. The prophets had long used the image of harvest to describe judgment and fulfillment. Joel spoke of the sickle swung at the end of days; Isaiah of the earth's fruit brought to maturity under God's care. Jesus was placing their daily labour within that cosmic horizon. Every harvest in Galilee became an image of the world's harvest—the moment when what God has sown in history reaches completion.

Mark's telling leaves room for silence. We are not told what the crowd felt or how the disciples responded. The story ends as abruptly as it began, as if the lesson itself must be discovered in time. That is the genius of this parable: it teaches through waiting. Its meaning ripens slowly, the way the seed does. The more one ponders it, the clearer it becomes that Jesus was not only describing the Kingdom but enacting it. His own ministry was the seed—scattered across hearts, hidden beneath misunderstanding, destined to rise in glory long after He had passed from view.

The crowd might not have understood all this that day by the sea, but they would have felt its truth. The rhythm of Jesus' voice matched the rhythm of their days—work and rest, night and morning, trust and uncertainty. As the light faded over Galilee and the Teacher's words lingered in the air, they were already living inside the parable: the seed had been sown, and though they knew not how, it had already begun to grow.

## The Surface Story

To the people who first heard it, the parable of the Growing Seed was not an idea to be debated; it was the mirror of their daily life. Every man and woman along that Galilean shoreline had known the feel of soil between the fingers or the ache of waiting for rain. Fields and seasons shaped their prayers, their debts, even their sense of God. When Jesus began to speak of seed and soil, He was speaking their language, translating divinity into the rhythm of their days.

A man scatters seed upon the ground. At once, the crowd can see it. In

## THE PARABLE OF THE GROWING SEED (MK 4:26–29)

first-century Galilee, sowing was as ordinary as breathing and as risky as faith. Most farmers were tenants labouring on estates owned by Herodian officials or wealthy patrons. They farmed rocky, narrow plots divided by low stone walls, trusting thin soil and the mercy of winter rain. Sowing was done by hand, a slow procession across the field: a rough sack slung across the body, the arm sweeping in wide arcs, the faint hiss of grain through air. Each handful was a wager. Too shallow, and birds would feast; too deep, and the seed would drown in darkness.

When Jesus begins, "The kingdom of God is as if a man should scatter seed upon the ground," His hearers can almost smell the earth after ploughing, can see the figure outlined against the sun. But the story turns strange in the next breath: "He sleeps and rises night and day, and the seed sprouts and grows—he knows not how." The shift is subtle but electric. The familiar becomes revelation.

No Galilean farmer was naïve about his craft. He read the sky, felt the wind, and knew the signs of blight and frost. Yet he also lived with the humility of ignorance. Beneath the soil was a mystery he could not master. Once the seed was covered, the rest was hidden. There were no pumps or irrigation canals in the hill country—only dew, prayer, and trust. When Jesus says, "he knows not how," His audience nods; they have seen green blades appear where yesterday there was dust. They know what it means to depend on what they cannot see.

The detail that he "sleeps and rises night and day" speaks not of laziness but of routine. It sketches the rhythm of peasant existence: the rooster's cry at dawn, the weight of sun and stone, the evening meal of lentils and bread, the sleep on a mat beside one's tools. Life goes on, day folding into night, and while he works, eats, and rests, something invisible unfolds beneath him. The parable's quiet power lies here: in the sanctification of the ordinary. The farmer's ignorance is not failure but faith in motion—trust that the unseen will bear fruit.

The soil itself, in that region, was a teacher. Galilee's volcanic earth looked barren until the rains came; then it seemed to breathe. Farmers turned it with wooden ploughs tipped with iron, guiding oxen through furrows cut by generations. They sowed wheat, barley, or lentils depending on the season's promise. The grain they threw was never anonymous. It was the seed saved from last year's harvest, stored in clay jars near the hearth—the same seed that had fed their families through the lean months. Each kernel carried memory and hope: what their fathers had planted, what their children might reap. When Jesus spoke of scattering seed, He was touching a gesture both economic and sacred, a continuity older than any empire.

Mark's description of growth captures that continuity in rhythm: "The earth produces of itself—first the blade, then the ear, then the full grain in the ear." The cadence itself sounds like time passing. The Greek word *automate*—"of itself"—suggests spontaneous life, but for Israel it meant something more profound: the earth cooperating with God. Anyone who had watched fields after rain could trace the stages—the tender green blades trembling in wind, the stalks stiffening as they draw strength, the pale grain swelling, then the heavy gold of ripeness bending toward harvest. Each stage was fragile, each a small miracle. "The earth produces of itself" was not a denial of God's power; it was an affirmation that creation still obeys His command.

For Israel, the image of harvest was never neutral. It was worship. The Torah had bound agriculture to liturgy: the Feast of Weeks for the first fruits, the Feast of Booths for the final ingathering. Every farmer knew the law that commanded them to leave the edges of their fields for the poor and the stranger. The harvest was therefore an act of justice as well as gratitude, a visible sign that the land belonged to God alone. So when Jesus spoke of "putting in the sickle," His audience would have thought not only of labour but of procession—pilgrims carrying sheaves, psalms rising on the road to Jerusalem.

Yet in this story the most striking thing is what the farmer *doesn't* do. He does not hurry or intervene. He does not dig up the earth to measure progress. He sleeps and rises, trusting that the hidden life is at work. For people whose survival depended on relentless effort, that picture was provocative. Ancient agriculture demanded vigilance—clearing stones, repairing walls, guarding against theft. But here the Kingdom's drama unfolds in stillness. The farmer's passivity becomes the parable's theology: the Kingdom grows while we rest.

To the peasants who strained under taxes and drought, that image was more than comfort; it was revolution. They lived on the edge of debt, their harvests monitored by stewards of Rome. The grain they sowed was both their livelihood and their liability. Yet Jesus describes a man who sleeps in peace. The parable's calm tone is itself the message: divine life does not depend on human control. The Kingdom advances while the anxious sleep.

The pacing of the story reinforces that calm. "First the blade, then the ear, then the full grain in the ear"—a sentence that breathes patience. No leaps, no haste. The rhythm mimics the slow work of grace. The people listening by the lake were attuned to that rhythm. They lived by seasons, not clocks; by the moon's waxing and the rains' return. They knew that time was something received, not managed. In that slow unfolding, they heard their own faith named back to them.

The farmer in Jesus' story is deliberately anonymous. He is not the righteous man or the wicked man, not the rich fool or the diligent steward. He has no moral label, no heroic title. He is simply "a man." That simplicity is part of the revelation. The Kingdom of God does not begin with the exceptional; it begins with the ordinary. The divine Word takes root in the everyday gestures of nameless people who keep sowing without understanding the mystery they serve. The silence of the parable is as instructive as its speech.

Hidden beneath its plain description is a quiet reversal of expectations. In most rabbinic parables, moral clarity dominates: the good servant is rewarded, the foolish man destroyed. Jesus removes all that scaffolding. He gives us no moral drama, no conflict, no villain—only process, trust, and time. The holiness of the Kingdom is not staged in triumph or judgment but in patience. That is its first miracle: the discovery that divine power hides in continuity, in the ordinary rhythm of sowing and sleeping.

This patience is not passivity. The farmer's stillness is active faith, an obedience to the mystery of creation. In the Scriptures, the earth was never inert. "You cause the grass to grow for the cattle," sings Psalm 104, "and plants for man to cultivate." Those words would have echoed in the minds of Jesus' hearers. They had recited them in festivals and remembered them in droughts. The psalmist's faith—that the land's fruitfulness is God's ongoing work—was the theology under their feet. When Jesus says, "the earth produces of itself," He is not inventing new doctrine; He is reminding them of an old one: creation is not machinery but covenant.

In that line—"the earth produces of itself"—something profound happens. The phrase does not mean that the world is autonomous. It means that the Creator has placed within creation a living energy that answers His Word. The soil is obedient. The seed listens. What begins in silence ends in abundance because creation itself participates in grace. This, to a people wearied by effort and failure, must have sounded like hope.

Even the image of the sickle, which closes the parable, carries the weight of reality. In a Galilean village, harvest was a communal feast of labour. At dawn, men and women went out together, cutting with curved blades, gathering sheaves by hand. Laughter mixed with work; neighbours sang as they bound the grain. "The harvest has come" was not metaphor—it was something shouted across the fields when gold replaced green. Yet every Israelite also knew that "harvest" carried another resonance. The prophets had used it to describe the final judgment—the day when God would gather His people and separate wheat from chaff. So when Jesus ends His story with the sickle, He lets that double meaning hang: reassurance for the faithful, warning for the indifferent.

The crowd that day would have understood the realism of the story before its mystery. They could see themselves in the nameless farmer: working the soil, living by trust, caught between exhaustion and expectancy. Jesus does not lift them into a heavenly abstraction; He reveals heaven already hidden in their labour. In His hands, the field becomes a sacrament of divine patience. Nothing spectacular happens—the miracle is precisely that it doesn't. Growth unfolds while the world sleeps. Grace, He tells them, is not thunder but germination.

## THE PARABLE OF THE GROWING SEED (MK 4:26–29)

That insight would have struck deeply at their fears. These were people living on the edge of survival. Their fields depended on unpredictable weather; their taxes fed empires. They had seen crops fail and neighbours lose land. Their lives oscillated between scarcity and endurance. Yet the man in the parable does not panic. He plants and sleeps. His calmness is a revelation of what trust looks like in a world of uncertainty. He cannot control growth, but he knows who gives it. That is what faith means in the Kingdom: not mastery, but surrender to a God who works beneath the surface.

The pacing of Jesus' words mirrors the slow heartbeat of creation itself. "First the blade, then the ear, then the full grain in the ear." Each phrase marks a season, a waiting, a proof that divine life ripens in stages. It is the same rhythm by which every soul grows into faith. We do not leap to holiness; we ripen toward it. The Kingdom does not erupt fully formed; it matures. In the farmer's patience we glimpse the patience of God Himself—the long mercy that waits for our hearts to yield fruit.

The harvest, then, becomes both symbol and sacrament. It is the fulfilment of the seed's promise and the revelation of divine timing. The man who began his work with uncertainty ends it in participation. He gathers what he did not make. The sickle is not judgment alone but joy— the moment when trust meets fulfilment. That is how the Kingdom moves through history: by ordinary hands reaping extraordinary grace.

For the first hearers, this story would have sounded like revelation spoken in their own dialect. They had always prayed for rain; Jesus told them that grace falls like rain—silent, sure, and sufficient. They had always planted seed without knowing what went on beneath the soil; Jesus said the Kingdom grows just so—beyond sight, beyond manipulation, yet certain in its outcome. The invisible, not the spectacular, is where divine power works.

What is astonishing is that Jesus does not moralize this mystery; He incarnates it. He speaks as one who Himself will soon be buried like seed in the earth. The rhythm of the parable is the rhythm of His Passion: sowing, hiddenness, growth, and harvest. The soil that hides the seed is the tomb that hides the Son. The world sleeps; God works. On the third day the seed breaks open, and the harvest begins. The resurrection is the parable's final image made flesh.

The people on that lakeshore could not have guessed that yet, but they felt the truth of it stirring. They understood that the life of God does not come through spectacle or force but through quiet fidelity. The parable dignified their existence: their fatigue, their patience, their waiting. It said that heaven was already at work in their dust.

This is why the story remains as alive for us as it was for them. The same divine patience governs every generation. The same seed still falls; the same soil still hides it; the same grace still grows unseen. The miracle is never absent; it is only hidden. Every act of faith, every prayer whispered into silence, every small good done without witness—all belong to this same mystery.

In the end, the surface story is not surface at all. It is the living skin of revelation. Through it, Jesus shows that God's Kingdom is not an interruption of life but its fulfilment. The earth still turns; people still sleep and rise; and beneath it all, the Word made flesh continues to germinate. The field of Galilee becomes the field of the world, the farmer's patience becomes God's patience, and every harvest is a rehearsal of eternity.

## The Hidden Fire

### a) Text, Translation, and Literary Context
**Greek (Mark 4:26–29):**

Καὶ ἔλεγεν· Οὕτως ἐστὶν ἡ βασιλεία τοῦ Θεοῦ ὡς ἄνθρωπος βάλλῃ τὸν σπόρον ἐπὶ τῆς γῆς, καὶ καθεύδῃ καὶ ἐγείρηται νύκτα καὶ ἡμέραν, καὶ ὁ σπόρος βλαστᾷ καὶ μηκύνηται ὡς οὐκ οἶδεν αὐτός. αὐτομάτη ἡ γῆ καρποφορεῖ, πρῶτον χόρτον, εἶτα στάχυν, εἶτα πλήρη σῖτον ἐν τῷ στάχυϊ· ὅταν δὲ παραδοῖ ὁ καρπός, εὐθὺς ἀποστέλλει τὸ δρέπανον, ὅτι παρέστηκεν ὁ θερισμός.

Mark's opening line—Καὶ ἔλεγεν· Οὕτως ἐστὶν ἡ βασιλεία τοῦ Θεοῦ—appears so plain that most readers glide over it. Yet within that small phrase lies

## THE PARABLE OF THE GROWING SEED (MK 4:26–29)

the evangelist's theology of revelation in miniature. *Houtōs estin* means more than "it's like this." It signals not mere comparison but identification through narrative. Jesus is not sketching an analogy; He is unveiling reality. What follows is not a fable about the Kingdom but a window into how it truly operates—in the world's soil, in the slow rhythm of days, in the heart that waits.

Mark's simplicity is deceptive. Beneath the quiet surface, his verbs throb with divine energy. Listen to their order and flow: βάλλῃ... καθεύδῃ... ἐγείρηται... βλαστᾷ... μηκύνηται... οὐκ οἶδεν... αὐτομάτη... καρποφορεῖ... πρῶτον... εἶτα... εἶτα... ὅταν... εὐθύς... ἀποστέλλει.

It is a slow, patient grammar of grace. The rhythm moves outward from human action to divine mystery: first the farmer's sowing, then his resting, then the seed's hidden movement, then the earth's own generative power, until finally the ripeness calls for reaping. Mark's syntax itself becomes a parable—the liturgy of cooperation between divine and human will.

At the centre stands a single, luminous word: αὐτομάτη (*automate*). Our English "of itself" hardly does justice to its strangeness. In classical Greek, the term described springs that flowed without being touched, doors that opened unforced, or events that unfolded under no visible cause. Mark dares to apply this word to the earth under God's reign: "automatically, the soil bears fruit." He is not denying divine causality but confessing it in a new register. The spontaneity is grace; the hidden agency is God's own. The earth's quiet obedience becomes the sign of divine sovereignty still at work within creation.

Two other details deserve careful attention. The first is ὡς οὐκ οἶδεν αὐτός—"he himself does not know how." That admission is not ignorance as failure but ignorance as faith. The farmer's unknowing is the humility proper to all co-workers of God: the recognition that life moves beneath awareness, that growth exceeds comprehension. The second phrase comes at the harvest: ὅταν δὲ παραδοῖ ὁ καρπός, literally "when the fruit hands itself over." The fruit is not seized or forced; it offers itself. Ripeness, in the Kingdom, is grace's self-presentation. Only then does the human agent re-enter the scene: εὐθὺς ἀποστέλλει τὸ δρέπανον—"immediately he sends the sickle." The verb *apostellei*—used elsewhere of apostolic mission—gives the reaper's action a quiet sacredness. Even harvesting is an act of being sent.

Mark's positioning of this parable within chapter 4 is deliberate. It stands between the Sower (vv. 3–9) and the Mustard Seed (vv. 30–32), forming the hinge between reception and fulfillment.

In the first parable, the Word meets the soils of human freedom: hearing becomes the decisive act.

In the second, the mystery deepens—the Word germinates unseen, the process unfolding "night and day."

In the third, the smallness of beginnings erupts into universality, the tiny seed growing into a tree for all nations.

The parable of the Growing Seed, poised between them, is the bridge of time itself: the long middle in which grace does its slow work. Between hearing and fruition, the Kingdom matures while we "sleep and rise."

Mark also frames it within his meditation on revelation. Just before, Jesus has spoken of the lamp hidden under a basket (4:21–25): "Nothing is hidden except to be made manifest." Immediately after, He tells of the mustard seed. Our passage sits between those two sayings like a heartbeat—showing that disclosure is not sudden brilliance but patient emergence. The lamp will shine, but first it must burn quietly under cover. The Kingdom's revelation is not a flash of spectacle; it is the steady unveiling of life itself.

The stylistic rhythm intensifies this theology. The farmer's verbs are few: he casts, he sleeps, he rises, he sends the sickle. The seed and the earth carry the active burden: it sprouts, it grows, it bears fruit. The pattern reveals a mystery dear to Christian thought—the cooperation of freedom and grace. Human action is real and required, yet divine causality is primary, quiet, and constant. Even the temporal adverbs—*night and day... first... then... then... at once*—convey a spirituality of sequence. Grace does not skip process; it respects time, ripening each stage toward fullness.

This grammar of patience reaches backward to Genesis and forward to Easter. The echo is unmistakable: Καὶ εἶπεν ὁ Θεός· ἐξαγαγέτω ἡ γῆ χόρτον—

## THE PARABLE OF THE GROWING SEED (MK 4:26–29)

"And God said, Let the earth bring forth grass" (Gen 1:11). Creation begins when God's Word entrusts fruitfulness to the earth. Now, in Mark's telling, that same Word speaks through the incarnate Christ: the soil still obeys, still produces *automate*—of itself, yet by Him. The farmer's cycle of sleeping and rising carries the same verbs that will describe the Passion: *He sleeps* in death and *He rises* in glory. The parable whispers the Paschal mystery before the Cross reveals it.

Mark's storytelling discipline is part of the revelation. Unlike Matthew or Luke, he offers no allegorical explanation, no moral summary, no audience reaction. The story ends abruptly with harvest, as though mid-thought. That silence is the point. The middle section—the time when "he knows not how"—is left unspoken because it is where every believer must live. We are given only the beginning and the end: sowing and reaping. Everything between belongs to the mystery of God's hidden work.

The literary voice itself slows to match that hidden tempo. There is no tension, no conflict, no miracle to prove divinity—only the divine patience within nature. The text is an invitation to consent, to trust the *automatos* of grace. What happens in the soil is what happens in the soul: Word received, silence, slow transformation, fruit in its season.

Even the closing word, "immediately," rings with Markan irony. In this Gospel, *euthys*—"immediately"—usually signals urgency, action, divine interruption. Here, it marks the moment of fulfilment after long delay. The Kingdom's "immediately" is never haste; it is readiness. When the fruit hands itself over, response must be swift—but only because grace has been patient.

In this short passage, every line becomes an icon of divine economy. The verbs form a kind of theology of time: sowing as obedience, sleeping as faith, rising as participation, growth as mystery, harvest as communion. The human and the divine are interwoven in a choreography too quiet for spectacle.

The field in the story is the world, but it is also the human heart. The seed is the Word that continues to act even when forgotten. The soil's life, *automate*, is the Holy Spirit working beneath awareness. The "first…

then… then…" of growth describes the unfolding of sanctification: grace taking hold, virtue maturing, charity ripening into glory. And when the fruit "hands itself over," it is the soul's surrender at last to the Sower's hand.

So Mark's parable is not agricultural advice but eschatological revelation. It shows us how divine life unfolds—in silence, in order, in time, in trust. The farmer's patience is the Church's vocation between Christ's Ascension and His return. We sow the Word, we sleep and rise, we watch the seasons pass; the rest belongs to the mystery.

In that rhythm, Mark offers the most consoling theology of all: the Kingdom's progress does not depend on our awareness. It grows while we sleep. Grace, hidden and unstoppable, continues to work in the dark. The grammar itself preaches it—each verb a heartbeat of faith: *he sows… he sleeps and rises… it sprouts… it grows… the earth bears fruit of itself… first… then… then… and when… at once he sends the sickle.* The language becomes a prayer, the structure a kind of psalm. It is the Gospel's quiet creed: God is still sowing, still ripening, still bringing His creation to harvest.

### b) Theological Interpretation

The Parable of the Growing Seed (Mark 4:26–29) is one of the most quietly astonishing statements in all of Scripture. It is short—barely a few verses—yet it contains a theology of divine action that could fill volumes. Its simplicity conceals profundity. Jesus does not speak here about human labour, repentance, or soil quality, as in the Sower. He speaks of something far more mysterious: a seed that grows on its own, silently and irresistibly, while the sower sleeps. The Kingdom, He says, is like that. Grace has a life of its own.

This parable sits midway through Mark's collection of seed parables, forming a bridge between the Sower and the Mustard Seed. If the first teaches receptivity and the last reveals universality, this one unveils *agency*: who actually causes the Kingdom to grow. Jesus' answer overturns both presumption and despair. The farmer does what he can—he scatters the seed—but the work that matters most occurs beyond his control. "Night and day," Mark says, "he sleeps and rises, and the seed sprouts and grows, *he knows not how.*" That single phrase is the heartbeat of the parable. The mystery of growth belongs to God.

Mark uses a rare Greek verb here: *automatē*—"of itself" or "spontaneously." The seed bears fruit *automatically*, not by the farmer's manipulation. The word appears elsewhere in Scripture only twice: in Acts 12:10, when Peter's chains fall and "the iron gate opened *of its own accord*," and in Leviticus 25:5, describing the Sabbatical year when the land produces "what grows of itself." In both contexts, it signals divine initiative—a moment when God acts without human interference. The same idea pulses here: grace has its own vitality, independent of human management. The Kingdom's growth is a divine miracle disguised as natural process.

This is the theology of *divine fecundity*. God's Word, once sown, contains the power of its own fulfillment. The prophet Isaiah foresaw this when he declared, "As the rain and the snow come down from heaven… so shall My word be that goes forth from My mouth; it shall not return to Me empty" (Isa 55:10–11). Jesus' parable is the fulfillment of that promise in miniature. The Word of God is not inert sound waiting for human permission; it is living seed. The Kingdom advances not because we manage it efficiently but because the Word bears fruit by the will of the One who spoke it. The farmer's ignorance—"he knows not how"—is not negligence; it is reverent humility. He plays his part and then yields to mystery.

At the centre of this mystery is divine patience. The farmer cannot dig up the soil each morning to check whether roots are forming. Growth happens too deeply, too gradually, to be observed. The Kingdom moves at the pace of life, not machinery. There are seasons of invisibility, long winters when nothing seems to happen. Yet under the surface, the process is unstoppable. The parable teaches us to trust the unseen rhythms of grace. We live in an age obsessed with immediacy, but God's Kingdom unfolds according to His eternal calendar. There is no fast-forward button for holiness. The silence between sowing and harvest is not emptiness but incubation. God works most profoundly when He appears to be doing nothing.

The three stages in the parable—blade, ear, full grain—trace the life of grace in both the individual soul and the Church as a whole. The blade is conversion: the first tender sign of life after the Word has entered the soil of the heart. The ear is sanctification: the slow, structured growth of virtue, often hidden beneath the surface of daily fidelity. The full grain is consummation: the maturity of love that prepares the soul for harvest, the final gathering into God's barn. These are not merely agricultural metaphors but a moral topography of the Christian life. The Kingdom's growth within us mirrors its growth in history—quiet, organic, patient, governed by the Spirit.

The farmer's two movements—sowing and harvesting—frame God's own economy of salvation. From creation to consummation, God sows His Word into the world and will one day reap it in glory. Between those two moments lies the long history of divine patience. The parable therefore sketches a theology of time. Human history is not an endless cycle but a field moving toward a harvest. The night-and-day rhythm of the farmer—his sleeping and rising—suggests the whole drama of salvation history: the darkness of sin, the dawn of revelation, the repeated pattern of apparent dormancy followed by renewal. God allows the field to rest, to lie fallow, before new growth. His mercy is measured in seasons.

Within that rhythm lies the mystery of human cooperation. The farmer's role is small but not insignificant. He cannot cause growth, yet the seed cannot be sown without him. Divine grace and human freedom meet in synergy. Augustine captures this beautifully: "God created you without you, but He will not save you without you." The parable safeguards both sides of that truth. It rejects Pelagian activism—the illusion that we can engineer holiness—and quietist passivity—the despair that nothing depends on us. The Kingdom requires human hands to scatter the seed but not human control to make it live. Our task is fidelity, not management. In every vocation—parent, teacher, priest, friend—we are called to scatter truth, love, and mercy into the world and then to trust the mysterious fertility of grace.

If we listen closely, the parable carries an implicit warning to every age that tries to domesticate grace. The modern Church, no less than Israel before it, is tempted to replace wonder with management. We plan, organize, and measure, often forgetting that the Kingdom is not a corporation but a living organism. Bureaucracy is not the enemy of holiness, but it can become its parody when we begin to act as if salvation depends on strategic planning. Jesus' story dismantles that illusion. The field grows because God breathes upon it. The Holy Spirit, not human technique, is the true principle of fruitfulness.

There is a paradox in the farmer's sleep. On the surface, it looks like inactivity; spiritually, it represents trust. His sleep is an act of faith that what he cannot see is still alive. In Scripture, sleep often symbolizes surrender into God's care. Adam sleeps, and creation is completed through him; Jacob sleeps, and heaven opens; Jonah sleeps amid the storm, trusting God's mercy; Christ Himself sleeps in the boat, calm amid chaos. In each instance, sleep is the posture of those who know that God works while we rest. The parable invites the same surrender. The farmer's sleep is the Sabbath of faith—the refusal to grasp at what only grace can give. Rest becomes the highest form of cooperation.

Mark's phrase "night and day" suggests the unbroken rhythm of God's providence. Even when the world seems dark, the divine process continues. The alternation of day and night echoes Genesis 1: "There was evening and morning, the first day." Creation's rhythm is still the Kingdom's rhythm. The same Word who said "Let there be light" now speaks into the furrows of the heart, and new creation begins again. The Gospel is not an interruption of creation but its renewal from within. Every act of grace is another sunrise over the field of the world. God's work is not divided into sacred and secular moments; He sanctifies all time.

The autonomy of the seed—its ability to grow *of itself*—does not imply separation from God but participation in His creative energy. Grace does not abolish nature; it perfects it. When Christ compares the Kingdom to a seed, He is affirming creation's sacramentality: the material world is capable of bearing divine life. The growth of a seed is not just a metaphor for spiritual progress but an icon of the divine will at work in matter. The soil, the rain, the hidden processes of germination—all obey the same Creator who formed them in the beginning. The universe itself is structured for grace. The parable teaches us to see the world as a living medium of revelation, not a neutral stage on which salvation happens.

This has profound implications for the moral and spiritual life. We often imagine holiness as self-improvement—an upward climb toward virtue. But in the logic of the seed, growth is not ascent but surrender. The seed must crack, decay, and yield before it can bear fruit. The law of the Kingdom is death that leads to life. To mature in grace is to become ever more dependent on divine nourishment. The stages of blade, ear, and full grain are not achievements of the ego but revelations of God's patience. Each stage requires letting go: the seed lets go of its shell, the stalk lets go of its greenness, the grain lets go of its moisture. In the same way, the soul must yield layer after layer of self-sufficiency until only love remains.

The image of harvest at the end of the parable introduces eschatological depth. When the grain is ripe, "he puts in the sickle, for the harvest has come." This echoes Joel 3:13 and Revelation 14:15, where the same phrase signals the final judgment. The parable therefore spans the entire arc of salvation—from the sowing of the Word in Christ's ministry to the reaping of souls at the world's end. The harvest is not sudden but cumulative; every moment of unseen growth prepares for it. To live in grace is to live in anticipation. The farmer's vigilance at harvest contrasts with his passivity during growth. When God's time arrives, we are called to act decisively. The same faith that rests must also be ready.

There is also an ecclesial dimension here. The Church herself is the field where the Word is sown and where the harvest is gathered. She grows through centuries of hidden sanctity, watered by the blood of martyrs, fertilized by the prayers of saints. Her history alternates between day and night—ages of light and ages of obscurity—but the life within never ceases. Councils, reforms, and revivals are moments when the blade becomes visible, yet the deepest growth remains unseen. The Church's vitality does not depend on cultural approval or statistical strength; it depends on the Word alive within her. Her endurance through persecution and scandal is proof of the seed's autonomy. The field may appear overgrown with weeds, but the harvest belongs to the Lord.

The theology of this parable culminates in its silence. Jesus offers no interpretation, no moral, no conclusion—only the image itself. The story ends as quietly as it began: a farmer, a field, a harvest. The absence of explanation is itself revelation. The Kingdom is not a problem to solve but a mystery to live within. By leaving the process unexplained, Jesus teaches that divine life cannot be reduced to technique or formula. God's grace operates in ways that elude observation, as certain and unmeasurable as growth itself. The task of the disciple is not to analyse the mystery but to trust it—to believe that beneath apparent barrenness, life is at work.

In this sense, the parable becomes a theology of hope. It assures us that grace is never idle, even when all seems dormant. Every field in winter looks dead, but under the frozen soil, roots are forming that will one day bear fruit. The same is true of the human soul, the Church, and the world. We often mistake God's patience for absence, yet patience is how He remains present. The delay of the harvest is not abandonment but mercy, giving time for all seeds to ripen. Divine timing is not slow; it is precise. "The Lord is not slow to fulfill His promise," Peter writes, "but is patient toward you, not wishing that any should perish" (2 Pet 3:9). The parable teaches us to see history not as stagnation but as gestation. What appears still is simply not yet complete.

The hiddenness of the Kingdom also reveals something about the hiddenness of God Himself. The same divine humility that entered a manger continues to govern the growth of grace. God does not impose His reign from above; He plants it within. His omnipotence hides in gentleness, His majesty in mercy. The entire Christian mystery could be summed up in that single rhythm: God working quietly through what seems ordinary. The Incarnation is the cosmic seed sown into the furrows of human history. From Bethlehem to Calvary, the divine life expands beneath the surface until the Resurrection brings the first fruits of the harvest. The parable, then, is not only about the Kingdom's progress but about Christ Himself—the Word sown, buried, and risen.

For the believer, this means that spiritual growth is less about visibility and more about fidelity. The work of God in us is seldom dramatic. Conversion may begin in a moment, but sanctification unfolds in seasons. Our part is to remain in the field—to stay rooted through dryness, temptation, and monotony, trusting that grace is at work. The most fruitful saints were not those who saw results but those who persevered through hidden years of faith. What matters is not that we understand *how* grace grows, but that we let it. The interior life matures through prayer, repentance, and love, but the energy that animates it is divine. We are soil, not architects; vessels, not engines. The most active cooperation with grace is consent.

The harvest imagery points finally toward joy. When the crop is ready, "he puts in the sickle." That is not a threat but a promise. The same Lord who sows in mercy will reap in glory. The sickle is the symbol of divine completion—the moment when everything hidden becomes manifest. Every prayer whispered, every act of mercy unseen, every hidden struggle will be gathered into God's barn. The harvest will reveal what history concealed. The end will not contradict the beginning but crown it. The patience of God will prove itself infinitely fruitful.

Thus, this small parable contains the theology of the entire Gospel: divine initiative, human cooperation, hidden growth, and final fulfillment. It teaches us that the Kingdom is neither spectacle nor stagnation, but steady life. The world demands evidence; God offers process. The world seeks speed; God sanctifies time. The world wants control; God invites trust. The seed sown in the field of the world continues to grow—quietly, automatically, inexorably—until the day when the Lord of the harvest comes. Then what was hidden will stand revealed: the field of creation transformed into the garden of resurrection, the silent seed of grace become the song of glory.

### c) Typological and Intertextual Parallels

## THE PARABLE OF THE GROWING SEED (MK 4:26–29)

The parable of the Growing Seed gathers into a few simple sentences the great symphony of Scripture—from the first "Let there be" of Genesis to the last harvest vision of Revelation. It may sound like a farmer's tale, yet every word—seed, earth, growth, harvest—vibrates with the language of creation and covenant. In these few lines, Jesus takes the whole story of God's interaction with the world and tells it again through the rhythm of nature.

The echo begins in Genesis. "Then God said, 'Let the earth bring forth vegetation, plants yielding seed, and fruit trees bearing fruit in which is their seed, each according to its kind'" (Gen 1:11). When that word was spoken, creation didn't just appear—it responded. The earth, receiving the divine command, became a living participant in its own fruitfulness. The Septuagint's phrasing—*exēnegken hē gē*, "the earth brought forth"—already hints at the mystery that Mark later names *automatos*: the earth acting "of itself," moved not by human hand but by divine impulse within. From the very beginning, God's sovereignty has been generative rather than mechanical. He rules by giving life its own share in His vitality.

When Jesus says, "The earth bears fruit of itself," He is recalling that first morning of creation. The same voice that called forth the fields of Eden now speaks from the lips of the Son of Man, walking Galilee's shores. What once was nature's obedience becomes grace's renewal. The field beneath the farmer's feet is the old earth still answering its Maker's word. Jesus' parable does not describe a different world from Genesis but the same world, transfigured by the Incarnation—the soil now quickened again by the presence of its Creator in flesh.

From creation we move to covenant. Hosea 2:21–23 gives one of the tenderest visions in the prophets: "I will answer the heavens, and they shall answer the earth; and the earth shall answer the grain, the wine, and the oil… and I will sow her for myself in the land." Here, heaven and earth are pictured in dialogue—a cosmic chain of response. Rain descends, soil replies, seed answers, and finally Israel herself becomes God's own sowing. In that poetic exchange, covenant is described as ecology: divine love circulating through creation.

Jesus' parable deepens that vision. The sower in Galilee is not merely God working upon His people but God entering into His people. The seed is now the Word made flesh, sown into humanity itself. Hosea promised that God would "sow Israel in mercy"; Christ fulfills it by sowing Himself. The "earth" that responds is no longer only the land but the human heart. The entire covenant has shifted inward. What was once symbolized by rain and soil now takes place in the soul: God speaking, the heart answering, the world being renewed from within.

Isaiah 55:10–11 adds another layer: "As the rain and the snow come down from heaven and do not return there until they have watered the earth… so shall my word be that goes out from my mouth." Divine revelation is described in agricultural language—God's speech descending, entering, vanishing from sight, and at last returning with fruit. Jesus' parable is Isaiah's image made visible. The Word falls like seed into the soil of history, disappears into its seasons, and returns not void but full of life. The process is not forced; it unfolds *automatos*, by the living power of the Word itself.

This movement from descent to fulfillment finds its final revelation in the Cross. John 12:24 gives the interpretive key: "Unless a grain of wheat falls into the earth and dies, it remains alone; but if it dies, it bears much fruit." Here the parable's pattern becomes flesh. The Son Himself is the seed that falls into the furrows of death. The three days in the tomb are the dark middle period—the hidden germination of salvation. The farmer in Jesus' story "sleeps and rises, night and day," and while he does, the seed works in silence. So too, while the world thought God absent in death, the automatos of redemption was already at work. The Resurrection is the sprouting, the moment when invisible life breaks the soil's crust and appears again in glory.

St. Paul translates the same vision into the life of the Church. "I planted, Apollos watered, but God gave the growth" (1 Cor 3:6). The apostolic mission is patterned on the same rhythm: human cooperation and divine causality, the visible and the hidden. Ministers can plant and water, but increase comes only from God. The field is now the Church herself, alive with the same mysterious fertility that animated the first earth. Paul's language of cultivation is not metaphorical convenience—it is theological realism. Grace works organically. The Church is not a factory but a field, not a mechanism but a living body that grows by divine life within it.

When Jesus speaks of harvest, the tone of the parable widens toward judgment and fulfillment. "When the fruit is ripe, at once he sends the sickle." The line cannot be heard without recalling Joel 3:13: "Put in the sickle, for the harvest is ripe. Go in, tread, for the winepress is full." The same image reappears in Revelation 14, where an angel cries, "Put in your sickle and reap, for the hour to reap has come." The imagery is consistent across the canon: harvest is both joy and reckoning. What has ripened in hiddenness will be gathered, and what has remained barren will be exposed. Jesus' parable, quiet though it seems, carries this apocalyptic undertone. The same patience that sustains growth will one day yield to decisive gathering.

In this way the story stretches across all time. Genesis shows the first sowing; the prophets promise the resowing of mercy; the Gospels show the divine Seed entering history; the Epistles speak of the Church's hidden growth; Revelation unveils the harvest. The whole arc of Scripture moves according to one rhythm—descent, concealment, fruition, and revelation. The "first the blade, then the ear, then the full grain in the ear" describes not only nature but the economy of salvation itself. Creation's gradual unfolding mirrors redemption's slow perfection.

The harvest is more than conclusion—it is disclosure. The grain that has silently ripened now hands itself over; the world reveals what grace has made of it. In this sense, the parable teaches not only patience but hope. The delay of harvest is not neglect but mercy. God waits so that the field may reach its full stature. Time itself becomes the instrument of compassion. Each passing season is grace given for repentance and growth. The delay of judgment is the generosity of divine patience stretched across history.

Through this long arc, the single word *automatos* binds the story together. The soil that once responded to God's first command still responds now, but through the mystery of Christ's indwelling. What was natural fertility becomes supernatural fruitfulness. The earth's obedience to creation's Word becomes the Church's obedience to grace. Every conversion, every act of love, every sacrament quietly celebrated in hidden places is a continuation of that ancient "Let the earth bring forth." The field of the world is still answering.

In Israel's liturgical memory, this entire pattern found ritual expression. The Feast of Weeks, celebrating the first fruits, was Israel's annual confession that the harvest belonged to God. Farmers brought the earliest sheaves to the temple as pledge and thanksgiving. For the Christian, Pentecost is that feast's fulfillment. The Spirit descends as the first fruits of the new creation, and the disciples become the ripened grain offered for the life of the world. Creation's cycle of sowing and reaping becomes the Church's rhythm of mission and sanctification. The soil of Galilee becomes the soul of humanity, now flowering with the fruits of the Spirit.

The Fathers of the Church loved this image because it revealed divine order as both cosmic and intimate. What the Greeks called *physis*—nature's self-movement—finds its fulfillment in *charis*, the grace that moves from within. God's oikonomia, His "housekeeping" of salvation, is not a series of interventions from outside but an ongoing cultivation from within. He governs history as a farmer governs his field: by patience, by presence, by trust in the vitality of His own seed. "First the blade, then the ear, then the full grain." This is not simply agricultural description—it is the grammar of redemption.

The pattern unfolds everywhere. In Israel's story, the Law was the blade—fresh, tender, defining form. The prophets were the ear—structure rising, filled with promise. The Gospel is the full grain—the Word Himself ripened into flesh, ready for the world's feeding. In the Church's life, too, the same rhythm holds. Catechesis is the blade, the first stirring of understanding. Faith and sacramental life form the ear. Charity—the fullness of love that feeds others—is the grain. In every generation the process repeats: the divine seed maturing through history toward its harvest in glory.

## THE PARABLE OF THE GROWING SEED (MK 4:26–29)

This rhythm is not merely temporal; it is ontological. The same divine energy that created continues to recreate. Grace does not replace nature—it perfects it. The soil of creation remains good, but it is now infused with the life of the Spirit. The "earth that bears fruit of itself" has become the Church bearing fruit of the Word. The parable therefore discloses the deepest continuity between creation and redemption: both are God's acts of fruitful speech. In Genesis, the Word calls forth the world; in the Gospel, the Word enters the world to bring it to completion. What began as "Let the earth bring forth" culminates in "Behold, I make all things new."

This continuity gives Christian hope its steadiness. The same patience that governs seasons governs salvation. The slow ripening of virtue, the hidden work of sanctity, the apparent silence of God in history—all are part of the same divine tempo. When Jesus describes the farmer "sleeping and rising," He sanctifies the rhythm of ordinary time. God works through time, not against it. The world's slowness is not resistance but participation in His method. The soil waits, the seed transforms, the harvest comes—each in its appointed hour.

Scripture closes the circle in Revelation's harvest vision: "Then another angel came out of the temple, calling… 'Put in your sickle and reap, for the hour to reap has come'" (Rev 14:15). The same earth that once "brought forth" at the Creator's word now offers back its fruit to the Redeemer. Between those two moments—Genesis and Apocalypse—lies all of history, the long season of divine patience. The parable of the Growing Seed stands at the centre of that arc. It is the heartbeat of the oikonomia itself: God speaking, creation responding, fruitfulness appearing at last as glory.

Every element of the image is charged with theological precision. The sower represents divine initiative—God's will entering the world. The soil stands for creation's freedom and receptivity. The growth that occurs unseen is the mystery of grace operating within history. The harvest is the manifestation of what has been forming all along: the deified creation, the communion of saints, the world transfigured in love. Nothing in this sequence is wasted; even the hidden seasons contribute to the final abundance.

In the end, the word *automatos* unites everything. It is the signature of divine trust. God so believes in His creation that He allows it to share in His own productivity. The soil bears fruit "of itself" because the Spirit dwells within it. The Kingdom's growth is therefore not an invasion but a maturation. God is not an engineer imposing order from above but a Father coaxing life from within. His omnipotence is expressed as patience, His sovereignty as confidence in the life He has sown.

That is why the parable feels so peaceful. There is no anxiety, no striving, no frantic labour—only sowing, waiting, and reaping. The field of the world rests secure under the gaze of its Lord. The same divine power that once turned dust to Eden now works quietly in the soil of human hearts, bringing forth holiness without spectacle. Every act of faith, every hidden deed of charity, every small victory of grace is another stalk in that great harvest.

Seen in this light, the Growing Seed is more than a rustic illustration; it is a miniature theology of everything. It holds together creation and new creation, history and eternity, nature and grace, time and fulfillment. It tells us that God's work is not frantic but faithful, not imposed but invited. The Kingdom does not break in with thunder; it rises like wheat. It grows because God has planted Himself in the world and will not abandon what He has made.

So the parable ends where all Scripture ends—in quiet confidence. The Sower has spoken. The earth is answering. Beneath the surface of every age, grace continues its hidden labour. The harvest will come, and when it does, it will be the flowering of everything that has ever lived by that first command: "Let the earth bring forth." In that fulfillment, the world will at last reveal what it has been becoming all along—the garden of God, bearing fruit *automatos*, filled with the glory of its Maker.

## d) Patristic and Theological Synthesis

The early Church Fathers read this brief parable as a revelation of the whole divine economy — the mystery of how grace operates in the world and in the soul. They recognised in its plain imagery of soil and seasons the deepest truths of faith: that growth belongs to God, that human cooperation is real but secondary, and that the silence between sowing and harvest is not emptiness but divine activity concealed.

Augustine often returned to the phrase *automatos hē gē karpophorei* — "the earth bears fruit of itself." For him, the "earth" is the human heart once softened by faith, now animated by the Spirit's quiet work. In his *Sermons on the Gospels*, he remarks, "The heart believes before it understands; the earth gives before it knows." That sentence captures his theology of prevenient grace: the soul begins to change before it even comprehends how. The mystery of growth, he says, is "the mercy of God working beneath our awareness." Augustine saw in the parable the structure of conversion itself — the moment when grace begins its secret germination long before the believer can name it. The "blade" is the first stir of desire for truth, the "ear" is the formation of virtue, and the "full grain" is charity brought to perfection. Every stage is God's work, yet none without human consent.

John Chrysostom, preaching to urban congregations impatient for visible results, used this parable to rebuke the illusion that holiness or mission could be forced. "Do not measure God's work by your reckoning," he told his hearers, "for the seed grows while you sleep." Chrysostom's pastoral realism shines here: he saw the farmer's ignorance as consolation for the weary and corrective for the proud. The preacher may sow doctrine, he said, but its fruit is born only when the Spirit wills. What appears barren may be ripening beneath the surface. His exegesis mirrors his theology of patience — a theme that pervades his homilies: divine timing is not slow but exact; the delay between sowing and reaping is mercy's interval.

Gregory the Great extended the same insight into the moral and ecclesial realm. In his *Moralia on Job*, he interprets the "earth that bears fruit of itself" as the Church sustained by grace rather than by human mastery. Bishops, he writes, are farmers, not engineers; they guard what they do not generate. Gregory links the "threefold growth" — blade, ear, full grain — to three ascending stages of virtue: compunction, progress, and contemplation. The Church's history, too, follows that arc: first purified by martyrdom's sharpness, then strengthened by doctrine's ear, and finally matured in the quiet fruit of charity. For Gregory, the parable teaches that divine providence guides not only individual sanctity but the slow unfolding of the Church's mission through centuries.

The Eastern Fathers often read the parable through a more mystical lens. Origen, in his *Homilies on Mark* (fragmentary though they are), saw in the growing seed the Logos Himself implanted within the soul. "The Word," he writes, "grows secretly in those who receive Him; while the senses sleep, the heart keeps watch." For Origen, the process is interior: the divine Logos, once sown in baptism and nourished by Scripture, expands from within until the entire person becomes fruitful with divine knowledge. This interpretation would later influence Maximus the Confessor, who saw in the "sleeping and rising" of the farmer the rhythm of the spiritual life — moments of rest and struggle, darkness and illumination — through which the Logos slowly unites the created and uncreated. For Maximus, *automatos* signified the mysterious cooperation of human freedom with divine energy: grace and will working together, yet grace always first.

The scholastic synthesis of Thomas Aquinas preserves this patristic inheritance in philosophical form. In the *Summa Theologiae* (I–II, q. 111), he teaches that grace acts as both cause and companion of human will. The parable, though he never comments on it directly, embodies his principle of *gratia praeveniens* — prevenient grace that precedes every good act. The earth cannot bear fruit until moved by the sun's warmth, but when warmed it acts truly, not passively. So the soul, once touched by God's initiative, becomes an active participant in its own sanctification. In Thomistic terms, *automatos* names not independence from God but participation in His causality: the soul moved by grace moves itself.

In modern theology, this same insight reappears in thinkers such as Henri de Lubac, who saw in the parable the pattern of "supernatural finality" — the idea that human nature is ordered beyond itself to divine participation. For de Lubac, the world's hidden fruitfulness is the signature of its supernatural destiny. Creation contains within it a call to be more than itself; grace does not violate nature but fulfills its deepest inclination.

## THE PARABLE OF THE GROWING SEED (MK 4:26–29)

"The earth bears fruit of itself," he writes, "because it has been spoken into being by a Word that never ceases to work within it." The parable thus bridges natural and supernatural orders: the physical process of growth becomes a visible icon of spiritual ascent.

The Fathers and theologians, across centuries, converge on one truth: the *automatos* of the Gospel is not a doctrine of self-sufficiency but of divine indwelling. The seed grows "by itself" because God's life animates what He has made. The world's fertility, the Church's holiness, and the soul's sanctification all unfold under the same quiet law — grace hidden yet unstoppable.

The parable also offered the Fathers a way to understand history itself. They saw in its progression — sowing, growing, harvest — the three ages of the world. The Patristic Age, like the blade, was the greening of revelation through martyrdom and faith. The Medieval and Apostolic maturation, like the ear, was the structuring of that faith into doctrine and liturgy. The final age, yet to come, is the full grain — when the world, ripened through centuries of divine patience, will be gathered into eternity.

At its deepest level, this parable became for the tradition a theology of stillness. Divine governance is not frantic. The Church's role, like the farmer's, is fidelity rather than control: to sow truth, water with prayer, and trust the hidden power that operates beneath perception. In a world enamoured of immediacy, the Fathers heard in Jesus' words an invitation to patience that is itself participation in God's eternity. "The harvest will come," wrote Augustine, "when the Lord who planted shall be seen in the fruit He ripened."

The Growing Seed thus closes the triad of Mark's agrarian parables— the Sower, the Growing Seed, and the Mustard Seed—by revealing the invisible middle of redemption's story: the time between hearing and fulfillment, between Word spoken and Word made glorious. Creation, covenant, and Church are all versions of the same mystery: God's life germinating in what seems inert.

Grace grows, says the Gospel, *automatos*. The earth bears fruit "of itself," yet not by itself. That paradox—divine action working through created freedom—became for the Fathers the very grammar of salvation. Growth through stillness, transformation through trust: this is the heartbeat of the Kingdom, and the secret rhythm of God at work in all things.

## The Shock and the Turn

To those who first heard it, the parable of the Growing Seed sounded almost anticlimactic. It lacked the drama of the Sower or the grandeur of the Mustard Tree. Jesus compared the Kingdom of God to a farmer scattering seed and then—simply—going about his life. He sleeps, he wakes, and without his knowledge the seed sprouts and grows. Nothing spectacular, no divine intervention, no miracles or armies or trumpets. The Kingdom, Jesus said, is like this. That sentence alone was enough to scandalize expectations.

The crowd wanted apocalypse. They imagined God's reign as a sudden invasion of power, a restoration of Israel through judgment and might. But Jesus gave them a story of patience and silence. In a culture longing for deliverance, He offered the image of a man asleep while salvation happens under the soil. The shock lies in that contrast: the Messiah they awaited was a revolutionary; the Messiah they received is a farmer who trusts the hidden processes of grace. This was not how kingdoms were supposed to come.

The scandal of the parable is divine restraint. God acts, but not as we would act. He works invisibly, through time, through nature, through the quiet persistence of His Word. The farmer cannot force the seed to grow; he cannot even explain how it grows. He must live with mystery. "He knows not how," Jesus says. That line dismantles both the religious pride of control and the secular illusion of mastery. We want a God we can understand and predict, a faith we can calculate. But the Kingdom resists explanation. It demands trust, not comprehension. The shock of the parable is that God is not transparent to human reason; the turn is that this mystery is not frustration but grace.

For the Pharisees, that was an affront. They imagined holiness as the product of precision—every rule observed, every impurity avoided, every outcome measured. Yet Jesus spoke of a Kingdom that unfolds without supervision. The Sower plants; God gives the growth. The Word carries within itself the energy of life. The parable thus strikes at the heart of religious control. It replaces calculation with surrender. The good soil of faith is not mastery but humility—the willingness to let God work unseen.

The same truth unsettles us today. We live in an age obsessed with measurable outcomes. We evaluate success by visibility and speed. Churches adopt marketing strategies, believers measure prayer by productivity, and spiritual life becomes another project to manage. Jesus' parable dismantles that entire mindset. The farmer's only task is to sow faithfully and wait. The mystery of growth belongs to God alone. He is Lord of the harvest, and His grace is never in crisis. This is the first great reversal: salvation does not advance through efficiency, but through fidelity.

The farmer's sleep is more than a practical detail—it is a theological symbol. He sleeps because he trusts. He knows that the field is alive even when it looks barren. In Scripture, sleep often marks surrender into divine care. Adam sleeps, and creation continues through him. Jacob sleeps, and heaven opens. Jonah sleeps in the storm, trusting that mercy will prevail. Christ Himself sleeps in the boat while the sea rages. Sleep is the posture of faith—rest in the sovereignty of God. The parable calls the anxious soul to learn this Sabbath rest. To live in the Kingdom is to believe that God is working even when we cannot see Him.

That truth also carries judgment. Many of us live as if everything depends on our awareness, our planning, our constant motion. We cannot rest because we do not trust. The field must be monitored, managed, measured. We dig up the soil to check whether the seed has germinated, and in our interference we destroy what God is doing. The parable rebukes that nervous piety. It teaches that spiritual control can become unbelief disguised as diligence. Faith is not hypervigilance; it is surrender. To sleep is to confess that the Kingdom grows by grace alone.

The Greek word Mark uses for "grows"—*automatē*—is the hinge of the parable. It means "of itself," the same term used in Acts 12 when the prison gate opens "of its own accord." This single word would have shocked ancient listeners. It implies that the divine Word possesses autonomy—that God's grace is self-moving, self-generating. The farmer contributes, but the process transcends him. It's not indifference; it's mystery. The Kingdom's progress is certain precisely because it does not depend on human strength. The God of Israel, who once thundered from Sinai, now works through the quiet fertility of soil. His omnipotence takes the form of patience.

Patience—that is the sting. The Jews expected urgency; the Romans respected efficiency; but Jesus reveals a God who takes His time. The Kingdom grows "night and day," at the rhythm of creation, not the pace of empire. The divine clock moves by seasons, not seconds. That reversal demands a conversion of imagination. We must learn to see time as grace, not obstacle. The long winter of waiting, the decades of apparent barrenness, are not evidence of failure but the slow unfolding of divine life. In the field of history, every delay conceals preparation. The silence between sowing and harvest is not absence; it is gestation.

And yet this patience is not passivity. The farmer does not withdraw from the field. He watches the horizon, ready for the signal of ripeness. "When the grain is ready," Jesus says, "he puts in the sickle." The moment of divine timing requires human readiness. The same man who once slept now moves with precision. That is the second shock: the Kingdom demands both rest and readiness. God's grace is sovereign, yet He entrusts its final moment to human obedience. The field will ripen without us, but the harvest waits for our response. The parable's moral inversion is complete—first, man learns to let go; then, he learns to act when called. True discipleship is not constant activity, but perfect attentiveness.

This tension between stillness and action lies at the heart of the Gospel. The parable of the Growing Seed teaches that holiness is neither restless labour nor passive waiting, but the union of both. The Kingdom grows in the quiet hours when nothing seems to change, yet the disciple must be awake when God's hour arrives. The sleep of trust and the harvest of obedience are two sides of the same faith. The one who learns to rest rightly will also know when to rise.

That is why Jesus gives this parable to His disciples in the midst of their impatience. They wanted signs that the Kingdom had arrived—proof that their following Him was not in vain. But Christ refused to stage a spectacle. His answer was agricultural: the seed is already in the ground. The process has begun, even if you cannot see it. The scandal is that God's work looks indistinguishable from ordinary life. No trumpet announces the Kingdom's growth. It moves through hidden conversions, quiet obediences, anonymous sacrifices. God reigns not from a throne in Jerusalem but from within the soil of human hearts. That inversion of expectation—the divine majesty revealed as meekness—is the Gospel's deepest shock.

To understand this, we must remember where the parable points. The seed will not remain above ground. It must be buried. The man who sleeps while the seed grows will one day see the Sower Himself sleep in the tomb. The growth of the Kingdom follows the same rhythm as the Passion: descent before ascent, death before life. When Christ's body was laid in the earth, the world thought the story was over. Yet in that darkness the greatest growth occurred. The soil of Calvary hid the germination of resurrection. The disciples slept in despair; God worked in silence. The parable was being fulfilled.

That connection would not have been lost on Mark's early readers. The same community that heard of the seed growing unseen also heard of a Messiah who rose before dawn, "while it was still dark." The Kingdom's power is resurrection power—life springing forth from death without fanfare. Every believer is invited into that same pattern. Our apparent failures, our unseen sufferings, our hidden faithfulness—these are not wasted. They are the buried seeds of glory. The grace that seems dormant is already alive.

The parable's turn, then, is existential. It calls for conversion from anxiety to trust, from obsession with control to peace in God's providence. Modern life conditions us to equate meaning with measurement. We demand to know what difference prayer makes, what results obedience brings. Jesus refuses to satisfy that hunger for data. He tells us instead that the seed grows "he knows not how." Faith is living with that ignorance. It is the courage to believe that unseen processes are not unreal ones. The greatest movements of grace often occur beneath the surface of ordinary fidelity.

For pastors, parents, and all who labour in God's field, this is both rebuke and consolation. The fruit you long for may take decades to appear—or it may ripen in ways you never witness. The soul you pray for may seem barren, but the Word you sow has its own life. You may rest before you ever see the harvest, but the Lord of the harvest will not forget your labour. The silence of results is not the absence of grace. Heaven measures fruit differently. What matters is not visibility, but faithfulness—the willingness to keep sowing while trusting that God keeps growing.

The parable also contains a prophetic warning for the Church. In every age, believers are tempted to confuse the Kingdom with influence, to trade the mystery of grace for the machinery of success. Yet every revival that has truly changed history has begun in obscurity: a few hearts aflame in prayer, a few souls obedient to the Spirit's prompting. The power of God still moves as it did in Galilee—quietly, automatically, irresistibly. The Church's health cannot be read from headlines or statistics; her vitality lies in the secret work of the Spirit. The fields of the world are full of hidden growth.

When Jesus ends the parable with the harvest, He leaves the conclusion deliberately understated. "When the grain is ripe, he puts in the sickle." No commentary, no explanation—just action at the appointed hour. That silence is both promise and warning. The day will come when the slow work of grace will stand revealed, when the invisible will become visible, and when the Lord of the harvest will gather what He has sown. Until then, the call is simple: sow generously, rest trustfully, wait patiently, and rise promptly when God calls.

That is the great reversal of this parable. The Kingdom of God is not achieved by striving but received by trust. It grows while we sleep, matures while we wait, and comes to fullness when we obey. The world's empires build monuments to their power; the Sower builds life in silence. When the harvest comes, it will not be to those who conquered but to those who trusted. The shock of the parable is that grace works while we rest. The turn is that faith means resting in that truth. The Kingdom of God is growing even now—quietly, invisibly, irresistibly—until the final dawn when the fields of the world are white for harvest.

## The Revelation in the Son

Every parable of the Kingdom is, in the end, a veiled revelation of the King. Beneath the imagery of soil and growth lies the mystery of Christ Himself—the divine life sown into the furrows of creation, growing silently until the world is transfigured. The parable of the Growing Seed, brief as it is, contains the whole Gospel in miniature. What it describes as process is fulfilled in the Person of Jesus. The Word He proclaims is the Word He is. The seed that grows unseen is nothing less than the divine life concealed in His humanity.

The entire Incarnation is captured in that single motion: God sowing Himself into the field of the world. The eternal Word, through whom all things were made, descends into the soil of His own creation. The Creator becomes a creature, not as a gesture of disguise but as an act of fertility. In Him the infinite becomes small, the luminous becomes hidden, the omnipotent becomes vulnerable. He is the living seed of divine love, buried in the ground of history. What the farmer in the parable does unthinkingly—casting seed upon the earth—God does intentionally: He entrusts His life to the dark and difficult soil of human existence. The Kingdom of God begins not with conquest but with conception. Mary's womb becomes the first field of redemption, and the seed planted there will one day ripen into the harvest of resurrection.

Mark's phrase "he knows not how" finds its ultimate meaning here. Humanity cannot comprehend how the infinite life of God can dwell in a finite body, how divinity and dust can coexist without confusion. The

Incarnation is the supreme "he knows not how." Yet in that incomprehension lies salvation. The mystery of Christ's person is the same mystery that governs the Kingdom: divine life hidden, yet active; invisible, yet inevitable. Just as the seed grows silently in the night, the Son grows in obscurity—thirty years of hidden labour in Nazareth, the Word of creation learning to speak in a human tongue. The power that upholds galaxies works unnoticed in a carpenter's shop. The Kingdom of God is already sprouting beneath the gaze of those who see nothing special.

The stages of the seed—blade, ear, full grain—trace the pattern of Christ's life. The blade is the Nativity, the first green sign of life breaking through the soil of time. The ear is His public ministry, when the Word emerges and multiplies, stretching toward heaven in the light of revelation. The full grain is His Passion and Resurrection, when divine life reaches maturity and is gathered into the eternal harvest. From Bethlehem to Golgotha to the empty tomb, the Kingdom unfolds organically, each stage growing out of the last. The parable's quiet rhythm—sowing, growing, reaping—is the rhythm of salvation history: Incarnation, sanctification, glorification. The Son of God moves through the same pattern He built into creation. Redemption is not an interruption of nature but its fulfillment.

Even Christ's death follows the law of the seed. "Unless a grain of wheat falls into the earth and dies, it remains alone," He tells His disciples; "but if it dies, it bears much fruit" (John 12:24). His burial is the sowing of divine life into the ultimate darkness. On Holy Saturday, the field of the world lay still. The disciples slept the sleep of despair, unaware that beneath the soil of silence the new creation was germinating. The Resurrection is the hidden growth brought to light—the first green blade of eternity breaking through the crust of death. In that moment, the parable of the Growing Seed becomes prophecy fulfilled: the Word, once buried in weakness, now rises in power.

The harvest that follows is Pentecost, the Spirit gathering the first fruits of the redeemed. The same vitality that caused the seed to grow now fills the Church. The Spirit is the sap of the risen Christ, flowing through the branches of His Body, carrying divine life into every corner of creation.

## THE PARABLE OF THE GROWING SEED (MK 4:26–29)

The growth of the Kingdom through history is nothing other than the expansion of the risen Lord's life. He continues to live, breathe, and bear fruit within His Church. The "automatic" power of the seed—its self-generating growth—finds its divine equivalent in the indwelling of the Spirit. The Church does not manufacture grace; she receives it and lets it grow. She sleeps and rises through centuries, but the seed within her never ceases to live.

In this way, the parable's imagery becomes Christological and sacramental at once. The field is the world redeemed, the seed is the Word incarnate, the growth is the Spirit's work, and the harvest is the Father's gathering of all things into His Kingdom. The Trinity is the farmer behind every motion. The Father sows the Son, the Son becomes the seed, and the Spirit animates the growth. Creation, Incarnation, and sanctification are not three acts of a divine drama but one movement of love. God's life flows outward in giving and returns inward in glory. The Kingdom of God is the circulation of the Trinity through creation—the life of heaven planted in the earth, drawing all things back to their source.

Seen in this light, the parable does not merely *describe* the Kingdom; it *reveals* the way God acts. The stillness of the soil, the mystery of unseen growth, the sudden ripeness of harvest—all are signs of divine style. God works from within, not from above. His power is not coercive but creative, not thunder but yeast. The Word who made the world does not command it from afar; He enters it, like seed entering soil, transforming from the inside out. What looks like absence is in truth the intimacy of divine indwelling. The same hidden process that brings a stalk of wheat to maturity brings a soul to sanctity. Grace operates according to the laws of love—quietly, persistently, and always toward fruitfulness.

This means that every fragment of creation, every moment of history, is charged with Christ's presence. The mystery of the Growing Seed is cosmic: it extends from Galilee to galaxies. The Incarnation was not a local episode but a universal seeding of divinity into matter. "Behold, I make all things new," He declares, and the statement is not metaphor but metaphysics. The whole universe is the field of God's self-giving. Every act of mercy, every conversion, every Eucharist is another shoot of the same life pushing toward the light. The Kingdom is not imposed upon the world; it grows from within it, like the pulse of resurrection beneath the surface of history.

In the Eucharist, this mystery becomes immediate. The bread on the altar is both fruit of the earth and the body of the Sower. What the parable foreshadowed—the union of divine and natural life—occurs each time the priest lifts the chalice and the faithful receive. The same Word that became flesh in Mary becomes food for the world, sown again into human hearts. The altar is the field renewed; the harvest and the sowing coincide. Each communicant leaves the table carrying within them the seed of eternal life, hidden but alive, destined to transform the landscape of the soul.

The Church herself is the continuation of this incarnate sowing. She is both field and farmer, both the soil where grace takes root and the hand through which it is scattered. Her saints are the visible harvest—ordinary lives ripened by extraordinary grace. From martyrs' blood to mothers' prayers, from the scholar's insight to the peasant's faith, each is a stalk of wheat bending toward the light of Christ. Their holiness is not heroic effort but divine growth received. They reveal what the parable promises: that the Word of God, when allowed to dwell deeply, bears fruit that the world cannot calculate.

The final image—"the harvest has come"—points beyond time. The Lord of the harvest is Christ returning in glory, gathering the fruits of His own sowing. The Kingdom's quiet expansion through centuries will culminate in a sudden revelation, the full ripeness of creation in the light of the Son. What has grown in secret will stand radiant and complete. The patient rhythms of grace will resolve into the music of glory. The fields of the world, watered by the blood of the Lamb, will blaze with the gold of divine fruition. Then the Sower, who once trusted His seed to the earth, will behold the earth transfigured.

Until that day, the parable remains the Church's compass. It tells her how her Lord reigns—in hiddenness, in patience, in love that never ceases to give itself. Christ is the seed still working in the soil of humanity, the quiet vitality that outlasts every empire and ideology. His Kingdom grows through the cracks of history until the whole world becomes Eucharist. To believe this is to see creation differently: the field of ordinary life shimmering with the presence of God, every moment heavy with unseen grace.

The revelation of the Son, then, is not a vision of power but of participation. The Word who once spoke light into existence now invites His creatures to shine with it. We live, move, and have our being within this divine agriculture. The parable of the Growing Seed is the story of the cosmos: God sowing Himself into time, humanity receiving and ripening into glory. The mystery that began in a Galilean field ends in a resurrected world where the harvest never ends.

In that final light, the parable becomes doxology. The Sower's patience, the seed's hidden power, the harvest's sudden joy—all are faces of the same love. The Kingdom of God is Christ Himself—planted, buried, risen, and now spreading through the soil of every heart that dares to trust the dark. Beneath the surface of all things, the divine life grows still, silent but unstoppable, until the whole creation stands golden in the morning of the Resurrection, and the Sower looks upon His field and says, "It is very good."

### The Word for Our Age

We live in a time that worships visibility. Success is measured by speed, productivity, and recognition. We want results we can track, numbers we can post, change we can quantify. Yet the Kingdom of God, Jesus says, grows in precisely the opposite way—quietly, mysteriously, "of itself." The farmer in the parable "sleeps and rises, night and day, and the seed sprouts and grows—he knows not how." In those few words, Jesus reveals both the dignity of human effort and the utter dependence of human life on grace. The farmer works, yes, but the miracle happens beyond him. His task is faithfulness, not control. The real fruit of the Kingdom—conversion, sanctity, renewal—cannot be forced, scheduled, or measured. It grows in the hidden places where God alone can see.

That message strikes directly at the anxiety of our age. We live with the illusion that everything depends on us: our success, our reputation, our ministries, even our children's faith. We plan, strategize, optimize—and then exhaust ourselves when growth does not appear on our timeline. But the parable reminds us that grace does not work by our metrics. God's Kingdom moves according to His tempo, not ours. The most powerful acts of God are usually the least observable. The Incarnation began in the silence of a young woman's "yes." The Resurrection began before dawn, with no witnesses. The Church itself began in an upper room of fear, not a stadium of triumph. Divine power prefers obscurity because only there can it preserve freedom.

In the field of the modern world, we often mistake noise for growth. We rush from one program to another, from one outrage to the next, convinced that the louder we shout, the more effective we become. But the Kingdom's rhythm is different. It advances in prayer whispered in hospital rooms, in parents teaching their children to forgive, in hidden acts of fidelity that never make headlines. The Gospel is not a product to promote; it is a life to receive and let grow. When the Church forgets this, she begins to imitate the world's obsession with outcomes. We measure parish vitality by attendance charts instead of repentance, evangelization by social media reach instead of sacramental fruit. Yet the true harvest— the sanctification of souls—ripens in silence. The farmer "knows not how," because holiness cannot be graphed.

This parable therefore calls for a spirituality of patience. The modern Christian must learn again to trust process rather than immediacy. Growth, whether in virtue or in community, requires time, seasons, and sometimes long winters of apparent barrenness. The farmer cannot dig up the seed each morning to check its progress. He waits because he believes in what he cannot see. That is the heart of faith. So much of our spiritual frustration arises from confusing God's slowness with His absence. We pray for change, but nothing seems to move. We evangelize, but hearts remain hard. Yet underground, grace is at work. The roots of conversion often grow in darkness long before shoots of faith appear above the surface.

For families, this parable offers deep consolation. Parents sow countless seeds—lessons, prayers, examples—that seem to vanish. A teenager drifts, a child loses interest in faith, a family member stops going to Mass. It feels like failure. Yet Jesus' farmer would say otherwise. The seed is still alive. It may be hidden under layers of distraction or pain, but it retains divine potential. God's Word does not return empty; it bides its time. A single memory of love, a quiet line of Scripture, a parent's steadfast forgiveness—these are the small deposits of grace that can germinate years later, often when least expected. The spiritual life moves on a longer timeline than our own. The harvest belongs to God.

For those working in ministry or evangelization, the parable also redefines success. We are not called to manufacture growth but to remain faithful in sowing. The early Church grew not through strategy but through sanctity. Its members prayed, loved the poor, forgave enemies, and shared bread—and the seed grew "of itself." Our task is the same: to till the soil of culture through witness, not force. The Kingdom spreads through contagion of holiness, not by campaign. Whenever the Church returns to hidden fidelity—adoration, confession, service—she regains her fertility. The power of the Gospel lies not in novelty but in constancy.

The same truth applies to personal holiness. Many modern Christians live under quiet discouragement. We confess the same sins, pray the same prayers, and feel unchanged. But spiritual growth is like the seed: imperceptible from day to day, evident only over seasons. Holiness is not self-improvement; it is divine life taking root in our weakness. You may not notice the transformation, but others will. Patience with oneself is therefore not laziness but humility—the recognition that sanctity is God's work more than ours. To pray daily, to forgive slowly, to begin again after failure—these are the farmer's routines that allow grace to work unseen.

If the parable of the Sower revealed the human conditions for grace, the parable of the Growing Seed reveals God's own faithfulness. The soil may seem indifferent, the weather unpredictable, yet the vitality within the seed never dies. That is why despair is always premature. God's Kingdom cannot fail because it does not depend on us. Even when the Church appears diminished or the world grows hostile, the divine life continues its quiet work. The Kingdom's future is as secure as the seed's DNA—Christ Himself, planted in the soil of humanity. The outcome is not in question; only our participation is.

In the public sphere, this insight restores hope. We look at culture's confusion—truth denied, life devalued, family eroded—and we fear the field is lost. Yet Jesus has already described this: the seed grows "night and day." The darkness is not obstacle but environment. God's light penetrates it precisely because it seems impenetrable. Every age of Christian history has known decay followed by renewal; every winter has yielded spring. The secret of resurrection is already written into creation itself. Our task is not to despair at the weeds but to keep sowing in faith. As Pope Benedict once said, "The Church does not grow by proselytism but by attraction"—the quiet magnetism of truth lived.

At the personal level, this parable heals the modern wound of restlessness. We live in a world addicted to progress reports, yet the Kingdom's most important work happens in silence. The hours spent in prayer that seem fruitless, the kindness no one sees, the suffering offered for others—these are not wasted. They are the slow fermentation of holiness. The field of your life may look empty now, but underground the seed of Christ is swelling. Patience is not passivity; it is participation in God's rhythm. The farmer's waiting is itself an act of trust. So too our waiting becomes worship.

The image of harvest gives the final word. "When the grain is ripe, at once he puts in the sickle, because the harvest has come." That moment belongs to God alone. The farmer does not predict the hour; he recognizes it when it arrives. Likewise, the final consummation of the Kingdom will come suddenly, when the hidden life of grace in every soul reaches its fullness. History will be revealed as one vast field, every act of faith a seed now blazing with fruit. Until then, the disciple's task is simple: sow generously, rest in trust, and keep watch for dawn. The Lord of the harvest is faithful. The same hands that sowed the seed of creation will gather it again into glory.

In the age of instant results, Jesus' parable stands as holy contradiction. The Kingdom of God does not unfold at the speed of technology but at the pace of love. It grows in the silence of prayer, in the slowness of forgiveness, in the daily fidelity that no algorithm can measure. Its success is certain because its seed is divine. For every heart willing to receive it, the promise remains: *the earth produces of itself, first the blade, then the ear, then the full grain in the ear.* The mystery of growth is still at work—within the Church, within the world, within you. Trust it, tend it, and wait for the harvest that will never end.

### Hearing that Becomes Doing

Sit with the silence that follows the parable. No thunder, no command—only a farmer watching a field that grows without him. This is the landscape of faith. The Kingdom, Jesus said, is like seed scattered on the ground. The man sleeps and rises, night and day, and the seed sprouts and grows—how, he does not know.

Begin there: *how, he does not know.*

Faith always begins with that admission. You do not understand how grace works, how hearts change, how time becomes eternity's servant. You only know that the seed has been given and that the soil of your life can receive it.

Let the image settle. You are the soil—ordinary, unremarkable, but capable of miracle. God asks no brilliance of you, only openness. Soil never commands the seed; it simply holds it, warms it, allows rain to soak it. In the same way, the soul's task is consent. Consent to be ploughed, to be watered, to rest under night's obscurity. The Kingdom grows there—in the unseen hours where nothing seems to happen.

Look back over your days and notice how much of God's work has occurred without your planning. Think of the peace that came unannounced after long struggle, the forgiveness that arose when you were too tired to argue, the quiet courage you did not know you had. These are the harvests of hidden grace. You did not manufacture them; they emerged because God was faithful beneath your awareness.

The world prizes visibility—effort, production, results. But the soil's wisdom is different. It keeps its labour secret. You cannot hear roots forming or stems pushing through darkness, yet life is advancing. The same is true in the interior life. Prayer that feels fruitless may be the richest season of germination. Silence that feels empty may be the night in which God is enlarging you. The Gospel farmer sleeps and rises, not because he is lazy but because he trusts. Sleep becomes faith's most eloquent act of surrender.

Ask yourself: where is God asking me to sleep and rise in trust? Perhaps in a relationship you cannot repair, a project that resists progress, a prayer unanswered for years. Each of these is a field sown with mystery. Your calling is not to force growth but to stay near the soil, to keep your hands open to rain. Growth is the Spirit's art, not yours.

Patience is not passivity; it is participation in divine timing. The seed knows what to do because life is in it. Grace has its own momentum. You can cooperate—weed distractions, guard against cynicism—but you cannot accelerate the sun. The Kingdom is never hurried. God loves the long story.

Let this awareness simplify your prayer. You do not need to manufacture emotion or insight. You need only to stay turned toward the light. Even when clouds hide it, the sun is still drawing the stem upward. Even when you feel nothing, Christ is still rising in you. The faith that waits becomes the faith that matures.

There will be moments of harvest—sudden recognitions when everything once obscure makes sense. A sin forgiven, a heart at peace, a vocation clear. When that happens, do not rush past the wonder. Gather the fruit with gratitude, and remember that it grew in darkness. Gratitude is how the soul stores its harvest. Without it, even grace spoils.

But most of life will not feel like harvest. It will feel like slow weather. Do not despise that pace. God is teaching you His rhythm—the steady

## THE PARABLE OF THE GROWING SEED (MK 4:26–29)

pulse of eternity that no clock can measure. Every morning you rise and every night you rest are sacraments of that rhythm. Sleep and waking, loss and renewal, silence and song—these are the seasons of the Kingdom within you.

The farmer's ignorance—"how, he does not know"—is freedom. You are not responsible for the mechanism of grace, only for its reception. The mystery belongs to God; the patience belongs to you. In that humility, peace returns. Anxiety fades because the outcome no longer depends on your mastery. You can let the field be a field again, and let God be God.

When prayer feels dry, imagine the seed under earth. Nothing to see, yet roots are forming. When work feels useless, remember that hiddenness is the birthplace of holiness. The saints you admire were once buried seeds, unseen in obscurity. Their greatness ripened through years of quiet fidelity. Let that console you: obscurity is not absence; it is preparation.

At times you will feel the plough again—the sharp turning of life that exposes what was hidden. Do not fear it. The ground must be broken for fruit to appear. Surrender to the blade; it is mercy in disguise. The wounds of change become furrows where grace can rest.

When you kneel at the Eucharist, recall this parable. The bread began as seed scattered, cut down, ground, and baked by fire. What looks like stillness on the altar is the history of every seed fulfilled: death turned to nourishment. To receive that bread is to receive the whole rhythm of the Kingdom—sown, buried, raised, given. In that moment, the field and the farmer, the seed and the harvest, become one.

You might end your reflection with this prayer:

### Prayer of the Hidden Field

Lord of the seed and the seasons,
teach me to trust the earth of my own heart.
When I see nothing growing, remind me that You are.
When I grow restless, steady me in Your timing.
Let my faith be patient, my hope quiet, my love enduring.
May I never dig up what You have planted.
When the harvest comes, make me grateful;

       when it delays, make me peaceful.
    Until the field is full and the sickle sings,
    keep me faithful in the work of waiting.
                  Amen.

Stay with the stillness after you pray. The silence itself is fertile. Beneath it, something living is already pushing upward—the Kingdom of God, growing of itself, first the blade, then the ear, then the full grain in the ear.

# II

# Mercy and Judgment

*"Be merciful, even as your Father is merciful."* (Lk 6:36)

# 5

# The Fire That Divides and Heals

The first parables spoke of beginnings—of seeds scattered, soil tested, growth unfolding by unseen grace. They showed how the Kingdom takes root. The next speak of what follows once the Word has entered the heart: how grace must bear fruit, and how fruit must be judged. The language changes now from field to road, from furrow to encounter. The Sower who once cast seed returns as the Lord who seeks a harvest. His patience has ripened into invitation and demand.

If Part I revealed the generosity of divine initiative, Part II reveals the gravity of human response. The Kingdom that once germinated in secret now stands before us in the open, calling for decision. The Word has moved from ear to conscience, from hearing to accountability. What was grace in seed becomes mercy in motion, and mercy, when resisted, becomes judgment.

The landscape of these parables is recognizably human: a roadside ditch, a palace court, a prosperous field. They unfold not in the abstract but in the very places where grace meets freedom and freedom hesitates. The wounded man, the indebted servant, the self-satisfied landowner—each stands in for the soul when the gift of God collides with the habits of self. The stories expose what has taken root within.

Yet beneath every confrontation beats the same rhythm of divine compassion. Judgment in Jesus' teaching is never vengeance but truth revealed, love meeting resistance. Mercy and justice are not competing forces; they are two faces of the same fire—one that purifies and one that burns. To the humble it comes as warmth, to the proud as heat. The same sun that coaxes wheat to golden ripeness hardens clay into brick.

The Gospel never treats mercy as leniency. It is the most demanding thing God has ever done. To forgive us, He must enter the full weight of our cruelty; to heal, He must open the wound. Divine mercy is not sentiment but surgery. It restores by exposure. It is tenderness that will not lie. The light that comforts the contrite will blind those who cling to illusion.

This second movement of parables reveals that inner dynamic through story. The Samaritan, moved with compassion, becomes the icon of Christ Himself—descending the road of human ruin to bind the wounds of Adam's race. The forgiving king prefigures the Father who cancels an impossible debt at the cost of His Son. The rich fool mirrors fallen man grasping at security while eternity waits at his door. Three scenes, one thread: divine generosity meeting human refusal. Each parable becomes a mirror, asking what we have done with mercy received.

The lawyer, the debtor, the landowner—each seeks the same thing: grace without conversion. They desire the gift without its claim. Yet grace, once given, demands circulation. Mercy kept becomes poison; love hoarded turns to loss. The Gospel's tenderness always arrives with a choice—to open or to close, to let the current of grace flow or to dam it up with pride.

This tension—between mercy offered and mercy refused—is the heartbeat of Scripture. From the song of Mary to the sermons of the Apostles, the melody never changes: "He has scattered the proud in the imagination of their hearts; He has filled the hungry with good things." Divine mercy lifts the lowly by lowering itself; divine justice humbles the exalted by exposing their emptiness. Both movements meet on the Cross, where the world's sentence of death becomes God's sentence of life.

These parables bring that mystery down to earth, where it can be seen and touched. They translate cosmic truths into ordinary acts: stopping to help a stranger, releasing a debt, surrendering one's wealth to eternity.

Through them, Jesus makes visible the invisible economy of grace—where every forgiven heart must become a channel of forgiveness, every healed soul a vessel of healing. They are lessons in reciprocity, parables of measure: as you measure, it will be measured back to you.

Historically, this section of the Gospel belongs to the sharpening edge of Jesus' public ministry. The confrontations with scribes and Pharisees have become open; opposition is no longer whispered but declared. Yet the Lord's response is not retreat but deeper invitation. He teaches in images that both disarm and demand. He refuses to condemn without first calling to conversion. The rebuke is always an act of rescue. The Samaritan's oil and wine, the king's forgiveness, the divine interruption of the fool's monologue—all reveal the same heart: truth spoken for the sake of mercy.

For the modern listener, the word *judgment* often feels alien, even cruel. Yet without judgment, mercy dissolves into sentimentality, and love loses its moral weight. To judge is not to crush but to clarify. Judgment is what happens when the light of mercy reveals what is real. The Gospel does not invent punishment; it unveils consequence. The Word that made the world now names what the world has become.

That is why these parables, for all their tenderness, carry such urgency. Grace is free but never cheap. The forgiveness that costs God His life cannot remain a trinket in ours. The field must yield a harvest. The forgiven must forgive. The blessed must become a blessing. Refusal does not cancel the invitation—it hardens it into warning.

Still, the tone remains one of hope. The same Lord who judges is the one who stoops to lift. The same fire that burns also purifies. To meet the judgment of Christ is to encounter the truth of love itself—terrible, beautiful, and liberating. He exposes sin only to heal it; He disciplines to restore communion. The divine verdict is not *depart from Me* but *become like Me*.

To enter Part II, then, is to approach the moral center of the Gospel, where patience gives way to decision and grace calls for fruit. The parables here are not threats but mercies sharpened into truth. They remind us that the Kingdom is not simply growth but response, not only gift but stewardship. The Sower who once cast seed now stands as Reaper—not with scythe in hand, but with open arms, asking what we have done with the love sown in us.

So pause again before reading. Picture the road between Jerusalem and Jericho, falling away through dust and stone. A man lies bleeding at its edge, half-dead, half-alive. Footsteps approach—the sound of mercy drawing near. This is the sound of judgment, because it is the sound of God refusing to pass by.

The same fire that divides also heals. It burns through hypocrisy, purifies affection, and leaves only what can endure. In its light we learn what we truly are—and more wondrously, who He is.

# 6

# The Good Samaritan (Lk 10:25–37)

*And behold, a lawyer stood up to put him to the test, saying, "Teacher, what shall I do to inherit eternal life?" He said to him, "What is written in the law? How do you read?" And he answered, "You shall love the Lord your God with all your heart, and with all your soul, and with all your strength, and with all your mind; and your neighbour as yourself." And he said to him, "You have answered right; do this, and you will live."*

*But he, desiring to justify himself, said to Jesus, "And who is my neighbour?" Jesus replied, "A man was going down from Jerusalem to Jericho, and he fell among robbers, who stripped him and beat him, and departed, leaving him half dead. Now by chance a priest was going down that road; and when he saw him he passed by on the other side. So likewise a Levite, when he came to the place and saw him, passed by on the other side. But a Samaritan, as he journeyed, came to where he was; and when he saw him, he had compassion, and went to him and bound up his wounds, pouring on oil and wine; then he set him on his own beast and brought him to an inn, and took care of him. And the next day he took out two denarii and gave them to the innkeeper, saying, 'Take care of him; and whatever more you spend, I will repay you when I come back.' Which of these three, do you think, proved neighbour to the man who fell among the robbers?" He said, "The one who showed mercy on him." And Jesus said to him, "Go and do likewise."*

## The Word Spoken

The road to Jerusalem wound upward through rock and scrub, a ribbon of white stone gleaming in the sun. It was the road of pilgrims and merchants, priests and soldiers, and it carried the stories of a nation—its prayers, its feasts, its weariness. Jesus was walking that way now, teaching as He went. Luke's Gospel has already told us that He "set His face toward Jerusalem." The phrase means more than direction; it is resolution. Every step is a step toward His Passion. The disciples follow, half elated, half anxious, the scent of dust and sweat clinging to their clothes. Crowds gather and dissolve around them like waves—some seeking healing, some waiting for a spark of blasphemy to accuse. The air hums with the tension of expectation.

He pauses near a village, perhaps one perched along the borderland between Judea and Samaria, where suspicion is a native language. The people come quickly—farmers wiping soil from their hands, widows leaning on staffs, children clutching their mothers' skirts. They have heard the rumours: this teacher heals the sick, casts out demons, eats with tax collectors, speaks of a Kingdom coming near. Some approach with faith, others with curiosity, a few with calculation. Standing among them is a man whose bearing sets him apart—a lawyer, a *nomikos*, scholar of the Mosaic Law. His robe is precise, his phylactery broad, his gaze keen. He has come not for healing but for a test.

Luke writes with deliberate simplicity: *kai idou nomikos tis anestē ekpeirazōn auton*—"And behold, a certain lawyer stood up to test Him." The verb *peirazō* carries a chill. It is the same used of the devil tempting Christ in the wilderness. This man rises not as student to master, but as examiner to defendant. His question, though polished, carries a barb.

"Teacher," he says, "what must I do to inherit eternal life?"

The phrase is formal, yet the undertone is challenge. *To inherit*—*klēronomēsai*—is covenant language. It is not about possession but belonging: who has claim to the promise made to Abraham. The lawyer wants Jesus to draw boundaries, to define the conditions of grace.

## THE GOOD SAMARITAN (LK 10:25–37)

The crowd senses it; they grow still, awaiting the rabbi's reply.

Jesus does not answer directly. He meets calculation with calm. "What is written in the Law?" He asks. "How do you read?"

It is a rabbinic counter-question, but more than that—it shifts the struggle from intellect to heart. The lawyer quotes with precision: "You shall love the Lord your God with all your heart, with all your soul, with all your strength, and with all your mind; and your neighbour as yourself." The Shema of Deuteronomy joined to the ethic of Leviticus. It is the perfect summary of the Law.

Jesus nods. "You have answered rightly. Do this, and you will live."

The conversation could have ended there—orthodoxy confirmed, question satisfied. But something in Jesus' tone unsettles him. The words *do this* land heavier than expected. The man had come to discuss theory; Jesus speaks of obedience. Luke tells us: *thelōn dikaiōsai heauton*—"wanting to justify himself." The lawyer feels the need to draw limits, to make love manageable.

"And who," he asks, "is my neighbour?"

The crowd stirs again. It is a good question, the sort that wins applause in debate. Who qualifies as neighbour? Fellow Israelite? Resident alien? The righteous only? The question conceals a wound: a fear of love without borders. To love indiscriminately would be to lose control of holiness itself.

Jesus does not argue. He tells a story. His voice slows, the cadence of the storyteller replacing the rhythm of dispute.

"A man was going down from Jerusalem to Jericho."

At once the listeners picture it—the treacherous road dropping through seventeen miles of barren hills. The path descends from the holy city into a wilderness of red rock, the haunt of jackals and thieves. To say "he went down" is to say he left safety for exposure, the realm of prayer for the realm of danger. The word *anthrōpos tis*—"a certain man"—strips him of identity. He could be anyone: Jew, Gentile, rich, poor, scholar, labourer. Jesus leaves him anonymous because the parable is universal.

"He fell among robbers, who stripped him, beat him, and went away, leaving him half dead."

The verbs strike like blows: stripped, beaten, left. The audience can see it—clothes torn, skin bruised, breath shallow. Silence falls as they imagine the body lying motionless on the stones. The rhythm of the story changes; the air thickens.

"By chance," Jesus continues, "a priest was going down that road."

At once the listeners' tension eases. A priest—surely, now, help has come. Yet the next line stuns them: "When he saw him, he passed by on the other side." The detail is chilling in its restraint. The priest sees and crosses over. Duty to purity outweighs mercy. The crowd murmurs uneasily; they know this logic too well.

"So likewise a Levite, when he came to the place and saw him, passed by on the other side."

The repetition sharpens the wound. Two men of holiness, two glances, two refusals. Seeing without compassion is another kind of blindness. The road remains empty; the half-dead man breathes alone.

Then Jesus utters a word that makes the air itself shift.

"But a Samaritan..."

A wave of discomfort ripples through the crowd. A Samaritan? The word itself is a scandal. Samaritans are the heretics of the north, descendants of schism and impurity, despised by Judeans as corrupters of the faith. To place one in a story beside a priest and a Levite is already provocation. To make him the hero is unthinkable.

"...as he journeyed, came near him; and when he saw him, he was moved with compassion."

The verb *splagchnistheis* carries the sense of a gut-twisting mercy, the kind of compassion attributed to God Himself. The crowd shifts uneasily. This outsider feels what the holy men could not. Jesus continues, each phrase simple, concrete, devastating.

"He went to him and bound up his wounds, pouring on oil and wine; then he set him on his own beast and brought him to an inn, and took care of him."

The rhythm of action becomes litany: *he went... he bound... he poured...*

## THE GOOD SAMARITAN (LK 10:25-37)

*he set... he brought... he cared.* The verbs march with calm tenderness, mirroring the gestures of a priest at altar. The Samaritan becomes a living liturgy: mercy enacted.

"When he departed, he took out two denarii and gave them to the innkeeper, saying, 'Take care of him, and whatever more you spend, I will repay you when I return.'"

Two denarii—two days' wages—enough for days of rest and recovery. The promise *when I return* lingers like prophecy, the language of one who will come again. The listeners feel the story closing around them, its moral pressure growing.

Then Jesus turns to the lawyer. His tone is still gentle, but the light in His eyes is unyielding. "Which of these three, do you think, proved neighbour to the man who fell among robbers?"

The question reverses the entire debate. The issue is no longer *who qualifies as neighbour* but *who acts as one*. The lawyer's face tightens. The answer is clear, yet unspeakable. He cannot bring himself to utter "Samaritan." Prejudice sticks in his throat. So he says, carefully, "The one who showed mercy on him."

Jesus nods, almost sadly. "Go, and do likewise."

The air falls still. The parable is over, but its silence speaks louder than the question that began it. The lawyer stands exposed, not humiliated but unmasked. He came to test the rabbi; instead, the rabbi has tested him. He sought to define love by boundaries, and has been shown love without measure. His intellect had asked for doctrine; his heart has been confronted by revelation.

The crowd around them hardly breathes. They had expected a sparring match between scholar and teacher. What they have witnessed is judgment wrapped in mercy. The question "Who is my neighbour?" has turned into a mirror held up to every soul present. The men who crossed the road, the one who stopped, the one who lies wounded—each of them now lives within the listener. It is not an allegory yet, but it is already an anatomy of conscience.

The scene itself is charged with irony. A priest and a Levite—symbols of the Temple—are found impotent on the road that leads away from Jerusalem, while a Samaritan, excommunicated from the Temple, becomes its true priest. Oil and wine flow not in liturgy but in mercy. The road to Jericho has become the new sanctuary. The hearers sense the inversion but cannot name it; it feels too dangerous, too close to blasphemy. Yet in Jesus' tone there is no bitterness, only the calm authority of truth spoken by love.

Some in the crowd turn away, shaking their heads. Others gaze downward, tracing patterns in the dust with their sandals. A few—the broken, the outcast—lift their faces with sudden hope. If a Samaritan can be neighbour, perhaps they can too. The boundaries of holiness have just shifted beneath their feet. The lawyer, who had come armed with certainty, now stands at the threshold of transformation. Whether he will cross it, Luke never says. The story leaves him poised between knowledge and obedience, as every hearer remains.

Jesus does not press him. The command *"Go and do likewise"* is not reprimand but invitation. The verb *poreuou*—"go"—is the same Luke uses when Jesus sends the seventy disciples to proclaim peace. The call is missionary: mercy must move. To understand the parable is to become part of it. The Kingdom does not grow through those who know the story but through those who live it.

He turns and begins to walk again, heading toward the next village, the next encounter, the next heart ready to hear. The crowd slowly disperses behind Him, murmuring. Yet something has changed. They have heard the Law as they have never heard it before—not as boundary but as invitation into God's own compassion. The command to love has taken on flesh and movement. The story will travel farther than any of them.

For a long moment the lawyer remains where he stands, the horizon before him blurred by heat. In his mind he sees again the road to Jericho: the fallen man, the passing priest, the Samaritan bending low. The image will not fade. He had wanted a formula; he has been given a face. The neighbour he sought to define now looks back at him from the ditch. The sound of Jesus' final words, *"Go and do likewise,"* beats like a pulse in his chest. He came to measure mercy and found it immeasurable.

Around him, the late light burns gold on the hills. Donkeys bray from the distance, and a trader's cart creaks past. Ordinary noises return, but the air still carries the weight of revelation. The crowd may forget, but the story will not. It will move from mouth to mouth, from synagogue to hearth, from memory to Gospel. In time, it will cross languages and continents, teaching strangers the shape of divine love. And long after the lawyer is gone, his question will remain alive wherever religion becomes comfortable and the poor still lie by the roadside.

The disciples catch up to Jesus on the path ahead. They walk in silence for a while, the dust swirling around their feet. None dare speak first. Finally Peter breaks it: "Rabbi, was that story about us?" Jesus glances at him, and though He says nothing, the faintest trace of a smile crosses His face. They walk on. Behind them, the sun dips lower, casting their shadows long across the stones. Each shadow looks, for a moment, like a man bent to lift another.

The road stretches on toward Jerusalem, that city where the story will find its truest fulfillment. For there, the Teacher Himself will become the traveler who descends from the holy place to the place of death. He will be stripped, beaten, and left half dead on the road of this world. And the One despised and rejected—"a Samaritan" in the eyes of the righteous—will be the one who binds the wounds of humanity with His own blood. The parable has already begun to unfold in His life; the hearers do not yet see it.

By the time the crowd disperses, twilight has settled. The lawyer returns to his lodging in silence, his lips moving as he repeats the words he cannot escape: *Who proved neighbour?* Somewhere in that question, the sound of mercy continues to echo, patient as the heartbeat of God. The conversation that began as test has become revelation. A man stood to trap the Word, and found himself trapped by love instead.

That night the village quiets. The stars come out above the ridge. The same constellations that once guided Israel through the desert now watch over a Teacher who has just redrawn the map of compassion. Tomorrow

He will move on—to dine with Martha and Mary, to heal ten lepers, to speak of lost sheep and lost sons. But this evening's story will linger in the hearts of those who heard it. The Kingdom has spoken in the language of mercy, and its sound will never be silenced.

The road is empty again. Yet in the silence after the crowd departs, one can almost imagine the scene reborn—the wounded man breathing faintly, the Samaritan bending down, the oil glistening in the fading light. It is an image the Gospel will carry forever, a portrait of what God Himself looks like bending over our wounds. The story's ending is not a conclusion but a commission: the command that echoes across centuries—*Go and do likewise.*

The Word has been spoken. It has entered history like seed into soil, carried on the breath of the One who is Himself the Word. It will grow through disciples and martyrs, through acts of mercy and hidden compassion, until every road from Jerusalem to Jericho becomes a path where God's love walks in human form.

## The Surface Story

The parable of the Good Samaritan opens inside a world thick with meaning. Jesus' audience lived close to the land and to the law; every word He spoke brushed against realities they could touch. To them, the road from Jerusalem to Jericho was not an abstraction but a line carved into memory. Seventeen miles of descent, more than three thousand feet down, twisting through barren hills scarred by wind and bandits. Travelers called it the *Way of Blood* because the red limestone looked stained even when no crime had occurred. Pilgrims took it after worship in the Temple, merchants after paying tax, priests after their two-week rotations of service. Everyone who went down that road knew the risk: steep ravines where sound echoed but help never came, caves where thieves waited for shadows long enough to hide them. To begin a story there was to invoke danger and vulnerability.

The listeners would have seen the anonymous traveller in their minds—

robes dusty, sandals worn, purse small but tempting enough. He leaves the holy city behind, its white stones fading into the haze. Perhaps he travels alone because he trusts his strength or his righteousness. Then the inevitable: an ambush, a rush of bodies, fists, the rip of cloth, and silence. To be stripped was to lose not only safety but identity; clothing revealed tribe and class. To be left half-dead was to hang between worlds—alive enough to suffer, too broken to rise.

Into this familiar violence Jesus places figures of equally familiar piety. First, a priest. There were thousands in first-century Judea, descendants of Aaron who rotated through the Temple for scheduled periods. When their turn ended, they returned home—often to Jericho, a priestly city where many served between assignments. The crowd would picture a man of dignity, carrying scrolls or food, head covered against the heat. He sees the wounded traveller. The Greek verb implies sustained looking: he does not glance; he assesses. Then, deliberately, he crosses to the other side. His choice feels reasonable in the logic of purity. The Law warned that touching a corpse rendered one unclean for seven days (Num 19:11). If the man were already dead, compassion would cost holiness. Better to preserve ritual readiness than to risk pollution. The priest acts from caution that masquerades as obedience.

Next comes a Levite, a temple servant responsible for music and maintenance, the bridge between clergy and laity. He too "came to the place, saw, and passed by." The repetition would have struck the crowd like an echo in a canyon. Two holy men, two refusals: seeing without stopping becomes the rhythm of neglect. Yet again, their behaviour is not cruelty so much as the by-product of a system that prized ceremonial purity above spontaneous mercy. The religious hierarchy of Israel had become a wall meant to guard holiness but now blocked compassion. The audience would feel both recognition and discomfort. This is what sin looks like when it dresses itself in reverence.

Then, with a single word—"But a Samaritan"—Jesus overturns centuries of assumption. Every listener would tense. The Samaritans were the descendants of northern tribes who intermarried with Assyrian settlers after Israel's exile (2 Kgs 17). They built their own temple on Mount Gerizim, rejected the prophets, and were regarded by Jews as heretics and half-breeds. The hostility was mutual: pilgrims traveling through Samaria often faced insult or assault. To speak "Samaritan" in Judea was to spit an insult. For the parable to make this man hero rather than villain was a rhetorical earthquake. The crowd expected condemnation; they received reversal.

This foreigner, Jesus says, "came near." That phrase alone breaks a barrier. He approaches what the holy avoided. He sees—not as the priest saw, calculating risk, but as one whose seeing moves the heart. Luke's Greek gives the verb *splagchnizomai*, mercy felt in the gut, the same word used for the father of the prodigal son and for Christ Himself when He looks on the crowds. To feel mercy so deeply is to participate in God's own compassion. What follows is not sentiment but deliberate, costly action. He bandages wounds, pours oil and wine—every traveller's simple provisions for cooking and worship—and turns them into instruments of healing. He lifts the man onto his own beast, walking beside him through the heat. To do this is to become ritually unclean, to risk reputation, to slow one's journey. The Samaritan sacrifices convenience, safety, and status. In the economy of the first century, such acts were not minor kindnesses; they were scandalous.

Even more startling is where he brings the injured man: an inn. In ancient Judea, *pandocheion*—"a place that receives all"—was a rare word. Inns were despised establishments, frequented by Gentiles, traders, and thieves. To lodge there was to cross social boundaries again. Yet the Samaritan stays the night, tending the man personally. By morning he entrusts him to the innkeeper, giving two denarii—two days' wages—and a promise to return. In a barter economy, that is extravagant generosity. To pledge repayment "when I come back" suggests ongoing responsibility: compassion extended beyond impulse into covenant.

The lawyer listening would have been forced to imagine the scene with uncomfortable precision. Here is a man he would not touch, rescuing one he would call brother, performing the duties that Torah ascribed to the righteous. The parable's realism bites because it is plausible. Nothing supernatural happens, no angels descend; only human decisions determine whether life continues. In this ordinary mercy, Jesus grounds divine command.

For those first-century listeners, every element carried weight. To be beaten and left on the roadside was not only a physical tragedy but a ritual and social collapse. Honor depended on reciprocity—help for help, family for family. This man has none. He is *naked*, which in Hebrew thought signifies both shame and vulnerability. He cannot declare his lineage; he cannot be identified as friend or foe. The Samaritan's decision to aid him, therefore, is not motivated by tribal duty or religious law. It is mercy untethered from calculation—precisely what the Law had always intended but what human interpretation had fenced in.

For the Jewish audience, the story also echoed older Scripture. They would remember Abraham running to meet strangers under the oaks of Mamre, binding their feet with water and feeding them bread (Gen 18). They would recall the prophets crying that true fasting is to clothe the naked and loose the bonds of wickedness (Isa 58). Jesus, by telling this story, gathers those fragments into one living image: hospitality not as ritual but as imitation of God's own kindness. Yet the setting—this desolate road—makes that theology visible in flesh and dust.

The geography itself sharpens the moral tension. Jerusalem stood on the heights, symbol of divine presence; Jericho lay below sea level, a lush oasis often linked with temptation. The descent from one to the other became an emblem of spiritual decline. When Jesus says, "A man was going down," His hearers would sense more than geography. The story begins in the movement from sacred to profane, from city of God to city of man. The road's physical danger mirrors Israel's moral condition: a world in which holiness is continually ambushed by sin.

The inclusion of a priest and a Levite is therefore more than realistic; it is diagnostic. They represent Israel's cultic system—good in its origin, weary in its practice. Their avoidance of the dying man is not born of malice but of a theology grown rigid. Purity codes designed to protect the holy place have metastasized into barriers against love. The listeners would feel the sting. For centuries, Israel's vocation had been to mediate mercy to the nations. Now its representatives shrink from mercy even within Israel.

The Samaritan's arrival shatters that order. In one gesture of compassion, the ancient rivalry between north and south, schism and orthodoxy, is inverted. The "outsider" becomes image of divine fidelity; the "insiders" become symbols of failure. It is the covenant drama replayed in miniature: God choosing the unlikely to shame the self-assured. The shock lies not only in the identity of the rescuer but in the implication that God's compassion is larger than human boundaries. The lawyer, trained to defend those boundaries, finds the Law turned inside out.

Even the inn carries resonance beyond its modest walls. In a culture where hospitality was sacred yet limited by kinship, a *pandocheion* was an anomaly—"receiving all," including foreigners. The Samaritan's act thus extends into social imagination: he creates community where none existed. By entrusting the wounded man to an innkeeper, he establishes continuity of care, suggesting that mercy must become institutional, not episodic. It is the seed of a new kind of fellowship, one that will later be embodied in the Church.

The final dialogue—"Which of these three proved neighbour?"—presses the realism into moral precision. Jesus does not ask which man *was* the neighbour but which *became* one. The verb *ginomai*—to become—suggests transformation. In first-century Jewish ethics, "neighbour" (Hebrew *reaʿ*) referred primarily to fellow Israelites. To extend it beyond covenant borders was unthinkable. Yet here, neighbourliness is no longer defined by blood or creed but by mercy enacted. The lawyer's careful answer—"The one who showed mercy on him"—is both correct and reluctant. He cannot say "Samaritan." The word would taste of surrender.

For the ordinary listener, however, the parable would have carried a more visceral hope. Many among Jesus' audience were the poor and despised—people who knew what it felt like to be passed by. They would hear in this story not condemnation but vindication: the possibility that

God's favour might rest on those long excluded. If a Samaritan can be conduit of divine mercy, perhaps a sinner, a tax collector, a woman, a leper might also be. The Kingdom is drawing near, not to the centre of power but to the margins where compassion still breathes.

At the same time, the story offers no cheap comfort. The Samaritan's mercy is not effortless. He risks his safety on a road where robbers may still lurk; he pays from his own purse; he promises to return. In a world governed by debt and honour, this generosity defies economics. It hints at the cost of divine compassion that will soon be revealed in Christ's own journey to Jerusalem. But for now, the crowd hears only the human tale, the unsettling realism that mercy always requires vulnerability.

By the time Jesus ends—"Go, and do likewise"—the listeners are caught between admiration and disquiet. The command is clear, yet the example impossible. To act as the Samaritan acted would mean transgressing the social and religious boundaries that shape their world. The parable thus exposes not only their failure but their hunger. They glimpse what true righteousness would look like and sense how far they are from it.

That tension is exactly where Jesus wants them. On the surface, the story has been about a traveller, a crime, and an unexpected rescuer. Beneath the surface, it has been about the slow undoing of exclusion. Every layer of ordinary life—road, robe, ritual, and coin—has become theatre for revelation. Yet at this stage, the audience does not know it. They stand at the edge of comprehension, hearts stirred but unconverted. The story's realism has drawn them in; its mercy will soon demand more than sympathy.

When Jesus finishes speaking, the lawyer lowers his eyes. The crowd murmurs softly. The dust of the road settles again. They have been shown their own world—its roads, its hierarchies, its fears—but with the light slightly tilted, enough for truth to shine through. What began as a test of doctrine has become an encounter with the living God disguised as a story about a man left half-dead.

This is the surface of the parable, but it is already trembling with depth. What the listeners heard as moral realism will soon unfold as divine revelation. For now, they return to their homes through the same streets and rituals, carrying a story that will not leave them in peace. The road from Jerusalem to Jericho remains unchanged, yet anyone who travels it after this day will see it differently.

## The Hidden Fire

### a) Text, Translation, and Literary Context
### Greek (Luke 10:25-37)

Καὶ ἰδοὺ νομικός τις ἀνέστη ἐκπειράζων αὐτὸν λέγων· Διδάσκαλε, τί ποιήσας ζωὴν αἰώνιον κληρονομήσω; ὁ δὲ εἶπεν πρὸς αὐτόν· ἐν τῷ νόμῳ τί γέγραπται; πῶς ἀναγινώσκεις; ὁ δὲ ἀποκριθεὶς εἶπεν· Ἀγαπήσεις Κύριον τὸν Θεόν σου ἐξ ὅλης τῆς καρδίας σου καὶ ἐξ ὅλης τῆς ψυχῆς σου καὶ ἐξ ὅλης τῆς ἰσχύος σου καὶ ἐξ ὅλης τῆς διανοίας σου, καὶ τὸν πλησίον σου ὡς σεαυτόν. εἶπεν δὲ αὐτῷ· Ὀρθῶς ἀπεκρίθης· τοῦτο ποίει καὶ ζήσῃ. ὁ δὲ θέλων δικαιῶσαι ἑαυτὸν εἶπεν πρὸς τὸν Ἰησοῦν· Καὶ τίς ἐστίν μου πλησίον; Ὑπολαβὼν ὁ Ἰησοῦς εἶπεν· Ἄνθρωπός τις κατέβαινεν ἀπὸ Ἰερουσαλὴμ εἰς Ἰεριχὼ καὶ λῃσταῖς περιέπεσεν· οἳ καὶ ἐκδύσαντες αὐτὸν καὶ πληγὰς ἐπιθέντες ἀπῆλθον, ἀφέντες ἡμιθανῆ. κατὰ συγκυρίαν δὲ ἱερεύς τις κατέβαινεν ἐν τῇ ὁδῷ ἐκείνῃ, καὶ ἰδὼν αὐτὸν ἀντιπαρῆλθεν· ὁμοίως δὲ καὶ Λευίτης, γενόμενος κατὰ τὸν τόπον ἐλθὼν καὶ ἰδὼν ἀντιπαρῆλθεν. Σαμαρίτης δέ τις ὁδεύων ἦλθεν κατ' αὐτόν, καὶ ἰδὼν ἐσπλαγχνίσθη· καὶ προσελθὼν κατέδησεν τὰ τραύματα αὐτοῦ, ἐπιχέων ἔλαιον καὶ οἶνον· ἐπιβιβάσας δὲ αὐτὸν ἐπὶ τὸ ἴδιον κτῆνος ἤγαγεν αὐτὸν εἰς πανδοχεῖον καὶ ἐπεμελήθη αὐτοῦ. καὶ ἐπὶ τὴν αὔριον ἐκβαλὼν δύο δηνάρια ἔδωκεν τῷ πανδοχεῖ καὶ εἶπεν· Ἐπιμελήθητι αὐτοῦ, καὶ ὅ τι ἂν προσδαπανήσῃς, ἐγὼ ἐν τῷ ἐπανέρχεσθαί με ἀποδώσω σοι. τίς τούτων τῶν τριῶν δοκεῖ σοι πλησίον γεγονέναι τοῦ ἐμπεσόντος εἰς τοὺς λῃστάς; ὁ δὲ εἶπεν· Ὁ ποιήσας τὸ ἔλεος μετ' αὐτοῦ. εἶπεν δὲ αὐτῷ ὁ Ἰησοῦς· Πορεύου, καὶ σὺ ποίει ὁμοίως.

Luke positions the Parable of the Good Samaritan at a decisive threshold in his Gospel. The dialogue that precedes it—between Jesus and the lawyer—sets the tone for the entire second act of Luke's narrative: revelation meeting religion. The story emerges as the first great teaching on the road

## THE GOOD SAMARITAN (LK 10:25–37)

to Jerusalem, introducing the theology of mercy that will culminate at the Cross. Its phrasing, rhythm, and placement reveal the logic of divine compassion long before the plot unfolds.

The opening verse announces tension in miniature: *kai idou nomikos tis anestē ekpeirazōn auton*—"And behold, a certain lawyer stood up to test Him." The conjunction *kai idou* ("and behold") marks the sudden intrusion of drama; Luke often uses it to shift the reader from calm description to moment of divine encounter. The participle *anestē* ("stood up") conveys deliberate formality—a scholar rising as in synagogue debate. But the participle is paired with the infinitive *ekpeirazōn* ("to test"), a word Luke reserves for hostility rather than curiosity. Its earlier use describes Satan's temptation in the wilderness (4:2). Already, then, the dialogue is charged with confrontation. The man's posture is reverent; his intent is adversarial.

Jesus' response in verse 26 is syntactically symmetrical and psychologically incisive: "What is written in the Law? How do you read?" The double question reflects the rabbinic method of argumentation but also disarms aggression. The lawyer arrives as examiner; Jesus returns the examination. The repetition of "Law" (*nomos*) and "read" (*anaginōskeis*) establishes a key contrast between text and interpretation, letter and spirit. Luke often plays with this duality—how the same Scripture can conceal or reveal the Word, depending on the heart that reads it.

When the lawyer answers by joining Deuteronomy 6:5 and Leviticus 19:18, Luke records the perfect formula of covenant love: "You shall love the Lord your God… and your neighbour as yourself." The syntax merges vertical and horizontal relationships into one breath. Jesus' affirmation—"You have answered rightly; do this and you will live"—echoes Deuteronomy's own cadence: "Do this and you shall live by it" (Lev 18:5). Yet Luke's word order introduces a quiet subversion. The Greek phrase *poiei touto kai zēsei* ("do this and you will live") places action before life. The sequence reverses the lawyer's implied theology of achievement; it suggests that life itself will flow from obedience, not precede it. The living Word is not tested by the Law; the Law is fulfilled in Him.

The hinge of the entire narrative rests on the next clause: *thelōn de dikaiōsai heauton*—"But wishing to justify himself." The participle *thelōn* indicates continuous desire, not momentary impulse; *dikaiōsai* (to justify) invokes forensic language, the courtroom of conscience. Luke exposes the inner motion of the man's soul with precision: he does not seek righteousness from God but validation from within. The reflexive pronoun *heauton* drives the point home—he becomes both plaintiff and judge. Thus, the story that follows is not about neighbourly ethics but about grace and self-justification.

The question that triggers the parable—"And who is my neighbour?"—is deceptively simple. In Greek, *kai tis estin mou ho plēsion;* The noun *plēsion* comes from *plēsios,* "near." The lawyer's concern, therefore, is spatial before it is moral. He seeks the perimeter of obligation: how far must love reach? The genius of the parable lies in how Jesus transforms an adjective ("near") into a verb ("to become near"). The Samaritan will not merely identify a neighbour but *become* one, converting geography into relationship.

Luke's narrative technique intensifies this reversal through a series of participial clauses that mirror descent, encounter, and mercy. The first half of the parable (vv. 30–32) is built on repetition—three travellers, three moments of "seeing," three responses. The verb *eidōn* ("seeing") occurs in each case, binding the episodes together like refrain. The priest "saw" and passed by; the Levite "saw" and passed by; the Samaritan "saw" and was moved with compassion. The rhythm of the prose is crucial: the identical openings heighten contrast by anticipation. The reader expects the same outcome a third time; Luke's change of predicate—*splagchnistheis* ("was moved with compassion")—breaks the pattern like a note of grace interrupting monotony.

The verb *splagchnizomai* belongs to Luke's theological vocabulary of mercy. It appears only in contexts where divine compassion pierces human indifference: Jesus before the widow of Nain (7:13), the father of the prodigal son (15:20). The Samaritan thus becomes Christ-like in grammar before he becomes so in symbol. The word's etymology—from *splagchna,* "inner organs"—expresses visceral empathy, mercy felt in the gut. Luke's choice turns compassion into almost physiological necessity:

it is something the righteous cannot not do.

The syntax that follows mirrors the care itself. Six main verbs in verse 34 form a chain of merciful activity: he went to him (*prosēlthen*), bound his wounds (*katedēsen*), poured on oil and wine (*epicheōn elaion kai oinon*), set him on his own animal (*epibibasas to idion ktēnos*), brought him to an inn (*ēgagen*), and took care of him (*epemelēthē*). The sequence creates a rhythm of immediacy—each action following the other without conjunctions, a literary equivalent of urgent compassion. The parataxis mimics the breathless flow of mercy in motion.

In contrast, the behaviour of the priest and Levite is expressed with distancing verbs: *antiparēlthen*—"passed by on the opposite side." The prefix *anti-* ("opposite") suggests not neutrality but counter-movement. The holy men do not merely fail to help; they enact opposition to mercy itself. Luke's verbal symmetry thus encodes moral theology: to love is to draw near, to sin is to move away.

The narrative's second half (vv. 35–37) shifts tense and tone. The Samaritan's night of care yields to the language of covenant promise. He gives two denarii to the innkeeper and pledges, "Whatever more you spend, I will repay you when I return." The future tense *apodōsō* ("I will repay") introduces eschatological resonance—a coming settlement that transcends transaction. Luke, who loves to foreshadow the Parousia through parables, lets this promise echo Christ's own pledge of return. Even grammatically, mercy points beyond the moment to the horizon of redemption.

The closing dialogue between Jesus and the lawyer repeats the key term *plēsion* but transposes its function. "Which of these three do you think became neighbour (*plēsion gegonenai*) to the man who fell among robbers?" The shift from static noun to dynamic verb—*gegonenai*, perfect tense of *ginomai*—marks conversion complete. The "neighbour" is no longer object but subject, not the one defined but the one who acts. The perfect tense indicates lasting identity: having shown mercy, he remains neighbour forever.

Luke ends with Jesus' imperative, *poreuou kai su poiei homoiōs*—"Go, and you do likewise." The phrase fuses motion (*poreuou*) with imitation (*homoiōs*). The command is not repetition but participation. The disciple must become the event he has just heard. Luke places this final line immediately before the story of Martha and Mary (10:38–42), where listening and doing meet again. The juxtaposition is deliberate: mercy and contemplation, action and hearing, form a single rhythm of discipleship.

The literary placement within the Lucan travel narrative reinforces this theology. From 9:51 onward, Jesus is "on the way" (*en tē hodo*), journeying toward Jerusalem. The parable of the Samaritan, told "on the road," mirrors the larger motif: Christ Himself is the Traveler descending from the heights of heaven to the wounded world. The repeated use of *hodos* ("way, road") throughout Luke's Gospel becomes both topography and theology—discipleship as shared movement along His path. Thus, even in structure, the parable participates in the Gospel's central metaphor.

Luke's prose, then, is doing theology at every level. His verbs define holiness not as separation but as proximity; his participles trace the heartbeat of grace; his syntax turns mercy into grammar. The passage begins with a man "standing up to test" and ends with a command "to go and do." Between those two movements lies conversion itself: from standing apart to walking alongside.

This is Luke's genius as storyteller-theologian. He never preaches abstract principles; he incarnates doctrine in language. The divine compassion that Christ reveals is already at work in the very grammar of the story—drawing near, binding, lifting, and promising return. The text's rhythm becomes revelation. Before theology comments on it, the text itself proclaims the Word that it contains.

## b. Theological Interpretation

The encounter between Jesus and the lawyer begins as an argument about the Law but ends as a revelation of the heart of God. The transition is the measure of Luke's theological genius: what opens in intellectual curiosity closes in the tenderness of mercy. The lawyer's question, "Who is my neighbour?" is not a search for information but for limits. He wants to know the boundaries of love, to place fences around obligation so that righteousness might be achievable. The entire history of Israel's covenant life echoes in that question—the long struggle to live a holiness that separates from defilement yet reflects God's own fidelity. Jesus answers not with definition but with narrative. The parable becomes His theology in miniature: divine compassion made visible, holiness redefined as communion, salvation enacted in motion.

The first movement of the parable concerns divine initiative. In every Gospel, Jesus' stories begin with a human actor but end by revealing God. The Sower, the King, the Shepherd—these are not merely analogies but disclosures. So too the Samaritan, who moves in the story with the calm, deliberate energy that belongs to grace itself. The road from Jerusalem to Jericho descends through seventeen miles of wilderness, but in Luke's hands it becomes a spiritual topography. Jerusalem is the place of divine presence; Jericho, the city first cursed in Israel's conquest. The traveller who "went down" thus mirrors humanity's own fall from communion to estrangement. His stripping and wounding describe not random misfortune but the condition of sin—humanity robbed of its likeness, left half-alive.

Into that desolation comes the Samaritan. The word alone would have jarred the audience like a cracked bell. To Jewish ears, the Samaritan was the archetype of the unclean, the false worshipper. Yet in this story he alone acts with the attributes of God. His compassion (*splagchnistheis*) is the same compassion Luke attributes to Christ when He sees the widow of Nain or the hungry crowds. Divine mercy has changed costume. The scandal lies not merely in who the Samaritan is but in what he reveals: that holiness in the New Covenant is no longer preserved by separation but manifested by nearness. Grace crosses the road.

This inversion lies at the heart of Luke's theology of mercy. In the Old Covenant, purity was maintained through boundaries; in the New, it is revealed through contact. The priest and the Levite preserve their ritual cleanness but lose their vocation. They represent the religion of form without fire—law guarded so tightly that life escapes. Jesus, through the Samaritan, announces a holiness that risks contamination to heal contamination. The movement toward the wounded man is the motion of the Incarnation itself: the divine Word crossing from eternity into time, from unapproachable light into human suffering. The Samaritan's descent from his animal is the Word's descent into flesh.

Luke's verbs reinforce this divine initiative. "He came near" (*ēlthen pros auton*) is the hinge of the story. It repeats the language of divine visitation that runs through Luke's Gospel: God "came to visit His people" (1:68), the Spirit "came upon" Mary (1:35), Jesus "came near" to the city and wept over it (19:41). Every act of salvation in Luke's theology is a movement of approach. The Samaritan's nearness is therefore sacramental: God's compassion becomes tangible through presence.

The care that follows unfolds like liturgy. The Samaritan "bound up his wounds, pouring on oil and wine." These were the ordinary provisions of travel, yet their combination evokes priestly ritual: oil for anointing, wine for libation. The Samaritan's gestures form a kind of roadside Eucharist—body and blood turned into medicine. In the economy of grace, ordinary materials become sacraments of healing because love transfigures their use. The Church Fathers will later read this instinctively: Origen sees in the oil the soothing grace of the Spirit, in the wine the cleansing sharpness of the Word. Basil the Great speaks of the Samaritan's mercy as the "divine philanthropy" that binds the wounds of fallen Adam. The literal realism of the parable becomes the language of redemption.

Yet before it becomes allegory, it is theology of action. The Samaritan does not speak until the end; his mercy is wordless, expressed entirely in verbs of movement. Luke's syntax mirrors this theology of doing: the short, coordinated clauses—he went, he bound, he poured, he lifted—move like heartbeat. Grace, when embodied, has rhythm. It is this rhythm that exposes the sterility of the priest and Levite. They see but do not move; their faith is paralysed by calculation. Luke thus juxtaposes two kinds of religion: one that analyses and one that acts. Only the latter participates in divine life.

The climax of divine initiative occurs in the Samaritan's promise to return. After entrusting the man to the innkeeper, he says, "Whatever more you spend, I will repay you when I return." The Greek *en tō epanerchesthai me* echoes eschatological language of Christ's own return. What begins as human charity ends as prophecy. Mercy, once given, becomes a pledge of restoration. The story does not end with healing but with expectation. The inn becomes the space between grace received and glory awaited—a figure of the Church itself, where the wounded are tended until the Samaritan comes again.

Through this divine initiative, the parable unveils God's nature not as distant judge but as neighbour. The lawyer's question—"Who is my neighbour?"—is answered by the God who draws near. In the Old Covenant, to love one's neighbour was to mirror God; in the New, to love one's neighbour is to encounter Him. The direction of grace has reversed. What the Law prescribed externally, Christ internalizes as presence. Mercy is no longer imitation of God from afar but participation in His own compassion.

This is why Jesus ends the parable not with instruction but with invitation: "Go, and do likewise." The command is not moralism; it is sacramental. It summons the hearer into the divine pattern just revealed. To do mercy is to share in God's own life. The Church will later express this mystery in the language of deification—*theosis*—but its seed lies here: the human called to become neighbour as God has become neighbour. The Samaritan's crossing of the road is the map of salvation history itself—God stepping across the abyss between holiness and sin, creation and Creator, and binding the wound with His own flesh.

If the Samaritan reveals divine initiative, the lawyer exposes the tragedy of human resistance. The question "Who is my neighbour?" is not a failure of intellect but of trust. It betrays the fear that love might demand too much, that grace might dissolve the boundaries that make identity secure. The lawyer wants to remain righteous on his own terms—to love within limits, forgive within measure, obey without surrender. His posture is that of fallen humanity seeking to justify itself. Luke's description—*wishing to justify himself*—is the anthropology of sin in one phrase: self as both defendant and judge.

Every moral system built apart from grace begins here. The human heart wants control over its holiness, measurable virtue instead of dependent love. The lawyer's question echoes Adam's evasion in Eden: "Am I my brother's keeper?" Both are strategies of distance—attempts to define righteousness as separation rather than communion. Jesus refuses the premise. By telling the parable, He shifts the centre of the Law from boundary to encounter. The command to "love your neighbour as yourself" is no longer a test of the self but the revelation of God's image within the self.

The anthropology that emerges is profoundly covenantal. Humanity, made in the image of divine love, finds its life only in relation. The man left half-dead is not simply an individual in distress; he is the image of Adam—humanity wounded by sin, stripped of glory, unable to rise. The road from Jerusalem to Jericho becomes the long descent of creation away from communion. The robbers are not merely thieves; they are sin and death, powers that plunder the image of God and leave only ruin. The priest and Levite pass by because law alone cannot save what sin has broken. Their purity codes preserve holiness but cannot restore life. The Samaritan's compassion, by contrast, acts with creative power. Where law defines, love recreates.

In this light, the parable is not only moral exhortation but revelation of salvation's economy. The Samaritan's descent to the wounded man mirrors the divine condescension of the Word made flesh. He "comes near" because God's mercy cannot remain abstract. His touch heals because God's holiness no longer destroys the unclean but sanctifies it by presence. The old boundaries collapse as grace enters contamination and turns it into communion.

Here Luke's theology converges with the great arc of Scripture. In the prophets, God's mercy is often described as womb-like compassion—*rachamim*—the love that moves from within God toward His children. Hosea imagines God bending down to feed His people; Isaiah depicts Him carrying them from the womb. Luke translates that ancient tenderness into historical reality. The Samaritan's compassion is the *rachamim* of

God walking on two feet. The oil and wine he pours become the tangible form of that mercy, transforming instruments of ritual into instruments of healing.

The inn, likewise, carries theological weight. The Greek *pandocheion* means "a place that receives all." Patristic readers heard in that universality an echo of the Church—the household of mercy open to Jew and Gentile alike. The innkeeper receives the wounded not by merit but by the Samaritan's command, just as the Church receives sinners not by worthiness but by grace. The Samaritan's promise to repay whatever is spent becomes the theology of providence: God entrusting His mercy to human hands, yet pledging to supply all that they lack. The Church is thus both inn and innkeeper—caretaker of wounds, steward of another's compassion.

The lawyer's perspective, however, prevents him from seeing this mystery. His question isolates "neighbour" as object; Jesus makes it vocation. In the logic of the Kingdom, love does not ask "Who is worthy of my care?" but "How can I become neighbour?" The transformation is ontological: the disciple becomes what he beholds. Mercy is not task but transfiguration.

This redefinition of holiness reaches beyond the parable into Luke's Gospel as a whole. When Jesus heals lepers, eats with sinners, or forgives the adulteress, He acts as the Samaritan acts—crossing boundaries, risking defilement, binding wounds. Each gesture reveals that divine holiness is self-expending love. The old economy of ritual separation has yielded to a new economy of communion. As Paul will later write, "He is our peace, who has made us both one and broken down the dividing wall of hostility." The parable of the Samaritan is that theology in narrative form: holiness made porous by love.

What the priest and Levite fail to understand is that purity without compassion ceases to be purity at all. Their avoidance of the dying man, though legally justified, violates the deeper intent of the Law. The Torah's holiness codes were never meant to isolate Israel from the world but to train her to mediate God's presence within it. By the first century, however, fear of defilement had hardened into self-protection. The Samaritan's act of mercy restores the Law to its original purpose: not exclusion but healing. He embodies what God had commanded through Moses—that Israel should "love the stranger, for you were strangers in the land of Egypt." The covenant's memory of deliverance becomes, in this story, the motive for compassion.

In this sense, the parable stands as commentary on Israel's vocation. The priest and Levite symbolize the failure of the covenant people to recognize their mission as mediators of grace; the Samaritan prefigures the inclusion of the nations. Yet Luke does not set them in opposition for condemnation but for revelation. Through the scandal of reversal, Jesus reveals the universality of mercy. God's faithfulness to Israel is not abolished but fulfilled when the outcast becomes the bearer of His compassion.

The divine irony is complete: the "heretic" becomes the true image of the Holy One. The categories of clean and unclean, insider and outsider, dissolve in the fire of mercy. The road to Jericho thus becomes the first field of mission, where the geography of holiness is rewritten by love. The Samaritan's mercy is not mere humanitarianism; it is the dawn of a new covenant, where every boundary becomes an invitation for grace to cross.

The story therefore presses the listener toward a new anthropology of grace. Humanity is not defined by tribe or ritual purity but by the capacity to receive and transmit mercy. The Samaritan acts in freedom because he has already abandoned the calculus of worthiness. His compassion arises not from duty but from communion with something deeper—a reflection of the divine image itself. To "go and do likewise" is not to imitate foreign behaviour but to rediscover one's own origin. Humanity is created to love as God loves, to draw near as God draws near. Sin is simply the refusal of proximity.

This revelation reframes the entire moral universe. The lawyer's desire to "justify himself" is the mirror opposite of divine mercy. Self-justification encloses the soul within its own verdict; mercy opens it to the infinite. Where the lawyer seeks to prove his goodness, the Samaritan demonstrates that goodness cannot be proven, only given. The human heart becomes righteous not by declaring itself innocent but by letting love act through it. This is why Jesus ends the encounter not with an answer but with a command. The path to understanding is obedience. The truth of mercy can only be known by doing it.

At its deepest level, the parable describes the meeting of divine and human freedom. God's mercy does not erase the Law but fulfills its purpose: love inscribed not on tablets but in hearts. The Samaritan's gestures—approach, binding, lifting, entrusting—outline the contours of the Incarnation itself. Christ will go farther still: He will not only tend the wounded but take the wound into Himself. Yet already in this story we glimpse the divine logic of salvation—God bending low, transforming helplessness into communion.

Luke's composition reinforces this theology by the way he frames the story within the Gospel's "journey narrative." From 9:51 onward, Jesus is on the way to Jerusalem, setting His face toward the city of rejection and redemption. The parable of the Samaritan, told on that road, becomes a self-portrait in parabolic form. He is the true traveller from the heights to the depths, the one who descends to bind the wounds of fallen humanity. The inn, with its open door and unfinished promise, prefigures the Church that will carry His work until He returns. Every element of the narrative anticipates the Passion: the descent, the wounds, the oil and wine, the pledge to come again. The theology of mercy is already the theology of the Cross.

The Fathers of the Church discerned this instinctively. Origen wrote that "the man who went down from Jerusalem to Jericho is Adam," and that "the Samaritan is Christ, who took pity on him." Ambrose saw in the binding of wounds the sacraments of the Church; Augustine called the inn "the Church, where travellers recover until the Samaritan returns." Though these interpretations differ in detail, they converge on the same vision: the parable is salvation history in miniature, the story of humanity redeemed by the compassion of God. Luke's artistry allows both readings to coexist—the moral and the mystical, the ethical and the cosmic—because they are one truth told at different scales.

Within this vision, mercy emerges not as sentiment but as participation in divine power. The compassion of God is creative: it restores what sin disfigures, it builds communion where hostility reigned. When Jesus commands, "Go, and do likewise," He extends to the disciple the dignity of cooperation. The same Spirit that moved the Samaritan moves now in the hearts of believers, empowering them to heal, forgive, and reconcile. The imitation of mercy is not human effort alone; it is grace reproducing itself. To act mercifully is to let the life of God circulate through human flesh.

This is why Luke's Gospel will later call the disciples to be "merciful, even as your Father is merciful." The standard of holiness is divine resemblance. The Samaritan's generosity, costly and unmeasured, prefigures the generosity of the Cross. His promise to repay what is spent foreshadows the inexhaustible sufficiency of grace. The wounded man represents every sinner carried into the Church, nursed by its sacraments, sustained by its hope until the Redeemer's return. The priest and Levite stand as warning: religion without compassion becomes the parody of holiness. The Samaritan stands as prophecy: love that crosses the road is the true image of God.

In the end, the lawyer's question dissolves. "Who is my neighbour?" becomes "Whose neighbour will I be?" Revelation shifts from knowledge to transformation, from boundary to gift. The heart of the Law is not principle but Person—the Word who became flesh to dwell among the wounded. To live this truth is to walk the same road as the Samaritan, knowing that every act of mercy is participation in the mercy that has already saved us.

The parable thus brings together heaven's initiative and earth's response. Grace descends; humanity rises by yielding. In the Samaritan, holiness bends toward the broken. In the wounded man, the world receives its healer. Between them lies the Church—the inn where divine generosity is still at work, spending and being repaid in love.

Luke closes the episode with quiet finality: "Go, and do likewise." The Greek imperative *poiei* stands in the present tense, continuous and habitual—keep doing, keep becoming. The command is not an ending but an open horizon, inviting every listener to step into the story. On that road from Jerusalem to Jericho, time and eternity meet. The mercy that moved once in a Samaritan now moves through every disciple who dares to cross the road.

This is the theology beating within the parable: God is neighbour. And to become neighbour is to share His life.

### c. Typological and Intertextual Parallels

Luke's parable breathes the air of Scripture. Every image within it—road, wound, oil, wine, mercy, and return—draws life from earlier revelation and gives it back transformed. The story unfolds like a miniature of salvation history: creation, fall, covenant, exile, and redemption replayed on a dusty road between Jerusalem and Jericho. To read it typologically is not to impose meaning but to recognize continuity—the one divine Author weaving the same pattern of descent and rescue through every age. What happens between the Samaritan and the wounded man has already happened between God and His people, and will happen again whenever grace stoops to lift the fallen.

The first echo is Genesis. The "man going down from Jerusalem to Jericho" is not merely a traveller but humanity itself descending from communion into alienation. Jerusalem, city of peace and presence, symbolizes the Garden—the place of divine fellowship. Jericho, lowest city on earth and first to fall under judgment, mirrors the world east of Eden. The verbs "went down," "fell among robbers," "was stripped," "was left half-dead" repeat the cadence of Genesis 3: humanity descending, being deceived, losing its garment of glory, and finding itself mortal. The robbers who "stripped and beat him" are the powers of sin and death. They do not kill outright but leave man half-alive—body surviving, soul wounded. The parable thus begins where the Bible begins: with man broken on the roadside of history.

Into that scene enters the Samaritan, bearing in his actions the pattern of divine visitation. He is the God who "walked in the garden in the cool of the day," seeking the lost Adam. His approach reverses the movement of the Fall: man fled from God's presence; now God draws near to man's pain. The moment the Samaritan "came near" recalls every divine descent—the Lord coming down to see the tower of Babel, to rescue Israel from Egypt, to speak with Moses face to face. The verbs of approach mark revelation's rhythm: the transcendent choosing proximity. The Incarnation will be the final and fullest expression of that same mercy that refuses distance.

The typology deepens through the Exodus lens. The road from Jerusalem to Jericho mirrors Israel's own wilderness journey—away from the temple's glory into the land of testing. The robbed traveller, helpless and stripped, recalls Israel enslaved in Egypt, wounded by oppression and unable to free itself. The Samaritan's descent to him mirrors the Lord's descent in Exodus 3:7–8: "I have seen the affliction of my people... I know their sufferings, and I have come down to deliver them." The oil and wine poured on the wounds replay the plagues' inversion: whereas Pharaoh's hardness brought blood and pestilence, divine compassion brings healing and blessing. In this reading, the Samaritan's mercy is the new Exodus—the deliverance of the individual soul from bondage to sin.

The oil and wine also echo the tabernacle's worship. Oil was used to anoint priests and vessels; wine was poured in thanksgiving offerings. Their use on the wounded man's flesh foreshadows a new temple in which the human body becomes altar. The Samaritan's mercy transforms ritual matter into sacrament. The Old Covenant's symbols are not discarded but fulfilled: priestly oil becomes the chrism of healing; wine once consecrated in libation becomes the blood of redemption. In that act of anointing, the Samaritan replays the divine pattern of consecration—turning the profane into the holy, the wounded into the blessed.

Psalm 23 hums quietly beneath the surface. "He restores my soul; He anoints my head with oil; my cup overflows." The wounded man lies in the valley of the shadow of death; the Samaritan leads him beside still waters, anoints him, and restores him. The shepherding God of Israel appears disguised as an outcast traveller. The "good shepherd" of John 10 will later give His own interpretation: "I lay down my life for the sheep." Luke's Samaritan foreshadows that same pastoral mercy. He does not offer doctrine but presence; he walks beside, bears the weight, ensures recovery. The shepherd's staff has become a traveller's bandage, yet the love guiding it is the same.

The priest and Levite, who "passed by on the other side," stand in the typological line of Israel's earlier failures. Their avoidance recalls the neglect denounced by the prophets—Israel's priests who "have not strengthened the weak, healed the sick, bound up the injured, or brought back the strayed" (Ezek 34:4). Their piety without mercy recapitulates the hardness of Pharaoh and the cold formalism Isaiah condemned: "This people honours Me with their lips, but their heart is far from Me." The Samaritan's act becomes prophetic reversal—the true shepherd arriving where the hirelings failed.

Yet the parable's most audacious echo comes from the prophets of mercy: Hosea and Isaiah. Hosea's God declares, "I will heal their faithlessness; I will love them freely." Isaiah's Servant "bears our griefs and carries our sorrows." Both images converge in the Samaritan who lifts the broken onto his own beast, bearing the weight of another's suffering. The substitution is deliberate: the strong exchanges places with the wounded, walking while the other rides. This is not benevolence but atonement in miniature. The mercy of God always carries the burden of the beloved. The same pattern will reach completion when Christ, the true Samaritan, carries the cross and humanity's weight upon it.

The inn, with its open door, draws together the typology of Zion and the eschatological banquet. The Psalmist sings, "The Lord sustains me on my sickbed; in my illness you heal me." Isaiah envisions a feast for all peoples where God "will wipe away tears from every face." In Luke's world, the inn anticipates that feast: a place of restoration between ruin and redemption. Its name, *pandocheion*—"receiving all"—is itself theology. It signifies the Church, the dwelling where God's hospitality continues through time. The innkeeper entrusted with care represents the apostolic ministry, receiving wounded souls from Christ's hands. Even the two denarii have found symbolic resonance in the Fathers: the two covenants, or the two great commandments of love. Yet before allegory, there is simple continuity—what God began with Israel now continues through the body of Christ.

Finally, the Samaritan's promise—"When I return, I will repay you"—extends the typology into the future. Every act of divine compassion in Scripture carries a promise of fulfillment. The Lord who came down in Exodus vowed to bring His people to the Promised Land; the Servant who bore sins promised to see the travail of His soul and be satisfied. In the same way, the Samaritan's future return prefigures the Parousia—the day when mercy will be completed in justice. Until then, the Church lives in the interval between departure and return, caring for the wounded with the resources of grace entrusted to her. The story thus stretches from Genesis to Revelation, from the first wound to the final healing.

The typological horizon widens even further when we consider how Luke's parable converses with the wisdom tradition of Israel. Proverbs had already taught that "whoever is kind to the poor lends to the Lord, and He will repay him" (Prov 19:17). That single verse anticipates the Samaritan's promise of repayment. What had been moral exhortation in the Wisdom books becomes revelation in action: God Himself identifies with the wounded, and to serve the suffering is to lend to the Lord who will repay at His coming. The pattern of divine reciprocity—mercy given, mercy returned—echoes across Scripture. Tobit counsels his son to give alms to all who live uprightly; Sirach declares that compassion "atones for sin." The parable enfolds these wisdom maxims into the logic of the Kingdom, where mercy is not transactional but participatory: one enters God's generosity by enacting it.

Another resonance lies with the story of Jonah, the reluctant prophet who would rather preserve national privilege than see God's mercy extended to enemies. Jonah's flight from Nineveh mirrors the priest and Levite passing by on the far side. Both recoil from the wideness of God's compassion. When Jesus makes a Samaritan—the very image of Israel's despised half-brother—the agent of salvation, He replays Jonah's lesson in miniature: mercy that does not offend our sense of justice is not yet divine. The God of Israel has always chosen scandalous instruments to reveal His love—Gentile kings, pagan magi, and now a Samaritan who out loves the righteous.

The contrast also reaches into the Book of Ruth, where a foreign woman's steadfast kindness becomes the seed of redemption. Ruth's loyalty to Naomi—"Where you go, I will go"—prefigures the Samaritan's solidarity with the fallen man. Both women and Samaritans occupied the margins of covenant identity, yet through their compassion the lineage of the Messiah is sustained. The typological rhythm persists: the outsider reveals the fidelity that insiders forget. The covenant expands not by abandoning Israel but by fulfilling her vocation to be a light to the nations.

Luke's parable also reverberates with the vision of Isaiah 58, the prophet's great liturgy of mercy. "Is not this the fast that I choose," God asks, "to loose the bonds of wickedness… to share your bread with the hungry and bring the homeless poor into your house?" Every imperative of that oracle finds embodiment in the Samaritan. He feeds, shelters, and binds up the broken; he turns the road of danger into a house of mercy. In him, true fasting—the turning from self to neighbour—takes bodily form. The same chapter promises that those who act so "shall be like a watered garden," an image fulfilled when Jesus tells of the Samaritan pouring oil and wine upon dry skin. The prophetic vision becomes incarnate compassion.

Yet the most profound parallel is Christological. The Samaritan is a living type of the Redeemer who "while we were still sinners… died for us." His nearness to the wounded man anticipates the mystery of Emmanuel—God with us. Every gesture foretells the Paschal mystery: he comes down from his own height, lays the man upon his beast as Christ bears the cross, pays the price of recovery, and promises to return. What the Samaritan does in parable, the Son of God will accomplish in history. The oil and wine, once signs of temple worship, will become the sacraments of anointing and Eucharist. The inn will become the Church, entrusted to continue His healing ministry through time. The parable thus moves from narrative to prophecy: what begins on a dusty road will end on Calvary and begin again at Pentecost.

Paul's theology later distils the same revelation in doctrinal form:

"Though He was rich, yet for your sake He became poor, that by His poverty you might become rich." The Samaritan's willingness to bear cost, risk, and loss is the grammar of the Cross itself. Divine love never calculates return; it spends itself entirely and trusts the Father to repay in resurrection. In that light, the Samaritan's two denarii resemble not mere payment but pledge—the double grace of water and blood that flow from Christ's side, or the twofold mission of word and sacrament by which the Church continues His compassion.

At the same time, the figure of the wounded man recapitulates Israel's prophetic laments. Isaiah spoke of the nation as "beaten from head to foot, no soundness in it, wounds and sores not pressed out or bound up." The Samaritan's bandaging fulfills what Israel long awaited: the divine physician who would bind up the crushed heart. Hosea promised, "He has torn, but He will heal us; He has struck down, but He will bind us up." Luke's language of binding (*katedēsen*) consciously echoes that promise. The parable is thus both national and personal redemption: the people of God restored through the compassion of the rejected one.

The innkeeper, too, belongs to this web of type and fulfillment. In Genesis, Joseph is entrusted with the care of Egypt's stores during famine; in Luke's parable, the innkeeper is entrusted with the wounded man's recovery. Both figures act as stewards of another's mercy. Their faithfulness becomes the hinge of providence—the quiet collaboration through which divine plans unfold. In the New Covenant, this stewardship becomes the ministry of the Church, called to tend humanity's wounds with the resources of grace until the Master's return. The parable thereby joins the genealogy of divine delegation: God entrusting creation, covenant, and now redemption to human hands that serve His purpose.

Even the Samaritan's departure and promise of return draw the story into the eschatological imagination of Revelation. The wounded world is still being healed; the Physician has gone ahead but will repay. The Church, like the inn, lives in that interval of faithfulness, sustained by memory and hope. The "two denarii" become the down payment of the Spirit, the guarantee of future completion. When the Samaritan returns, the care will be rewarded; when the Son of Man comes, every act of mercy will be revealed as participation in His own.

The typological threads converge finally in one radiant centre: divine mercy as the grammar of all Scripture. The God who clothed Adam, led Israel, wept through prophets, and bore flesh in Bethlehem is the same God who bends over the dying on the Jericho road. The parable gathers Genesis, Exodus, Psalms, Prophets, and Gospel into one movement of compassion. Every descent of God toward His people finds its human analogue in the Samaritan's act; every return to God of the healed sinner fulfills the story's end. It is, in essence, a microcosm of the covenant—God's fidelity meeting human need until the two become one life.

In this way, Luke's parable stands as a hinge between Testaments. The Old prepares for the One who will cross every boundary; the New reveals that crossing accomplished. The wounded man of Genesis becomes the healed humanity of Revelation. The God who once asked, "Where are you?" now answers His own question in flesh: "Here I am, beside you." The Samaritan's mercy is the exegesis of divine history. In his approach, Scripture itself draws near.

### d. Patristic and Theological Synthesis

The Fathers of the Church read the Parable of the Good Samaritan not merely as moral instruction but as the Gospel itself in miniature. In its simple narrative they heard the whole symphony of salvation—creation, fall, incarnation, redemption, and the Church's continuing ministry. For them, this was not an edifying tale about human kindness but a divine self-portrait. The Samaritan was Christ; the wounded man was Adam; the inn was the Church; the oil and wine were the sacraments. What Jesus described in story, He would soon enact in flesh.

Origen, writing in the third century, first unfolded this vision with characteristic daring. "The man going down from Jerusalem to Jericho," he says, "is Adam descending from Paradise to the world." The robbers are the hostile powers that wound the soul; the Samaritan is the Savior who "binds the wounds" through His commandments and pours on the healing oil of the Spirit and the wine of the Eucharist. The inn, Origen continues, is the Church "which receives all who wish to enter," and the innkeeper is the Apostle who cares for souls until the Lord's return. In Origen's reading, the parable becomes an icon of the whole economy of salvation—grace that descends, heals, entrusts, and promises to complete what it has begun. The story's realism yields to cosmic scope: Adam's fall meets Christ's descent.

Ambrose of Milan, echoing this tradition a century later, reads the Samaritan's compassion as the manifestation of divine "philanthropy"—the love by which God stoops to the misery of His creatures. "Who is this Samaritan," he asks, "but He who came not as neighbour to the righteous but to sinners?" The oil signifies mercy that soothes; the wine, judgment that purifies; the beast, the humanity Christ assumed to bear us. The two denarii represent the knowledge of Father and Son, or the double commandment of love. For Ambrose, every element of the parable is Christological and sacramental. The Redeemer not only pities but restores, and the Church becomes the dwelling where that restoration continues.

Augustine, with his characteristic synthesis, sees in the Samaritan the pattern of *caritas*—love that is both divine and human. The priest and Levite signify the old dispensation of Law and prophecy, capable of diagnosing sin but powerless to cure it. The Samaritan, an outcast among men, reveals God's compassion for the excluded. His descent from the heights of the road to the depths of the ditch mirrors the Word's descent from heaven to earth. When Augustine reaches the Samaritan's promise to return, he lifts the parable into eschatology: "He will come again to judge the living and the dead; He will repay what He owes, for He owes mercy." The inn, again, is the Church, a hospital of grace where the wounded are healed until the Physician returns. In Augustine's imagination, the parable becomes not allegory for its own sake but sacramental realism—the visible world transfigured into sign of divine love.

Gregory the Great later adds the pastoral dimension that will shape medieval theology. "The Samaritan bound the wounds with oil and wine," he writes, "for He tempered the spirit of compassion with the discipline of correction." Mercy and truth, in other words, are not opposites but complements. The Church, like the innkeeper, must imitate both: she heals with tenderness but also teaches with firmness. Gregory's synthesis guards against the moral sentimentalism that later ages would mistake for mercy. Compassion that abandons truth ceases to heal; it only numbs. The Samaritan's medicine is costly because love is honest.

By the high Middle Ages, the parable had become a theological grammar of redemption. Thomas Aquinas, gathering the patristic inheritance, interprets the story within his doctrine of charity. Charity, he writes, is "friendship of man with God," and therefore the principle of all right action. The Samaritan's mercy is charity in motion—grace uniting the lover and the beloved. In refusing to pass by the wounded, he mirrors the inner life of the Trinity itself, where love eternally moves outward without ceasing to return. For Aquinas, the moral command "Go and do likewise" is a summons to participate in that Trinitarian dynamism. The parable thus joins moral theology to mystical theology: what begins as ethical imitation becomes deification. To act mercifully is to share in God's own act of love.

The modern magisterium retains this patristic inheritance with renewed clarity. In *Dives in Misericordia*, John Paul II calls the Samaritan "the living icon of Christ's mercy" and "the measure of every human relationship." Mercy, he insists, is "love's second name." In the Samaritan's gesture, humanity sees what divine justice truly looks like: the power that bends down to raise up. Benedict XVI, in *Deus Caritas Est*, returns to the same text, observing that the Samaritan's compassion "shows that seeing and stopping are the essence of love." The priest and Levite see but do not stop; their religion is intact but sterile. Only the Samaritan allows sight to become sympathy, sympathy to become service, service to become communion. The parable thus becomes the perennial test of authentic faith: orthodoxy without mercy is unrecognizable to God.

When these voices are heard together—from Origen's cosmic vision to Benedict's modern meditation—the unity of Christian interpretation emerges. The parable is not exhausted by any single moral or mystical reading; it contains them all. It is at once Christ's biography, the Church's mission, and the soul's pilgrimage. The Samaritan is God stooping to heal; the wounded man is the world awaiting redemption; the inn is the communion of saints where divine compassion continues through human hands. The oil and wine are not merely symbols but the real grace poured out in sacraments; the promise to return anchors Christian hope. The entire drama of salvation is condensed into one ordinary act of mercy.

The theological synthesis that flows from this tradition is luminous in its simplicity: mercy is the form that divine love takes in a fallen world. Justice alone restores order; mercy restores relationship. The priest and Levite maintain order, but only the Samaritan rebuilds communion. The Fathers and Doctors agree that this is the very logic of the Incarnation. God does not save by decree but by descent. He crosses the road of eternity into time, assumes our wounds, and makes His compassion the law of a new creation. To be Christian is to enter that same movement—to live as innkeepers of grace, tending the broken with the resources of the Spirit and the promise of the Son's return.

Thus, when Jesus concludes, "Go and do likewise," He is not closing a parable but opening a vocation. The Church hears in those words her own commission: to become, for every age, the Samaritan who stops, binds, and carries. The Fathers understood that the story will end only when the Samaritan returns and every wound is healed in His light. Until then, mercy remains the Church's path and proof. The parable of the Good Samaritan, read through the centuries, becomes the unbroken homily of God's compassion—love descending, healing, and promising always to come again.

## The Shock and the Turn

The parable begins with a question and ends with another. It opens in calculation and closes in command. "Who is my neighbour?" the lawyer asks, hoping to define compassion by proximity. Jesus answers by dismantling the question itself. The story does not tell him who to love; it

## THE GOOD SAMARITAN (LK 10:25–37)

shows him what love looks like. When the final words fall—"Go and do likewise"—the lawyer is left exposed, stripped of the distance he had tried to keep between doctrine and duty. The road from Jerusalem to Jericho has become the landscape of his soul.

The first jolt for those listening was the inversion of virtue. The men who pass by are the very ones expected to embody compassion. Their purity, their respectability, their knowledge—all the things that should have prepared them to help—become the reasons they turn away. They see the broken body and measure the risk. They count the cost in time, reputation, and safety. Mercy, they decide, is not worth the danger. The scene would have landed with quiet recognition. Everyone had seen this happen before. Everyone had done it. The shock was not in the description but in the mirror.

Then came the second turn, more cutting still. The one who stops is a man from the wrong side of history. His presence on that road is almost an intrusion. The story could have worked without him; it would have been safer, tidier. Instead, Jesus places him at the centre, and with that choice He turns the world inside out. The least expected becomes the likeness of God. The story's grace lies in that unlooked-for mercy: goodness emerging from where it was not supposed to dwell. What the crowd had dismissed as unworthy becomes the vessel of healing.

The listeners would have felt the air change. It was not a pleasant surprise. The Samaritan's act was too generous, too unguarded. It exposed every boundary built to keep love manageable. His mercy had no filter of kinship or belonging. He did not weigh the man's worth or ask who he was. He simply saw, stopped, and gave. That simplicity is the scandal of holiness. It shows how complicated our self-protection has become.

The story presses deeper still. The Samaritan does not merely assist; he involves himself. He touches wounds, lifts dead weight, walks beside the animal that now carries another in his place. He pays what is owed and promises to return. In each gesture, a quiet light falls on the lawyer's question. Love, it turns out, cannot be contained within definitions. It must spend itself. The moment we begin to measure it, it has already ceased to be love.

For those gathered around Jesus, the image of a wounded traveller would have stirred memories of their own vulnerability. The road from Jerusalem to Jericho was notorious for ambushes. Many had walked it with fear. Now they see themselves in the ditch. That recognition is the parable's sharpest turn. The lawyer began by asking whom he should help; he ends by realizing he is the one who needs to be helped. The distance between benefactor and beggar collapses. The one who shows mercy becomes the measure of divine action, and the one who receives it discovers his poverty. Every hearer is forced into both roles.

The silence that follows must have been heavy. The Teacher had not argued, accused, or condemned. He had only told a story, and yet the story leaves no place to hide. The question "Who proved neighbour to the man who fell among thieves?" demands an answer that cannot be evaded. "The one who showed mercy." The lawyer cannot bring himself to speak the Samaritan's name. He acknowledges the truth without embracing it. That hesitation is the moment of judgment. Mercy has been revealed, but not yet accepted.

This is how truth confronts the heart—not with thunder, but with exposure. The parable ends without applause or conclusion. There is no assurance that the lawyer obeyed, no evidence that understanding turned to imitation. The story lingers, unfinished, waiting for the listener to complete it. The command "Go and do likewise" is not advice but unveiling. It declares that compassion is not an optional virtue but the shape of salvation itself.

For us, the shock remains. The roles may have changed, but the temptation endures—to admire compassion from a safe distance, to analyse rather than to act, to believe that love's work belongs to someone else. The road to Jericho runs through every modern city, every digital space, every closed heart. The wounded man still lies in the dust; he simply looks different now. His wounds may be loneliness, poverty, or despair; his robbers may be addiction or betrayal. The question is the same: who will stop?

## THE GOOD SAMARITAN (LK 10:25–37)

The parable also speaks to another subtle wound—the injury of superiority. The priest and Levite do not see themselves as cruel. They see themselves as responsible, practical, perhaps even prudent. They have become professionals of goodness who can no longer risk being good. The Samaritan, untrained in such calculation, acts from something deeper than duty. His mercy arises from recognition: he sees in the broken body another self. Compassion begins there, where the heart discovers that every stranger is somehow familiar.

The story turns again in its final image: the Samaritan departing, trusting another to continue the care. Mercy does not end with one gesture; it multiplies through others. The innkeeper's quiet service becomes part of the same current of grace. Jesus leaves the listeners with that unfinished chain of responsibility. The Samaritan has done his part; who will take the next watch? The parable thus moves from description to vocation. It ends, as all revelation does, with invitation disguised as demand.

The deeper one listens, the more the parable unsettles. The wound on the roadside is not only the traveller's; it is the wound of the world. The violence that left him half-dead is the same impulse that runs through every age—the instinct to protect oneself at the expense of another. The priest and the Levite are not villains; they are portraits of ordinary avoidance. They represent what happens when caution eclipses compassion, when moral order replaces living love. Their passing is the quiet tragedy of self-preservation: the desire to stay clean rather than to become holy.

What unsettled the first hearers was the discovery that holiness could look unrefined. The Samaritan's mercy is messy. It breaks rules of separation and contaminates the neat boundaries of social piety. He touches, lifts, binds, spends. His goodness is not careful; it is costly. The listeners would have understood that such love threatens the entire hierarchy of worth. It levels every distinction built on bloodline, learning, or law. The story's true revolution lies there—in the revelation that neighbourliness is not a category but a conversion of vision. One becomes neighbour not by proximity but by compassion.

When the story falls silent, the crowd stands before a mirror. The lawyer's question has been answered by exposure: he asked for a rule and received a revelation of himself. The same happens to every hearer who lets the parable in. Beneath its calm surface lies a judgment more searching than any commandment: to know mercy is to be obligated by it. Grace, once recognized, demands response. We cannot receive what we refuse to give. The heart that withholds compassion discovers that it has shut itself off from the very mercy it needs.

This is why the parable does not close with comfort. Its ending is deliberately abrupt, like a sentence left hanging. "Go and do likewise." No blessing, no benediction—just the weight of a choice. The road stretches out again before every listener. Some will take it back toward safety; others will find themselves, perhaps unwillingly, walking toward the wounded. The parable waits for that decision, and in that waiting, it judges.

Yet even this judgment is mercy. The exposure it brings is not meant to condemn but to awaken. The story's knife cuts only to heal. It reveals how small our love has become, not to shame us, but to call us into something larger. The Samaritan's act is not heroic exception but divine invitation. What he does once, God does always—drawing near, lifting the fallen, paying the cost, promising to return. The story's final word is therefore not duty but possibility: the possibility that human hearts, when seized by grace, can begin to love as God loves.

The true turn of the parable comes when the listener recognizes that the Samaritan is not merely model but mirror. The one who tells the story will soon live it. Jesus Himself is the traveller who descends from the heavenly Jerusalem into the world's Jericho, who is stripped, beaten, and left for dead by sin, and who rises to become the healer of all. He is also the Samaritan who kneels beside every fallen soul. The story circles until it meets its teller. In Him, mercy and need are joined, the wounded and the healer made one.

For the lawyer, and for us, that realization is the final shock. We are not asked to admire the Samaritan but to become him—to let Christ's compassion take possession of our own hearts. The parable's demand is not moral effort but spiritual conversion. We cannot "go and do likewise" by willpower; we can only do so by participation in the love we have received. The road to Jericho thus becomes the road of discipleship: a path where mercy both wounds and heals, where love costs everything and gives more than it takes.

When the story ends, Jesus does not move to another topic. He simply looks at the lawyer—and through him, at us. The silence between question and command is the space of decision, the pause where grace waits for consent. Somewhere in that silence lies the hinge of eternity. Whether we will pass by or stop is the question every age must answer anew.

The parable leaves no applause behind it, only the echo of footsteps continuing down the road, and the faint sound of someone breathing, alive again. The mercy that once seemed impossible has taken flesh and begun to move. The fire of divine love has crossed the road. It still does.

### The Revelation in the Son

The parable of the Good Samaritan, when allowed to breathe in the full atmosphere of revelation, discloses not merely a moral example but a vision of God Himself. It is Christ speaking of Christ, the eternal Word revealing His own form under the veil of a story. Every gesture of the Samaritan—the seeing, the stopping, the stooping, the carrying—unfolds the logic of the Incarnation. What philosophy strains to name as *the descent of Being into the finite* becomes, in this image, the drama of mercy made visible.

The Samaritan's movement from height to depth mirrors the Trinitarian rhythm at the heart of reality. The Father eternally generates the Son; the Son eternally proceeds in self-gift; the Spirit is that Gift personified. The descent from Jerusalem to Jericho is the procession of divine love into the far country of sin and death. It is *kenosis*—the self-emptying that does not diminish glory but reveals what glory truly is. For God's splendour is not sterile transcendence but radiant nearness. In Jesus of Nazareth the infinite bends, and the bending itself is beauty.

To "see" the wounded man, the Samaritan must allow his gaze to be seized by compassion. So too, the eternal Word looks upon creation not with cold inspection but with creative pity. *Compatiens Deus*—a God who suffers with—does not mean a deity who loses majesty, but One whose majesty consists in perfect empathy. In Christ's eyes fixed upon the sinner we glimpse what Aquinas called the *convenientia Dei*: the fittingness of divine love stooping to restore the image it made. The world's wounds become the mirror in which God's mercy recognises itself.

He draws near, touches, binds, lifts. Each verb is a miniature theology of the Incarnation. To draw near is the Word's assumption of flesh; to touch is the sacraments' tactile grace; to bind is the Passion's redemptive constraint; to lift is the Resurrection's exaltation. The Samaritan's compassion is not simply analogous to God's action—it *is* that action translated into human terms. Here we glimpse what Balthasar called "the form of Christ": divine splendour appearing under the aspect of service. The beauty of God reveals itself as love willing to be soiled by the dust of the road.

When the Samaritan pours oil and wine upon the man's wounds, the imagery passes effortlessly from symbol to sacrament. Oil is the Spirit's anointing; wine is the blood of the covenant. The two together compose the Church's economy of healing: *spiritus et sanguis*, breath and blood, the very circulation of divine life through history. What is poured out on the roadside will flow again from the pierced side of Christ. The parable thus anticipates Calvary: mercy as the expenditure of the divine heart.

The carrying of the wounded man upon the Samaritan's beast gathers the mystery into one gesture. The Fathers saw in it the *theandric exchange*—God taking humanity upon Himself, humanity borne within God. The Word walks while we ride. The Creator assumes the burden of the creature, not as condescension but as solidarity. This is what it means for the Son to be "made sin," as Paul dares to say: love so complete that it enters the condition of the loveless. The Samaritan does not delegate compassion; he becomes the vehicle of another's life. The Cross is this image writ large—the divine shoulders stooping beneath the world.

At the inn, mercy assumes institutional form. The Samaritan entrusts the healed man to an innkeeper, giving him the means to continue care and promising to return. Here the parable opens into ecclesiology. The inn is not a metaphor but a prophecy of the Church: a place of hospitality where wounded existence is tended by grace until the Lord's return. The two denarii, modest in appearance, signify abundance in reality—the double treasury of Word and Sacrament through which divine compassion endures in time. The innkeeper is every bishop, every disciple, every soul who receives from Christ the charge: "Take care of him." The mercy begun by God is perpetuated by those who bear His Spirit.

The Samaritan's final promise—"When I return, I will repay you"—draws the entire scene toward eschatological light. The story does not end in this world. The One who departed will come again, and the measure of recompense will be mercy's own plenitude. What is begun in tenderness will be completed in transfiguration. The parable is therefore both historical and prophetic: it narrates the Incarnation and anticipates the Parousia. The same Love that descends to bind wounds will return to glorify what it has healed.

In this vision the moral and the metaphysical coincide. Love is not simply commanded; it is ontologically real. To act mercifully is to participate in the very being of God, for *Deus caritas est*. The Samaritan's compassion is not an ethical addition to an indifferent universe; it is the universe's secret law. The cosmos itself, in its ordered generosity, reflects the same logic of self-gift. Stars burn by surrendering energy; lives flourish by losing themselves in love. Christ, the radiant centre of creation, is this law made visible. To see Him is to understand that mercy is the grammar of existence.

What emerges, then, is a theology of light. The Samaritan's mercy is luminous because it reveals what the divine essence is like when expressed in time. The Greek Fathers called this *theophany*: God showing Himself not through domination but through radiant humility. On the road from Jerusalem to Jericho, the eternal Logos becomes visible as beauty bending downward. The true form of glory is the shape of a man stooping over a stranger. To contemplate that form is to glimpse the inner movement of the Trinity: love proceeding outward, returning inward, never ceasing to give.

In Christ, the parable's narrative structure becomes ontology. The Word's seeing is the Father's eternal knowing of the Son; His drawing near is the Incarnation; His binding is the Passion; His carrying is the Resurrection; His return is the Ascension toward the promise of final restoration. Each gesture within the story is an event in salvation history, but also a window into the being of God. Compassion is not merely one attribute among others—it is the grammar through which divine life communicates itself. The Cross, therefore, is not an interruption of glory but its fullest disclosure.

The Samaritan's movement also discloses the paradox of divine justice. In human terms, justice distributes; in divine terms, it restores. The act of mercy is God's justice made visible, for it returns creation to its proper harmony. This is why Aquinas insists that mercy is "the greatest of the virtues": it does not abolish righteousness but perfects it. On the Cross, that perfection blazes. The Infinite settles accounts by forgiveness; the Judge heals rather than condemns. The Samaritan's promise to repay is the logic of Easter—justice fulfilled in joy.

If we follow this revelation to its depth, the parable becomes icon of the hypostatic union. The Samaritan's descent and ascent trace the rhythm of the *theandric exchange*: God takes what is ours and gives what is His. He bears our weakness, and we share His strength. The creature, once half-dead, is now made alive in participation with the divine. The journey from ditch to inn is the itinerary of deification. We are not rescued to be merely well; we are raised to communion. The wounded man awakens in the house of God, and his restored heartbeat is the pulse of grace within creation.

This vision opens into beauty. For the Fathers and the scholastics alike, beauty is the splendour of form—the radiant clarity of order fulfilled in love. The Samaritan's mercy is beautiful because it renders the invisible visible. What philosophy named the *transcendentals*—truth, goodness, beauty—here converge. Truth becomes credible in compassion; goodness becomes radiant in tenderness; beauty becomes redemptive in sacrifice.

## THE GOOD SAMARITAN (LK 10:25–37)

The story is not a moral anecdote but a revelation of the world's aesthetic centre: the Crucified as the loveliest of the sons of men.

In this light, holiness ceases to be moral decorum and becomes ontological transparency. To be holy is to allow divine light to pass through the material of one's life as through stained glass—coloured, yes, but illuminated from within. The Samaritan, anonymous and ordinary, becomes translucent to the glory that moves him. His hands shine with borrowed splendour. Every disciple is called to that same transparency, to become a conduit of the light that has bound our wounds. The imitation of Christ is not mimicry but participation: we act as He acts because His Spirit animates us.

The promise of return, finally, gathers the whole cosmos into hope. The One who descended into the world's ditch will not abandon it unfinished. He will return, not as passerby, but as King, to consummate what His mercy began. Then the inn—the Church scattered through time—will be revealed as the City of God, the home of the healed. The wounds of history will become the luminous scars of glory, reminders that love's descent was not in vain. Every act of compassion, every hidden service, will be shown as participation in that single mercy that once crossed the road.

To read the Good Samaritan in this way is to see that theology itself is an act of praise. The parable is not a lesson appended to doctrine; it *is* doctrine sung in narrative form. It shows that the Word who orders galaxies also binds wounds, and that the hand that shaped the stars now rests on the broken body of the world. The universe, in the end, is the road upon which God has knelt. The Samaritan's mercy is the Incarnation's secret told in plain speech: divine splendour disguised as kindness.

When the story closes, the question remains: who proved neighbour to the man who fell among thieves? The answer, uttered once and for all, is Christ Himself. He is the neighbour who never passes by, the stranger who becomes saviour, the light that enters every darkness. To behold Him is to see the fire that both heals and judges, the mercy that is the very majesty of God. The world's wound, once its shame, has become the place of revelation—the radiant scar through which the glory of the Son forever shines.

## The Word for Our Age

The road from Jerusalem to Jericho has not disappeared. It runs now through every city and neighbourhood, through our screens and schedules, through the quiet distances between people who live side by side yet remain strangers. The man lying wounded by the roadside is not a relic of ancient travel; he is the person right in front of us—overlooked, inconvenient, easily passed by. The question Jesus asked the lawyer, "Which of these proved neighbour?" still confronts us with disarming simplicity. The parable is not meant to be admired. It is meant to be lived.

We live in an age that prizes compassion in theory but resists it in practice. We post sympathy online but seldom stop in our stride. The priest and the Levite live on in every hurried step past another's pain, every scroll past a plea for help, every clever justification for keeping distance. We convince ourselves that mercy belongs to specialists—charities, institutions, professionals. Yet Jesus' story leaves no such loophole. Mercy is not delegated; it is embodied. It is what love looks like when it meets suffering. The Samaritan was not moved because he had a plan; he was moved because he had a heart that could still be moved.

The deeper challenge is not that we fail to see need but that we no longer wish to see it. Compassion costs attention, and attention is what modern life spends most carelessly. Our world forms us to avert our gaze—to protect time, comfort, and reputation. But the parable insists that love begins with sight. "He saw him and was moved with compassion." That single line describes the entire moral revolution of Christianity. To see as Christ sees means allowing ourselves to be interrupted. The Samaritan's schedule was derailed; so was his safety. But grace always travels at the speed of interruption.

What might this look like for us? Sometimes mercy is as small as noticing—the colleague withdrawn at work, the family member quietly carrying burdens, the friend whose silence hides struggle. Sometimes it is as demanding as forgiving the one who has wounded us. In every case, the pattern is the same: seeing, stopping, serving. Each moment of compassion is a return to the road of the Gospel. Holiness is not built on extraordinary deeds but on ordinary love offered consistently. As Mother Teresa said, "Do small things with great love." The Samaritan's greatness lies not in grandeur but in faithfulness—he simply does not look away.

The Church today stands, again, as the inn along this road. Our parishes, our homes, our friendships are meant to be places of restoration where people encounter the healing of God. Yet for that to happen, we must rediscover what it means to be innkeepers of mercy. It begins with presence. We cannot heal what we will not touch, and we cannot touch what we will not approach. The Incarnation teaches us that love is always embodied; it requires time, listening, and the willingness to share another's weakness. The Samaritan's tenderness—binding wounds, lifting, walking alongside—is the model of every Christian vocation, from parenting to priesthood. Wherever someone says, "I will stay with you," the Gospel is happening again.

The parable also speaks powerfully to the divisions that scar our society. We define people by race, ideology, income, and nationality, and we guard those borders fiercely. The Samaritan crossed every one of them. His compassion ignored the categories that divide. In doing so, he revealed the heart of God, who "makes His sun rise on the evil and on the good." Mercy refuses to play by the world's rules of belonging. It looks first not at difference but at dignity. Every human person, no matter how broken, carries the image of the One who became our neighbour. That is why indifference is never neutral—it denies something sacred. To pass by is to forget God's own face reflected in another.

The Church's mission in the twenty-first century must therefore be marked by proximity. Programs and plans matter, but the deepest evangelization happens when mercy becomes personal. The world listens to witnesses more than to teachers. What convinces hearts is not argument but encounter—the moment when someone feels truly seen and loved. This is how the Samaritan preaches without words. His homily is his hands. When believers begin to love like that, the credibility of the Gospel is restored.

We might also notice how the Samaritan's compassion is both immediate and enduring. He doesn't only act in the moment; he ensures the wounded man's recovery continues. "Take care of him," he tells the innkeeper, "and I will repay you." Here we find a model for Christian service that balances spontaneity with commitment. Mercy begins with impulse but matures through perseverance. It means not only helping but staying—walking with those we serve long after the first gesture of aid. True love, as St. John Paul II reminded us, "is never something ready-made; it is something we must build together."

Our culture often prizes efficiency over fidelity. We prefer quick solutions, measurable outcomes, and minimal inconvenience. But mercy refuses those terms. It is inefficient by design because people are not projects. The Samaritan could have satisfied his conscience with a token effort; instead, he gives his time, his possessions, his trust. In doing so, he models the very excess of divine love. God, too, gives not according to our need alone but according to His abundance. Every act of mercy shares in that excess—it hints at heaven's generosity breaking into the world.

There is another dimension to the Samaritan's act that speaks urgently to our own moment. He does not ask who caused the man's suffering. He does not weigh guilt or innocence. He simply responds to what is before him. Our culture, by contrast, often confuses compassion with analysis. We debate who is at fault, who deserves help, who qualifies for sympathy. In doing so, we lose the immediacy of love. Mercy begins not with judgment but with recognition. The wounded man does not need an explanation; he needs a neighbour.

This does not mean indifference to truth. The Samaritan's compassion is not sentimental; it is costly and clear-eyed. He does not ignore the reality of suffering; he engages it. Likewise, Christian mercy holds together truth and tenderness. It seeks to heal without compromising moral clarity. When the Church tends the wounds of our age—the wounds of family breakdown, addiction, despair, and loneliness—she does so by offering both balm and direction. Grace does not merely console; it transforms. To be merciful is to love people enough to lead them toward freedom.

Every disciple must learn that rhythm: receive, then give. Before we can bind another's wounds, we must let Christ bind our own. Before we can carry another, we must first be carried. The Samaritan's mercy is, in this sense, a portrait of grace itself—freely received, freely given. Each of us is both the traveller and the rescuer, the one in need and the one sent to help. Our capacity to show compassion flows directly from how deeply we have allowed ourselves to be healed by God's compassion. The Eucharist, the confessional, the moments of prayer when we meet His gaze—these are where we learn how to love.

If this parable were told today, the priest and the Levite might not walk a physical road. They might scroll past an image, change the channel, or close the tab. The temptation to keep moving has only multiplied. Yet the remedy is the same: to stop, to see, to draw near. The Samaritan's act cuts through every age because it describes the only path that leads to life—self-giving love. Our task is not to invent new moral strategies but to let this ancient simplicity re-enter our modern hearts.

We can begin small. A phone call to someone forgotten. A meal for the isolated. A moment of patient listening where the world has grown loud. The road to Jericho may seem long, but every act of mercy shortens it. The Church will renew the world not through cleverness but through closeness—through millions of small encounters where the love of Christ becomes visible again. Each time we stop for the wounded, we proclaim that God has not passed us by.

The Samaritan's promise to return also anchors hope in the midst of fatigue. It reminds us that we are not alone in carrying the world's pain. Christ has already gone before us and will come again to complete what we begin. Every act of mercy participates in His greater work of restoration. This is what gives courage to persevere when compassion feels costly. The innkeeper's quiet care, unseen by the world, matters infinitely because it shares in God's own patience. One day, the account will be settled—not in payment but in joy.

The parable, then, becomes a kind of moral compass for the Church's mission in an age of indifference. The neighbour is not chosen; he is given. The question is not, "Who deserves my love?" but, "Will I love as I have been loved?" This is the measure of discipleship. Christianity is not first about ideas or even ethics; it is about imitation of a Person whose mercy knew no limits. The Gospel will always scandalize the efficient and inconvenience the comfortable, but it is precisely there—in the costly, unspectacular work of compassion—that holiness takes root.

When Jesus says, "Go and do likewise," He is not offering advice for moral improvement. He is inviting us into participation with His own heart. To "go" means to enter His movement of self-giving love; to "do likewise" means to become transparent to the mercy we have received. The world will change only when Christians take that invitation seriously—when we stop calculating and start caring, when our seeing becomes compassion, and our compassion becomes communion.

The road remains the same, the wounds familiar, the invitation unchanged. Christ still walks ahead of us as the Good Samaritan of every age, asking each heart the same quiet question: Will you cross the road? The answer begins whenever we dare to see.

### Hearing that Becomes Doing

You know the road now. You have walked it in imagination, from Jerusalem's height down through the rock-cut turns toward Jericho. You have seen the dust, the silence, the figure crumpled in the ditch. But the story does not end when the Samaritan rides away; it ends when you realise the road is still beneath your own feet. The parable was never meant to be admired. It was meant to be lived.

Begin here, in stillness. Close your eyes and bring the scene before you. The wounded man lies just beyond reach, the world passing by in its haste. You can feel your own pulse quicken—the instinct to step back, to protect, to move on. The priest and the Levite are not villains; they are the anxious part of you that fears interruption, that clings to order. Notice how familiar they feel. The Lord's first invitation is not to condemn them, but to recognise them within yourself.

Now let the Samaritan draw near. He does not speak first. He looks. Compassion begins with seeing. Let that gaze fall through you. Every act of mercy begins when you allow yourself to be moved. In the Samaritan's eyes you glimpse the eyes of Christ, seeing you where you lie half-dead in your own failures. This is where love starts—not in strength but in recognition.

Take time to feel what mercy costs. The Samaritan risks his safety, his reputation, his coin. He gives without question, without counting. He stops because he cannot pass by. That is the rhythm of Christ's own heart. He stops before every human wound, even when the world looks away. To follow Him is to let your pace be broken, your plans rewritten by compassion.

Ask quietly: who lies on the roadside of your life? Whose suffering have you passed by with polite avoidance? It may not be a stranger at all. It may be someone in your home, a colleague quietly fading under pressure, a friend whose silence hides exhaustion. The wounded are closer than they appear. The parable begins on a road, but it is fulfilled in the ordinary corridors of your day.

Forgiveness was the lesson of the previous chapter; now it becomes movement. To love the neighbour is to forgive before being asked, to act before being thanked. Mercy is not sentiment; it is participation in God's own descent toward the broken. Each time you draw near to another's pain, you re-enact the Incarnation. You carry Christ into flesh once more.

Let prayer be your training ground for this descent. In the quiet of the heart, picture those whose wounds frighten you—the addict, the enemy, the family member whose life feels like chaos. Name them before the Lord, not with analysis but with compassion. Say only, "Jesus, go to them." Prayer is not a way of avoiding action; it is how action begins purified of ego. The Samaritan's journey started in his gut—in the *splagchna*, the deep place of mercy. Prayer cultivates that place in you.

Then look at your own wounds. Every person who loves will eventually discover exhaustion. The road is long, and compassion without rest becomes resentment. The inn in the parable is not only a symbol of the Church; it is the soul's sabbath. Even mercy must be renewed. Let Christ carry you there. When you kneel in confession, when you receive the Eucharist, when you simply rest in prayer, you are the wounded man being tended again. Only the healed can heal.

The Samaritan promised, "When I return, I will repay you." That promise belongs to Christ. He has entrusted to you certain wounded ones—people, situations, the fragile world itself—and He will come back for them. Until then, you are the innkeeper of His mercy. Care for what He has placed in your hands. Love those He has brought to your door. You do not need to fix everything; you need only to remain faithful in tending. The denarii He leaves—grace and sacrament—are enough.

Sometimes the neighbour you must love will not receive your care. Sometimes they will reject it, even wound you in return. Then you will understand more deeply the Samaritan's journey, and Christ's. Do not turn away. Love that costs nothing is not yet divine. To be neighbour in the Gospel sense is to love without return, to remain merciful in the face of indifference. That is how Christ loves you still.

Let mercy shape the small habits of your day. Slow down at the person in need of conversation. Listen without preparing your answer. Give quietly when you could draw attention. Speak blessing instead of complaint. Compassion is not heroic gesture but accumulated gentleness. The kingdom grows through a thousand unnoticed kindnesses that echo the Samaritan's first step toward the wounded man.

In the evening, review your day as one who has walked the Jericho road again. Where did you pass by? Where did you stop? Both moments matter. The first reveals where fear still governs; the second where love has begun to rule. Bring both to the Lord. He will not shame you. He will simply say again, "Go and do likewise." That is not command but invitation—to continue His own mission of mercy.

You might pray with these words:

## THE GOOD SAMARITAN (LK 10:25–37)

Lord Jesus,
You are the Good Samaritan who found me on the road.
You bound my wounds with Your compassion
and carried me when I could not walk.
Teach me to recognise Your face in every traveller I meet.
When I am tempted to pass by, slow my steps.
When I grow weary, bring me to Your inn and restore my heart.
Let my hands become Your hands for the wounded,
and my eyes see as Yours see.
May I never forget that I live because You stopped for me.
Amen.

When the prayer fades and silence returns, stay there a while. Picture again the Samaritan lifting the wounded man onto his beast. Now let the faces merge until you can no longer tell who carries whom. That is the mystery of mercy: the moment you stoop to lift another, you discover Christ has been carrying you all along.

# 7

# The Unforgiving Servant (Mt 18:21–35)

*Then Peter came up and said to him,*
 *"Lord, how often shall my brother sin against me, and I forgive him? As many as seven times?"*
 *Jesus said to him,*
 *"I do not say to you seven times, but seventy times seven.*
 *Therefore the kingdom of heaven may be compared to a king who wished to settle accounts with his servants.*
 *When he began the reckoning, one was brought to him who owed him ten thousand talents;*
 *and as he could not pay, his lord ordered him to be sold, with his wife and children and all that he had, and payment to be made.*
 *So the servant fell on his knees, imploring him,*
 *'Lord, have patience with me, and I will pay you everything.'*
 *And out of pity for him the lord of that servant released him and forgave him the debt.*
 *But that same servant, as he went out, came upon one of his fellow servants who owed him a hundred denarii;*
 *and seizing him by the throat he said,*
 *'Pay what you owe.'*
 *So his fellow servant fell down and besought him,*
 *'Have patience with me, and I will pay you.'*

# THE UNFORGIVING SERVANT (MT 18:21–35)

*He refused and went and put him in prison till he should pay the debt.*

*When his fellow servants saw what had taken place, they were greatly distressed,*

*and they went and reported to their lord all that had taken place.*

*Then his lord summoned him and said to him,*

*'You wicked servant! I forgave you all that debt because you besought me;*

*and should not you have had mercy on your fellow servant, as I had mercy on you?'*

*And in anger his lord delivered him to the jailers, till he should pay all his debt.*

*So also my heavenly Father will do to every one of you,*

*if you do not forgive your brother from your heart."*

## The Word Spoken

The afternoon light in Capernaum was beginning to turn gold when Peter broke the silence. The dust from the morning's crowd still hung in the air, drifting through the open doorway of the house where Jesus had gathered them. They were tired—days of walking, preaching, and the endless press of questions had left their faces drawn. The Teacher had just finished speaking about forgiveness: what to do when a brother sins, how to seek reconciliation, how to treat the unrepentant. His words had carried both comfort and sting.

Peter sat near the front, one hand on his knee, thinking. Forgiveness was fine in theory. He had done it plenty of times. But there had to be limits. Every fisherman on the Sea of Galilee knew that if you let someone cheat you too often, you went hungry. Mercy might keep a soul clean, but it never kept a net full.

He shifted his weight and cleared his throat. The others looked up—Peter's voice always carried authority even when he was uncertain.

"Lord," he asked, "how often shall my brother sin against me, and I forgive him? As many as seven times?"

The number felt generous. Seven was the number of completion, the sacred rhythm of creation itself. Surely, Peter thought, that would impress the Master—large-hearted yet reasonable. Forgive seven times and then you've done your duty.

The house grew quiet. Jesus looked at him for a long moment, not sternly but with something like sadness. The kind of look that saw straight through good intentions to the fear behind them. The disciples waited, half-expecting praise for Peter's balance of mercy and caution.

"Not seven times," Jesus said softly, "but seventy-seven times."

The words hung in the air like a change in the weather. Seventy-seven—so high it ceased to be a number at all. It wasn't a command to keep count but a call to stop counting. The disciples glanced at each other, unsure whether they had heard right. Andrew frowned. Thomas looked down at his hands, calculating. Judas raised an eyebrow. Only John seemed to understand that something far deeper had just been revealed.

Forgiveness without measure. Mercy without ledger. It was beautiful—and impossible.

Peter looked away toward the open window. Outside, a donkey brayed somewhere in the street, and a child laughed. He felt the heat on his neck and the dryness of his throat. He wanted to say something clever, to make sense of the number, but all that came was a nervous chuckle. It was the kind of answer that made you dizzy, as though the solid ground of law had suddenly given way to open water.

The other disciples were restless too. They knew the Scriptures well enough to recall the old story of Lamech, who had vowed vengeance seventy-seven times. Jesus had reversed it. Infinite retaliation had become infinite forgiveness. But who could live that way? Who could forgive endlessly and survive in this world?

The silence lengthened. Jesus let it. He often did. He never rushed to explain Himself; He allowed truth to settle like seed on the ground, trusting it to take root in time. His gaze moved slowly around the room—face to face, heart to heart—until even the most self-assured disciple felt unmasked.

Peter shifted again. He thought of his brother Andrew, of the small arguments that had piled up between them over the years: missed turns at the oars, forgotten repairs, debts of labour repaid with sighs. He thought of the Samaritans who mocked them on the road, the Pharisees who called their Teacher blasphemer, the Romans who taxed their catch until there was little left to bring home. How many times was he supposed to forgive them all? Seventy-seven? Seven hundred? Always?

His stomach tightened. He could almost feel the weight of so much mercy pressing on him like a net too full to lift.

Jesus stood then. The movement was simple, unhurried. He stepped closer to the window where the light fell on the wall in a thin golden band. Dust floated through it like small galaxies. His hands were relaxed at His sides. When He spoke again, His tone was steady, not angry, but heavy with meaning.

"The kingdom of heaven," He began, "may be compared to a king who wished to settle accounts with his servants."

Every man in the room straightened. They knew that tone—the beginning of a story. When Jesus spoke in parables, the ordinary world grew transparent. What was familiar—seed, field, coin, fish—suddenly carried the weight of eternity. But this time the air felt different. There was tension in the stillness, as though mercy itself were about to be put on trial.

Matthew, sitting near the back, felt his stomach twist. He had been a tax collector once. He knew what "settling accounts" meant: names on scrolls, debts shouted aloud, guards dragging men away. The phrase brought the sound of weeping wives and the smell of ink and fear. He lowered his eyes.

Jesus continued, His voice low but clear enough for those outside to fall quiet too. The open door framed faces leaning in—the curious, the sceptical, the poor who had no ledgers but plenty of unpaid debts of their own. A few Pharisees stood at the edge of the crowd, arms folded, watching the Teacher spin another tale.

The disciples drew closer, caught between fascination and unease. Peter, who had asked the question, could already feel it coming back toward him like a wave.

He had wanted a rule—something neat to measure holiness. Instead he was being drawn into a story. That was how Jesus always answered when the question was too small.

He began to describe the king and the servant, the impossible sum, the plea, the release. The words carried a rhythm, calm and terrible. As He spoke, Peter saw the faces: the ruler seated in judgment, the servant trembling before him, the sweat on his neck, the desperate eyes. He could almost hear the gasps of the crowd in the story within the story.

By the time Jesus reached the moment of mercy—the king moved with compassion, cancelling the unimaginable debt—the room itself seemed to exhale. Even the Pharisees at the door looked unsettled. They prided themselves on fairness, on knowing the measure of righteousness. But this king was not fair. He was impossible.

The Teacher paused, letting that impossibility sink in. He glanced toward Peter again, and Peter felt his chest tighten. The look was not rebuke but invitation. As if to say: *This is the world you asked about, Simon. This is how it works in heaven's kingdom.*

Then Jesus went on, His voice quiet, describing how the forgiven man went out and found another servant who owed him little. The story turned darker. The listeners leaned forward, instinctively sensing where it was heading.

When He reached the end—"Should you not have had mercy on your fellow servant, as I had mercy on you?"—the room was completely silent. Outside, a dog barked somewhere in the distance, breaking the tension.

Jesus' eyes moved again across His disciples. None met His gaze. Even Peter, bold and brash, stared at the floor. It was as though each man had been weighed and found owing. The Teacher said nothing more. He simply turned back toward the light, the lines of fatigue at the corners of His face softened by compassion.

For several moments, no one spoke. The story still echoed inside them. *Seventy-seven times.* The words no longer sounded like arithmetic. They had become a measure of heart, an invitation into something far larger than law—a mercy that asked for nothing in return.

Peter opened his mouth, then closed it. What answer could he give? The question he had thought so practical had turned into revelation. The kingdom he sought was not a place of balance but of grace.

Later, when they walked out into the evening air, the sun had dipped low over the lake, staining the water with fire. The men walked quietly, their sandals crunching in the dust. Peter trailed behind, turning the story over in his mind. The rhythm of it stayed with him—the plea, the pardon, the failure, the judgment.

He did not yet know that the story would one day be his own, that he too would stand before the Master with a debt he could never pay, and that forgiveness would come not from a throne but from a cross. For now, he only knew that mercy had no measure, and that the voice which had spoken of kings and servants was already forgiving them all.

## The Surface Story

The question still hung in the air—how many times must I forgive?—when Jesus began His story. The disciples sat close, dust clinging to their feet from the road. They were men who knew debt, not as metaphor but as survival. Galilee lived on borrowed seed and borrowed mercy. Behind every field of barley stood a creditor's account. Harvests could fail, taxes never did. To fall behind was to lose everything. A man could be sold for a sum he once hoped to earn. Every face in the circle had seen that happen.

So when Jesus said, *"The kingdom of heaven may be compared to a king who wished to settle accounts with his servants,"* they understood the tone at once. A reckoning. It was the kind of summons that could end a life. The king in His parable is not an oriental despot but a ruler with the power of Rome itself—one whose word was law, whose ledger was fate. To be called before such a master meant that the time for excuses was over.

The servant in the story owes what no man could possibly owe. *Myriōn talantōn*—ten thousand talents. The number drew laughter, then unease. It was the largest numeral in their tongue joined to the largest measure of money. A single talent equalled fifteen years of labour; ten thousand was a mountain of gold. Jesus' listeners did the math, then stopped—there was no math for this. It was not economics but impossibility. The servant's debt was absurd, cosmic, the weight of human guilt told in silver.

The court grows still. The king commands that the man, his wife, his children, and all he owns be sold. That was justice as they knew it—harsh but expected. Every village had seen a debtor's household divided, their belongings auctioned in the marketplace, their shame displayed for all to witness. The crowd around Jesus nods; this is how the world works.

But the servant collapses. He does not argue the figure or protest unfairness. He falls to the floor, face in the dust, and begs, *"Have patience with me, and I will repay you everything."* It is a promise as ridiculous as the debt itself. He cannot pay in a hundred lifetimes. Yet his desperation is recognisable: every sinner believes that more time will fix what guilt has broken.

Then the impossible happens. The king's face changes. Matthew's word is visceral—*splagchnistheis*—a movement from the gut. The ruler who holds power over life and death feels compassion. He does not renegotiate terms or extend the deadline. He releases the man entirely. *Aphēken*, says the text—"he let it go." The chains fall, the debt vanishes. A silence must have swept the courtyard. No king behaves this way. Justice has not been delayed but overturned.

For the hearers, the shock is physical. Mercy of that magnitude threatened to unravel the order they depended on. If debts could simply be erased, what became of responsibility, honour, law? They could almost feel the ground shift beneath their sandals.

The servant staggers out into the sunlight, free—yet not free. The story moves quickly now. In the narrow street outside the palace, he finds a fellow servant, a man like himself, owing a hundred denarii—three months' wages. It is not nothing, but compared to ten thousand talents it is dust on a scale. The newly released man seizes his neighbour by the throat. The verbs in Greek are sharp and choking: *ekratēsen... epnigen*. He grips and strangles, spitting the same words he had spoken moments earlier: *"Pay me what you owe."*

## THE UNFORGIVING SERVANT (MT 18:21–35)

The scene is brutally familiar. In every Galilean market, debt collection was public theatre. Creditors grabbed their victims by the collar and shouted their claims for all to hear. The smell of sweat and fear filled the air. People turned away, embarrassed, pretending not to see. Jesus' listeners could picture it—the same humiliation they had pitied in the first scene repeated now with roles reversed.

The second servant pleads with identical words: *"Have patience with me, and I will repay you."* The echo must have stung the ears of the disciples. It is as though a mirror were placed in the story itself. The first man's freedom has evaporated in seconds. The mercy that was supposed to remake him has left no trace. He throws his fellow servant into prison until payment can be made—a grim joke, for prisoners earn nothing. The onlookers exchange glances of disbelief.

Those onlookers, the "fellow servants," are the moral conscience of the tale. They are neither heroes nor informers but witnesses to the collapse of grace. Matthew says they are *lypēthēsan sphodra*—"greatly grieved." It is a word for sorrow more than outrage. They cannot bear to see mercy mocked. They go and tell their lord what has happened.

The king summons the man again. The courtroom that had been a place of mercy becomes a place of reckoning once more. The ruler's words cut with grief as much as anger: *"You wicked servant! I forgave you all that debt because you begged me. Should you not have had mercy on your fellow servant, as I had mercy on you?"* The question carries no malice; it is the aching logic of grace betrayed.

The sentence follows: the man is handed over to the *basanistai*, the tormentors—those who extract truth through pain. For Jesus' audience, the image was grimly familiar. Debtors' prisons existed in every province; torture was not cruelty but policy. Yet here it carries deeper weight. The punishment is not simple retribution but exposure. The unmerciful servant must live in the same system he imposed on others: a world without mercy. What he demanded is now demanded of him.

The listeners fall quiet. They had expected a parable of divine justice; they received a revelation of divine character. The king's wrath is not vengeance but reflection—the mirror of the servant's own heart. Mercy rejected becomes judgment. The same grace that could have freed him now burns within as torment.

For a moment, the disciples can almost hear the echoes of their own lives in the story. They know what it is to owe, to plead, to promise the impossible. They also know how quickly gratitude can fade, how easily one forgiven moment turns into the next complaint. The parable's realism is its snare: before condemning the servant, they have already recognised themselves.

Jesus lets the silence work. Then He ends without commentary: *"So also my heavenly Father will do to every one of you, if you do not forgive your brother from your heart."* No parable in Matthew closes more abruptly. There is no soft landing, no moral platitude. The story stops like a door slammed. The hearers are left blinking in the light, uncertain whether they have just witnessed justice or mercy, or something that transcends both.

Every detail of the scene is drawn from their world. Kings and tenants, ledgers and prisons, chains and markets—none of it symbolic yet all of it transparent to the divine. Jesus takes the machinery of empire and turns it into a mirror for the soul. The kingdom of heaven, He implies, is not a distant dream but a reversal of the systems they inhabit daily.

You can imagine Peter still staring at the ground, counting perhaps, as if numbers could make sense of it. Seven times? Seventy-seven? How do you measure mercy when the debts are infinite? Behind him, the others are silent. They have seen what forgiveness looks like when it is wasted.

The story lingers in their imagination long after Jesus stops speaking. In the days ahead, as they argue over greatness and stumble through rivalry, fragments of it will return: a man clutching another by the throat, the echo of words once spoken in desperation, the king's grief at mercy refused. They will not yet realise that the story is about them all—that soon they will watch their own Master pay the debt none could repay.

For now, they only know the realism of the tale. The dust, the ledger, the pleading voice, the gasp of choking, the sound of keys turning in a cell. These are not metaphors; they are the scaffolding of ordinary sin.

The difference between the two servants is only a heartbeat—the space between receiving mercy and remembering it.

When Jesus finishes, the crowd exhales. Some shake their heads, unsettled. Others glance at their neighbours, half-smiling, half-ashamed. Everyone knows someone who owes them something. Everyone knows someone to whom they owe more.

And so the story ends where it began, in the economy of human hearts—accounts open, ledgers waiting, the King's question still unanswered. Beneath the dust of daily fairness, a fire has begun to glow: if the kingdom of heaven runs on mercy, who can afford to keep counting?

### The Hidden Fire

### a) Text, Translation, and Literary Context
#### Greek (Luke 10:25-37)

Διὰ τοῦτο ὡμοιώθη ἡ βασιλεία τῶν οὐρανῶν ἀνθρώπῳ βασιλεῖ ὃς ἠθέλησεν συνᾶραι λόγον μετὰ τῶν δούλων αὐτοῦ.

Ἀρξαμένου δὲ αὐτοῦ συνᾶραι προσηνέχθη αὐτῷ εἷς ὀφειλέτης μυρίων ταλάντων.

μὴ ἔχοντος δὲ αὐτοῦ ἀποδοῦναι ἐκέλευσεν αὐτὸν ὁ κύριος αὐτοῦ πραθῆναι καὶ τὴν γυναῖκα καὶ τὰ τέκνα καὶ πάντα ὅσα ἔχει, καὶ ἀποδοθῆναι.

πεσὼν οὖν ὁ δοῦλος προσεκύνει αὐτῷ λέγων· Μακροθύμησον ἐπ' ἐμοί, καὶ πάντα σοι ἀποδώσω.

σπλαγχνισθεὶς δὲ ὁ κύριος τοῦ δούλου ἐκείνου ἀπέλυσεν αὐτὸν καὶ τὸ δάνειον ἀφῆκεν αὐτῷ.

ἐξελθὼν δὲ ὁ δοῦλος ἐκεῖνος εὗρεν ἕνα τῶν συνδούλων αὐτοῦ ὃς ὤφειλεν αὐτῷ ἑκατὸν δηνάρια, καὶ κρατήσας αὐτὸν ἔπνιγεν λέγων· Ἀπόδος εἴ τι ὀφείλεις.

πεσὼν οὖν ὁ σύνδουλος αὐτοῦ παρεκάλει αὐτὸν λέγων· Μακροθύμησον ἐπ' ἐμοί, καὶ ἀποδώσω σοι.

ὁ δὲ οὐκ ἤθελεν, ἀλλὰ ἀπελθὼν ἔβαλεν αὐτὸν εἰς φυλακὴν ἕως οὗ ἀποδῷ τὸ ὀφειλόμενον.

ἰδόντες οὖν οἱ σύνδουλοι αὐτοῦ τὰ γενόμενα ἐλυπήθησαν σφόδρα, καὶ ἐλθόντες διεσάφησαν τῷ κυρίῳ ἑαυτῶν πάντα τὰ γενόμενα.

τότε προσκαλεσάμενος αὐτὸν ὁ κύριος αὐτοῦ λέγει αὐτῷ· Δοῦλε πονηρέ, πᾶσαν τὴν ὀφειλὴν ἐκείνην ἀφῆκά σοι ἐπεὶ παρεκάλεσάς με·

οὐκ ἔδει καὶ σὲ ἐλεῆσαι τὸν σύνδουλόν σου ὡς κἀγὼ σὲ ἠλέησα;

καὶ ὀργισθεὶς ὁ κύριος αὐτοῦ παρέδωκεν αὐτὸν τοῖς βασανισταῖς ἕως οὗ ἀποδῷ πᾶν τὸ ὀφειλόμενον.

Οὕτως καὶ ὁ Πατήρ μου ὁ οὐράνιος ποιήσει ὑμῖν, ἐὰν μὴ ἀφῆτε ἕκαστος τῷ ἀδελφῷ αὐτοῦ ἀπὸ τῶν καρδιῶν ὑμῶν.

Matthew's Greek tells the story like a heartbeat—steady, deliberate, then suddenly racing. It begins in the language of ledgers and ends in the language of love. The opening phrase, ἠθέλησεν συνᾶραι λόγον—"he wished to settle accounts"—sets the tone of judgment. This was the phrase used for royal audits or official reckonings, when a king called his stewards to give an account of their management. In Matthew's hands, it becomes a parable of divine justice: God calling humanity to face the truth of its life. Yet before long, the tone softens. When the servant falls to his knees, the king is described as σπλαγχνισθείς—"moved with compassion." That word, drawn from σπλάγχνα, literally means the inward parts, the gut. In the Old Testament Greek translation, it's the same word used for God's mercy toward His people. So the story moves from the head to the heart, from calculation to compassion. The shift is not sentimental; it's theological. Matthew shows that the kingdom of heaven begins with justice but is fulfilled in mercy.

The verbs themselves trace that journey. The king "willed" (ἠθέλησεν), the servant "was brought" (προσηνέχθη), "was unable to pay" (οὐκ εἶχεν ἀποδοῦναι), "fell down" (πεσών), "begged" (προσεκύνει), the king "was moved with compassion" (σπλαγχνισθείς), "released him" (ἀπέλυσεν), and "forgave" (ἀφῆκεν). Each action opens the story wider until grace flows freely. But then, as the forgiven man refuses mercy to another, the verbs twist back: "he seized" (κρατήσας), "choked" (ἔπνιγεν), "threw into prison" (ἔβαλεν εἰς φυλακήν). What began with release ends with restraint. The pattern itself is the parable's argument: grace that is not passed on collapses into violence.

The sums of money add another layer of meaning. The servant's debt—

μυρίων ταλάντων, "ten thousand talents"—is beyond reason. A single talent equalled about fifteen years of wages; ten thousand meant more than the empire's yearly income. Jesus isn't describing a careless borrower but an impossible debtor. The number points to the nature of sin. It isn't a list of misdeeds that could be balanced with good deeds; it's a rupture so vast that only divine mercy can bridge it. When the king forgives that debt, he doesn't cancel a bill—he restores a relationship. The scale is absurd because mercy is absurd by human standards.

Then comes the smaller debt: ἑκατὸν δηνάρια, "a hundred denarii." It's about three months' wages—tiny beside the other. Yet the first servant cannot forgive even that. He grabs his fellow by the throat, echoing the violence that sin always breeds when grace is refused. The contrast is deliberate. Jesus wants the hearer to feel the obscenity of proportion. How could someone forgiven of everything imprison another over a fraction? The exaggeration is the moral microscope through which the story burns its truth: if we withhold mercy, it proves we have not understood mercy.

The verbs Matthew chooses for forgiveness carry deep theological weight. The king ἀφῆκεν αὐτῷ τὸ δάνειον—"forgave him the loan." The root verb ἀφίημι means "to release, to let go." It's the same word Jesus uses in the Lord's Prayer: ἄφες ἡμῖν τὰ ὀφειλήματα ἡμῶν—"forgive us our debts." The connection is intentional. What God does for us, we must mirror toward others. The parable, then, is not only about the danger of an unforgiving heart but about the shape of divine forgiveness itself: complete release. In this way, Matthew ties the story to Israel's *Jubilee* tradition, when debts were cancelled and slaves set free every fifty years (Leviticus 25). The king's act is a personal Jubilee—an image of God's eternal rhythm of mercy.

Yet the story darkens again with παρέδωκεν αὐτὸν τοῖς βασανισταῖς—"he handed him over to the torturers." The Greek βασανισταί originally meant examiners or testers of metal, those who tested purity by fire. Matthew's use suggests not demonic tormentors but the torment of a conscience that has failed mercy's test. The prison becomes a symbol of self-enslavement. The man is bound by the very thing he refused to release. What he did to another becomes the law that now governs him. Forgiveness withheld becomes its own punishment.

Matthew's sentence rhythm mirrors this moral rhythm. The early lines move with long, steady phrases: the king deliberates, the servant pleads, the lord relents. Then the pace shortens. The verbs come hard and fast—seized, choked, cast. Grammar turns violent. Even the sound of the Greek tightens: κρατήσας... ἔπνιγεν... ἔβαλεν. The very cadence of the language feels suffocating. Matthew's syntax makes the sin audible.

Placed within Matthew chapter 18, the parable crowns the discourse on community and forgiveness. Peter has just asked, "How often must I forgive my brother? Up to seven times?" Jesus replies, "Not seven, but seventy times seven"—a deliberate echo of Genesis 4:24, where Lamech boasts that vengeance will be repaid seventy-sevenfold. Jesus turns the arithmetic of revenge into the arithmetic of mercy. The old human instinct—escalating violence—is replaced by a divine instinct—escalating forgiveness. Within that frame, the parable becomes the living proof of the saying.

Every image fits the logic of the kingdom. The βασιλεύς (king) represents God, whose justice expresses itself not by erasing debt but by transforming it through compassion. The δοῦλος (servant) is humanity, standing bankrupt before the divine Judge yet embraced instead of condemned. The ὀφείλημα (debt) is sin itself—unpayable, not because God is cruel, but because only love can repair what sin has broken. The ἄφεσις (release, forgiveness) is grace—the free act that remakes the bond. The σύνδουλος (fellow servant) is every other human being, the mirror in which the truth of our forgiveness is tested. And the φυλακή (prison) is the soul that clings to resentment, a cell built from its own bitterness.

Matthew ends with words that cut to the core: Οὕτως καὶ ὁ Πατήρ μου ὁ οὐράνιος ποιήσει ὑμῖν, ἐὰν μὴ ἀφῆτε ἕκαστος τῷ ἀδελφῷ αὐτοῦ ἀπὸ τῶν καρδιῶν ὑμῶν. "So will my heavenly Father do to you, unless each of you forgives your brother from your hearts." The warning is not a threat of divine cruelty but a statement of spiritual physics. The heart that shuts out mercy shuts itself off from God, because God is mercy. The verbs that began with reckoning and release end here with revelation: the kingdom operates by the rhythm of the heart, not the ledger.

In this compressed story, Matthew captures the whole movement of salvation. Justice calls the account. Compassion interrupts it. Mercy is offered. Refusal turns mercy into judgment. The grammar itself mirrors the Gospel: calculation gives way to compassion; compassion rejected returns as consequence. Every verb, every image, every number carries the same truth—mercy received must become mercy given, or it ceases to be mercy at all.

**b) Theological Interpretation**

The parable of the Unforgiving Servant opens a doorway into the inner architecture of the Gospel itself. Beneath its surface drama of kings, debts, and anger lies a theology as vast as the kingdom it reveals. Matthew places the story directly after Peter's question about forgiveness because what Jesus addresses is not manners or community etiquette but the metaphysics of divine government. Peter asks how far mercy must go; Christ answers by showing what kind of world comes into being when God reigns.

"The kingdom of heaven," Jesus begins, "may be compared to a king who wished to settle accounts with his servants." The phrase "settle accounts"—ἠθέλησεν συνᾶραι λόγον—is drawn from the world of imperial administration, the language of taxation and tribute. Yet on Jesus' lips it becomes an image of revelation. When God "settles accounts," He is not behaving like a bureaucrat tallying errors; He is unveiling truth. In Scripture, divine judgment (*krisis*) means that the hidden order of things comes into view. To judge, in the biblical sense, is not merely to punish but to set right, to restore harmony. That is why the word for justice, *dikaiosynē*, does not describe retaliation but righteousness—the state in which all things stand in their proper relation to God and one another.

The king's reckoning, then, is not the cold balance of legalism but the moment creation is brought back into tune with its Maker. To call God just is to say He repairs reality. Mercy is not a deviation from that justice; it is its perfection. The Fathers called it *iustitia misericordiae*—the justice of mercy—because in God, truth and love are not opposites but two movements of the same will: truth naming what is broken, love healing what it names. In plain terms, divine justice does not mean giving us what we deserve; it means making us whole again. Mercy is the means by which God repairs what fairness alone could never heal. Law reveals the fracture; grace resets the bone.

The servant's debt—μυρίων ταλάντων, ten thousand talents—is the first shock of the story. A single talent equaled roughly fifteen years of wages for a labourer; ten thousand was beyond imagination, more than the annual revenue of several provinces combined. Jesus' exaggeration is deliberate. He wants His listeners to experience the futility of calculation. Sin is not a bookkeeping error; it is an abyss. Every attempt to measure its weight only proves the absurdity of repayment. The servant's plea, "Have patience with me, and I will pay you everything," (μακροθύμησον ἐπ᾽ ἐμοὶ καὶ πάντα σοι ἀποδώσω) captures the perennial illusion of fallen humanity—that time, effort, or willpower could ever close the gap between creature and Creator. This is the polite heresy of moralism: the fantasy that salvation can be earned in instalments.

The king's answer destroys that illusion. Matthew writes, σπλαγχνισθεὶς ὁ κύριος—"moved with compassion, the lord..." The verb *splagchnizomai* comes from *splagchna*, the inward organs, the seat of visceral emotion. In biblical language, it describes the movement from interior to exterior, from divine feeling to divine action. Mercy, therefore, is not a mood in God; it is motion. The Creator's inner life spills outward into history, seeking its lost children. The king's compassion issues in two decisive verbs: ἀπέλυσεν ("he released him") and ἀφῆκεν ("he forgave"). Both belong to the vocabulary of Exodus. To forgive is literally "to let go," the same word Jesus will teach in the Lord's Prayer—ἄφες ἡμῖν τὰ ὀφειλήματα ("forgive us our debts"). The echo is no accident. What the king does in miniature anticipates what the Father will do on Calvary. Forgiveness is not leniency but liberation; it is the unbinding of what sin has chained.

At the centre of the Gospel stands this pattern—justice fulfilled in compassion. The Cross is the king's gesture writ large: God assumes the debt He does not owe to restore debtors who cannot pay. In forgiving, God does not suspend justice; He enters it. He becomes the place where justice and mercy coincide. Saint Paul names this mystery when he says God is "just and the justifier" (Rom 3:26). Truth is not annulled but transfigured. The scales of the world are not tipped but remade; balance gives way to communion. The parable thus becomes a small version of the Incarnation's logic: divinity descending into human reckoning to change the meaning of justice itself.

To grasp that transformation is to understand the difference between moralism and grace. Moralism ends where fairness is achieved; grace begins where fairness fails. In the logic of the Kingdom, mercy is not the loosening of standards but the revelation of divine abundance. The law can expose sin but cannot erase it. Only love that enters the wound can heal it. This is why the king does not defer payment, renegotiate terms, or lower expectations—he cancels the debt entirely. Nothing partial would suffice. God's forgiveness does not calculate; it creates.

The servant, released into this new economy, steps out carrying the imprint of grace yet still thinking in the arithmetic of fear. His mind has been freed no more than his hands. He meets a fellow servant who owes him *hekaton dēnaria*—a hundred denarii, roughly three months' wages. The debt is not trivial. The Gospel's realism matters here: Jesus never mocks the weight of genuine injury. Some wrongs do wound deeply; some reparations cannot be quick. Yet the contrast is crushing. What is finite cannot be measured against what is infinite. The tragedy of the unforgiving servant is not that he remembers his pain but that he forgets his pardon.

Matthew's verbs reverse the king's: ἐκράτησεν—he seized him; ἔπνιγεν—he choked him. Where the king released, the servant restrains; where God let go, man grips tighter. Grace has escaped the courtroom but has not yet entered the heart. The man who was forgiven refuses to forgive, proving that the deepest captivity is not external but interior. The drama of redemption turns back on itself, revealing that salvation unaccepted becomes judgment.

The king's question on the man's return is the theological axis of the entire parable: Οὐκ ἔδει καὶ σὲ ἐλεῆσαι ὡς κἀγὼ σὲ ἠλέησα;—"Should you not have had mercy on your fellow servant as I had mercy on you?" The little word *hōs*—"as"—runs like a thread through the New Testament: *Be merciful as your Father is merciful; love one another as I have loved you.* The comparison is not rhetorical but creative. To be forgiven is to be drawn into the very rhythm of divine life. Grace reproduces its own likeness. The Fathers saw in this word the seed of *theosis*—participation in the nature of God. Forgiveness is not merely moral imitation; it is ontological transformation. The one who forgives as God forgives begins to live in God's own mode of being.

Saint Thomas Aquinas gave this paradox its classical form: "Mercy is the fullness of justice." Justice restores right order; mercy accomplishes that restoration by entering the disorder and transforming it from within. The king's act is therefore not a suspension of the law but its fulfilment in love. Every debt is acknowledged, every truth named, every relationship reopened. In that movement we glimpse the economy of salvation itself: truth embraced, cost absorbed, communion renewed. To withhold mercy, by contrast, is to deny reality. The human person is made in the *eikōn*—the image—of a God who gives; when we refuse to give, we deform that image and take on the likeness of the Accuser.

The parable thus becomes anthropology as well as theology. It shows what humanity is and what it becomes apart from grace. Forgiveness is not an optional virtue but the form of divine life shared with us. The servant's violence, therefore, is not simply cruelty; it is self-destruction—the refusal to be what he already is. Hell begins there, not as fire but as the collapse of the self into its own measure.

When the king hears of what has happened, his response is swift but not irrational. Matthew writes, παρέδωκεν αὐτὸν τοῖς βασανισταῖς—"he handed him over to the tormentors." The word *basanistēs* first meant one who tests metal on a touchstone. What follows, then, is not arbitrary cruelty but exposure. The servant is given over to the measure he has chosen, tested against the standard he himself applied. Jesus has already declared the principle: *"With the measure you use, it will be measured back to you"* (Matt 7:2). The unforgiving man has demanded a world of repayment and has received it. His punishment is to inhabit the economy he created.

In Catholic theology this image touches both mystery and warning. The same divine fire that purifies also reveals. For the soul open to grace, that fire is purgation; for the heart closed to mercy, it becomes torment. Heaven, purgatory, and hell are not three kinds of God but three responses to the same love. What melts wax hardens clay. The judgment of the king, then, is not vengeance but veracity: the revelation of what the man has become. He has chosen isolation over communion, control over compassion, arithmetic over gift. The tormentors are not new executioners sent by an angry monarch; they are the servant's own desires turned inward. Hell is simply the mathematics of unforgiveness carried to its conclusion.

This same principle animates every sacrament and moral act in the Church. The Eucharist, the reconciliation of penitent and priest, even the quiet act of asking pardon—all are designed to retrain the human heart in divine proportion. Each time a believer forgives, the balance of the world shifts slightly back toward Eden. Each time we refuse, the old captivity tightens. Mercy is not sentiment but structure; it is how reality works when governed by God. That is why Matthew situates this parable in the very heart of Jesus' community discourse. The Sermon on the Mount revealed the inner logic of the Kingdom; this discourse reveals the architecture of the Church. The Church lives not by efficiency but by mercy. Her governance, her discipline, her very survival depend upon it.

Read in that light, the parable's closing exchange—*"Should you not have had mercy as I had mercy on you?"*—is not merely personal; it is ecclesial. It defines the DNA of discipleship. Every ministry, every community, every family that calls itself Christian stands or falls by that comparison. The king's "as" becomes the charter of the baptized. To live in Christ is to forgive in His measure. Anything less is to step back into slavery.

Saint Augustine heard in that "as" the echo of the Lord's Prayer. "When we say, 'Forgive us our debts as we forgive our debtors,'" he writes, "we bind ourselves before God with our own words." The petition becomes a self-imposed prophecy. Either we forgive and are forgiven, or we refuse and are bound by the logic of our refusal. Augustine calls this not threat but mercy—a divine pedagogy that trains the heart for heaven. God desires to make His children merciful, because only the merciful can enjoy eternity. In that sense, forgiveness is not a moral duty but the skill of eternity itself. The saints will not need to forgive in heaven, but they will carry its habit as the muscle memory of love.

Thomas Aquinas follows this logic to its metaphysical depth. In him, mercy is not weakness but the perfection of justice. Justice, he says, "renders to each his due"; mercy, by going beyond the due, completes the act. To forgive is to act more justly than justice alone would allow. That is why the king's mercy is not lawless—it is super-legal, operating from a plane higher than law. The Incarnation itself follows this pattern: God does not abolish justice but assumes it, satisfying its truth from within by love. The Cross is justice in act, mercy in form.

In the parable, this truth appears as a pattern of exchange: debt, release, refusal, judgment. The Gospel reveals that these are not four stages of a story but the continual rhythm of spiritual life. Every soul oscillates between them. We are always somewhere between being forgiven and forgiving. The health of the Church depends upon that movement not stopping. Grace is like breath—once held, it suffocates. The unforgiving servant dies of spiritual asphyxiation.

Matthew's placement of this teaching within the community discourse reinforces the point. The chapter begins with a child—symbol of humility—then moves through the warning against scandal, the shepherd seeking the lost, and the procedure for reconciliation among believers. The parable of the Unforgiving Servant crowns these instructions. It shows in story form what each of the earlier teachings implies: that divine life is a circulation of mercy. Stop the flow and death enters.

This rhythm is also the pattern of the sacraments. Baptism initiates mercy by cleansing debt; the Eucharist sustains mercy by feeding communion; confession restores mercy when it falters. The Church is, in essence, a society of forgiven debtors learning to imitate their King. Her discipline, therefore, is not contrary to grace but in service of it. Excommunication, penance, reconciliation—all are forms of the king's question: "Will you share the mercy you have received?"

When viewed in the wider frame of salvation history, the parable becomes a rehearsal for the Passion. The king who cancels the debt prefigures the Son who will absorb it into Himself. The servant's choking grasp foreshadows every human refusal of grace—the hands that will seize, strike, and crucify. The king's grief anticipates the sorrow of the Father watching His mercy rejected. Even the final handing-over to the tormentors mirrors the mystery of divine permission: God allowing human freedom to run its course. The Cross is the parable enacted—the King paying the debt His servants cannot, even as they choke Him for payment.

And yet, the story does not end in despair. Behind its severity stands a radiant hope. The king's justice, though fierce, aims at restoration. The debt may be infinite, but so is the mercy that cancels it. In Christ, the reckoning of accounts becomes the reconciliation of hearts. The books are not burned but rewritten in the blood of the Lamb. What was once owed is now offered; what was once demanded is now given. The economy of heaven begins where the economy of earth collapses.

To hear the parable in that light is to recognize oneself within it. Every Christian stands as that first servant—forever indebted yet infinitely loved. Each time we recite the Lord's Prayer, we speak our own story again: forgiven and asked to forgive, freed and called to free. The measure we extend is the measure we inhabit. The kingdom's currency is compassion; its mathematics are mercy squared.

Matthew ends the passage abruptly: *"So will my heavenly Father do to every one of you, if you do not forgive your brother from your heart."* The line sounds harsh until one hears the tenderness beneath it. It is not a threat but a description of reality. To live without mercy is to live without God. The heart that refuses forgiveness closes itself to the air it needs to breathe. The Gospel's warning is therefore an invitation: open the window, let mercy flow, and live.

The justice of God is terrifying only from outside. Step into it, and it becomes the atmosphere of love. The King who settles accounts does so not to condemn but to create communion. His kingdom is not a court but a household where every debtor, once released, becomes a child. The parable ends where it began—in the motion of mercy. The books are balanced only when every page reads the same word: *forgiven*.

### c) Typological and Intertextual Parallels

Every parable Jesus tells is a thread drawn through centuries of revelation. The Unforgiving Servant is no exception. Beneath its Roman imagery of debts and prisons runs the older music of Israel—the law of release, the rhythm of mercy that pulsed through the Torah. To hear it rightly, one must stand not in a palace court but on Sinai.

When the king begins to "settle accounts," the echo is unmistakable. The Hebrew Scriptures had already spoken of a divine reckoning that is not destruction but restoration. In Leviticus 25 the Lord commands a *Jubilee* year, every fiftieth year when debts are cancelled, slaves freed, and ancestral land returned. "You shall proclaim liberty throughout the land to all its inhabitants," He says, "for it is a jubilee" (Lev 25:10). The Jubilee was not economic policy; it was theology enacted. It declared that Israel's true King owns everything and that mercy, not accumulation, sustains creation. By shaping His parable around debt and release, Jesus places Himself within that jubilee tradition—and then surpasses it. His king does not wait fifty years; He acts immediately. The perpetual Jubilee arrives in the person of the Son.

Deuteronomy 15 deepens the resonance. There Moses commands the *šĕmittāh*, the remission of debts every seventh year: "Every creditor shall release what he has lent to his neighbour; he shall not exact it of his brother, because the Lord's release has been proclaimed." The same Hebrew root—*šāmaṭ*, to let drop—is the conceptual ancestor of Matthew's *aphienai*, to forgive. When Jesus tells of a ruler who "lets go" of what is owed, He is reenacting the divine *šĕmittāh* on an infinite scale. The kingdom is a land

## THE UNFORGIVING SERVANT (MT 18:21–35)

where release is the permanent state of affairs.

Even the number "seventy-seven" from Peter's question draws its genealogy from Genesis. Lamech, descendant of Cain, once boasted, "If Cain is avenged sevenfold, then Lamech seventy-sevenfold" (Gen 4:24). Humanity's history began with vengeance multiplied; Jesus reverses it with mercy multiplied. The arithmetic of sin becomes the arithmetic of grace. Where the first murderer's lineage escalated violence, the Son's lineage—His Church—will escalate forgiveness. The parable, following directly on that saying, becomes the narrative embodiment of this reversal.

Another ancient pattern underlies the king's compassion. When Moses intercedes after the golden-calf rebellion, he appeals to God's own nature: "The Lord, the Lord, a God merciful and gracious, slow to anger and abounding in steadfast love" (Exod 34:6). The Greek translation renders "merciful" as *oiktirmōn*—from the same root that will later form *splagchnizomai*. The divine bowels of mercy that spare Israel on Sinai are the same depths that stir the king in Jesus' story. The parable thus re-enacts Exodus 32–34 in miniature: idolatry answered by intercession, guilt eclipsed by compassion, covenant renewed through mercy. Every audience steeped in Torah would have heard the allusion.

The Psalms turn this theology into song. "If you, O Lord, should mark iniquities, Lord, who could stand? But with you there is forgiveness" (Ps 130:3–4). The line could serve as the forgiven servant's own confession—had he remembered it. Psalm 32 likewise celebrates the blessedness of remission: "Blessed is he whose transgression is forgiven, whose sin is covered." The psalmist's joy stands in tragic contrast to the servant's hardness. Where David rejoices that his debt is erased, the parable's man forgets his ledger has even been burned.

Prophecy continues the melody. Isaiah 55:7 announces the same divine logic that governs the king's courtroom: "Let the wicked forsake his way... and let him return to the Lord, that he may have mercy on him; for he will abundantly pardon." The Hebrew verb *rabbāh*—to multiply—is paired with *sĕlīḥāh*, pardon. God's forgiveness is exponential. That arithmetic again meets the parable's "ten thousand talents." The magnitude of guilt is answered by a magnitude of grace. Isaiah 1 adds another layer: "Though your sins are like scarlet, they shall be white as snow." The cleansing of debt becomes the cleansing of stain. Both are metaphors of unpayable imbalance rectified only by divine generosity.

By the time Jesus speaks, these images had accumulated into a theology of release awaiting fulfilment. The Jubilee had lapsed into memory; debtors' prisons were back. The Roman system of tribute weighed heavier than Pharaoh's bricks. Israel longed for the divine audit that would wipe the slate clean. Into that weariness Jesus tells His story of a king who does precisely that. The hearers would not have missed the implication: the messianic age of release had begun.

Between the Testaments, this hope continued to ferment. The wisdom book of *Sirach* almost preaches the parable in advance: "Forgive your neighbour the wrong he has done, and then your sins will be pardoned when you pray. Does a man harbour anger against another, and yet seek healing from the Lord?" (Sir 28:2–3). The Greek text even repeats Matthew's logic of measure: "If he, being flesh, keeps wrath forever, who will make atonement for his sins?" In Tobit 4:15 we hear the positive formulation of the same principle: "Do to no one what you yourself hate." These intertestamental voices set the stage for Jesus' teaching. They articulate mercy as covenant duty but stop short of showing how such mercy becomes possible. Grace is preached, not yet embodied.

When Jesus, therefore, turns that moral exhortation into a parable of divine initiative, He completes the trajectory. What Sirach commands— "Forgive your neighbour"—the king performs. What the pious Israelite could only imitate, God Himself now enacts. The Old Covenant's mirror becomes the New Covenant's window: through it the face of the merciful King looks out.

The scene of the fellow servant's violence also echoes Scripture's darker moments. It recalls Exodus 2, where Moses, having been spared, strikes down an Egyptian; the man who has known deliverance repeats oppression. Human history, the Bible insists, tends to replay its chains. The forgiven servant is Israel forgetting Egypt, the Church forgetting Calvary, the individual forgetting baptism. The story exposes the perennial amnesia of grace.

The prophetic writings return again in the king's question: "Should you not have had mercy as I had mercy on you?" The phrase *as I had mercy* re-sounds Hosea 6:6: "I desire mercy and not sacrifice." Jesus had already quoted that verse earlier in Matthew to defend His table-fellowship with sinners. Here He enacts it in narrative form. The servant performs the sacrifice of strictness; the king embodies the mercy God desires. The parable thus becomes Hosea rewritten for the heart's interior altar.

The structure of this parable also reverberates through Israel's Wisdom tradition. Proverbs 11:4 warns, "Riches do not profit in the day of wrath, but righteousness delivers from death." The saying captures the parable's underlying paradox: wealth cannot purchase security, yet mercy—righteousness in action—saves. In Proverbs 19:17, mercy even becomes investment: "He who is kind to the poor lends to the Lord, and He will repay him." Jesus inverts that line with divine irony: the king forgives debt not because repayment will come, but because God Himself becomes the repayment. The lender becomes Redeemer.

The same reversal appears in Psalm 49, the meditation on mortality that haunts so many of Jesus' teachings: "Truly no man can ransom another, or give to God the price of his life, for the ransom of his soul is costly and can never suffice." The psalm's hopeless tone—no man can pay—forms the backdrop against which the parable's good news erupts: what no man can pay, the King remits. Grace answers what gold cannot. The psalmist's despair finds its reply in the Lord who forgives.

Within the New Testament itself the network of allusion tightens. The Lord's Prayer, taught only a few chapters earlier in Matthew, becomes the interpretive key. *"Forgive us our debts, as we also have forgiven our debtors."* The prayer is not commentary but seed; the parable is that seed in bloom. Every clause of the prayer echoes here—debts owed, forgiveness extended, measure mirrored. The difference is that in the parable the debtor's refusal exposes the logic implicit in the prayer: if forgiveness halts, so does life. Mercy must circulate or die.

The Beatitudes amplify the same truth. "Blessed are the merciful, for they shall obtain mercy." The saying is not transactional; it describes the circular movement of divine love. The merciful receive mercy because they live in its stream; the unmerciful are dry because they have dammed it. Jesus' story of the servant who blocks the flow is thus a narrative gloss on the Beatitude. His inner drought becomes outer judgment.

Other evangelists join the chorus. Luke's version of the Lord's Prayer substitutes "sins" for "debts," making explicit what Matthew implies. James restates the parable's moral in a single aphorism: "Judgment will be without mercy to anyone who has shown no mercy; mercy triumphs over judgment" (Jas 2:13). The final clause, *katakauchatai*, "boasts over," evokes triumphal imagery. Mercy is the victor standing over judgment's corpse. Paul likewise renders the same theology cosmic: "Where sin increased, grace abounded all the more" (Rom 5:20). The ten-thousand-talent debt meets its counterweight in the infinite treasury of the Cross.

John's Gospel, though never recounting this parable, assumes its substance. The foot-washing in John 13—one forgiven cleansing another—enacts the same logic of participatory mercy. "As I have done, so you also must do." That "as" again; the king's question becomes Christ's command. The typological web is complete: Torah's Jubilee, Wisdom's mercy, Prophets' call, Jesus' parable, the Church's sacrament—all variations of a single theme, the divine economy of gift.

Beneath the ethical instruction, a deeper typology stirs. The king in the story is not merely a metaphor for God but a figure of the Father seen through the Son's eyes. The servant's unpayable debt mirrors humanity's collective estrangement, the weight of sin from Adam onward. The fellow servant's smaller debt represents the injuries we inflict on each other inside that fallen world. The king's cancellation therefore prefigures not only divine pardon but the entire economy of redemption. When the Son of God enters history, He does what the king does—He assumes the loss. "He cancelled the bond which stood against us with its legal demands; this He set aside, nailing it to the cross" (Col 2:14). Paul's language almost paraphrases the parable's climax. The royal ledger becomes the wooden tablet of Calvary.

Even the violent imagery of "handing over" (*paredōken*) recurs in the Passion narratives. Judas hands over Jesus; the chief priests hand Him over to Pilate; Pilate to the crowd. In each case, divine mercy subjects itself to human calculation. The King becomes the servant; the debt-payer becomes the debtor. The irony is devastating: the one Person who owes nothing is treated as though He owed all. On the Cross the motion of the parable reverses—man strangles God for payment, yet God responds with forgiveness. The story's moral failure becomes history's salvation.

The figure of Joseph in Genesis offers the clearest Old Testament foreshadowing. Sold by his brothers, he later rises to power in Egypt and holds their lives in his hands. When they come pleading for grain, he forgives them with the same words the king might have spoken: "Do not be afraid… you meant evil against me, but God meant it for good." Joseph's mercy transforms betrayal into providence. His forgiveness is the seed of Israel's survival. Jesus, descended from that lineage, becomes the greater Joseph—the one who feeds a starving world by giving Himself. The grain of Egypt becomes the Eucharistic wheat of the Kingdom.

Another figure, Jonah, offers a foil. Jonah flees because he knows God is merciful and cannot bear to see Nineveh forgiven. The prophet's resentment of grace mirrors the servant's. Both sulk outside the circle of mercy, preferring justice on their own terms to joy in God's. Their isolation anticipates the outer darkness of the parable's end. Each becomes an image of the sinner who cannot rejoice in another's pardon.

By weaving these strands together, Matthew presents Jesus not as an isolated moralist but as the fulfilment of Israel's entire narrative. The Torah's Jubilee, the Prophets' mercy, Wisdom's counsel, and the Writings' songs all converge on Him. He is the living Jubilee, the embodied *aphesis*, the forgiveness that once came by proclamation now walking in flesh. His blood is the new currency of atonement, the payment that cancels all ledgers.

In that light, the parable's ending is not despair but prelude. The king's wrath reveals the stakes of freedom. The measure of mercy refused becomes the measure of mercy received at the Cross. Humanity's failure inside the story prepares the stage for God's victory beyond it. The unforgiving servant is Adam replayed; the merciful king is Christ prefigured. The first Adam grips, the second releases; the first demands, the second gives. The history of salvation is the conversion of possession into gift.

The typological current finally carries us to Revelation, where John sees "books opened" before the throne. There, every account is settled—not by calculation but by the Lamb who was slain. The "tormentors" of the parable reappear as the self-exclusion of the damned; the "release" reappears as the eternal Sabbath of the redeemed. The Bible ends where the parable began: with a King and His servants, with accounts and release, with justice transfigured by love.

And so the Scripture circle closes. From Leviticus to the Apocalypse, the same heartbeat sounds: debt forgiven, mercy multiplied, creation restored. The parable of the Unforgiving Servant is not a footnote in that story—it is its summary. What the law prefigured and the prophets foresaw, Jesus narrates and then enacts. The king's voice, still echoing through every age, asks each generation the same quiet question: *Should you not have had mercy, as I have had mercy on you?*

## d) Patristic and Theological Synthesis

From the earliest centuries, the Fathers of the Church read the Parable of the Unforgiving Servant not as a moral anecdote but as a miniature of the Gospel itself—its anthropology, its soteriology, and its eschatology compressed into a single scene. They saw in the king's mercy the movement of the Incarnation; in the servant's refusal, the tragedy of a heart untouched by grace. For them, the story's power lay not in its warning alone but in its revelation of what divine life looks like when translated into human action.

Origen was among the first to treat the parable as a mirror of salvation history. The king's reckoning of accounts signified, for him, the divine judgment by which every soul must come to truth. Yet judgment, Origen insisted, is mercy's instrument. "The Lord settles accounts," he wrote, "not to condemn but to heal." The unpayable debt represents not a numeric excess but the boundless distance between creature and Creator, which only the Word made flesh can cross. For Origen, the servant's failure to forgive reveals the failure to participate in the divine nature offered through the Logos. Grace had entered him externally but not yet taken root within—the difference between being absolved and being transformed.

John Chrysostom, preaching to his congregation in Antioch, brought the parable down to the level of everyday discipleship. "You have been forgiven ten thousand talents," he thundered, "will you not forgive a hundred denarii?" For him, the parable was an antidote to the illusion of self-righteousness. The servant's cruelty was not ignorance but pride—the refusal to see oneself as debtor first. Chrysostom's reading retains the realism of Matthew's story: mercy is not sentimental leniency but the soul's likeness to God. "Nothing makes us so like God," he said, "as to be always ready to forgive." That likeness, once refused, becomes deformity; the unmerciful servant is not punished so much as unmade.

Augustine read the same story through the lens of interior grace. He saw in the servant a man who had indeed received forgiveness, but only juridically, not ontologically. "He was forgiven," Augustine writes, "but he was not healed." The king's act removes the guilt of sin; the transformation of the heart requires consent to love. For Augustine, every Christian lives between those two moments—the absolution already granted and the healing still being wrought. The servant's fate warns that justification cannot remain external. Grace, to be saving, must penetrate the will.

Gregory the Great and later Bede saw the parable as an image of the Church's sacramental life. The king's forgiveness prefigures baptismal grace; his renewed reckoning after the servant's refusal mirrors the ongoing call to repentance within the baptized. Gregory noted that the servant is not cast out immediately after receiving mercy but only when he refuses to extend it. The delay signifies divine patience: God waits for the forgiven to become forgiving. Only when that patience is despised does judgment reveal itself as self-chosen isolation.

Aquinas, inheriting the patristic tradition, drew the theology into its metaphysical clarity. Mercy, he argued, is "the fullness of justice," because justice aims at right order and mercy restores it. In the parable, the king's act of remission is therefore not the suspension of law but its perfection. The servant's violence, conversely, represents the perversion of justice into cruelty. The *Summa's* famous line—*"It belongs to God to have mercy, and whoever exercises mercy acts in likeness to God"*—finds its narrative proof in this story. The servant's refusal to forgive is, in Thomistic terms, a refusal of *theosis*: the invitation to share in the divine manner of being.

Eastern theologians, reading through the lens of deification, pressed this point further. The forgiveness granted by the king is not only juridical pardon but participation in divine life. To forgive as God forgives is to enter into His energy of love. The servant's tragedy is that he remains an outsider within grace—redeemed in name but unchanged in nature. In the words of Maximus the Confessor, "He who receives love and does not become love has received it in vain." The parable thus discloses the dynamic of theosis in negative relief: what happens when the gift is received without transformation.

Across all these readings, a single pattern emerges. The Fathers agree that the parable is not about arithmetic mercy but ontological participation. The king's act reveals what God does; the servant's response reveals whether the divine image has become likeness. The entire Christian life is suspended between those two motions—being forgiven and becoming forgiving.

Within that synthesis, the moral becomes mystical. Forgiveness is not an optional virtue or a therapeutic strategy but the visible sign that one has entered the divine economy. To forgive "from the heart" is to allow grace to become nature, mercy to become the rhythm of one's being. Refusal, by contrast, is not mere disobedience; it is the soul's withdrawal from the life of God.

Thus the parable stands as both catechism and icon. It teaches that the justice of the kingdom is mercy fulfilled, that salvation is transformation, and that judgment is the unveiling of what we have chosen to resemble.

# THE UNFORGIVING SERVANT (MT 18:21–35)

The king who releases his servant is Christ Himself; the debt forgiven is the cross; the call to "have mercy as I had mercy" is the invitation to share His life. In the end, the story's warning and its promise are the same: to forgive is to live in God.

## The Shock and the Turn

When Jesus began this parable, His listeners thought they recognised the pattern. A king settling accounts was a familiar image—a trope of judgment in Jewish imagination. The Day of the Lord would be like that: the divine Judge calling Israel to render an account, the guilty condemned, the righteous vindicated. Even Peter's question that introduced the story belonged to that same logic: "How often must I forgive my brother?" He was not being cynical; he was being faithful. The rabbis taught that forgiving three times fulfilled the law's generosity. Peter, doubling it and adding one for good measure, thought himself merciful. Mercy, in Israel's moral grammar, was real but finite. Justice built the world; mercy decorated it.

So when Jesus began, "The kingdom of heaven may be compared to a king who wished to settle accounts with his servants," everyone expected a sober moral tale about accountability. But almost immediately, the world they knew began to slip.

The servant's debt—ten thousand talents—was impossible. One talent equalled nearly twenty years' wages. Ten thousand was the largest numeral in common Greek, *myrioi*, a word that meant not precision but absurdity. The crowd would have laughed. No such debt existed. Jesus was teasing them past mathematics into theology. The point was not bookkeeping but the chasm between humanity and God: an unpayable obligation of love, a fracture no labour could mend. The hearers could predict the next move. The debtor would be sold; justice would be done.

But instead, the king forgives. Without negotiation, collateral, or probation—he releases the man entirely. Matthew's verb *aphēken* means to let go, to send away, to release a bond. It is the same word Jesus uses for the forgiveness of sins: "Forgive us our debts." To those schooled in covenant law, the gesture was reckless. The Torah required restitution: life for life, measure for measure. Mercy could cover sin but never cancel it outright. To erase such a sum was to act as though law itself no longer ruled the kingdom. That was the first shock.

Yet in this scandal lies revelation. The king's mercy does not violate justice; it fulfils it. Forgiveness, in Jesus' vision, is not amnesia but assumption. The loss is not ignored but absorbed. The cost falls back upon the giver. The crowd could not know it yet, but this image pointed toward Golgotha, where the divine King would pay His servants' debt in His own blood. The moral story was becoming a prophecy.

The reversal deepens when the servant, freshly released, meets a fellow servant who owes him a hundred denarii—three months' wages. A real debt, but hardly ruinous. The smaller debtor falls to his knees and pleads with the same words the first man had just uttered: "Have patience with me, and I will repay you." The echo is deliberate, the symmetry perfect. The audience braces for gratitude made visible. Surely a man forgiven the impossible will forgive the manageable.

Instead, he seizes the debtor by the throat. The verbs harden: *ekratēsen*—he gripped; *epnigen*—he choked. Mercy stops at the lips. Grace has not entered the bloodstream. The one who was released now imprisons another.

At that moment, the parable turns from amusing to accusing. The villain is not a pagan tyrant or a corrupt tax collector but a servant of the king—a man inside the covenant, someone who has tasted mercy and withheld it. The story's mirror tilts toward the listener. This is Israel in miniature: the nation forgiven at Sinai, sustained in the wilderness, restored from exile, yet still measuring others by law. But the portrait is larger still. The unmerciful servant is humanity in every age—the sinner who loves the idea of divine patience but refuses to extend it. The parable's indictment reaches far beyond its first audience. It names the quiet hypocrisy of the religious heart: wanting grace for oneself and justice for others.

Here lies the second shock. In Israel's imagination, holiness meant separation—drawing clear lines between clean and unclean, faithful and unfaithful. Forgiveness could be granted, but only once repentance proved genuine. Jesus inverts that logic. In His kingdom, holiness is not distance preserved but mercy shared. The king's perfection lies not in the precision of his accounts but in the abundance of his compassion. Divine justice, Jesus implies, is not balance restored but communion renewed.

This is no sentimental mercy. It has edges. When the king hears of the servant's cruelty, he recalls him, not to renegotiate but to reveal. The man's heart has remained a courtroom while the king's has become a home. Matthew writes that the servant is handed over to the *basanistai*—the tormentors. The word originally described the "touchstone" used to test the purity of metal. The punishment, then, is not caprice but exposure. The servant is tested by the standard he demanded. What he inflicted on others becomes his own condition.

The torment is not external. It is the suffocation of a heart that will not breathe mercy. In refusing to forgive, he has chosen to live by exact repayment; the king merely lets him inhabit that choice. Justice without mercy becomes its own prison. The fire that purifies gold burns up straw. The same light that softens wax hardens clay.

The parable's sting is quiet but devastating. The hearers expected a story in which sinners are punished; they receive one in which the unforgiving are condemned. God's wrath turns out to be mercy refused. Judgment is simply the reflection of the heart's measure. Divine anger, in this parable, is not an emotion but a mirror.

The scandal is therefore twofold. First, that divine forgiveness is total, preceding repayment, erasing every calculus of worth. Second, that such forgiveness demands imitation. To receive mercy without passing it on is to cancel its meaning. The servant's failure is not misbehaviour but metaphysical contradiction: he denies in action what he has received in being. Mercy unshared ceases to be mercy at all.

The parable's terror lies here. It forces every listener into the story. One cannot admire it from a distance. To remain within the safe world of desert and reward is to remain outside the kingdom altogether. The economy of grace is not a moral upgrade to justice; it is an entirely new world where debts no longer define reality.

For those who longed for the coming Messiah, this reversal would have felt intolerable. They expected a king who would settle accounts by punishing the wicked and vindicating the faithful. Jesus presents a king who settles accounts by erasing them. He does not vindicate Israel's superiority; He exposes her shared need for mercy. The chosen people are summoned into an economy where chosenness is measured not by obedience but by forgiveness. The law remains, but it is transfigured. What the commandments outlined in stone, the king now writes into the flesh of the heart.

When Jesus ends, His words fall with the weight of finality: "So will my heavenly Father do to every one of you, if you do not forgive your brother from your heart." The phrase *from your heart* is crucial. Jesus is not demanding sentiment but surrender. Forgiveness in Scripture is an act of will grounded in truth—it names the offence and releases the claim to vengeance. The heart that refuses such release is not punished from outside; it collapses from within. The parable is not warning of arbitrary damnation but describing a spiritual law as inevitable as gravity: what you measure, you live by.

For the first listeners, the ground would have shifted beneath them. The God they had imagined as a cosmic accountant had revealed Himself as a Father whose authority flows from compassion. The world they knew, built on honour and restitution, had been replaced by one built on grace. Justice remained, but it was now radiant with mercy.

The story ends not with moral tidiness but with revelation. The king's justice merges into compassion; human righteousness dissolves before divine generosity. The hearers are left standing in that exposed silence between judgment and mercy, where all pretence dies.

In that silence, the meaning of the kingdom becomes clear. The God who forgives all demands that His forgiveness take form in His children. The atmosphere of heaven must become the air they breathe. The kingdom of heaven is not a distant realm reached after death; it is the present climate of mercy in which the forgiven learn to live.

This is the scandal of grace: that God cancels the unpayable and commands us to do the same. The cross will make visible what the parable made imaginable—the King paying His servant's debt, not by decree but by self-offering. The justice of God will be revealed as love crucified, and the measure of mercy will be nothing less than His own heart.

For those who heard Jesus that day, the story must have lingered long after the crowd dispersed. A God who erases ledgers is harder to serve than one who keeps them. Yet this is the kingdom's unrelenting demand: that those who have been set free learn to set others free. The divine economy is gift upon gift, and its only currency is mercy.

### The Revelation in the Son

Every parable conceals a face. Beneath the characters and metaphors, the Word made flesh is speaking about Himself. In the story of the Unforgiving Servant, that hidden face is Christ—the King who settles accounts not by condemnation, but by substitution. What is revealed here is not only how God forgives, but who God is: a Father whose justice is mercy embodied in His Son.

From the opening line, "The kingdom of heaven may be compared to a king who wished to settle accounts," Jesus is speaking of His own mission. He is that King come into His world. He does not send auditors or prophets to collect debts; He comes personally to reconcile His servants. The Incarnation is the great accounting—the divine initiative to make visible the invisible balance between love owed and love given. Humanity's moral debt, symbolised by the ten thousand talents, is not numerical but ontological: a rift between creature and Creator that cannot be closed from below. The King's entrance into His kingdom is thus the first act of mercy, the divine descent into the economy of sin.

In Christ, the storyteller and the story become one. The parable's drama of debt and release is transposed into history: God Himself becomes the servant who assumes what cannot be repaid. On Calvary, the King kneels before His own justice and takes the place of His debtor. The Cross is the ledger where divine mathematics is rewritten—the place where mercy and justice cease to be opposites and become two movements of the same love. Justice demands restoration; mercy provides it through self-giving. The Crucified does not abolish the law of repayment; He fulfils it by paying the debt Himself.

Theologians have long called this the *mirabile commercium*, the wondrous exchange: the rich becoming poor, the blameless taking the blame, the sovereign kneeling as servant. Saint Paul describes it with stunning simplicity: "For your sake He became poor, that by His poverty you might become rich" (2 Cor 8:9). What in the parable seemed unthinkable—a King absorbing His servant's loss—becomes, in the Gospel, the central mystery of redemption. The ruler's pity becomes Passion. His compassion becomes crucifixion.

At the Cross, the verb *aphienai*—"to release"—is fulfilled not in speech but in blood. The King does not merely declare amnesty; He accomplishes it. He releases creation by allowing Himself to be bound. He cancels the note of debt by nailing it to the wood, as Saint Paul writes: "He cancelled the bond which stood against us with its legal demands; this He set aside, nailing it to the cross" (Col 2:14). Forgiveness is thus not an abstraction but a transaction of divine life. The treasury of heaven is emptied; the price is Himself.

This is why the Church calls the Cross the throne of Christ. It is there that the parable's paradox—the King who pays—becomes revelation. The justice of God, long feared as a scale of exact retribution, is unveiled as the radiant symmetry of self-giving love. Mercy is not weakness; it is the highest form of power. In human kingdoms, the monarch demands satisfaction from subjects; in God's kingdom, the Monarch provides it. The authority of heaven is exercised not through coercion but through kenosis—through the self-emptying of the Son.

In that light, the figure of the unmerciful servant becomes the negative icon of fallen humanity. He represents what creation becomes when it receives grace but refuses to transmit it—when it breaks the current of divine generosity. The Son, by contrast, is the perfect Servant who receives everything from the Father and returns everything to Him. He is mercy without obstruction, love in uninterrupted motion. Where the first servant hoards what he was given, Christ pours out what He receives. His very being is the eternal circulation of gift—the Son eternally receiving from the Father and eternally returning that gift in love. This is what makes the Cross not a tragedy but a revelation of the inner life of God.

For in the Passion, the eternal relation between Father and Son is displayed within history. The Father gives; the Son receives and returns; the Spirit is the breath of that exchange. The economy of salvation reveals the theology of the Trinity. The Father is not an impersonal judge but the source of mercy; the Son is not an appeaser but the embodiment of the Father's compassion; the Spirit is not sentiment but power—the living current by which divine forgiveness reaches creation. When the Son says from the Cross, "Father, forgive them," He is not begging for a reluctant pardon; He is articulating the eternal will of the Father in human words.

Seen in this light, the parable's closing warning—"So will my heavenly Father do to every one of you, if you do not forgive your brother from your hearts"—is not a threat but an invitation. It is the voice of the Son calling humanity into His own pattern of life. To forgive is not merely to obey; it is to participate in the divine circulation of love. Grace received must become grace given, or it dies. The Cross is both the source and the standard of that flow. As Saint John writes, "By this we know love, that He laid down His life for us; and we ought to lay down our lives for one another" (1 Jn 3:16).

The parable's imagery of debt and release finds its sacramental fulfilment in the Eucharist. Every Mass is the King's act repeated: His Body given, His Blood poured out "for the forgiveness of sins." The Church stands as the household of the forgiven, gathered around the table of mercy. In that liturgical exchange, the economy of grace continues: we offer bread and wine—the tokens of human work—and receive in return the infinite gift of divine life. The Eucharist is the ongoing settlement of accounts where every loss is turned to gain, every debt into communion.

The forgiveness enacted in the parable also becomes tangible in the Sacrament of Reconciliation. There the King's mercy descends again, not metaphorically but personally. The confessor speaks the same Greek verb: *Ego te absolvo*—"I release you." Each absolution is the king's gesture renewed, the letting-go that creates life. The Church's power to forgive is not an administrative privilege; it is participation in the life of the Forgiver. She binds and looses not as judge but as midwife of new creation.

Yet Christ's revelation does not stop at the altar or the confessional. The divine logic of mercy must extend into the world through His mystical Body. The Church herself is meant to be the visible sign of that King who forgives. She is not the fortress of the perfect but the inn of the healed—the place where those once bound by debt learn to bind up others' wounds. The parable's inn from the Good Samaritan finds its complement here: the community of believers entrusted with the oil and wine of mercy. The Church's credibility lies not in her perfection but in her proximity to human pain. She is to be, in every generation, the field hospital of grace where the unpayable is cancelled again and again.

This participation extends to every believer. In baptism, each Christian is drawn into the King's own compassion. The Spirit imprints the pattern of divine mercy into the soul, making it capable of what nature alone cannot do. To forgive the unforgivable is not weakness but the sign that the divine life is truly operative within. Grace is not a moral bonus; it is the transfiguration of the heart into likeness with Christ.

The parable, then, is not simply a warning against resentment. It is a revelation of divine ontology: to exist in Christ is to live as forgiven and forgiving. The refusal of mercy is not merely sin; it is a rejection of participation in being itself. The servant who strangles his brother lives as though the Incarnation never happened. He clings to the old world of equivalence, while the King has already inaugurated the new world of gift.

At the deepest level, the story unveils the mystery of divine substitution. The King bears the servant's debt, and in doing so, invites the servant to become like Him. The economy of redemption is mimetic: we are transformed by the mercy we imitate. The more one forgives, the more one becomes capable of divine love. The imitation of Christ is not external effort but internal participation; it is the Spirit drawing the human will into the rhythm of Trinitarian exchange.

The end of the parable, where the unmerciful servant is handed over to the tormentors, should be read in the light of this mystery. Hell is not imposed by God; it is the final refusal of the Son's pattern. The tormentors represent the soul's own resistance to the divine flow. The saved are those who allow themselves to be carried by mercy; the damned are those who resist its current. The same river of love runs through both; it is welcomed by some, rejected by others.

In Christ, the King's reckoning becomes revelation. The Cross shows that divine justice is not the destruction of the sinner but the destruction of sin through love. The resurrection, in turn, is the proof that this justice is victorious. When the risen Christ breathes peace upon His disciples and says, "Whose sins you forgive, they are forgiven," He extends the parable's logic to the whole Church. The economy of mercy now moves through human hands. The same breath that raised Him from the tomb becomes the air the Church breathes.

In this way, the Unforgiving Servant is not merely a moral tale; it is a portrait of the Paschal mystery. The King who forgives at His own expense is none other than the Son who dies to make that forgiveness real. The servant who refuses mercy is Adam's race trapped in self-justification. And the new humanity born from Christ's side is the kingdom where debts are no longer counted, because love itself has become the law.

The final revelation of the Son, therefore, is not that God occasionally forgives but that He *is* forgiveness. His being is the eternal act of giving and releasing. To know Him is to be drawn into that act. When the Gospel says, "Be merciful as your Father is merciful," it is not prescribing imitation from afar but describing participation from within. The believer's life becomes an extension of the Son's own compassion—a human continuation of divine logic.

In Christ, the story of the King and His servant reaches its fulfilment. The accounts are settled not by destruction but by self-offering. The books are closed, not because justice has been ignored, but because justice has been transfigured into love. The King has become the Servant, the Servant a son, and the world—once defined by debt—is now defined by grace.

One line gathers it all: The Judge has become the debtor, so that debt might die forever.

### The Word for Our Age

Every generation finds itself somewhere in this parable. The details of economy and empire may have changed, but the inner logic of debt and demand still governs modern life. We live surrounded by ledgers—digital ones, emotional ones, moral ones. We count followers, hours, calories, mistakes. We speak of "owing" apologies and "deserving" love. Our culture's imagination, like the servant's, is formed by accounting. Nothing is free; everything must be earned or cancelled. In such a world, forgiveness feels almost unnatural, even naïve.

The spirit of the age trains us to measure everything. Success is quantified, failure documented, offense archived forever. The smartphone in our hands is a portable ledger: every post recorded, every word judged. Public life has become a courtroom where the sentence is perpetual outrage. In that environment, mercy looks like weakness, and forgetting an offense seems immoral. The world insists that justice means exposure, that healing comes through revenge, that forgiveness betrays the victim. The parable of the Unforgiving Servant speaks directly into this climate. It warns that a society which refuses mercy ends up strangling itself.

Our modern tormentors are not ancient jailers but inner ones: anxiety, resentment, and fear of being forgotten. They keep us awake in the night rehearsing wrongs, counting what others owe us. They feed the illusion of control. Yet beneath them lies exhaustion. The servant's hands around his fellow's throat are our clenched hearts—tight, guarded, unable to let go. We are not cruel so much as terrified: afraid that if we release the debt, we will lose the last proof of our worth.

The Gospel proposes a different economy. It tells us that life is gift from start to finish. What we possess—time, talent, even breath—is borrowed. Nothing we have is earned; everything is entrusted. To live in grace is to stop calculating. Forgiveness becomes possible when we remember that we ourselves live by it. The one who forgives does not condone evil but imitates God's way of overcoming it. Mercy does not erase justice; it perfects it by restoring communion where division once reigned.

If the parable exposes the disease of modern life, Christ offers the cure. His Cross reveals that the deepest freedom is not the power to control but the power to release. The world worships autonomy; the Gospel calls us to communion. The modern self says, "I am my own." The Christian says, "I am His, and therefore yours." True freedom is not the ability to stand apart but the grace to love without measure.

We can see this contrast everywhere. Our economy prizes competition; the kingdom prizes generosity. Social media rewards outrage; Christ blesses peacemakers. Politics runs on grievance; the Gospel runs on gratitude. The old servant still lives in every system that counts worth by output and status. We live surrounded by small prisons of merit. Yet the king's gesture remains—an open hand inviting us to step into a new arithmetic where everything is gift.

The Church's task in such an age is to make that arithmetic visible. She must not merely preach mercy but model it. When the world weaponizes failure, the Church must be the place where sinners are restored. When society divides into tribes of resentment, the Church must be the space where enemies meet as brothers. The credibility of the Gospel today will not rest on argument but on presence—on communities that practise forgiveness as a way of life. A parish that reconciles divided families, a monastery that prays for its persecutors, a household that refuses to pass down bitterness—these are the living commentaries on the parable.

Yet mercy cannot remain institutional. It begins at the smallest scale: the home, the marriage, the workplace. Forgiveness is not an event but a discipline, a daily choice to let go of the claim we hold against another. It may start with silence rather than speech, with restraint rather than reconciliation. Sometimes the most merciful act is to stop rehearsing the story of the wound. The servant's tragedy was that he kept his hands on another's throat; ours is that we keep wrongs alive in memory and conversation. To forgive is to allow God to edit the narrative—to let His version of the story replace ours.

This interior freedom does not ignore justice; it trusts God to accomplish it. Forgiveness is not denial of pain but the refusal to become its prisoner. It says, "This hurt belongs to God now; He will do what is right." Such surrender is not passive. It is active participation in Christ's own work of redemption. Every time we release another, we open a channel for grace to flow through the world again. The kingdom advances one forgiven debt at a time.

In the public square, this witness matters urgently. The modern mind confuses forgiveness with compromise and tolerance with indifference. But Christian mercy is neither. It is truth in love—naming the wound yet refusing to weaponize it. A society that has forgotten how to forgive cannot hold together. Its only tools are law and punishment. The Gospel alone teaches the power of restoration. The Church's task is to remind the world that justice without mercy is not justice but vengeance delayed.

The same principle applies within our digital lives. Online culture is built on the thrill of judgment. We scroll through headlines and scandals, absolving ourselves by condemning others. Yet behind that cycle lies a deep hunger for grace. People long for a word that says, "You are forgiven." The Christian in the digital world must become that word. To speak kindly when others mock, to resist gossip disguised as concern, to assume the best when the crowd assumes the worst—these small acts of restraint become modern works of mercy. They reintroduce oxygen into a suffocating environment.

In relationships, the parable invites examination. Where do we still hold accounts? What names come to mind when we pray, "Forgive us our debts"? The Gospel does not require that we forget harm or forego boundaries, but it insists that bitterness has no home in a redeemed heart. Every grudge is a small exile from God's kingdom. The measure we use becomes the measure we live in. The only safe measure is mercy.

Practically, the path of forgiveness begins with memory transformed by prayer. To bring the wound before God is to place it in the furnace of His love, where pain can become intercession. The saints often prayed most earnestly for those who wronged them, not because they enjoyed suffering but because they understood its redemptive power. In doing so, they entered the logic of the Cross: evil answered with blessing, hatred converted into offering. The Christian life is impossible without that pattern; it is the bloodstream of grace.

Modern discipleship, then, is not about maintaining moral superiority but about staying in the flow of divine mercy. The Christian who forgives becomes a living sign that God has entered history. Nothing preaches Christ more convincingly than a heart that refuses to retaliate. When a mother forgives an absent father, when a friend refuses to return gossip for gossip, when a parish welcomes back someone who once left in anger—heaven touches earth again. These are not small gestures; they are sacraments of a healed humanity.

This spirit must also shape how the Church addresses conflict and scandal within her own body. A community that talks of grace must live it. Accountability is essential, but its goal must always be restoration. The Church's strength will not lie in spotless reputation but in transparent repentance. Her saints are not those who never failed, but those who never stopped forgiving. Only a Church that forgives from the heart can speak credibly of the God who does the same.

For the world beyond her walls, this witness is desperately needed. Ours is an age both saturated with guilt and starved of absolution. People confess online to strangers but rarely hear the words, "You are forgiven." They seek therapy for wounds that only grace can heal. The Church must stand again as the voice of that grace, not merely pronouncing pardon but embodying it. Her mission is not to win arguments but to build reconciled lives—to make visible a love stronger than resentment.

The parable's relevance could not be clearer. The unforgiving servant lives wherever people define themselves by comparison and control. The King lives wherever people entrust their wounds to God and let mercy have the last word. The world's future depends on which story we inhabit.

Forgiveness will never trend. It has no audience, no algorithm. Yet it remains the quiet revolution by which God renews the earth. To forgive is to proclaim, in miniature, the Resurrection: that evil does not have the final word. Every act of mercy is a small Easter morning, a victory of light over calculation.

The call is personal and immediate. Somewhere today, a conversation can be healed, a silence broken, a heart released. The King who settled accounts long ago still walks among His servants, looking for those willing to live in His generosity. The choice lies before every disciple: to keep the ledger open or to let it burn in the fire of grace.

When we forgive, we allow the world to glimpse the nature of God Himself. The ledger closes, not because we are indifferent to truth, but because truth has already been fulfilled in love. That is the word for our age: that mercy is not weakness, but the new order of creation. Every time a believer forgives, the kingdom of heaven draws near again, and the King's heart beats once more in human flesh.

## Hearing that Becomes Doing

You have heard the story many times. A king, a servant, a debt, a mercy refused. But now the voices fade, the crowd disperses, and the parable remains like an echo inside you. The question is no longer what it meant then, but what it asks of you now. The Gospel does not end at the page; it waits in the heart for response.

Let the scene return in silence. Imagine yourself before the King. There are no witnesses, no excuses, no hiding of the record. You stand with the weight of unpayable things—words spoken in haste, love withheld, wounds you caused and would rather forget. Yet the King's eyes are not calculating. They are steady and kind. You expect a demand; He offers release. The ledger between you is closed by His own hand. The mercy that once seemed distant now looks at you and calls you by name.

Stay there a moment. The temptation is to hurry on, to fill the quiet with thanksgiving or guilt. But mercy must first be received before it can be shared. The servant's tragedy was not that he failed to act, but that he never let forgiveness sink beneath his skin. He left the throne room unchanged, still thinking in the language of debt. Let the King's gesture reach deeper in you than that. Let it unmake your inner accountant.

If you listen closely, forgiveness has a sound: the faint tearing of old pages. It is the noise of ledgers being burned, of weights lifting, of chains dropping quietly onto stone floors. That sound belongs not only to heaven but to the human heart. When you forgive, that same sound is heard again. The parable is not finished until it echoes there.

Begin, then, with the small debts. They are everywhere—those who forgot you, misunderstood you, disappointed you. Forgive them in detail. Name them before God and release them. You do not need to feel affection; you need only to will their good. Forgiveness is not an emotion; it is a decision to hand the matter over to the King. Whisper it if you must: "I release this debt into Your mercy." In that moment, you step back into the story and allow it to live through you.

Some debts are heavier. There are wounds that do not close easily—betrayal, injustice, cruelty. These are the debts that feel too costly to forgive. Yet remember the scale of your own pardon. The ten thousand talents are not there to shame you, but to remind you of abundance. You are not being asked to give what you lack, but to share what you have received. When forgiveness seems impossible, bring the person into prayer and place them beside you before the King. Let His gaze fall on both of you. It is impossible to hate long in that light.

The practice of mercy begins in this interior dialogue. Each time resentment rises, bring it into the presence of the One who cancelled your debt. The old habit will resist. The heart prefers its grudges; they feel like protection. But protection built on bitterness becomes a prison. The tormentors of the parable still exist—resentment, shame, pride—and they wait at the door of every unhealed memory. Only mercy opens the cell.

There will be days when forgiveness must be renewed hour by hour. That constancy is not failure; it is participation in the Cross. The King forgives once for all, yet we learn to live that forgiveness slowly, like a seed breaking open under the soil. Each act of release is a small resurrection, proof that the old world of measure is dying and the new world of grace is being born.

If you wish to know whether mercy has taken root, listen to how you speak about those who hurt you. When stories of injury no longer need retelling, when you can bless the one who wronged you, when gratitude begins to replace grievance, then forgiveness has become flesh in you. You have entered the kingdom's air.

The world will not understand this logic. It will tell you to protect your dignity, to remember the offense, to claim your justice. There is wisdom in that, but not life. The King you serve measures greatness not by control but by compassion. Each time you forgive, you stand beside Him at His throne, continuing His work of restoration. You become the place where the divine economy touches earth.

Forgiveness also transforms how you receive others' mercy. Some people long to forgive you, but you keep them away, certain you must repay before you deserve it. Let them forgive. Let their mercy teach you something of God's. The pride that refuses to receive grace is the first debt that must be cancelled. The humility that allows itself to be loved is the beginning of heaven.

Bring all of this to prayer in the quiet moments of the day. Sit in stillness and recall someone who owes you nothing yet gives you kindness. Let gratitude rise. Then recall someone who owes you something—a word, an apology, a debt of affection—and imagine handing their name to Christ. Watch Him take it, as He once took your own name, and see His hands close around it with the gentleness that once closed the wound in His side. This is how forgiveness moves from hearing to doing: not by grand gestures but by small surrenders.

At night, before sleep, examine your heart. Ask where resentment still lodges. Offer it as the last prayer of the day. The Lord who watches will recognise the pattern; it is the same movement that brought Him from heaven to the Cross. Your forgiveness joins His. That is the secret rhythm of the kingdom.

And when you fail—when anger returns, when the ledger reopens—do not despair. Go back to the throne room. Begin again. The King does not grow weary of releasing debts. His mercy is the atmosphere you breathe; even your failures are carried in it. The only defeat is to stop returning.

Let this prayer rise quietly from that awareness:

Lord Jesus Christ,
You who carried the weight of every unpayable debt,
teach me to live as one forgiven.
When I am wronged, remind me of Your patience.
When I am hardened, soften me with Your tears.
When I cannot release, let Your hands open mine.
Breathe into me the freedom You won for all.
May those I forgive glimpse in me Your face,
and may I never forget that I live only by Your mercy.
Amen.

Now let the story end as it began—in silence before the King. No words, no calculations, only presence. The debt is gone. The air is clear. You are free to love again. That freedom is the true conclusion of the parable, and it is written not in books but in hearts that have learned to forgive.

# 8

# The Rich Fool (Lk 12:13–21)

*One of the multitude said to him, "Teacher, bid my brother divide the inheritance with me."*

*But he said to him, "Man, who made me a judge or divider over you?"*

*And he said to them, "Take heed, and beware of all covetousness; for a man's life does not consist in the abundance of his possessions."*

*And he told them a parable, saying,*

*"The land of a rich man brought forth plentifully;*

*and he thought to himself, 'What shall I do, for I have nowhere to store my crops?'*

*And he said, 'I will do this: I will pull down my barns, and build larger ones; and there I will store all my grain and my goods.*

*And I will say to my soul, Soul, you have ample goods laid up for many years; take your ease, eat, drink, be merry.'*

*But God said to him, 'Fool! This night your soul is required of you; and the things you have prepared, whose will they be?'*

*So is he who lays up treasure for himself, and is not rich toward God."*

**The Word Spoken**

The crowd had followed Him since dawn. Dust hung in the heat like smoke. Along the road from the villages of the Decapolis to Jerusalem,

## THE RICH FOOL (LK 12:13-21)

thousands pressed together—farmers, merchants, mothers with children on their hips—each trying to catch a glimpse of the man who spoke with authority yet carried no weapon, wore no insignia, and took nothing for Himself. They called Him *rabbi*, though He had never studied under the famous teachers. He spoke of the Kingdom of God as if He had seen it with His own eyes.

He had been teaching for hours. His voice, steady but unhurried, drifted over the multitude. "Do not fear those who kill the body," He said, "but fear Him who, after He has killed, has power to cast into Gehenna." The words fell heavy in the air, and yet the tone was not threat but pity. He warned of hypocrisy, of hearts hidden behind pious faces, of treasure stored in heaven. The crowd listened with mixed minds—some stirred, others uneasy. Every phrase seemed to pierce.

Near the front stood a man in his thirties, his tunic well woven, his sandals clean. His eyes flicked between Jesus and another man farther back—his brother. They had come not together but out of the same family quarrel. Their father had died months ago, leaving land and olive groves. The inheritance had been divided, but not fairly, or so each thought. The argument had dragged through neighbours, then elders, now here—perhaps the new teacher could resolve what the rabbis had not.

The man waited for a pause, then shouted above the murmuring:

"Teacher! Tell my brother to divide the inheritance with me!"

The sound broke across the assembly like a stone through still water. Conversations stopped. Heads turned. Some frowned at the intrusion; others leaned forward, curious. Disputes over property were common. Many expected Jesus to quote Torah, to arbitrate as a respected *rabbi* might. It was the kind of question that gave teachers a chance to display wisdom. But Jesus did not answer immediately. He looked at the man for a long moment, His face unreadable.

Behind the question lay an entire world—the weight of family, the ache of fairness, the endless struggle for more. The man's voice had carried not hatred but desperation, the tone of one who believes he has been wronged. His brother lowered his gaze, embarrassed. The crowd began to whisper again: "What will He say? The Law of Moses divides the estate; surely He knows that."

But Jesus' eyes moved slowly across the faces before Him. The sun caught the edge of His hair, turning it bronze. "Man," He said, His voice clear but without anger, "who made Me a judge or divider over you?"

The sentence struck oddly—neither approval nor refusal, but something deeper, unsettling. Those closest to Him felt the shift in the air. He was not dismissing the man; He was addressing the sickness behind the question. The man blinked, confused. He had expected arbitration, not inquiry.

Jesus turned from him and raised His voice so that all could hear. "Take care," He said, "and be on your guard against all covetousness, for a person's life does not consist in the abundance of possessions."

The warning rippled outward. Farmers glanced at one another. A woman clutched the purse at her belt. The word He used—*pleonexia*, the hunger for more—touched everyone. In a land where most survived on little, the desire for plenty was not vice but survival. Yet Jesus spoke as if it were poison. His tone was sorrowful, not severe, as though He pitied those enslaved by their own need.

A silence followed. Even the children stopped fidgeting. Jesus stepped toward a patch of shade cast by a sycamore tree. He looked beyond the crowd toward the hills, where terraces of barley shimmered in the light. The land itself seemed to answer His gaze—a vast field of gold ready for harvest.

"The land of a rich man," He began slowly, "brought forth plentifully…"

People leaned forward. It was the familiar opening of a story, the rhythm they had come to love. He would speak now in images they could understand. His parables were mirrors; in them, each person saw themselves. A murmur ran through the crowd as they settled, some squatting on the ground, others resting on their walking sticks. Even the man who had asked the question stayed rooted, torn between resentment and curiosity.

Jesus' hands moved as He spoke, tracing shapes in the air. He described the man's fields swelling with grain, the barns already full, the decision

## THE RICH FOOL (LK 12:13–21)

to build bigger ones. The listeners nodded—they had seen such wealth. Many worked the estates of men like that, labouring for a handful of coins while their masters counted harvests from balconies. But Jesus' tone was not one of envy; it was warning mixed with compassion, as if He grieved what success could do to the soul.

Behind Him, the Sea of Galilee shimmered, a mirror of white light. The breeze carried the smell of salt and fish. Birds circled above the fields, their cries mingling with His voice. "And he said to himself," Jesus continued, "'What shall I do, for I have nowhere to store my crops?'"

The crowd smiled faintly. They knew the type—men so rich their problems were inventions. Some laughed quietly; others waited, sensing where the story was heading. But Jesus' expression did not change. He let the laughter fade on its own.

"I will do this," He said, quoting the man. "'I will tear down my barns and build larger ones, and there I will store all my grain and my goods. And I will say to my soul, Soul, you have ample goods laid up for many years; relax, eat, drink, be merry.'"

The cadence was familiar—wealth's lullaby. The listeners could almost hear it in their own hearts: *if only I had enough, then I would rest.* The rich man in the story sounded content, even wise. He had planned, built, secured. The audience might have nodded—until Jesus' tone sharpened like a blade drawn across stone.

"But God said to him, Fool! This night your soul is required of you, and the things you have prepared, whose will they be?"

The word *Fool* fell like thunder. Some gasped. Others turned their faces away. It was rare to hear that word on the lips of a teacher; in their culture, it was an accusation of spiritual blindness, not stupidity. The man in the story had done nothing illegal. He had simply forgotten that his breath was borrowed.

Jesus paused, letting the silence do its work. The only sound was the rustle of robes, the shifting of feet on dust. The earlier question about inheritance now hung like a shadow. Everyone felt its reach—brothers quarrelling, neighbours comparing, farmers counting their grain by lamplight. The parable was about one man, yet everyone knew it was about them.

Jesus spoke again, softly now, almost to Himself: "So is the one who lays up treasure for himself and is not rich toward God."

The last words carried through the stillness and disappeared into the wind that swept across the lake. For a moment, no one moved. The brothers who had argued over land could not meet each other's eyes. Some looked at their hands, calloused and empty, and wondered whether they too were poor in the wrong way. Others glanced toward the hills, where the rich man's barns might have stood, and felt a pang of envy turning into unease.

Jesus looked over them one last time. His gaze did not accuse; it invited. He seemed to be asking not for surrender of possessions but for freedom from their weight. Then He turned and began walking toward the next village. The crowd hesitated, then followed—still silent, each carrying the story like a mirror. The man who had shouted the first question lingered behind, torn between resentment and awe. The answer he had received was not the one he wanted, but it was the truth he needed.

As they walked, the sun began to sink. The long shadows of olive trees stretched across the path like dark rivers. Somewhere in the distance, a dog barked; a child laughed; the hum of life returned. Yet within each heart the echo remained: *This night your soul is required of you.*

They would remember those words long after the dust settled. Some would think of them while counting coins, others while staring at their empty fields. For once the story was told, it kept telling itself—in barns, in marketplaces, in the quiet reckoning of conscience. The kingdom had entered their imaginations like seed into soil. It would grow there, slowly, until one day each would hear the same divine question: *What have you done with your life?*

The evening wind carried the faint smell of harvest. The Sower of stories had walked on, leaving His words behind to root where they would.

**The Surface Story**

## THE RICH FOOL (LK 12:13–21)

When Jesus began this parable, His listeners recognised the world He described. The "rich man" was not a villain from imagination but a familiar figure in Galilee and Judea. In a land where most people worked as tenant farmers or day labourers, a handful of large landowners controlled the fertile valleys and plains. They owned not only fields but the threshing floors, granaries, and contracts that governed distribution. The wealth of such men came not from luxury but from management — grain, oil, and wine converted into trade and rent.

In that society, a man's land was his identity. Property was covenantal, tied to family inheritance and divine promise. Every Israelite knew the ancient law that the land ultimately belonged to God (Lev 25:23). To be a "rich man" in Jesus' story, therefore, was not automatically to be corrupt. It simply meant one whose harvest had been generous, whose estate had prospered under favourable seasons and skilled labour. His success would have been read as blessing. Those in the crowd who had worked other men's fields would have nodded in recognition. They knew the mixture of admiration and envy such abundance inspired.

When Jesus said, "The land of a rich man brought forth plentifully," His audience would have pictured a good year — steady rain from late autumn to spring, mild heat through the summer, no locusts, no disease in the crop. Harvest meant long days of cutting, binding, threshing, and winnowing. At the end of it all came the practical concern every farmer understood: storage. There were no mechanical silos or sealed bins. Grain was kept in stone or clay granaries, or in pits plastered with lime, where moisture and rodents were constant threats. Every year, a portion spoiled. Too little storage meant waste; too much meant risk of theft. So when the parable's farmer surveys his overflowing barns and says, "What shall I do?" he is voicing a real agricultural dilemma. It is the question of success.

The listeners could imagine his thought process. If the barns were full and the new crop exceeded their capacity, the choices were limited. He could sell quickly — but that would flood the market and lower prices. He could distribute to the poor, but that would reduce his surplus. He could build larger barns and store for lean years, turning the harvest into security. That final option would have seemed sensible, even virtuous. A prudent man saved; a fool squandered. No one in that crowd, hearing the story for the first time, would have suspected that the rich man was about to become a warning.

The man's internal monologue would have sounded familiar too. He speaks like a responsible patriarch: "I will tear down my barns and build larger ones, and there I will store all my grain and my goods." In the culture of the ancient Near East, first-person reflection like this was a sign of reasoned planning. In the wisdom literature of Israel, the diligent man stores up in summer while the sluggard begs at harvest (Prov 6:6–8). The man in Jesus' story is not lazy; he is industrious. His plans are not unlawful; they are intelligent. To most listeners, he would have seemed the model of prosperity — one who had earned rest after years of toil.

When he says, "Soul, you have many goods laid up for many years; eat, drink, be merry," the words echo common Hebrew idioms. "Eat and drink" was shorthand for living in contentment, not excess. The phrase could appear in Psalms and Ecclesiastes alike. To the villagers gathered around Jesus, this line would have sounded almost proverbial — the reasonable satisfaction of a man enjoying what God had given him. If there was any fault here, it was invisible. The story so far belonged entirely to the logic of their world.

That is what made the turn so abrupt. "But God said to him, 'Fool! This night your soul is required of you.'" The declaration would have silenced the crowd. In the Hebrew Scriptures, to be called "fool" — *nabal* — was not a comment on intelligence but on blindness to God. The book of Proverbs contrasts the wise, who see their lives in covenantal relation to the Lord, with the fool, who lives as though self-sufficient. Suddenly, Jesus' rich man, so prudent a moment before, becomes the very opposite. His flaw was not his barns but his boundaries. He had spoken only to himself; his plans included no one else. He had forgotten that harvests are never private property but gifts entrusted for the sake of the community.

Those who heard Jesus knew this instinctively. In their villages, the Law required that edges of the field remain unharvested so the poor and the foreigner might glean (Lev 19:9–10). Offerings from the first fruits were to be brought to the Temple as thanksgiving (Deut 26:1–11). Generosity was not charity but worship — acknowledgment that abundance came from God. The man in the parable had done what the world called wise but had failed to do what faith called right.

The phrase "this night" would have chilled them. In a culture where life expectancy was uncertain and sudden death common, that warning felt near. They had buried neighbours who seemed strong the day before. The audience would have felt the truth of it without explanation: all the calculations, the building, the striving, could end between one sunset and the next.

When Jesus finished the story with the line, "So is the one who lays up treasure for himself and is not rich toward God," the sense was clear on the surface. To be "rich toward God" was a phrase drawn from ordinary worship. It meant being generous in almsgiving, faithful in offerings, thankful in prosperity. Every hearer could translate it into daily terms: honour God first, hold possessions lightly, remember the poor. Nothing in this teaching was abstract. It was covenant realism—practical holiness expressed in the economy of village life.

The power of the parable lay in its plausibility. Jesus did not describe a monster of greed but an average man of success. His listeners would have seen him in the mirrors of their own hopes: the farmer praying for a larger crop, the merchant saving against famine, the father wishing to provide for his children. In a culture shaped by scarcity, security seemed the highest good. Yet beneath that normality lay the discomfort of the divine interruption. God calls the prudent man *fool*, not because he is evil, but because he has forgotten dependence. His world, so carefully arranged, collapses under the weight of that single truth: *life itself is not ours to store.*

The crowd understood what Jesus was describing because they lived it daily. They knew the pressure of survival under Roman taxation and the temptation to measure worth by what one could keep. They also knew the wisdom tradition that taught the opposite—that to hoard was to lose, to give was to gain. On the surface, the parable spoke their language. Only later, as its words echoed in memory, would they realise that the story's realism had concealed revelation.

For now, they would have walked away nodding quietly, thinking about their own barns, their own provisions. The story had sounded like a lesson in prudence, but something about it unsettled them. The man's reasoning had been so familiar, yet the verdict had reversed it completely. In that quiet tension, the seed of divine wisdom had been planted. The surface story had done its work.

**Hidden Fire**

## a) Text, Translation, and Literary Context
### Greek (Luke 12:13–21):

εἶπεν δέ τις ἐκ τοῦ ὄχλου αὐτῷ· Διδάσκαλε, εἰπὲ τῷ ἀδελφῷ μου μερισθῆναι μετ' ἐμοῦ τὴν κληρονομίαν.

ὁ δὲ εἶπεν αὐτῷ· Ἄνθρωπε, τίς με κατέστησεν κριτὴν ἢ μεριστὴν ἐφ' ὑμᾶς;

εἶπεν δὲ πρὸς αὐτούς· Ὁρᾶτε καὶ φυλάσσεσθε ἀπὸ πάσης πλεονεξίας, ὅτι οὐκ ἐν τῷ περισσεύειν τινὶ ἡ ζωὴ αὐτοῦ ἐστιν ἐκ τῶν ὑπαρχόντων αὐτῷ.

εἶπεν δὲ παραβολὴν πρὸς αὐτοὺς λέγων· Ἀνθρώπου τινὸς πλουσίου εὐφόρησεν ἡ χώρα.

καὶ διελογίζετο ἐν ἑαυτῷ λέγων· Τί ποιήσω, ὅτι οὐκ ἔχω ποῦ συνάξω τοὺς καρπούς μου;

καὶ εἶπεν· Τοῦτο ποιήσω· καθελῶ μου τὰς ἀποθήκας καὶ μείζονας οἰκοδομήσω, καὶ συνάξω ἐκεῖ πάντα τὸν σῖτον καὶ τὰ ἀγαθά μου,

καὶ ἐρῶ τῇ ψυχῇ μου· Ψυχή, ἔχεις πολλὰ ἀγαθὰ κείμενα εἰς ἔτη πολλά· ἀναπαύου, φάγε, πίε, εὐφραίνου.

εἶπεν δὲ αὐτῷ ὁ Θεός· Ἄφρων, ταύτῃ τῇ νυκτὶ τὴν ψυχήν σου ἀπαιτοῦσιν ἀπὸ σοῦ· ἃ δὲ ἡτοίμασας, τίνι ἔσται;

οὕτως ὁ θησαυρίζων ἑαυτῷ καὶ μὴ εἰς Θεὸν πλουτῶν.

Luke's Greek opens in ordinary language and ends in divine address, moving from a public interruption to a cosmic verdict. The precision of its vocabulary and syntax guides the reader from the external to the interior, from dispute to revelation.

The scene begins with the request: Διδάσκαλε, εἰπὲ τῷ ἀδελφῷ μου μερισθῆναι μετ᾽ ἐμοῦ τὴν κληρονομίαν — "Teacher, tell my brother to divide the inheritance with me."

The key verb μερισθῆναι (aorist passive infinitive of μερίζω, "to divide, apportion") comes from legal and priestly vocabulary; it was used of the distribution of land among the tribes in the Septuagint (e.g. Num 26:55). Luke thereby situates the question within Israel's covenantal world — inheritance as sacred allotment. The man's request is not criminal; it is covenantal language used self-servingly. Jesus' reply refuses that role: τίς με κατέστησεν κριτὴν ἢ μεριστὴν ἐφ᾽ ὑμᾶς; The paired nouns κριτής (judge) and μεριστής (divider, arbitrator) define the limits of His earthly mission. Luke's diction echoes Ex 2:14 (Moses' rejection by the Israelites: "Who made you ruler and judge over us?"). The resonance quietly identifies Jesus as a new Moses who declines to repeat the old role of legal adjudication; His kingdom will judge hearts, not estates.

Immediately follows the warning: Ὁρᾶτε καὶ φυλάσσεσθε ἀπὸ πάσης πλεονεξίας — "Take heed and guard yourselves from all covetousness."

The doubled imperatives (ὁρᾶτε, φυλάσσεσθε) form a Hebrew-style intensification, recalling Deuteronomy's admonitions to "keep" and "watch." The noun πλεονεξία (pleonexia) literally means "the desire to have more," from *pleon* (more) and *echo* (to have). In Greek ethics it denoted greed, but in Jewish wisdom literature it implied idolatry — an appetite that displaces trust in God. Luke thus introduces the parable with a psychological diagnosis: the issue is not inheritance but insatiability.

The rationale is given in a tight aphorism: οὐκ ἐν τῷ περισσεύειν τινὶ ἡ ζωὴ αὐτοῦ ἐστιν ἐκ τῶν ὑπαρχόντων αὐτῷ — "a person's life is not in the abundance of his possessions."

The verb περισσεύειν (to abound, overflow) carries physical and spiritual connotations; Luke uses it elsewhere for grace and joy (e.g. Acts 16:5). Here, ironically, the overflow enslaves. Ζωή (life) is set against ὑπάρχοντα (possessions), creating a rhythmic antithesis: what truly exists (ζωή) is not derived from what one happens to have (ὑπάρχει). The sentence establishes the contrast that will structure the parable: existence vs. accumulation.

The parable proper begins: Ἀνθρώπου τινὸς πλουσίου εὐφόρησεν ἡ χώρα.

Luke's syntax foregrounds the land, not the man: literally, "The land of a certain rich man produced plentifully." The verb εὐφορεῖν (to bear fruit abundantly) appears in Genesis 1 LXX for the earth's fertility; the passive absence of the farmer highlights divine agency. The soil, not the owner, is the subject of prosperity. Thus before the rich man speaks, the narrative already hints at grace preceding possession.

Then comes the interior dialogue: καὶ διελογίζετο ἐν ἑαυτῷ λέγων· Τί ποιήσω... — "He reasoned within himself, saying, What shall I do...?"

Luke often uses διαλογίζεσθαι ἐν ἑαυτῷ to describe inward deliberation that replaces prayer (cf. 7:39; 16:3). The prepositional phrase ἐν ἑαυτῷ isolates him: literally "in himself." It signals the self-enclosure that will define his folly. His first verb ποιήσω (future active) begins a sequence of first-person futures — καθελῶ, οἰκοδομήσω, συνάξω, ἐρῶ — six in total. The monologue is grammatically self-absorbed; every clause begins with "I" or "my." Luke structures the passage as a crescendo of possession culminating in the soliloquy to the soul. The repetition of the first-person pronoun (μου, ἐγώ) creates what patristic commentators later called the "liturgy of the self."

The key noun of his plan is ἀποθήκη (apothēkē), "storehouse" or "barn." The compound of *apo* (away) and *thēkē* (a receptacle, chest) conveys removal and containment. Classical writers used it for granaries; in later usage it could mean treasury or vault. Its imagery is spatial — keeping things apart, locking them away — and thus already expresses the opposite of generosity. The verb καθελῶ ("I will tear down") and οἰκοδομήσω ("I will build") form a deliberate antithesis: destruction for expansion. The grammar mirrors his logic of replacement — old structures undone not for need but for more.

In verse 19 the monologue reaches its centre: καὶ ἐρῶ τῇ ψυχῇ μου· Ψυχή, ἔχεις πολλὰ ἀγαθὰ κείμενα εἰς ἔτη πολλά· ἀναπαύου, φάγε, πίε, εὐφραίνου.

Here Luke condenses an entire anthropology into one sentence. The word ψυχή (psychē) denotes the living self, the seat of desire and consciousness. In the Septuagint it translates *nephesh*, the life-breath that belongs to God (Gen 2:7). To speak to one's ψυχή is to assume mastery over it — a gesture of self-possession. The participle κείμενα ("laid up, stored") is used elsewhere for the dead lying in tombs (Luke 23:53); the echo suggests that what he calls security already smells of burial. The four imperatives — ἀναπαύου (rest), φάγε (eat), πίε (drink), εὐφραίνου (rejoice) — reproduce the hedonistic refrain of Ecclesiastes 8:15 but stripped of its final clause, "for this is from the hand of God." The omission is Luke's irony: self-congratulation replaces thanksgiving.

The divine reply reverses every verb. Ἄφρων — "Fool" — introduces the only direct speech of God in the parable. The adjective derives from *phrēn* (mind, understanding) with the privative prefix *a-*: literally, "mindless." In wisdom literature, the *aphrōn* is not intellectually weak but morally senseless, the one who "says in his heart, there is no God" (Ps 14:1 LXX). The phrase ταύτῃ τῇ νυκτὶ ("this very night") uses demonstrative immediacy; the doom is not future but imminent.

God's verb ἀπαιτοῦσιν ("they demand back") is plural and impersonal — literally, "they are requiring." The implied subject may be the angels or the cosmic creditors of life. The verb comes from financial contexts: to demand repayment of a loan. Life (ψυχή) is thus portrayed as something lent, not owned. What follows — ἃ δὲ ἡτοίμασας, τίνι ἔσται; — closes the structure with a rhetorical question. The relative pronoun ἃ (the things which) reduces possessions to impersonal objects; the dative τίνι (to whom) contrasts with the earlier "for myself." Luke ends the divine speech with economy: no curse, no thunder, only exposure of futility.

The final verse summarizes the moral logic in participial form: οὕτως ὁ θησαυρίζων ἑαυτῷ καὶ μὴ εἰς Θεὸν πλουτῶν.

The participle θησαυρίζων ("hoarding, storing treasure") echoes Jesus' later teaching in 12:33 about storing treasure in heaven. The contrastive construction ἑαυτῷ... εἰς Θεόν marks the decisive orientation of life: inward accumulation versus outward communion. The verb πλουτῶν (present active participle of πλουτέω, "to be rich") is continuous — one may go on "being rich" either for self or toward God. Luke's grammar leaves the reader standing between those directions.

Literary placement deepens the meaning. The pericope sits in Luke's long "travel narrative" (9:51–19:27), a section structured by teaching on discipleship and detachment. Immediately before, Jesus has spoken against hypocrisy (12:1–12) and for trust in divine care (12:22–34). The parable functions as hinge: from warning against public pretence to warning against private greed. Thematically, it mirrors the story of the rich ruler in 18:18–23, forming an inclusion around the travel narrative: both men seek security in possession and depart sorrowful.

Stylistically, Luke juxtaposes two voices — the self-talk of the rich man and the abrupt divine address. The rhythm moves from reflective prose to prophetic oracle. Between the man's "I will say to my soul" and God's "Fool, this night..." lies the decisive silence of death. The narrative's energy is in the contrast between monologue and dialogue: the man speaks only to himself until God speaks *to him*. What he never utters becomes his undoing — no blessing, no thanksgiving, no neighbour.

Within Luke's Gospel the passage also anticipates Jesus' subsequent teaching in 12:22–31: "Do not be anxious... seek (ζητεῖτε) His kingdom." The same root verb contrasts with θησαυρίζων ἑαυτῷ — seeking versus storing. The literary symmetry ties the parable to its antidote: trust replaces possession.

Luke's Greek, read attentively, already contains the theology that will unfold in the following sections. The movement from *pleonexia* to *aphrōn*, from abundance to demand, exposes the inner logic of sin: the attempt to secure the self against the Giver. Yet even within the grammar, grace lingers — the divine voice interrupts but does not annihilate; it calls. The text closes not in condemnation but in unfinished tension, leaving space for response. The story's syntax holds open the invitation that theology will now explore.

### b) Theological Interpretation

The parable of the Rich Fool reveals the theology of possession turned inward. Beneath the surface realism of barns and grain lies a vision of

## THE RICH FOOL (LK 12:13–21)

what happens when human life forgets its source. Jesus does not condemn wealth itself, nor the prudence of saving, but the delusion that abundance equals existence. In the parable's inner grammar, ownership expands while being contracts. The man's fields yield more, yet his world shrinks until it contains only one voice—his own.

Luke has placed this story within a chain of teachings on trust and dependence: first the warning against hypocrisy, then the call to fearless witness before God, and finally the invitation to seek the Kingdom without anxiety. The parable sits at the centre like a diagnostic mirror. It exposes the pathology that makes all the other commands impossible—the refusal to live as creature. Every word the rich man speaks is a distortion of the covenant language Israel knew by heart. Where the Psalms cry, "Bless the Lord, O my soul," he says instead, "Soul, you have many goods." The shift is subtle and fatal: God has been replaced by goods, the Giver by the gift.

At its core, this story is not about money but about anthropology. The rich man's sin is not greed in the modern sense but idolatry in the biblical one—the worship of the self through accumulation. He is not punished for enjoying a harvest but for mistaking the harvest as self-made. When he says, "My barns... my grain... my goods," the possessive pronoun becomes a litany of alienation. In biblical logic, to name something "mine" apart from God's blessing is to pronounce its death sentence. What is grasped ceases to live. The man's possessions have become his theology: he believes in his barns.

The divine interruption—"Fool! This very night your soul is demanded of you"—is not arbitrary judgment but revelation. It unveils the truth that the man's entire economy rests on borrowed breath. The Greek verb *apaitousin* (they demand back) evokes the creditor's claim; life itself is a loan to be returned. This recalls Job's confession: "The Lord gave, and the Lord has taken away; blessed be the name of the Lord" (Job 1:21). The fool's tragedy is that he never learned that prayer. He lived as if *psychē*, his life, were an asset under management rather than a mystery held in trust.

In biblical theology, *psychē* does not mean a detachable soul floating within the body. It is the person as living breath—life received from

Another. Thus, when God "demands back the soul," it is not vengeance but truth: the return of life to its rightful owner. The man's barns were designed to store what could never be kept. His sin is not so much that he hoarded wealth but that he attempted to hoard time. He says, "You have goods for many years," yet there is no "many years" outside the divine will. His crime is temporal arrogance—the presumption of tomorrows ungraced.

This theme echoes throughout Scripture. Ecclesiastes warns of the man who "toils and stores up for himself" only to leave it to another who did not labour for it (Eccl 2:21). Jeremiah mocks those who build houses by injustice, "cutting out windows" for comfort while neglecting righteousness (Jer 22:13–17). The prophets saw the same pattern Jesus names: when the heart seeks permanence through possession, it turns covenant into contract. The result is isolation. The rich man's monologue—his "I will say to my soul"—is the opposite of dialogue with God. Sin's essence, as the Fathers loved to say, is *autarkeia*—self-sufficiency. It is the fantasy of being one's own origin.

Yet the parable's theology cuts deeper than a moral warning. It unveils the structure of divine judgment itself. God does not destroy the fool; He simply reveals him. The moment of death exposes the fiction he has lived by. The man who thought himself secure discovers that everything he owned was, in fact, borrowed. The barns crumble because they were built on the false foundation of autonomy. Judgment, in Luke's hands, is never divine cruelty but divine clarity. As light unmasks shadows, so grace unmasks self-deception.

This moment also discloses a profound truth about God's character. The divine voice calls him "Fool," not "enemy." The tone is not fury but sorrow. The fool is pitiable because he has reduced the infinite exchange of grace to the arithmetic of possession. In refusing to live for others, he has made himself unfit for heaven, where all life is shared. The tragedy of the rich fool is that he is invited to communion but has trained his soul for solitude.

"Rich toward God" (*ploutein eis Theon*) is Luke's summative phrase and the heart of the parable's theology. It describes not a quantity but a direction. To be "rich toward God" means to turn the motion of life outward—to recognise that every gift exists to be given again. The verb *ploutein* (to be rich) appears elsewhere in Luke only in the Magnificat, where Mary sings that God "has filled the hungry with good things and sent the rich away empty." In both cases, richness is a spiritual orientation, not a status. Mary is "poor toward self and rich toward God"; the fool is her inversion.

In this light, the parable becomes a microcosm of salvation history. Humanity, made rich in creation, has turned its abundance inward, building barns of pride and fear. The divine interruption—"This night your soul is required"—is the Cross's logic in miniature. Christ, the true Rich One, will later hear a similar demand in Gethsemane: "Father, into your hands I commend my spirit." The contrast is total. The fool clutches what was loaned; the Son returns what was given. The first loses everything; the second receives everything anew.

This is why the Fathers often read the parable as moral anatomy of the fall. St. Basil the Great asks, "What are your barns but the stomachs of the poor?"—exposing the social dimension of the story. For Basil, the man's folly is the refusal of communion: he severs himself from neighbour, and therefore from God. St. Augustine sees the same drama inwardly: "The rich man's field had brought forth abundantly, yet he was impoverished in God." Augustine calls this the "poverty of abundance," the soul so full of goods that it has no room for grace.

The pattern reaches beyond economics. The fool represents the spiritual condition of every person who tries to secure joy through control. Whether through wealth, reputation, or ideology, we all attempt to build barns against loss. The divine word still interrupts: *apaitousin*—"your life is required back." The Gospel insists that life cannot be insured; it can only be offered. Every Eucharist is that reversal enacted: what we receive, we return. The Christian life is the ongoing dismantling of barns.

Luke's closing sentence—"so is the one who lays up treasure for himself and is not rich toward God"—contains the quiet metaphysics of the

Kingdom. It defines salvation as relationship, not possession. The self-accumulating man stands outside communion; the self-giving disciple lives within divine abundance. The parable, then, is not about punishment but participation: the tragedy of one who refuses to live the life he was created for—the life of shared gift.

The story of the Rich Fool reaches into the very heart of covenant theology. It is not a parable about business ethics or financial planning but about relationship—what happens when the creature forgets the Creator, when gift is mistaken for possession. The man in Jesus' story isn't wicked or criminal. He's ordinary. That is what makes the warning so urgent. He represents the believer who still prays, still works hard, but has quietly come to believe that security is something he can build with his own hands. His barns are the symbol of self-sufficiency, the illusion that we can store tomorrow.

In Israel's Scriptures, land and harvest were never neutral. They were signs of covenant faithfulness, sacraments of God's promise. When Moses led the people into Canaan, he told them to bring the first fruits to the altar and confess: *"My father was a wandering Aramean... and the Lord brought us into this land"* (Deut 26:5–9). The offering was not mere custom; it was theology in motion. Every harvest was to remind Israel that abundance comes from God's hand, not human calculation. Gratitude was the fence that kept blessing from turning into idolatry.

The rich man in Luke's parable tears down that fence. His soil yields plentifully, but there is no thanksgiving, no offering, no neighbour in sight. The land is fruitful; his soul is barren. He sees only the crop, not the covenant. "What shall I do?" he says. The words sound practical, but they are the wrong question. The biblical farmer was meant to ask, "What will I give?" Instead, this man asks, "Where will I keep?" The problem is not his success but his solitude. The verbs pile up: *I will tear down, I will build, I will store, I will say.* He speaks as though God and neighbour have disappeared. It is the litany of the self-made man—the religion of the solitary "I."

Luke lets the man's monologue expose the sickness that runs through

## THE RICH FOOL (LK 12:13–21)

fallen humanity: we trust storage more than stewardship. The moment we think of blessing as something to keep, it begins to rot. That is why the manna in the wilderness spoiled when hoarded. God wanted His people to depend on daily bread, not stored bread. In the same way, the fool's barns overflow because he has forgotten the law of dependence. What he calls wisdom, Scripture calls *pleonexia*—the desire to have more. Jesus names it explicitly before telling the story: *"Beware of all covetousness."* Greed, in biblical thought, isn't just about money. It's about control. It's the refusal to live in trust.

When God speaks, the entire world of the parable reverses: *"Fool! This night your soul is required of you."* In the ancient world, to be called *aphrōn*—fool—was not an insult to intelligence but a diagnosis of spiritual blindness. The fool is the one who lives as if God were irrelevant. The divine word does not condemn the man so much as expose his delusion. He has mistaken the temporary for the permanent. The Greek verb *apaitousin*—"they demand back"—evokes repayment of a loan. The breath in his lungs, the time he presumes to own, were never his to begin with. Life, the parable teaches, is covenantal property. It belongs to the Lord, who gives and who recalls.

This logic runs through all of Scripture. Adam was given dominion over creation, yet only as steward, never as owner. Israel was given land, but it was "the Lord's land," lent under the condition of obedience (Lev 25:23). The prophets thundered against those who built houses without justice and stored grain while the poor starved (Amos 8:4–6). Each story told the same truth: blessing without gratitude becomes curse. When the gift is cut off from the Giver, it begins to die.

The fool's barns, then, are not merely a sign of greed—they are the architecture of unbelief. He builds as if the covenant were void, as if God no longer sustains the world day by day. His real sin is theological: he has replaced providence with planning. "Soul, you have many goods laid up for many years," he tells himself. Yet he cannot control even the night. The barns promise a future that will never come.

In that moment of revelation, the rich man's story becomes the mirror of our own. We may not have granaries, but we build our own versions—bank accounts, insurances, reputations, digital archives—all meant to secure us against loss. None of these are evil in themselves, yet all become idols when they stop being instruments of communion. The man's tragedy is not that he was rich but that he was alone. He stored his harvest but not his heart. He had no one to bless because he had built no relationships of love. Wealth without gift becomes isolation, and isolation is death rehearsed.

The parable's final line gathers all of this into one sentence: *"So is the one who lays up treasure for himself and is not rich toward God."* The phrase *rich toward God* sounds simple, but it is the key to the whole Gospel. Luke uses the same verb later for the "treasure in heaven" that never fails. To be rich toward God is to live within His covenant economy—the economy of grace, not grasping. The law of that Kingdom is always the same: what you give multiplies, what you hoard decays. As Proverbs says, "One man gives freely, yet grows all the richer; another withholds what he should give, and only suffers want."

This logic culminates in Christ Himself. The parable of the Rich Fool points toward the Cross, though no one in the crowd could see it yet. Jesus will later become the true rich man who loses everything—not because of folly, but because of love. He will have no barns to store His life, only the open hands of surrender: "Father, into your hands I commend my spirit." The fool tries to preserve his soul and loses it. Christ gives His soul and gains the world. The two stand as mirror images: one clings, one offers; one builds barns, the other becomes bread.

In that reversal lies the law of the Kingdom. The more we give, the more we become ourselves. God's judgment on the fool is not revenge but revelation: to cling to life is to lose it. To be rich toward God is to enter the pattern of divine generosity that sustains the universe. Every Eucharist proclaims this exchange: "Take, eat, this is my body given for you." Heaven's storehouses are filled by the hands that give.

The story of the Rich Fool does not end with condemnation; it ends with invitation. God's question—*"The things you have prepared, whose will they be?"*—isn't a sneer. It is mercy disguised as reckoning. The Lord confronts the man not to crush him but to call him back into reality. Everything he thought was his own is revealed to be borrowed. The barns, the grain, the years ahead—they all belong to God. The question lingers for the listener, too. The crowd that day would have gone home thinking not about a stranger's greed but about their own trust. "Whose will my life be?"

That question has haunted every generation. The fool's delusion did not die with him. It is the same spirit that tempted Israel in the wilderness to hoard manna, that led David to count his soldiers, that whispered to the Pharisee in the Temple, "You are secure." Each is a variation of the same heresy—the belief that safety can be achieved without surrender. Yet the whole logic of the covenant is the opposite: security comes only through dependence. Israel's history, from Abraham to Mary, is the slow education of the human heart in that truth. The barns of Egypt and Babylon always fall. The jars of flour in the widow's kitchen never run out.

To be "rich toward God" means learning this rhythm of dependence. It's not about financial poverty but spiritual posture. The saints live with open hands because they know that ownership is an illusion. Everything is gift, and gift only remains gift when it's given again. That is why the early Church in Acts lived by a pattern that seemed economically impossible: *"They had all things in common, and there was not a needy person among them."* They were not communists; they were covenantal. Their wealth was not abolished but transfigured. The rich gave freely; the poor received gratefully; all rejoiced together. That is what the Rich Fool never knew—that joy is the only form of wealth that multiplies when shared.

The Church Fathers understood this well. St. Basil the Great asked his congregation, "When you give to the poor, are you not simply returning what was never yours? The bread you hoard belongs to the hungry." For Basil, charity is not generosity in the modern sense but justice in the divine sense. God entrusts resources to His children so that grace may circulate through them. To block that flow is to break the covenant. The barns we build in our hearts are not neutral—they either store up love or suffocate it.

Every age builds its own barns. In the ancient world, they were filled with grain; in ours, with data, savings, and control. The technology has changed; the temptation hasn't. We measure life by what we can quantify. Jesus dismantles that illusion with one sentence: *"Life does not consist in the abundance of possessions."* In Greek, the word for life here is *zoē*—not mere biological existence but the life that comes from communion with God. That kind of life cannot be earned, bought, or stored. It must be received moment by moment, like breath. The fool dies because he has mistaken storage for security and quantity for meaning.

Yet the Gospel's answer is not disdain for material goods but their redemption. Creation itself is good; the problem lies in disordered attachment. God delights in fruitfulness, in the joy of His creatures sharing in His abundance. What the parable exposes is the danger of trying to possess what can only be shared. The rich man's barns are full of grain, but his heart is empty because he has forgotten what grain is for—to feed. The purpose of abundance is communion. Every time we share our resources, we restore creation to its original order: everything flowing from the Father through the Son to the Spirit, and back again.

The Cross makes this restoration possible. Christ is the opposite of the Rich Fool because He holds nothing back. He does not build barns; He becomes bread. On Calvary, He gives even His breath—the *psychē* the fool tried to keep. Where the fool hears, "Your life is demanded back," the Son says, "Father, into your hands I commend My spirit." The contrast is complete. The man's life is taken from him; Christ's life is offered. The first loses everything; the second gains all. In that offering, the barns of heaven are filled—the storehouse of grace opened for all who live as He lived: in total gift.

Every disciple must face this same reversal. The Gospel asks: do we live by the world's arithmetic or by heaven's? The world says, "Keep, and you'll be safe." The Kingdom says, "Give, and you'll live." That choice is presented anew in every age—in families, in workplaces, even in the Church herself. Communities die when they start guarding what they have instead of giving who they are. The only wealth that survives judgment is love made visible. "Where your treasure is, there will your heart be also."

That is not sentimental poetry; it is ontological fact. The heart clings to what it treasures, and in the end, it becomes what it clings to.

To be rich toward God, then, is not to despise barns but to fill them with what endures—acts of mercy, generosity, prayer, and service. These are the harvest that will not rot. St. Paul calls them "the fruit that increases to your credit." When a mother gives her patience, when a worker offers honesty, when a believer forgives, each is adding to a storehouse in heaven. That is the new agriculture of the Kingdom—the only economy that survives the night when souls are required.

The parable ends not in despair but in decision. Jesus leaves His hearers standing between two worlds: the world of the barn and the world of the altar. One is built on fear; the other on trust. One isolates; the other unites. One perishes; the other endures. The choice is not made once but daily. Each day we are asked, "Whose will these things be?" Every prayer, every gift, every sacrifice answers that question anew. The fool's story becomes the disciple's conversion when we learn to say, "Lord, all that I have is yours."

At the end of the day, that is the Gospel's real economy. Salvation is not a transfer of assets but a transformation of attachment. Heaven is not the reward for giving—it is the place where giving never ends. The barns of this world crumble, but the storehouse of love stands forever. And the One who first told this parable, the true Rich Man of heaven, has already given everything to make us heirs of that endless abundance.

### c) Typological and Intertextual Parallels

The parable of the Rich Fool stands within a long biblical conversation about wealth, wisdom, and worship. Jesus isn't introducing a new theme but fulfilling one that runs from Genesis to the prophets and into the apostolic Church. From the beginning, Scripture treats possessions not as evil but as tests of the heart. What we do with abundance reveals what—or whom—we trust. When Jesus warns against building bigger barns, He is drawing on centuries of divine instruction about the dangers of forgetting the Giver while enjoying the gift.

The first echo sounds in Genesis, where Adam and Eve reach for the fruit God had not given. Their sin is not hunger but grasping. They wanted to secure knowledge, to take rather than to receive. In that moment, they became the first hoarders of grace. The pattern repeats in Cain, who withholds his best offering, and in Babel, where humanity builds upward to make a name for itself. Every story of the early chapters of Genesis is the same story: human beings trying to store what should have been shared. The barns keep getting bigger, and the hearts keep getting smaller.

Later, God entrusts His people with a new kind of abundance: the Promised Land. Its fields and vineyards are meant to be both home and sacrament. The land belongs to the Lord; Israel is the tenant. "The land shall not be sold in perpetuity," God declares, "for the land is mine; you are strangers and sojourners with me" (Lev 25:23). In this covenant, ownership is stewardship. When Israel forgets that and begins to treat blessing as entitlement, prophets arise to remind them. Amos thunders against those who "store up violence and robbery in their strongholds" (Amos 3:10). Isaiah mourns the houses "joined field to field until there is no more room" (Isa 5:8). Jeremiah, centuries later, denounces the king who builds his palace with unjust gain, asking, "Did not your father eat and drink and do justice? Then it was well with him. But you have eyes and heart only for dishonest gain" (Jer 22:15–17). In each case, the sin is the same as the fool's: abundance without thanksgiving, prosperity without mercy, faith turned into possession.

The manna in the wilderness offers another typological thread. God feeds His people daily but forbids them to store the bread overnight. When they disobey, it breeds worms and stench (Exod 16:20). The manna is heaven's way of teaching trust—grace as daily bread, not long-term investment. The Rich Fool repeats the same error on a grander scale. He takes what is meant for today and tries to turn it into tomorrow. His grain becomes the new manna that spoils because it was hoarded.

The wisdom literature of Israel also anticipates this parable. Ecclesiastes laments the man who labours and heaps up wealth only for someone else to enjoy it: "What has a man from all the toil and striving of heart with

## THE RICH FOOL (LK 12:13–21)

which he toils beneath the sun? For all his days are full of sorrow, and his work is a vexation" (Eccl 2:22–23). Psalm 49 delivers the same verdict: "When he dies he will carry nothing away; his glory will not go down after him." These reflections don't despise wealth—they despise the illusion that wealth is life. They prepare for the day when the true Wisdom will stand among men and say, "Life does not consist in the abundance of possessions."

Even the fool's inner dialogue has roots in the Old Testament. His words—"Eat, drink, and be merry"—echo Ecclesiastes 8:15, but Jesus deliberately strips the line of its final phrase: "for this is from the hand of God." The rich man repeats the wisdom of Scripture but removes its source. His sin is not new; it is the perennial temptation to enjoy the fruit while denying the tree.

Against these shadows, Jesus' parable shines like a final commentary on all of Israel's history. Every earlier story now converges in this one moment. The rich man's land "brought forth plentifully"—a blessing of creation. But he responds with Babel's self-talk, Pharaoh's hoarding, Israel's forgetfulness. He becomes the sum of all covenant failures in miniature. The tragedy of the fool is that he is Israel without worship, Adam without gratitude, humanity without trust.

At the same time, Jesus is also drawing on the prophetic hope of restoration. The prophets promised that one day God would write His law not on stone but on hearts (Jer 31:33), that greed would give way to generosity, that a new creation would flow with justice "like an ever-flowing stream" (Amos 5:24). The parable hints at this promise by its very contrast: the fool's barns will fall, but a new harvest will rise where grace, not grain, is stored.

In the Gospel of Luke, this pattern of reversal runs like a thread. The Magnificat already announced it: "He has filled the hungry with good things and sent the rich away empty." The fool embodies the latter half of that line. He is the man sent away empty not because God withheld, but because he would not open his hands. In Luke's theology, wealth is never condemned outright, but it is always dangerous because it tempts the heart to forget that it is creaturely. The fool's abundance is his undoing precisely because he misreads blessing as possession.

There is also a striking typological contrast with Joseph, the son of Jacob. In Genesis 41, Joseph stores grain in Egypt during the seven years of plenty to feed the nations during the famine. He builds barns, too, but in obedience and service. His storage becomes salvation. The fool's storage becomes suffocation. Joseph gives away; the fool locks away. One acts in covenant partnership with God; the other acts as his own god. Both men gather abundance, but only one turns it into gift.

Jesus' audience would also have heard the faint echo of Daniel's warning to Nebuchadnezzar. The proud king of Babylon says, "Is not this great Babylon, which I have built by my mighty power?" (Dan 4:30). The words are almost identical in tone to the fool's monologue. That night, Nebuchadnezzar loses his sanity and becomes like a beast until he looks to heaven and gives glory to God. The parable's verdict—"This night your soul is required of you"—is a gentler version of the same divine reversal. Pride in possession always ends in exile until gratitude is restored.

Moving forward through Scripture, the apostolic writings echo Jesus' teaching. James warns the wealthy merchants of his day: "Come now, you who say, 'Today or tomorrow we will go into such and such a town…'—you do not know what tomorrow will bring" (Jas 4:13–14). Like the rich fool, they plan without acknowledging God's will. James continues: "You have laid up treasure in the last days." His image of hoarded gold corroding in their hands is a direct descendant of this parable. Paul likewise tells Timothy, "As for the rich in this present age… they are to do good, to be rich in good works, generous and ready to share, thus storing up treasure for themselves as a good foundation for the future" (1 Tim 6:17–19). The contrast between the fool's barns and the believer's charity becomes the apostolic standard for Christian stewardship.

But no typological reading is complete without turning toward Christ Himself. Every parable, every Old Testament echo, converges on the Cross. There, the Son of God lives the exact opposite of the fool's logic. He does not keep but gives; He does not build barns but opens His body.

## THE RICH FOOL (LK 12:13–21)

Where the fool's soul is demanded back, Christ's soul is freely offered. The parable thus becomes prophecy fulfilled: humanity's hoarding meets God's outpouring. The one who clung to life loses it; the one who surrenders life restores it to the world.

The Eucharist completes the pattern. At every Mass, we bring our little offerings—bread, wine, work, suffering—and the Lord receives them, multiplies them, and returns them as His very life. It is the divine reversal of the fool's economy. What we give is not lost; what we withhold decays. Heaven's storehouse operates on the opposite law: generosity is gain. The altar is the anti-barn. It is the place where we learn that security lies not in storing but in surrender.

This same rhythm continues into eternity. The fool dies because he has nowhere to take his treasure. The saints live forever because their treasure is in God. The book of Revelation describes the heavenly city as a place where "nothing unclean shall enter," not because it is exclusionary, but because selfishness has no currency there. Heaven is what happens when every heart has become rich toward God.

Through this lens, the parable ceases to be a warning only and becomes a promise. The barns that fall are not the end but the clearing for a new field. The Lord who demands the fool's soul is also the Lord who will give it back transfigured. What is lost in self-preservation is found in self-gift. The covenant that began in Eden ends at a table where the true Rich Man of heaven feeds His poor with Himself. The "many goods laid up for many years" are replaced by one inexhaustible gift: Christ, "the Bread that endures to eternal life."

The story of the Rich Fool, then, is not just a moral parable about greed but the gospel in miniature. It traces the entire arc of salvation history: creation as gift, sin as grasping, redemption as surrender. It calls us to live now in the economy of the Kingdom—to trade fear for faith, barns for altars, storage for service. Every act of generosity, every thank-you, every relinquishment of control is a small participation in Christ's own self-offering. The parable ends where Scripture began: in the call to trust the Giver more than the gift, to remember that life itself is borrowed breath—and that every breath, returned in love, becomes eternal.

### d) Patristic and Theological Synthesis

The early Church never read the parable of the Rich Fool as a story about economics. They read it as a mirror for the soul. To them, the barns of the fool were not fields or buildings but hearts swollen with self-love. Every Father of the Church, from Basil to Augustine, saw in this man the reflection of fallen humanity—graced by God, blessed with abundance, yet tempted to keep what was given for communion. The Fathers understood that greed is not simply love of money; it is forgetfulness of grace. When Jesus said, "So is the one who lays up treasure for himself and is not rich toward God," they heard the call to recover the covenant rhythm of gift and gratitude that defines true faith.

St. Basil the Great, preaching in Cappadocia amid a famine, gave perhaps the most famous homily on this passage. His words are as piercing now as when they first echoed through the basilica:

"The bread in your cupboard belongs to the hungry; the cloak in your wardrobe belongs to the naked; the shoes you let rot belong to the barefoot; the silver you keep hidden is the property of the needy."

For Basil, the fool's barns were not simply excessive; they were unjust. In God's economy, surplus is never private property but entrusted mercy. Wealth, he said, is given so that generosity might circulate through the body of Christ. The fool sinned not by prospering, but by damming the river of grace that should have flowed through him. In hoarding what was meant to be shared, he robbed both the poor and himself. The true tragedy was spiritual starvation amid material plenty.

St. John Chrysostom echoed this logic in his fiery sermons at Antioch. Preaching before wealthy merchants and bureaucrats, he said, "The rich man's barns burst not because of their smallness, but because of his greed. The stomachs of the poor were larger and safer storehouses." For Chrysostom, charity was not optional. It was the visible form of justice under grace—the sign that the heart had been converted. His words gave flesh to the Lord's command to "be rich toward God." The fool's barns symbolized the false worship of possession; the poor man's stomach symbolized the true temple of the Spirit. When we feed others, he said, we become God's coworkers in creation, turning the dust of earth into the bread of heaven.

St. Augustine, preaching on this same text, called the rich fool "a man busy planning for tomorrow while God was calling him today." He saw in the man's self-talk the great illusion of sin: the belief that life's timeline belongs to us. Augustine urged his listeners to treat every possession as borrowed breath. "You are a steward," he said, "not the owner. The Giver may demand His goods when He will." In his vision, the barns of the fool were the soul's compartments filled with anxieties, plans, and unoffered prayers. The only safe storage, Augustine said, is in heaven's treasury—acts of mercy laid up where neither moth nor rust destroy.

St. Gregory the Great took the image further. He compared the "barns" to the mind that collects knowledge but withholds love. "When understanding swells without charity," he wrote, "it becomes a burden, not a blessing." For Gregory, the fool's sin was not only greed but pride—the intellect storing wisdom without giving praise. His insight widens the parable's meaning: the temptation to hoard does not belong only to the wealthy. Scholars, preachers, and even the pious can become rich fools when they gather truth but refuse to let it bear fruit in humility and compassion.

This patristic chorus all sings one refrain: every gift becomes dangerous when it ceases to serve communion. The fool's barns, whether filled with grain, gold, or glory, stand for the soul turned inward. The Fathers called this *philautia*—the love of self that bends every blessing toward one's own comfort. Against this sickness, they proposed the remedy of *agapē*—the love that gives without measure. In their eyes, salvation was not simply deliverance from sin's penalty but liberation from this self-enclosure. Grace breaks open the barns of the heart so that God's life can circulate through His people again.

The medieval doctors would later continue this line of thought. Thomas Aquinas, reflecting on this parable in his *Commentary on Luke*, describes the fool's sin as *avaritia spiritualis*—spiritual greed. Even holy works, he warns, can be sought as possessions. True virtue always refers back to God and neighbour; otherwise, it becomes self-glorification. Aquinas saw divine judgment in this story not as vengeance but purification: "He is called fool because he mistook time for eternity." To cling to temporal goods as permanent is, in Thomistic language, a failure of reason and of worship. Wisdom, by contrast, begins in ordering all things toward the last end—God Himself.

The Church's magisterial teaching echoes these ancient insights. The Second Vatican Council's *Gaudium et Spes* warned that "man is more precious for what he is than for what he has." St. John Paul II, in *Centesimus Annus*, explained that material progress without moral progress becomes regression. Possession must serve participation; wealth must serve communion. The Council Fathers were simply rephrasing the Gospel's own verdict: "So it is with one who stores up treasure for himself but is not rich toward God." Modern Catholic social teaching stands as the contemporary echo of Basil and Chrysostom. It is not anti-wealth; it is pro-love. Every resource is meant to be sacramental—a sign that points beyond itself to the generosity of the Creator.

Pope Benedict XVI expressed this beautifully in *Deus Caritas Est*. "Love," he wrote, "is divine in origin. It is the light—and in the end, the only light—that can always illuminate a world grown dim." The fool's barns are dark precisely because they contain only his light. True abundance shines outward. When the heart opens to God's love, possessions become instruments of that love, not competitors to it. The fool's error, in the Pope's language, is the refusal of *caritas*. He has wealth but not joy, storage but no song.

The Church's liturgical tradition also carries this teaching into prayer. In the Roman lectionary, the parable of the Rich Fool often appears alongside the reading from Ecclesiastes—"Vanity of vanities, all is vanity." The liturgy places the wisdom of Israel beside the wisdom of Christ to remind believers that detachment is not disdain but freedom. Every time the Church prays, "Give us this day our daily bread," she is rejecting the fool's philosophy.

We do not ask for barns; we ask for manna. We do not cling to surplus; we trust in sufficiency.

Read together, the Fathers and the Magisterium speak with one voice: the call to generosity is not an extra-credit option for the spiritually advanced; it is the very form of discipleship. To be Christian is to live in the circulation of grace. When Jesus warns against building bigger barns, He is not commanding poverty for its own sake but inviting participation in divine abundance. The God who gives Himself entirely asks us to reflect that same pattern in our use of everything we hold—our time, our goods, our words, even our knowledge.

At the end of the parable, the fool's barns collapse, and the Fathers invite us to imagine what might rise in their place. Basil would say: the storehouse of mercy. Chrysostom would answer: the temple of the poor. Augustine would add: the heart at peace because it trusts. Gregory would whisper: the mind illumined by charity. All agree that when a believer begins to give, heaven begins to dwell within. The dismantling of the barns is not destruction; it is transfiguration. Grace breaks the locks we've built around ourselves so that love can do what it was made to do—overflow.

And so, the early Church read this parable as a promise as much as a warning. The fool's fall reveals the path to wisdom: to hold all things lightly, to give all things gladly, to remember that everything stored up for self is lost, but everything given in love is kept forever. The barns of this world will fall; the storehouses of mercy will remain.

As the Fathers would say, every heart must choose its architecture. Either we build barns that crumble or altars that endure. The voice that called the fool that night still calls us today—not with condemnation, but with invitation: "Be rich toward God." Those four words sum up the entire moral theology of the Gospel. They describe the life of Christ, the pattern of the saints, and the destiny of every soul that learns to live by the generosity of heaven.

## The Shock and the Turn

The crowd that gathered around Jesus that day did not expect to be unsettled. The request that began the conversation—"Teacher, tell my brother to divide the inheritance with me"—was ordinary. In their world, disputes over inheritance were part of daily life. Wealth meant stability, land meant legacy. Rabbis were often asked to settle such matters, and people expected justice: fairness, restitution, the right outcome. Jesus refuses to arbitrate. Instead, He tells a parable that overturns the whole conversation.

The listeners leaned in expecting moral clarity; what they heard was judgment wrapped in irony. A man prospers. His land yields beyond expectation. He has not cheated or oppressed anyone. By the measure of Israel's wisdom, this man is blessed. The Law promised abundance to those who obeyed. The psalms sang of the righteous flourishing like trees planted by streams of water. The patriarchs were men of herds and harvests. In the covenant imagination, fullness was the language of favour.

But Jesus begins to draw a quiet line through that assumption. The man's fields yield richly, yet his words reveal poverty. He does not speak to God, nor to neighbour, nor even of gratitude. He speaks only to himself. His monologue is filled with the smallest pronoun: *I*. "What shall I do? I will tear down my barns, I will build larger ones, I will store my grain, I will say to my soul..." It is the liturgy of self-sufficiency. The listeners who had nodded at his prosperity begin to feel unease.

Then comes the reversal. God enters the story—but not as the approving blesser of diligence. He enters as the voice of judgment: "Fool! This night your soul is required of you." The word falls like thunder on the calm field of worldly reason. The man who had planned for "many years" discovers that his years have run out. The divine verdict undoes the entire logic of his life. In a single breath, Jesus transforms what seemed wisdom into folly.

For the crowd, this was more than moral instruction; it was theological shock. Israel's tradition had long equated visible blessing with divine approval. But here, the man most blessed is the one most blind. His wealth becomes the veil that hides his dependence. The God of abundance, it turns out, is not the guarantor of human security but the Giver who demands remembrance. The "fool" is not condemned for his barns but for his forgetfulness.

That is the turn—the deep reversal of divine economy. The people expected the Messiah to vindicate the diligent, to reward the faithful, to bless those whose barns overflowed. Instead, the Son of Man declares that such fullness may conceal famine of the soul. Heaven measures differently. The kingdom of God is not an economy of accumulation but of participation, not storage but surrender.

"This night your soul is required." The Greek verb *apaitousin* carries the sense of calling back what was lent. The shock lies in that discovery: life is borrowed breath. The farmer has mistaken stewardship for ownership. Everything he counts as *mine*—land, grain, time, even soul—was never his in the first place. The illusion of control shatters under that single word *required*.

The listeners would have recognized the echo of Ecclesiastes: "Vanity of vanities, all is vanity." Yet Jesus is not repeating the old lament of meaninglessness. He is revealing the deeper cause of it. Vanity comes not from mortality itself but from the refusal to live in gratitude. The fool's barns are monuments to a life without reference to God. That is the tragedy. He has everything but communion.

For the devout Jews around Jesus, this message would have sounded dangerously close to blasphemy. Did not Moses teach that obedience brings prosperity? Did not Deuteronomy say that faithfulness would cause "barns to be filled with plenty"? How could the Messiah now condemn the very abundance God had once promised? But Jesus is not abolishing the Law; He is unveiling its heart. The blessings of the covenant were never meant to end in possession. They were signs pointing to communion with the Giver. When Israel treated them as permanent rather than provisional, grace hardened into idolatry.

That is the great shock of the Gospel—the shift from covenant as contract to covenant as communion. Israel expected the Day of the Lord to settle accounts: the righteous vindicated, the wicked destroyed. Yet in this parable, God does not divide estates or balance ledgers. He interrupts them. Judgment arrives not as retribution but revelation. The measure of the heart is shown to be love, not ledger.

The turn slices through every layer of piety. The rich fool is not a villain; he is respectable, cautious, prudent. That is the sting. He represents not the notorious sinner but the complacent believer, the man who keeps his religion within the safety of calculation. His downfall is the silence of prayer. He never asks, "What does God will?" Only, "What shall I do?" That small shift of reference—from God to self—marks the whole tragedy of fallen man.

Jesus' audience expected the righteous to be justified by their labour; instead, He calls them to surrender their labour to love. "Be rich toward God," He concludes. The phrase has no precedent in Jewish teaching. Wealth toward God means giving back to the One who needs nothing—living in gratitude so radical that it turns possession into praise. The man's barns stand as symbols of every life built on the illusion that security can be stored.

In the silence that must have followed, the listeners would have felt the parable turning back on them. Every family in that crowd knew the tension of inheritance, the struggle to keep land, the anxiety of survival under Roman taxation. They worked hard, prayed hard, and longed for a Messiah who would restore prosperity to Israel. Now this Teacher speaks as though prosperity itself is the danger. He is dismantling the old calculus of merit. The Day of the Lord will not reward the careful accumulator but the open-handed giver.

The reversal runs deeper still. Israel's wisdom tradition had long praised prudence—the ability to prepare for the future. Joseph in Egypt built storehouses and saved nations. Proverbs commended the ant who gathers in summer. Yet Jesus presents a man who does exactly that—and calls him a fool. The difference is interior. Joseph's barns fed the hungry; this man's barns feed no one. Wisdom without generosity decays into greed. The fool's prudence becomes parody.

What scandalized the first listeners is what still unsettles the modern soul: that God measures wealth in generosity, not in gain. The barns we build—our careers, our savings, our reputations—can become the walls that block heaven's light. The reversal is not only about money. It touches every attempt to secure life apart from God's providence. The fool's error lies in trusting management over mercy, permanence over presence.

The silence after Jesus' final words must have been heavy. The crowd that had begun by demanding fairness now faced an invitation far more demanding: to live as receivers, not owners. The parable does not condemn work or harvest; it reorders them. Every field must become altar. Every yield must become offering. To be rich toward God is to live with one's barns open—to hold everything as if it already belongs to heaven.

In this way, the shock becomes mercy. God calls the man "fool" not to shame him but to wake him. The divine rebuke is a rescue from delusion. Jesus does not want His listeners to despise the world's goods but to see them truthfully: as gifts meant to pass through the hands, not remain clutched within them. The barns will fall; the Kingdom will not.

By the time Jesus' voice fades, the crowd's idea of blessing has been reversed. The God they thought rewarded prudence has revealed Himself as the God who delights in generosity. The man they pitied at first—dying without heirs—becomes their mirror. The treasure of heaven is not built on accumulation but participation. The soul that clings loses; the soul that gives finds abundance.

That is the great turn of this parable: the moment when divine logic overturns human logic, when the barns of self-sufficiency collapse and the horizon of eternity opens. It is the point where judgment becomes invitation, and fear becomes freedom. "So is he who lays up treasure for himself and is not rich toward God." With those words, Jesus leaves His hearers standing at the threshold of decision—between the comfort of full barns and the joy of empty hands.

### The Revelation in the Son

Every parable, like stained glass, is most truly seen when the light of Christ passes through it. Luke's story of the Rich Fool is not merely a moral fable about money; it is, in its deepest register, a Christological icon. It reveals by contrast who Jesus is and, by fulfillment, what He comes to bestow. The man who builds bigger barns to secure his life is the negative image; the Son who "emptied himself" (Phil 2:7) unto the Cross is the positive form, the radiant antithesis. Between the clenched fist of the fool and the open hands of the Crucified, the Gospel displays the decisive alternative that orders all existence.

Consider first the fool's interior monologue: "I will" ... "my crops" ... "my barns" ... "my grain" ... "my goods" ... "my soul." The grammar is centripetal, curving back upon the ego. His life collapses into the pronoun. He speaks to himself as if he were his own origin and end, as though his breath did not arrive moment by moment from Another. This is why the divine interruption cuts like lightning: "Fool! This night your soul is required of you." The verb suggests a loan recalled. Life is not possession; it is gift on loan from the Giver. Christ, the eternal Son, is the contrary movement: "The Son can do nothing of His own accord, but only what He sees the Father doing" (John 5:19). Where the fool encloses, the Son receives. Where the fool amasses, the Son surrenders. Where the fool speaks to himself, the Son speaks to the Father: "Into your hands I commend my spirit."

Luke situates this parable on the journey to Jerusalem, the long arc in which Jesus advances toward His Pasch. The path itself interprets the story. Every step of the Lord is an exodus from self-enclosure toward self-donation. "Foxes have holes... but the Son of Man has nowhere to lay his head" (Luke 9:58): no barns, no storehouses, because the true wealth of the Son is relation—His unbroken communion with the Father, poured out for the life of the world. The Rich Fool imagines a future secured by insulation; the Son walks into a future secured by love. On Calvary, He will be stripped of garment and reputation, bereft even of consolations, and yet in that poverty reveal a wealth that moth cannot eat and thieves cannot steal: the wealth of divine charity.

The parable's divine question, "The things you have prepared, whose

## THE RICH FOOL (LK 12:13–21)

will they be?" receives its most luminous answer at the Cross and in the Eucharist. "Whose will they be?"—they will be the Father's, because the Son, priest and victim, returns all things. In the Eucharist, the Church learns Christ's logic of wealth: take, bless, break, give. The Rich Fool's logic—take, keep, enlarge, store—cannot become sacrament; it cannot be lifted in thanksgiving because it curves toward the self. But bread placed in Christ's hands becomes an economy of superabundance. Five loaves, once blessed and broken, feed thousands; a chalice, once consecrated, contains the very self-gift of God. The barns that burst are replaced by baskets that overflow—not because of accumulation, but because of donation.

Here the Christological antithesis becomes clear. The fool says to his soul, "Relax, eat, drink, be merry." Christ says to His disciples, "Take, eat... this is my body given for you." One invites the self to feast upon stored goods; the Other makes Himself food. One seeks to ensure tomorrow by hoarding; the Other secures eternity by handing Himself over "for you and for many." The parable, read in the light of the Son, is not a scold against planning; it is a summons into the Eucharistic pattern by which the world is saved.

Luke's Gospel reinforces this vision through a gallery of figures who orbit the parable like satellites around a sun. The Rich Young Ruler goes away sad because he has great possessions—an echo of the barn-builder's sorrowful arithmetic. Zacchaeus, by contrast, receives Christ with joy and spontaneously moves from storage to gift: half to the poor, fourfold restitution to the defrauded. The widow's mite, small in quantity yet massive in quality, reveals the true currency of the Kingdom: not the amount kept but the love released. All of these scenes are Christological reflections: when the Word draws near, the gravitational field shifts. Possessions loosen their grip, hands open, praise rises—because Someone greater than barns has arrived.

To name Jesus as the fulfilment is to say more than that He exemplifies generosity. He is not simply a moral teacher urging almsgiving. Rather, He is the metaphysical heart of the parable: the Logos through whom all things were made and in whom they subsist. If the fool's error is to absolutize the finite, Jesus reveals the proper ontology of things: every good is a participation, not a god. "In Him all things hold together" (Col 1:17). Severed from Him, they disintegrate into dust or devour their possessors. Received through Him and returned in Him, they become luminous—signs that lead upward.

Therefore the Church reads this parable on the horizon of the Resurrection. Death is the test that exposes the truth of one's wealth. The fool's barns cannot cross the threshold; the Son's wounds do, shining as trophies in the new creation. In the Risen Christ, we glimpse the imperishable treasure promised to those "rich toward God": communion, not commodity; glory, not grain. He stands as the world's counter-barn—an inexhaustible store of mercy into which the poor, the anxious, and the overburdened may step and find rest.

Seen from this height, the parable also discloses the drama of freedom. God is not a rival hoarder, competing with human happiness. He is the Giver whose very being is gift—Father begetting Son in the love of the Spirit. When the Son enters history, He invites us into that trinitarian circulation: "As the Father has loved me, so have I loved you... abide in my love" (John 15:9). Abiding is the antithesis of hoarding. Hoarding isolates; abiding communicates. Hoarding cages goods; abiding transfigures them into gifts. The fool chooses isolation. Christ draws us, through His Paschal Mystery, into communion.

This is why the saints are the true exegesis of the parable. In Francis of Assisi, barns dissolve into fraternity with every creature; in Elizabeth of Hungary, dynastic wealth becomes bread for the poor; in Mother Teresa, time itself is emptied into presence with the dying. None of this is mere moral heroism. It is Christ's own life replicated in His members—an ontological shift wherein the ego, formerly the centre of gravity, is displaced by the living Christ. "It is no longer I who live, but Christ who lives in me" (Gal 2:20): that is the richest sentence ever spoken by a human being, and it is the exact inversion of the fool's monologue.

A specifically Marian note belongs here, for Mary is the first and fullest realisation of the parable's fulfillment. Confronted not with a windfall harvest but with the Word Himself, she does not build barns; she opens space: "Be it done unto me." Her womb becomes hospitality to the Infinite; her Magnificat sings the overthrow of proud self-regard and the filling of the hungry with good things. In Mary the Church learns the grammar of true wealth: receptivity that generates mission, praise that becomes justice, treasure that is always shared. If the fool says, "My goods, my soul," Mary sings, "His mercy... His servant... His promise."

The Church's sacramental life is the institutionalization of this Christological logic. Baptism breaks the dam of self-possession and grafts us onto the Son's relational life. Confirmation strengthens the outgoing current. Penance releases what we have clutched and restores us to the flow. Matrimony turns eros into gift; Orders makes a life into service; Anointing entrusts even weakness to divine purpose. And at the centre, the Eucharist—Christ present as Victim and Priest—unceasingly converts barns into altars. The disciple who brings bread and wine, the very symbols of labour and harvest, watches them become the Body and Blood. What we were tempted to store, the Lord dares us to offer—and by offering, we receive it back transfigured.

There is, finally, an eschatological sharpness to Christ's fulfillment. "This night your soul is required of you" is not divine caprice but the unveiling of proportion. A life wrapped around itself cannot stretch into the breadth of eternity; it has no room for God because it has made no room for the neighbour. Heaven is not a reward for generous bookkeeping; it is the habitat of self-giving love. Christ, risen and glorified, is that habitat made visible. To be "rich toward God" is to be conformed to Him now, so that death becomes not loss but entrance—like stepping from a dim barn into the bright feast of the Father.

What, then, does the Son finally reveal through this parable? That the decisive question is not "How much do I have?" but "To whom do I belong?" The rich man belonged to his barns; the Son belongs to the Father and, in the Father, to us. "Having loved His own who were in the world, He loved them to the end" (John 13:1): there is the opposite of the fool's soliloquy, the divine answer to the divine question, "Whose will they be?" All that

Christ has—His teaching, His power, His very life—He places into the Father's hands for our sake, and then places us, with all we are and have, back into those same hands.

The invitation, therefore, is not moralism but mysticism: to live eucharistically. Wake to the borrowed sunlight and say, "Yours." Receive the day's talents—time, strength, influence—and say, "For others." Meet the poor and say, "For Christ." Stand at the altar and say, "Take, bless, break, give." In such a life there is no need of bigger barns, because the store is inexhaustible; the Giver is present. The soul learns at last the paradox sung by the saints: what we keep we lose, what we give we possess, and what we place in the Father's hands returns a hundredfold, pressed down, shaken together, running over.

In the radiant face of the Son, the parable's warning becomes a promise. Leave the barns. Enter the banquet. Be rich toward God—and discover that His riches are Himself.

### The Word for Our Age

If Jesus were to tell the parable of the Rich Fool today, He wouldn't need to change much—only the scenery. The barns would become high-rise apartments, investment portfolios, social media accounts, or online shopping carts. The same restless pursuit of "more" would remain. Modern life, like the fool's monologue, hums with the same anxious refrain: *What shall I do to secure myself? How can I make sure I have enough?*

Our world has perfected the art of building barns. We save, store, upgrade, and insure everything—our money, our time, even our image. We track our steps, monitor our heart rate, and curate our digital selves. None of these things are evil; they can even be wise. Yet Jesus' words still pierce the modern heart because our barns keep growing and our peace keeps shrinking. Beneath all the progress and control lies the same fragility: the fear of not having enough, of not being enough.

The fool in the parable is not a monster. He's us on a good day: hardworking, prudent, organized. The tragedy is not his success but his forgetfulness. He treats blessing as possession, not participation. He forgets that everything he has—from his field to his breath—is borrowed. That's the heart of the modern problem too. We have learned to measure life by productivity, wealth, and recognition. Yet Jesus gently calls us to see that the good life is not the one filled with things, but the one filled with thanksgiving.

The spiritual poverty of our age is not material lack but the illusion of control. We think that if we just manage the variables—income, health, reputation—we can secure happiness. But life doesn't work that way. As Christ reminds us, "This night your soul is required of you." Not because God is cruel, but because everything, even life itself, is a gift we can't own. The wise disciple lives with open hands.

Being "rich toward God" means seeing every blessing as something to be received and shared, not seized and stored. It doesn't mean rejecting money or planning for the future. It means surrendering the illusion that we're the source of our own security. It means trusting that what we give will not be lost, because the Giver is faithful. Gratitude becomes the antidote to fear; generosity, the proof of faith.

Jesus invites us into this new way of living every day. When we wake, we can begin by saying, "Thank You, Lord, for another breath." When we plan our week, we can ask, "Lord, how can I use what You've given to bless someone else?" When we face anxiety about the future, we can echo His words: "Father, into Your hands I commend my spirit." In a culture that tells us to take control, Christ teaches us to release control—and find joy in doing so.

For many of us, the barns we build aren't made of wood or stone. They're built out of the need to be seen and approved. Social media has become a mirror for our souls. We store up likes, followers, and achievements like the fool's grain. We look at our digital reflection and say, "Soul, you have ample goods stored up—relax, be content." Yet the more we chase affirmation, the emptier we feel. Jesus' words confront this new idolatry just as sharply as they did in Galilee: *Life does not consist in the abundance of possessions*—or the abundance of attention.

There's a freedom that comes when we let go of trying to be our own saviour. That's what this parable offers our generation—a freedom rooted in trust. God's love does not need to be earned, and our worth does not depend on accumulation. When we finally allow that truth to sink in, we stop building barns and start building relationships. We stop storing up security and start investing in love.

This is what holiness looks like in an age of excess: living simply, giving generously, and trusting radically. It's about re-learning how to receive every moment as grace. The disciple's life becomes a rhythm of thanksgiving. Each act of generosity—every hour given to prayer, every meal shared, every quiet act of mercy—becomes a way of being rich toward God.

Jesus' warning, "This night your soul is required of you," is not meant to frighten us—it's meant to wake us up. Every day could be that night. Every breath is grace on loan. That's not morbid; it's liberating. It reminds us that the purpose of life is not to extend it indefinitely but to fill it meaningfully. The fool's barns were full, yet his heart was empty. The saint's hands may be empty, yet his heart overflows.

The Christian answer to the anxiety of our age is not detachment for its own sake, but trustful surrender—the confidence that God provides what we truly need. The saints show us that security does not come from what we hold but from Who holds us. Think of Francis of Assisi leaving behind wealth and finding joy, or Elizabeth of Hungary using her resources to feed the poor, or Josephine Bakhita who, after years of slavery, could say, "I am loved, and so I am free." Their lives are living commentaries on this parable.

The Gospel asks us to make the same shift in our own world. The businessman who measures success by service rather than profit, the mother who offers sleepless nights as prayer, the student who chooses integrity over advantage—these are the new saints of the mustard field, quietly sowing trust in a world obsessed with control. They have discovered what the fool never did: that what you give away, you keep forever.

To be rich toward God today means living *eucharistically*—seeing life itself as thanksgiving. Each breath becomes an offering, each task a chance to glorify the Giver. When we live this way, even the smallest acts carry eternal weight: a kind word to a stranger, forgiveness offered before sleep, a simple meal shared without hurry. These things are the currency of heaven. They don't appear on ledgers or screens, but they build the only treasure that lasts.

The Church, too, must live this parable in her own body. When she seeks influence or comfort instead of conversion, she risks becoming another barn—safe, stocked, but spiritually stale. The call of Christ is always outward and downward: to give, to pour, to serve. The true riches of the Church are not her buildings or institutions but her saints, her sacraments, her witness of mercy in a weary world. Every parish, every family that gives without calculation becomes a sign of the Kingdom that money can't buy.

Our modern barns are larger than ever—economies, technologies, even ideologies that promise security. Yet the soul of humanity is restless. We keep building but seldom resting, producing but seldom worshiping. Jesus' parable reminds us that all striving without surrender ends in solitude. The only antidote is to recover the posture of dependence—like a child who trusts that his father knows what he needs. That's the heart of discipleship: not ownership but relationship.

Practical steps help us live this truth. Set aside regular time for gratitude—perhaps each evening recalling three graces from the day. Practice almsgiving not as obligation but as delight, learning to love the freedom of generosity. Keep a Sabbath rhythm that says with your body what your heart believes: that you are not your own provider. And above all, cultivate awareness of God's presence in the ordinary. The simplest moments—a morning coffee, a conversation, a breath—can become altars of thanksgiving.

The parable of the Rich Fool ends abruptly, but its unfinishedness is the point. It hands the listener a mirror. Each of us must decide whether our life will be a barn or a blessing, a monologue or a dialogue with God. Jesus doesn't condemn success; He redefines it. True abundance is measured not by what we store but by what we surrender.

If you listen closely, you can still hear His question cutting through every age: *"This night your soul is required of you; and the things you have prepared—whose will they be?"* The answer is not despair but invitation. They will be God's, if we place them in His hands. They will be heaven's, if we let love use them first.

To be rich toward God is not a burden; it is freedom. It means living with the quiet joy of those who know that everything is gift. It means dying with empty hands but a full heart. It means walking through this world without fear, because we already belong to the One who cannot be lost. In the end, the only barn that endures is the heart that has become a dwelling place for Him.

## Hearing that Becomes Doing

The story is over, yet its echo remains. The field is quiet, the barns stand empty, and the question of Jesus still hovers in the air: *"This night your soul is required of you."* Do not hear those words as a threat; hear them as a truth that sets you free. Each day is that night. Each breath is that summons. What will you hold—and what will you offer?

Let the parable pass through your imagination like evening light over a field. See the man surveying his harvest, the satisfaction on his face, the sudden darkness that silences his plans. Then let the scene turn inward. You have barns too; everyone does. They may not hold grain, but they hold fears, ambitions, unfinished stories, and small illusions of control. Jesus stands before those doors, not angry but waiting. He does not shout; He knocks.

When you sense His presence, do not hide what you fear He will see. Invite Him in. Picture Him walking through the rooms of your interior life, touching the things you cling to most. He does not destroy—He blesses, He transforms. What you hand to Him is never lost; it is returned transfigured. The grain He breaks becomes bread; the treasure He empties becomes freedom. Ask quietly: *"Lord, what am I afraid to give You?"* Sit in the pause that follows. That hesitation often names the very place where grace wants to begin.

Do not rush. The Holy Spirit speaks in subtleties—through unease, through memory, through the face of someone you've avoided. Notice what stirs. The fool in the story died alone not because God abandoned him, but because he confused possession with communion. Salvation begins the moment you step out of that solitude—first toward God, then toward another person. Think of one relationship that needs reconnection, one conversation postponed too long. Begin there. Mercy is always personal before it becomes universal.

Each day offers chances to dismantle your barns one board at a time. Offer a word of gratitude instead of complaint. Give away something quietly. Write a note of encouragement; return a call you've delayed; take a slower walk and let creation praise God through your stillness. These small acts are the cracks where divine light enters. The Kingdom begins in gestures so simple that only love recognizes them.

When anxiety rises again—and it will—return to the image of Jesus lifting His eyes to the Father: *"Into Your hands I commend My spirit."* These are the richest words ever spoken by human lips, the answer to every fear of loss. Whisper them whenever control tempts you: while checking your finances, waiting for test results, standing in traffic. Let them become breath prayer—short enough for a heartbeat, deep enough for eternity. To live this way is to be rich toward God.

Prayer becomes practice when gratitude anchors it. Tonight, before sleep, name aloud three gifts from the day. Thank Him for what delighted you, and also for what stretched you. Thank Him for the interruptions that reminded you you're not the centre. Gratitude loosens the fist; it teaches the soul to live open-handed. The fool thought rest would come once his barns were full; the disciple discovers rest when his hands are empty and his heart is full of thanks.

If restlessness persists, make it physical. Light a candle and watch its steady flame; let it remind you that what burns in love is not consumed.

Or hold your palms upward in silence and simply breathe. Each exhale can become a surrender, each inhale a reception of mercy. Such small bodily prayers train the heart to trust. The Spirit sanctifies the ordinary until even breathing becomes Eucharistic.

In the morning, begin again. As soon as you wake, open your hands—literally if you can—and say, *"Everything is gift."* That single gesture reorders the day before it starts. When you plan your schedule, invite the Lord into the margins. Ask where He wants to interrupt your efficiency with love. Leave space for a person, a pause, a prayer. The barns of tomorrow are built or dismantled in these small decisions.

You might also set one tangible rhythm of generosity. Choose a percentage of income, or a slice of time each week, to give without recognition. Treat it not as obligation but as joy. The fool's tragedy was isolation; the disciple's joy is participation. To give is to discover that we are part of a larger circulation—the river of grace that flows from the Father through the Son to the world. When you step into that current, fear begins to lose its grip.

Remember too that surrender is learned through relationship. Share your spiritual discoveries with a trusted friend or confessor. Speak honestly of the barns still standing inside you. When another person listens with compassion, your hidden places meet the light. Confession, conversation, community—these are all ways the Lord helps us live what we pray. No one dismantles barns alone.

At night, return to simplicity. Let the day's noise drift away until only presence remains. Sit with Christ as you would with a friend at dusk. No eloquence is needed—only attention. The barns, the tasks, the future—they recede. What remains is His steady gaze and the quiet rhythm of His breath within yours. That is the true rest the fool never found.

Before sleep, pray:

Lord Jesus,
You who left the riches of heaven to dwell among the poor,
teach me to rest not in what I can build,
but in what You freely give.

## THE RICH FOOL (LK 12:13–21)

Empty my barns of fear,
fill them with love.
When I cling to possessions or pride,
whisper that all is Yours and all is grace.
Grant me a generous spirit,
a quiet heart,
and hands open enough to receive and to give.
May I live this day as thanksgiving
and fall asleep each night in Your care.
Amen.

Now let the night return to silence. The barns are open to the wind; the fields gleam faintly under starlight. You are safe, not because you have secured yourself, but because you are already held within the mercy of God. The fool built barns to rest; the disciple rests by giving. That is the reversal that remakes the world. Let that truth settle into your breathing. Let it carry you into sleep—unafraid, unguarded, free.

# III

# Banquets and Invitations

*"Blessed is he who shall eat bread in the Kingdom of God."*
(Luke 14:15)

# 9

# The Table of the King

Every story of salvation ends with a meal.

From Eden's garden to the marriage supper of the Lamb, the divine plan moves toward communion—the sharing of life between Creator and creature. In Scripture, food is never only nourishment; it is covenant made tangible. To eat what God provides is to consent to relationship; to refuse His meal is to decline His mercy. That is why the next group of parables gathers around a single image: the table.

If the earlier parables spoke of seed and soil—how grace begins and grows—these speak of invitation and readiness—how grace is offered and received. The field has yielded its crop; now the harvest becomes feast. The Sower has become the Host, the Word has become bread, and the question that echoes through every story is no longer *Will you hear?* but *Will you come?*

In the world Jesus knew, the banquet was the highest expression of fellowship. To eat with someone was to recognize them as kin. Table-fellowship drew the invisible lines of belonging: who was in covenant, who was not. Yet when the Word made flesh began to recline at table, He redrew every line. He ate with tax collectors and sinners, broke bread with betrayers, allowed a penitent woman to wash His feet with tears. Every meal He shared was an enacted prophecy of the Kingdom—heaven's hospitality invading earth's exclusion.

It is this shocking generosity that forms the heartbeat of the banquet parables. In them, grace takes the shape of invitation, and judgment takes the shape of refusal. The Host is always God, though He appears under many guises—a master preparing a feast, a king celebrating his son's wedding, a bridegroom delayed yet returning in joy. Those invited represent Israel, humanity, each soul in turn. The invitation is free, but never casual. To accept it requires readiness; to neglect it is to reject not only the meal but the giver Himself.

Luke places the first of these stories at a dinner table in the house of a Pharisee. Jesus has just healed a man of dropsy on the Sabbath—a foretaste of the healing He intends for the world. Around the table sit men who love precedence and protocol. They measure holiness by seating order. Into that setting He speaks of a banquet where the honored seats remain empty because the guests will not come. The outcasts, the maimed, the blind, and the poor take their places instead. The reversal is total: pride yields to hunger, status to gratitude. The Kingdom is not a meritocracy but a meal.

Matthew continues the theme with the parable of the Wedding Feast. Here the invitation carries royal weight—a king's summons to celebrate his son. Refusal becomes rebellion; indifference turns into violence. The story intensifies from neglect to outrage, from mere disinterest to murder. Yet even after judgment falls, the king's generosity persists. The servants are sent "into the highways" to gather all they find, "both good and bad." Grace never quits; the table must be filled. But another twist awaits: among the guests sits one without a wedding garment—one who accepts the invitation but refuses transformation. It is not enough to enter; one must also be clothed. Mercy received must become mercy worn.

Finally comes the midnight scene of the Ten Virgins. The imagery shifts from banquet hall to threshold, from host to bridegroom. Ten lamps flicker in the dark; ten hearts wait for the sound of arrival. All are invited; only some are ready. The foolish carry no oil, presuming on time they do not control. The wise keep watch, their flame fed by faith and perseverance. The door that finally opens and closes is not arbitrary punishment—it is the manifestation of choice. Those who have kept their lamps burning enter the joy prepared for them; those who let light die find only the silence of their own delay.

Across these three parables runs a single thread: divine hospitality and human readiness. God never ceases to invite; man never ceases to hesitate. The tension between generosity and response defines the drama of salvation. The table is set, the feast is prepared, but each heart must decide whether to sit or to stand outside.

These stories unfold not as sentimental metaphors but as the very logic of covenant. From Abraham's tent where three visitors dined, to Sinai's banquet where elders ate and drank before God, to the Eucharistic table where Christ gives His body as bread, every divine promise culminates in shared food. To "eat bread in the Kingdom" is to live in reconciled communion. Refusal, therefore, is not impoliteness; it is apostasy.

Yet the tone of these parables is not despair but *hope that burns*. The Host never ceases to call. He sends servants again and again, widening the guest list until the highways and hedges resound with invitation. In the logic of mercy, every refusal becomes occasion for a new outreach. The joy of the King is not in exclusivity but fullness—"that my house may be filled."

Still, the stories end with urgency. Each carries an unspoken refrain: *Come while the door is open.* The guest without the garment, the foolish virgins shut outside, the complacent who promise to attend "tomorrow"—all reveal the same peril: grace delayed becomes grace declined. The door of the Kingdom is wide but not weightless; it turns on the hinge of readiness.

This section of *Hidden Fire* will trace that hinge in three movements.

- In **The Great Banquet (Luke 14:15–24)**, we watch divine hospitality overturn human hierarchy—how the lowly and forgotten become honored guests while the self-satisfied stay hungry.
- In **The Wedding Feast and the Proper Garment (Matthew 22:1–14)**, we enter the royal feast where inclusion without conversion becomes its own condemnation.

- In **The Ten Virgins (Matthew 25:1–13)**, we stand at the doorway between time and eternity, where vigilance becomes the measure of love.

Each narrative begins with invitation and ends with revelation: the state of the heart exposed by the way it responds. Each reveals that grace is not a static gift but a summons into communion.

To read these parables, then, is to stand again before the Eucharistic mystery. Christ is both Host and Food, both Bridegroom and Feast. He invites not merely to a table but to His own life. The garments of readiness are baptismal; the oil in the lamps is the flame of charity. The stories are not about manners but about the Mass—the wedding supper that begins in this world and is perfected in the next.

As we move from field to table, from sowing to celebrating, the divine pedagogy comes full circle. What was planted in the soil of parable now ripens into sacrament. The Word once scattered as seed now becomes bread broken and shared. The Kingdom no longer hides in furrows; it gleams on the chalice's rim.

To approach these next chapters, imagine the sound of invitation still echoing through time: *Come, for all is now ready.* The same voice that spoke over Galilee speaks still in every Eucharist, every act of mercy, every whisper of conscience that calls the soul home. The question is no longer whether God will feed us, but whether we will come hungry enough to eat.

So take your place at the beginning of Part III. The lamps are trimmed; the table is being laid. The Master's servants have gone out into the streets, calling every name, yours among them. What remains is to rise, to wash, to put on the garment of joy, and to step through the open door before the night grows quiet.

The Kingdom is not distant.

It is the invitation in your hand.

It is the light spilling from a door still unclosed.

It is the meal waiting on the other side of obedience.

# 10

# The Great Banquet (Lk 14:15–24)

*When one of those reclining at table with Him heard this, he said, "Blessed is he who shall eat bread in the kingdom of God." Jesus replied, "A man once gave a great banquet and invited many. When the time came for the banquet, he sent his servant to say to those who had been invited, 'Come, for everything is now ready.' But they all alike began to make excuses.*

*The first said, 'I have bought a field, and I must go and see it; please have me excused.' Another said, 'I have bought five yoke of oxen, and I am going to examine them; please have me excused.'*

*Another said, 'I have married a wife, and therefore I cannot come.' So the servant returned and reported this to his master.*

*Then the master of the house became angry and said to his servant, 'Go out quickly into the streets and lanes of the city, and bring in the poor and the maimed and the blind and the lame.'*

*The servant said, 'Sir, what you commanded has been done, and still there is room.' The master replied, 'Go out to the highways and hedges and compel people to come in, that my house may be filled.*

*For I tell you, none of those men who were invited shall taste my banquet.'"*

### The Word Spoken

It is the Sabbath. Late afternoon light slants through the lattice of a

Pharisee's house somewhere in the upper quarter of Jerusalem. The seventh-day meal has begun, the most honoured meal of the week. Everything smells of order and preparation—bread baked before sunset, herbs crushed, lamb seasoned early so that no labour breaks the law. Servants move quietly; their steps are rehearsed, each motion careful not to draw attention. The water jars stand near the doorway; the couches curve around a low table polished smooth by generations of feasts.

Jesus is there because He has been invited. That fact alone has everyone on edge. It is not an ordinary invitation but a test wrapped in courtesy. Earlier that day, they had watched Him heal a man swollen with dropsy. He had done it deliberately, in their sight, on the Sabbath, and then silenced their objections with a question that none dared answer: *"Which of you, having a son or an ox that has fallen into a well, will not immediately pull him out on the Sabbath day?"* The silence that followed still lingers now.

Around the table recline the invited men—Pharisees, scribes, one or two elders of the synagogue, and the host himself, a ruler among them. Their robes are clean, their fringes long, their greetings precise. The atmosphere is heavy with manners. Every guest knows where he sits in relation to the others. The couches form a hierarchy in crescent shape, the host at the centre, the most honoured on his right and left, the lesser guests tapering outward. Earlier there had been an unspoken rush for the best positions. Jesus had watched, saying nothing until they settled; then He had spoken a parable about choosing the lowest seat so that one might be raised higher. The words had cut through the quiet like a knife, yet He had said them with such ease that even offense sounded like invitation.

Now the meal continues. Dishes of lentils, dates, and figs have replaced the first course. The wine is sweet and diluted with water, as law requires. The guests keep their tone light, but the room carries the feel of scrutiny. They study Him in half-glances. Everything He does seems to reveal something about them.

Outside, voices drift from the street—children playing, merchants calling the last sales before nightfall. Inside, time slows. It is the Sabbath rest, but no one seems rested. They speak of Torah, of the prophets, of the

## THE GREAT BANQUET (LK 14:15–24)

resurrection of the righteous. The host, eager to keep dignity, remarks that generosity to the poor is a virtue rewarded by God. Jesus answers with another parable—about a man who invited the poor and lame to his feast rather than friends who could repay him. The idea unsettles the table. Such giving without return runs against everything social life depends on.

A pause follows. Cups are refilled. The smell of spiced wine mingles with unease. Then, from halfway down the couch line, a man clears his throat and tries to recover the mood. He lifts his cup, smiling toward Jesus with a blend of admiration and distance.

"Blessed is he who shall eat bread in the kingdom of God!"

The words land like incense—pleasant, safe, orthodox. Heads nod automatically. It is a respectable saying, something every Jew at that table believes: when the Messiah comes, there will be a feast, a table spread in Zion for the righteous. It is the kind of line that ends discussion neatly, returning things to piety. But the way the man says it carries assumption—*we* will be there, of course; *we* will eat that bread.

Jesus looks at him. He does not answer right away. His gaze moves around the table, over the silks, the jewels, the careful gestures of men who have spent a lifetime mastering holiness. He sees the host, proud but nervous; the scholars, confident in their citations; the servant waiting at the door with downcast eyes. He sees the empty place reserved for the late-arriving guest of honour. And He sees, beyond the wall, the narrow streets where beggars wait for what is left when the pious are finished.

The silence deepens. One of the younger scribes shifts uncomfortably. Another coughs to cover the tension. Jesus draws a slow breath and begins to speak.

"A certain man," He says, "gave a great banquet and invited many."

The phrase falls into the room with quiet weight. Everyone knows the rhythm—*a certain man* is how the rabbis begin stories that hide truth in plain sight. The listeners lean slightly forward. They expect instruction about hospitality or wisdom in planning. But His tone is different: not clever, not rhetorical—gentle, deliberate, as if the story were already happening before their eyes.

"When the time for the banquet came," He continues, "he sent his servant to say to those who had been invited, 'Come, for everything is now ready.'"

The guests imagine the scene easily; they have all given such feasts themselves. Invitations in their world come twice: first to announce the day, then again when the food is prepared. To refuse the second call is public insult. No excuse can soften it. Everyone knows that.

Jesus' eyes remain on the man who spoke the blessing. "But they all alike began to make excuses," He says. "The first said, 'I have bought a field, and I must go and see it; I pray you, have me excused.' Another said, 'I have bought five yoke of oxen, and I go to examine them.' Another said, 'I have married a wife, and therefore I cannot come.'"

A ripple of discomfort passes around the room. The examples sound almost comic in their impossibility—who inspects land after buying it, or oxen after payment? Yet everyone feels the sting. The politeness of refusal is their own language.

"The servant came," Jesus goes on, "and reported this to his master. Then the master of the house became angry and said to his servant, 'Go out quickly into the streets and lanes of the city, and bring in the poor and maimed and blind and lame.'"

Now the listeners stiffen. The poor and the lame do not recline with the learned. To invite them to a feast would overturn every social order. But Jesus speaks as if it were obvious, inevitable.

"And the servant said, 'Sir, what you commanded has been done, and still there is room.' And the master said to the servant, 'Go out to the highways and hedges and compel people to come in, that my house may be filled.'"

His voice remains calm, but there is urgency beneath it—the urgency of a heart that cannot bear an empty table. The Pharisees recognize the imagery: Isaiah had promised a banquet for all peoples on the mountain of the Lord. Yet the picture forming in their minds is not the mountain but the crossroads, not the pure but the unclean.

Jesus pauses. No one moves. Then He says the final line: "For I tell you, none of those men who were invited shall taste my banquet."

The sentence falls heavy, like a door closing. A murmur begins at the far end of the couches and dies quickly. The man who had spoken the blessing looks away. The host forces a thin smile and gestures for fruit to be brought, as though the conversation has ended. But the silence holds. It has the weight of judgment, though Jesus' eyes show only sadness.

The servants clear the table. The lamps sputter; oil pools at their base. Outside, the Sabbath dusk deepens to night. Somewhere in the distance a ram's horn sounds—the signal that the day of rest has ended. The guests rise slowly, adjusting their robes, speaking again of neutral things. Yet every man leaves with the echo of that sentence inside him.

None of those men who were invited shall taste my banquet.

They will remember it later, when they hear Him speak of bread broken and wine poured out. They will remember it when He dines with tax collectors and sinners, when the outcasts come running while the righteous hesitate. But for now, the meaning stays lodged in the silence.

Jesus steps into the cool air outside. The street smells of dust and oil lamps and distant baking. A few beggars linger near the doorway; He nods to them as He passes. Behind Him, the house hums again with conversation—anxious, respectable, unchanged. The feast they imagined for the righteous has already begun elsewhere. Somewhere in the darkness, hearts they have never noticed are being drawn to the table of God.

### The Surface Story

When Jesus began this parable, His listeners recognised the world He described. A banquet was the highest expression of honour in first-century Judea. Invitations marked one's standing; acceptance reaffirmed friendship and status; refusal was more than rudeness—it was rupture. To be welcomed to a table was to belong.

Meals in that world were covenantal symbols. From Abraham's hospitality beneath the terebinths to the Passover of Moses, shared food sealed peace. To recline with a man was to share his blessing. Every village, from Jerusalem's quarters to the hamlets of Galilee, echoed that conviction: table fellowship meant communion.

So when Jesus said, "A man gave a great banquet and invited many," His audience imagined a patriarch of means—an elder whose generosity sustained a household and whose honour rested on reciprocity. A feast of that scale required weeks of preparation. Animals were slaughtered, wine measured, bread kneaded in quantity, musicians hired. Invitations went out in two stages. The first was a pledge of intent: guests signified their agreement to attend. The second, delivered by servants once everything was ready, was not a request but a reminder—an announcement that the hour had come.

No guest of standing would decline that second call. To do so after having already consented was a grave public insult. It implied contempt for the host's generosity and questioned his dignity before the community. Such an act could end alliances, rupture marriages, even cause lawsuits. In a culture ordered by honour and reciprocity, the double invitation was sacred social glue.

That is what makes the refusals in Jesus' story immediately scandalous. His hearers would have felt the shock before He explained a word. One says he has bought a field and must inspect it. Another claims to have purchased oxen and needs to test them. A third appeals to marriage. Each excuse sounds plausible in isolation, yet all are transparent evasions. No one in that society buys land without prior inspection, or oxen without trial. Marriage is celebrated publicly and rarely coincides with great feasts hosted by others. Beneath the politeness lies rejection.

To refuse a man's feast was to declare independence from him. The audience at that Pharisee's table knew what such rejection meant: the host loses face, the social order trembles. Yet Jesus gives the master in His parable an unexpected dignity. The man does not retaliate; he widens his generosity. His honour, rather than shrinking, expands into mercy.

"Go quickly into the streets and lanes of the city," he commands, "and bring in the poor and the maimed and the blind and the lame."

That list would have startled His hearers. These were the categories of exclusion. In the ritual purity codes of Leviticus and in the social practice of the time, those with visible infirmities or poverty were often kept apart from formal banquets and from Temple participation. Physical defect symbolised impurity; economic want implied divine disfavour. To fill one's dining couches with such guests was to turn the ladder of honour upside down.

Listeners would have pictured the servant moving from marble courtyard to back alley: from those who feast to those who beg. It was a reversal almost comic in its impossibility. No nobleman in Judea would stake his reputation on the company of beggars. A feast was meant to confirm boundaries, not erase them. The host's decision in Jesus' story defied the very function of a banquet.

Still the parable moves further. Even after the poor and lame are brought in, the servant reports that "there is still room." The master's answer—"Go out to the highways and hedges and compel them to come in"—pushes the image beyond the city's limits. The roads and hedgerows lay outside the walls, in the realm of travellers, shepherds, and foreigners. The hearers would have understood: these are outsiders altogether, people without citizenship in the town, strangers to its feasts. To invite them is to dissolve the distinction between insider and alien.

The verb "compel" would not have sounded sinister to them. It meant to urge earnestly, to persuade those who feel unworthy to accept a gift they cannot repay. The host's generosity has reached absurd proportion; he will rather risk ridicule than see his hall half-empty.

All of this, at the surface level, is social realism. The story follows the logic of ancient hospitality until it breaks it open. The first listeners, reclining with Jesus at a Sabbath meal, would have sensed both the familiarity and the threat. He was describing their world with such precision that it became mirror and critique at once.

Banquets like the one Jesus depicts were central to public life. Roman officials hosted them to secure loyalty; local elders used them to reinforce rank. Seating arrangements were statements of hierarchy—the most honoured nearest the host, the least at the edges. Luke has already shown Jesus noticing how guests chose places of prestige. Now He deepens the lesson: honour itself can become a form of blindness. The story of the

Great Banquet exposes the fragility of a system built on invitation and repayment.

To the Pharisees, the details would have carried theological weight as well. Scripture often pictured the kingdom of God as a meal: Isaiah spoke of a feast of rich food for all peoples; the psalmist sang of a table prepared by the Lord. Every Sabbath meal was a small rehearsal of that promise. To share bread in righteousness was to taste, in advance, the age to come. When the man at the table said, "Blessed is he who shall eat bread in the kingdom of God," he was repeating a hope woven into Israel's prayers.

Yet Jesus' parable unsettles that expectation at its root. The ones who presume to belong decline the summons; the ones who could never imagine inclusion find themselves inside. The narrative itself, without interpretation, carries the sting. No moral need be added. The reversal is enough.

Those listening that day would have shifted uneasily. The host in the story behaves not as a prudent patriarch but as someone possessed by reckless generosity. His decisions violate custom after custom. In their world, such behaviour could only invite mockery or ruin. To invite the ritually unfit into a nobleman's hall was to contaminate the meal. To go out to the highways was to court scandal. Yet in Jesus' telling the host seems unconcerned with propriety. What matters is fullness—the house overflowing with guests, the food consumed, the invitation answered.

At the literal level, then, the parable dramatizes two truths of their culture: first, that refusal of hospitality is a mortal insult; second, that hospitality itself is the measure of greatness. The master's greatness is not diminished by rejection; it is revealed in how far he will extend welcome.

Every villager and scholar at that Sabbath table knew the cost of maintaining purity. They had built boundaries around their meals, their homes, their worship, believing such fences protected holiness. Jesus describes a host who tears down the fences rather than endure an empty hall. Even before theological meaning enters, the story is revolutionary in its realism.

The final sentence—"None of those men who were invited shall taste my banquet"—would have rung as a verdict of social consequence. To spurn a feast was to forfeit friendship. No second invitation would come. The insult cuts both ways: the proud lose honour, and the humble inherit it. Within the plain realism of the narrative, justice has been done.

Nothing here requires allegory to startle. On its surface, the parable is a study in the customs of invitation and response, a miniature of Israel's daily life. Yet those customs themselves already hold tension between law and mercy, purity and compassion. Jesus exploits that tension without explaining it. The men listening could recognise every gesture of the story; they could find no error in its details. That is why it disarmed them. The world it portrays is their own, yet its conclusion defies their logic.

They would have left the meal that day thinking of the insult of refusal, the shame of an empty banquet hall, the audacity of a host who turns disgrace into open-handed grace. The parable's surface required no interpretation: it was a portrait of their society drawn so truthfully that it began to expose them.

**The Hidden Fire**

### a) Text, Translation, and Literary Context
### Greek Text (Luke 14 : 15 – 24):

Ἀκούσας δέ τις τῶν συνανακειμένων ταῦτα εἶπεν αὐτῷ· Μακάριος ὅστις φάγεται ἄρτον ἐν τῇ βασιλείᾳ τοῦ θεοῦ.

ὁ δὲ εἶπεν αὐτῷ· Ἄνθρωπός τις ἐποίησεν δεῖπνον μέγα καὶ ἐκάλεσεν πολλούς, καὶ ἀπέστειλεν τὸν δοῦλον αὐτοῦ τῇ ὥρᾳ τοῦ δείπνου εἰπεῖν τοῖς κεκλημένοις· Ἔρχεσθε, ὅτι ἤδη ἕτοιμά ἐστιν.

καὶ ἤρξαντο ἀπὸ μιᾶς πάντες παραιτεῖσθαι. ὁ πρῶτος εἶπεν αὐτῷ· Ἀγρὸν ἠγόρασα καὶ ἔχω ἀνάγκην ἐξελθεῖν καὶ ἰδεῖν αὐτόν· ἐρωτῶ σε, ἔχε με παρῃτημένον.

καὶ ἕτερος εἶπεν· Ζεύγη βοῶν ἠγόρασα πέντε καὶ πορεύομαι δοκιμάσαι αὐτά· ἐρωτῶ σε, ἔχε με παρῃτημένον.

καὶ ἕτερος εἶπεν· Γυναῖκα ἔγημα, καὶ διὰ τοῦτο οὐ δύναμαι ἐλθεῖν.

καὶ παραγενόμενος ὁ δοῦλος ἀπήγγειλεν τῷ κυρίῳ αὐτοῦ ταῦτα. Τότε ὀργισθεὶς ὁ οἰκοδεσπότης εἶπεν τῷ δούλῳ αὐτοῦ· Ἔξελθε ταχέως εἰς τὰς πλατείας καὶ ῥύμας τῆς πόλεως, καὶ τοὺς πτωχοὺς καὶ ἀναπήρους καὶ τυφλοὺς καὶ χωλοὺς εἰσάγαγε ὧδε.

καὶ εἶπεν ὁ δοῦλος· Κύριε, γέγονεν ὃ ἐπέταξας, καὶ ἔτι τόπος ἐστίν.

καὶ εἶπεν ὁ κύριος πρὸς τὸν δοῦλον· Ἔξελθε εἰς τὰς ὁδοὺς καὶ φραγμοὺς καὶ ἀνάγκασον εἰσελθεῖν, ἵνα γεμισθῇ μου ὁ οἶκος· λέγω γὰρ ὑμῖν ὅτι οὐδεὶς τῶν ἀνδρῶν ἐκείνων τῶν κεκλημένων γεύσεταί μου τοῦ δείπνου.

Luke's narrative opens in courtesy and closes in confrontation. The language begins with a compliment—"Blessed is he who shall eat bread in the kingdom of God"—and ends with a sentence of exclusion—"None of those who were invited shall taste my banquet." Between those lines the vocabulary shifts from human politeness to divine speech. The syntax of social convention becomes the grammar of judgment.

The parable's first sentence, "A certain man made a great dinner and invited many," uses the ordinary diction of hospitality, yet each term carries deeper resonance. The verb *made* (ἐποίησεν) is the same used in Genesis and Exodus for God's creative acts. Luke's choice hints that the host's preparation mirrors the divine act of ordering creation toward communion. The noun *dinner* (δεῖπνον) names not the casual midday meal but the principal evening feast. In biblical idiom it evokes culmination—the point at which work ceases and fellowship begins. The addition of *great* (μέγα) intensifies the image: abundance bordering on excess. Luke thereby sets the scale from the start—the story concerns not a man's table but the generosity of God Himself.

The key verb *invited* (ἐκάλεσεν) frames the entire narrative. The Greek root καλέω, "to call," underlies Israel's entire covenant history. God "called" Abraham from Ur, "called" Israel out of Egypt, "called" the prophets to speak His word. Every call created relationship. Luke repeats the root six times in this short passage—those invited (κεκλημένοι), those later rejected, those newly summoned. The word's liturgical echo is unmistakable: *ecclesia*, the Church, literally means "the called." Before any refusal is uttered, the grammar already locates the parable in the sphere of election.

## THE GREAT BANQUET (LK 14:15-24)

The second movement introduces the servant and the second summons: "He sent his servant at the hour of the dinner to say to those who had been invited, 'Come, for everything is now ready.'" The combination of *sent* and *say* compresses the pattern of biblical revelation—God sending messengers to announce fulfillment. The temporal phrase "at the hour of the dinner" transforms ordinary time into kairos, the decisive moment. The declaration "all is ready" mirrors the liturgical formula of sacrifice: what was prepared in promise now stands complete in offering. In this small sentence the evangelist condenses salvation history—promise, sending, invitation, fulfillment.

Then comes the disruption. "They all alike began to make excuses." Luke's phrase *from the first, all began* (ἀπὸ μιᾶς πάντες ἤρξαντο) fuses individual refusals into collective rebellion. The participle ἤρξαντο ("they began") gives the action a ritual rhythm, as though rejection itself were liturgy. The verb *make excuses* (παραιτεῖσθαι) literally means "to refuse by pretext." In classical Greek it described a lawyer declining a case or a petitioner declining a gift; in Luke's world it implies evasion disguised as respect. The tone is the same civility with which the Pharisees mask hostility toward Jesus. Syntax and psychology align: politeness becomes resistance.

Each excuse is formulaic but revealing. The first says, "I have bought a field and must go to see it." The juxtaposition of *bought* and *must* captures self-imposed necessity—the bondage of possession. The Greek ἀγρός, "field," recalls the land promised to Abraham, the inheritance of Israel. By using that word, Luke frames the man's preoccupation as theological irony: he abandons the feast of covenant to inspect its symbol. The second guest claims to have purchased "five yoke of oxen" to test them. The number five evokes the Torah, the five books of Moses; what he treats as property once represented divine guidance. The third says simply, "I have married a wife, and therefore I cannot come." Marriage, a covenant of joy, becomes here an excuse for absence. Luke's arrangement moves from possession to power to pleasure—three faces of the same refusal. Each is rational, each courteous, and each denies communion.

The servant returns, and the narrative pivot occurs: "Then the master of the house, being angry, said to his servant..." The phrase *master of the house* (οἰκοδεσπότης) carries Old Testament overtones of divine lordship; God is often portrayed as head of His household Israel. His "anger" (ὀργή) does not imply volatility but the moral energy of love rejected. What follows is not revenge but redirection. "Go out quickly into the streets and lanes of the city and bring in the poor, the crippled, the blind, and the lame." The command inverts the order of social respectability. The verbs *go out* and *bring in* form a chiasm of mission: the host's mercy now extends outward precisely where human fellowship withdraws.

Luke's choice of epithets—poor, crippled, blind, lame—repeats the earlier teaching in this same chapter (14:13) where Jesus told the Pharisee to invite those very groups. The repetition unites narrative and discourse: what was moral counsel becomes divine action. Each term recalls exclusion under Levitical law. Those with defects could not offer sacrifice or approach the altar; now they become the honoured guests. Grammar itself becomes theology: the rejected objects of purity legislation become subjects of divine sentence.

The servant obeys. His report—"Lord, what you commanded has been done, and still there is room"—introduces the language of fulfillment. The perfect tense *has been done* (γέγονεν) suggests completion, yet the following clause—*and still there is room*—adds eschatological surplus. Divine generosity, unlike human honour, cannot be exhausted. In a single verse, Luke turns household management into revelation: obedience accomplishes command but discovers abundance beyond command.

The master's next order expands the geography again: "Go out into the roads and hedges, and compel them to come in, that my house may be filled." The nouns *roads* (ὁδοί) and *hedges* (φραγμοί) mark the boundaries of settled life—the margins where travellers, strangers, and beggars linger. The imperative *compel* (ἀνάγκασον) has been misread across history; in Luke's idiom it means not coercion but urgent persuasion, the holy insistence of hospitality. The purpose clause "that my house may be filled" reveals the heart of the story. The host's aim is not retribution but fullness.

His house is an image of divine will—the desire that none should be lost, that every place at the table be taken. The syntax of command is the language of mercy.

The final declaration closes the circle: "For I tell you, none of those who were invited shall taste my dinner." The conjunction *for* (γάρ) links the verdict to the mission; exclusion and inclusion stand in causal relation. The verb *taste* (γεύσεται) appears elsewhere in Scripture for experiential knowledge—"taste and see that the Lord is good." To "taste" the dinner, then, is to participate in divine life; to lose that taste is to lose communion. The possessive pronoun "my" recurs three times in the final clause—*my banquet, my house, my servant*—each repetition underlining ownership not of property but of grace. The tragedy is not that the unworthy entered but that the invited refused what was theirs.

Stylistically, Luke moves from descriptive narration to oracular tone. The parable begins with the rhythm of storytelling—verbs in the aorist, concrete actions, social realism—and ends with the solemn present of divine speech: "I tell you, none shall taste." The shift from past to present turns narrative into warning. Time itself narrows. What happened in story now stands before the hearer. The grammar transforms polite dinner conversation into eschatological address.

Within the larger Gospel, the passage sits at the heart of Luke's theology of table fellowship. Meals are the theatre of revelation: Levi's banquet of repentance (5:29), Simon's dinner of forgiveness (7:36), Martha and Mary's meal of contemplation (10:38), Zacchaeus's feast of salvation (19:6). Each episode enacts a dimension of the kingdom. The Great Banquet gathers them all into one scene. Here the table becomes not metaphor but mission—the sign of God's relentless pursuit of communion. The setting within the "travel narrative" (9:51–19:27) intensifies this meaning. Jesus is moving toward Jerusalem, where He will preside at another supper and pour Himself out as host and meal. The literary placement is deliberate: before the Last Supper comes this story of invitations declined and others extended. The syntax of the parable anticipates the words of institution. What the master says—"all is ready"—Jesus will say again over bread and wine.

Luke's arrangement of clauses mirrors this theology. Each section begins with human initiative and ends with divine reversal. The pattern—invitation, excuse, command, fulfillment—becomes a linguistic map of salvation history: call of Israel, rejection of prophets, mission to the poor, gathering of the nations. The verbs of sending (ἀπέστειλεν), bringing (εἰσάγαγε), and compelling (ἀνάγκασον) form a triple progression from inner city to outer world. Language and geography expand together. By the final verse, the narrative has moved from the dining room of a Pharisee to the highways of the world. The grammar has become catholic—universal in scope.

Luke's artistry lies in balance. His sentences hold the tension between divine sovereignty and human freedom. Every "invitation" implies response; every refusal provokes wider mercy. Even the anger of the host propels salvation outward. The text's structure thus performs what it proclaims: rejection becomes mission, failure becomes fruitfulness. The words themselves enact redemption.

By the close of the passage, the tone that began as table conversation has become prophetic decree. The voice that once told a story now addresses the listener directly. Luke's diction, precise and economical, has traced the transformation of grace from offer to outcome. Within the music of his syntax we hear the drama of salvation—God calling, man refusing, God calling again with even wider arms. The story's movement from invitation to inclusion is not only narrative but grammatical; the verbs themselves widen like the master's heart.

Read closely, Luke's prose already contains the theology that will follow. The progression from sending to summoning, from guests to outcasts, reveals the logic of divine mercy: grace that refuses to die when rejected. Even within the structure of the sentences, there is room—room for response, room for repentance, room for joy. The parable's words end, but its grammar remains open. The last verb is not refusal but fullness: "that my house may be filled." Luke leaves the reader standing before that house, hearing the echo of the servant's cry: *Come, for everything is now ready.*

## b) Theological Interpretation

The parable of the Great Banquet unfolds as one of the most theologically charged moments in Luke's Gospel, a living parable of the Kingdom's inner logic: grace offered, grace refused, grace extended until it fills the world. Beneath its social realism—a dinner party, invitations, excuses—lies a portrait of the divine economy itself. The God of Israel, who prepared His covenant people as the chosen guests, now opens His house to the unworthy and forgotten. Jesus tells this story not as moral instruction but as revelation. The host in the parable is not merely generous; he acts with a kind of holy insistence that mirrors the restlessness of divine mercy. The feast must be filled because the Father's joy is incomplete until it is shared.

Luke situates the parable at a Sabbath meal in the house of a leading Pharisee, amid discussions about humility and hospitality. The context matters deeply. The Sabbath meal was the microcosm of Israel's covenant life—the place where holiness met bread and wine, where blessing was recited, and where identity as God's people was renewed. To break bread at a Pharisee's table was to sit at the symbolic centre of Israel's religious order. When one of the guests exclaims, "Blessed is he who shall eat bread in the kingdom of God," his words are not irony; they are expectation. He echoes Isaiah's vision of the messianic banquet on the mountain of the Lord, when God would "swallow up death forever" and "prepare for all peoples a feast of rich food and well-aged wine" (Is 25:6–8). To that man's pious remark, Jesus replies with a story that will upend everything his audience assumes about who will actually sit at that table.

The host of the parable represents the divine initiative that has always driven salvation history. "A man once gave a great banquet and invited many." The covenant with Abraham, the Exodus, the Law, the Prophets— all were invitations leading toward this moment. God has been preparing the feast for centuries; Israel has been rehearsing its blessing in every Passover and every Sabbath meal. The phrase "when the time came for the banquet" signals the arrival of the kairos, the appointed hour in which all divine preparation converges. The servant's announcement—"Come, for all is now ready"—is the Gospel itself in miniature. It is not advice or information but proclamation: the work is finished, the table is set, the Kingdom is present. Nothing remains but response.

The first invited guests represent those who were closest to that covenant promise: the religious elite of Israel, the very audience around Jesus' table. Yet when the call arrives, they decline with polite indifference. The tragedy of the parable is not overt rebellion but domesticated refusal. The first man cites property, the second profession, the third family—each a good thing in itself. The excuses are respectable, reasonable, and deadly. They reveal how idolatry often enters through good gifts misplaced. The first guest's field represents possession—the attempt to find permanence through ownership. The second guest's oxen represent productivity—the need to test, manage, and measure one's worth. The third guest's marriage represents intimacy—the desire to secure love on one's own terms. Each chooses creation over Creator, stewardship without thanksgiving. The covenantal order—gift returning to Giver—is inverted.

Jesus' listeners would have recognised the echo of Deuteronomy's warnings: "Take care lest you forget the Lord your God… when your herds multiply and your silver and gold increase" (Deut 8:11–13). Forgetfulness, not hatred, is the seed of apostasy. The guests' refusals are the refined form of unbelief, the respectable atheism of people too occupied with blessings to attend the Blesser. The first-century Jew knew that meals were sacred acts; to decline such an invitation was more than rudeness—it was covenantal breach. In refusing to come, they reject not a party but communion itself.

The host's anger is therefore not caprice but covenantal grief. Divine wrath in Scripture is the form love takes when refused. It is the sorrow of abundance unshared, generosity turned into judgment by human resistance. "The master of the house became angry and said to his servant, 'Go quickly into the streets and lanes of the city.'" The "quickly" signals the urgency of divine mercy. The feast will not be postponed. God's plan does not collapse because of human rejection; it expands. The failure of the

## THE GREAT BANQUET (LK 14:15-24)

first invitees becomes the door through which the excluded enter. This is the paradox at the heart of salvation history: Israel's no becomes the world's yes.

The list of new guests—the poor, the crippled, the blind, and the lame—reaches back to Isaiah 61 and the Jubilee imagery that frames Jesus' entire ministry: "The Spirit of the Lord is upon me... he has sent me to proclaim good news to the poor." These are the very ones barred from temple worship in Leviticus, the ritually unfit, the social untouchables. In bringing them to his table, the host inverts Israel's purity code. What religion excluded, grace embraces. The Kingdom is revealed as reversal, not of morality but of status. The poor do not enter because they are innocent, but because they are empty-handed enough to receive. The feast becomes the visible expression of the Beatitudes: "Blessed are you who hunger now, for you shall be satisfied."

The theology of reversal, however, is not mere social critique; it is sacramental. To be brought to the table is to share in divine life. Eating, in biblical language, always implies covenant participation. In Exodus 24, the elders of Israel "beheld God, and ate and drank." At Sinai, a meal sealed the covenant in blood. In Deuteronomy 27, blessings and curses were ratified by shared sacrifice. Every ancient covenant ended at table. The host of the parable therefore acts as God once did with Moses: he calls His people to communion. Refusal is apostasy, acceptance is worship. The table is the new Sinai; bread and wine have become the place where God meets His people.

Luke's narrative structure mirrors that theology. The parable's expansion—from the city's lanes to the highways beyond—replays salvation history in miniature. First Israel, then the poor within Israel, then the Gentiles. Each wave of invitation widens the circle of covenant blessing. When the servant reports, "There is still room," he voices the eschatological truth that the divine hospitality can never be exhausted. God's desire exceeds human sin; His house is larger than our refusals. The command to "compel them to come in" has often been abused, but in Luke's Greek the verb anankasō carries the sense of urging or pressing by persuasion, not force. Grace insists, it does not coerce. The only pressure the servants apply is the pressure of love on wounded hearts.

Patristic commentators read this as the mystery of evangelization. Augustine saw in the servants' persistence the zeal of the apostles crossing frontiers; Gregory the Great saw in the poor and maimed the spiritual ailments healed by the Gospel. Both understood the parable as prophecy of the Church's mission. The host's house is the Church herself—one table, many guests. Her vocation is not to curate an elite dining room but to fill heaven with the undeserving. She goes into the highways of history not because she is superior but because she carries bread that is not hers.

The Eucharistic dimension of the story thus stands inescapable. "Everything is now ready" is the hidden announcement of the Last Supper. The same voice that sends the servant now speaks through the priest: "Blessed are those called to the supper of the Lamb." What Isaiah foresaw and Jesus prefigured, the liturgy enacts. The Mass is the great banquet made present in sacramental form—the divine meal at which the poor, the repentant, the hungry of every age are fed by the flesh of the Host Himself. In that light, every refusal to come to the Eucharist, whether through indifference or mortal sin, repeats the parable's sadness. Each "I cannot come" echoes across centuries of altars, the polite tragedy of souls too busy to eat.

The Church Fathers dwelt on this point with both tenderness and terror. St. John Chrysostom warned his hearers that to neglect the Eucharist was to imitate the first invitees: "They excused themselves with fields and oxen; you excuse yourself with business or sleep." St. Basil saw in the poor guests the very body of Christ: "When you feed the hungry, you serve the Master at His own table." For the Fathers, the banquet was never metaphorical; it was the concrete reality of the Church's worship and charity. To eat Christ's body without feeding Christ's poor was to betray the feast's meaning.

Yet the parable's theology stretches beyond ecclesial life into the very structure of creation. All of reality is, in a sense, a banquet—an act of divine self-giving that calls for participation. The cosmos exists as the overflow of Trinitarian love, a table spread by the Father through the Son in the Spirit. Every created good is a dish offered to be blessed, broken, and shared. Sin disfigures this order by turning participation into possession. The field, the oxen, and the wife are not evil; they are misused when torn from the rhythm of thanksgiving. The Kingdom restores that rhythm. In Christ, creation becomes Eucharistic again—the world offered back to God as praise.

The parable's conclusion—"None of those who were invited shall taste my banquet"—is therefore not vengeance but revelation. It exposes what sin finally becomes: exclusion from joy. The punishment fits the crime, because the crime was refusal of joy itself. The door closes not on those who were uninvited, but on those who would not enter. In the moral world of Scripture, judgment is simply the solidification of choice. Heaven is communion sustained forever; hell is self-sufficiency left to itself. The host's sadness lies in the fact that both are forms of freedom respected by God.

The theological core of the parable thus lies in the doctrine of grace and freedom intertwined. God's will is universal invitation—"that my house may be filled." Yet the human response must be real, not automatic. Love cannot be forced without ceasing to be love. Augustine captured the paradox: "He who created you without you will not save you without you." Every excuse in the parable—every "I cannot come"—is the small echo of that deeper refusal. The drama of salvation is not God's reluctance but ours.

The host's persistence after rejection reveals the very nature of divine providence. Grace does not halt at human boundaries; it overflows them. The history of salvation itself is the story of God's invitations widening through every refusal. Abraham is called out of Ur, Israel is called out of Egypt, the prophets are sent to call Israel back, and when all have turned aside, the Word Himself "becomes flesh and dwells among us." The banquet image gathers all these callings into one table. The God who once rained manna in the wilderness now offers the living bread come down from heaven. The meal He prepares is not a symbol of reconciliation but reconciliation itself made edible.

Each servant sent in the parable becomes a figure of the missionary Church. "Go out quickly" echoes Christ's Great Commission, an imperative charged with urgency because the feast already stands ready. There is no time to lose; the host's food cannot remain uneaten. Evangelization in this light is not recruitment but rescue, not a marketing campaign but a homecoming. The Church goes to the margins not to prove her relevance but to gather the Father's children for dinner. Even the verb "go" in Luke's Greek (exelthe) resonates with the Sower's movement earlier in the Gospel—the same divine impulse that scatters seed now sends servants. The Word sown in the world blossoms as bread; the harvest is communion.

The banquet also reveals something profound about divine justice. God's anger does not contradict His mercy but serves it. When the host declares that those who refused "shall not taste my banquet," he is not exacting revenge; he is affirming truth. The Kingdom cannot be entered by indifference. The food of divine life cannot nourish a closed heart. In biblical thought, tasting always implies participation: "Taste and see that the Lord is good." To be barred from tasting is to be excluded from experience itself, not by decree but by disposition. The door of the banquet hall is the threshold of the human heart.

In the ancient Near East, to accept an invitation was to pledge loyalty; to decline was to sever relationship. Jesus' audience would have understood the weight of that rejection. Covenant was always sealed by shared meals—from Abraham's hospitality under the oaks of Mamre to the blood-sprinkled feast at Sinai. When Moses and the elders "beheld God, and ate and drank" (Ex 24:11), they prefigured the communion that now stands open to all. The Eucharist is therefore not a new ritual but the perfection of the oldest one. God's self-gift, once symbolised in lamb and manna, is consummated in the Lamb who is Host and Meal in one. The parable of the banquet anticipates this sacramental climax: the Father prepares, the Son serves, the Spirit compels.

The Trinity itself is mirrored in the narrative. The host embodies the Father's inexhaustible generosity; the servant who carries the invitation mirrors the Son's mission; the compelling grace that draws the poor inward is the Spirit's work in the world. The triune God is not a static deity watching from afar but a communion in motion, a hospitality turned outward. The house of the host is an image of the Father's heart; its open doors are the pierced side of Christ; the fragrance of food within is the breath of the Spirit. To speak of the "Kingdom of God" is to speak of the inner life of the Trinity extended into time.

Within that mystery, the poor and maimed gathered from the streets become more than social guests. They are the visible form of redeemed humanity. In them, the parable's theology of grace takes flesh. They bring nothing, contribute nothing, and yet are honoured beyond measure. The divine economy operates not by equivalence but by exchange—poverty for abundance, shame for glory, exile for homecoming. Each guest is an enacted beatitude, a life that testifies that God's strength is perfected in weakness. The crippled who once could not approach the Temple now reclines at the table of the King. The blind who never saw the altar now see the face of the Host. The lame who could not enter Jerusalem now enter the wedding feast of the Lamb.

The Church lives perpetually in this banquet dynamic. She is both guest and servant—fed by grace, yet sent to invite others. Every sacrament she celebrates is an extension of the invitation; every act of charity is an echo of the host's command, "Go out." Her holiness is not separateness but hospitality. Whenever she closes her doors, she forgets her Master's anger and her mission's urgency. The Church's mission field is as wide as the host's desire: "that my house may be filled." The measure of her faithfulness is not her decorum but her welcome.

Yet the parable also stands as mirror and warning for those within. The first invitees were not pagans; they were insiders. The story therefore judges complacency within the covenant community. The greater danger for believers is not rebellion but routine—being so accustomed to the things of God that one forgets their weight. The excuses of the first guests—fields, oxen, marriage—are timeless. They name the idolatries of comfort and control that dull spiritual hunger. Many live at the threshold of the banquet hall yet never step in, satisfied with observing rather than tasting.

The tragedy of spiritual life is not ignorance but apathy.

Luke's structure intensifies this diagnosis. Just before this parable, Jesus told the Pharisees to invite "the poor, the crippled, the lame, the blind" (14:13). When they refused, He made them characters in a story where their own neglect becomes judgment. The parable therefore functions as revelation in narrative form. God's Kingdom does not merely critique social exclusion; it reveals divine inclusion as the measure of holiness. To eat at the Lord's table means to live as He lives—receiving everything as gift and giving it again as gift.

The early Church understood this connection instinctively. In the Acts of the Apostles, the first Christians "devoted themselves to the apostles' teaching and fellowship, to the breaking of bread and the prayers." The phrase "breaking of bread" was shorthand for the Eucharist—the continual participation in the banquet of the new covenant. Their communal sharing of goods flowed directly from that table; their unity was not sociological but sacramental. They were, in effect, the living continuation of Luke's parable—the poor gathered from every nation, seated together in the house of God. The Didache, one of the earliest Christian writings, echoes this rhythm: "As this broken bread was scattered upon the mountains and was gathered together, so let Your Church be gathered into Your Kingdom." The Eucharistic meal was the centripetal force of the new creation.

As the centuries unfolded, the Fathers deepened this theology. For Irenaeus, the banquet symbolised recapitulation: humanity restored to its original vocation of thanksgiving. For Augustine, it was the City of God formed around the altar, history itself moving from the scattered fields of self-love to the single table of divine charity. For Gregory of Nyssa, the feast prefigured the soul's eternal ascent, always tasting more deeply the infinite goodness of the Host. Each saw in the parable the same truth: salvation is not an escape from creation but its transfiguration into communion.

The anthropology embedded in the image of eating is decisive. In Scripture, to eat is to enter into covenant. The first sin was a meal without thanksgiving; redemption begins with a meal that restores gratitude. The tree of knowledge becomes the table of the Lord. To consume without blessing is to grasp; to eat with thanksgiving is to receive. The invited guests in the parable refuse not because they are starving but because they are full—full of themselves, of possessions, of plans. The poor enter precisely because they are hungry. Hunger is the only condition grace requires.

At this level, the parable also speaks to the spiritual life of every disciple. The "fields" we tend are the attachments we cultivate; the "oxen" are our projects and ambitions; the "wife" is our network of affections that often binds us to the familiar rather than to faith. Each must be offered back if we are to be free for the feast. Detachment in Christian tradition is not contempt for the world but readiness for the banquet. It is the soul's capacity to move when the servant calls, to say, "I come, Lord," without delay. The saints are those who live in that posture of readiness, always packed for joy.

The theology of the Great Banquet reaches its summit in the mystery of divine joy. At the story's centre stands a host who will not accept an empty table. His anger is holy because it defends delight. The feast represents not a human obligation but the happiness of God Himself—the blessedness that longs to be shared. From eternity, the Father's joy has been the Son, and the Son's joy the Father, their love spiralling outward as the Spirit. Creation is simply that love taking the form of invitation. The world exists so that creatures might sit at that table. Every covenant, every prophet, every sacrament is one more messenger sent down the road, repeating the same call: "Come, for all is ready."

This is why the parable cannot be reduced to social ethics. It is ontological. The banquet is the meaning of being. The universe itself is a divine meal in motion—the Father preparing, the Son serving, the Spirit gathering. Sin is refusal to eat; salvation is hunger restored. When humanity turned from God, it was not rejecting a task but declining an invitation. The Incarnation is therefore God's act of sending His Servant not merely with words but with Himself as food. The Host becomes the meal. The Bread of Heaven is the Host's own body; the wine poured out is His blood. The parable of the banquet is fulfilled in the upper room, where Christ says, "Take, eat." The command is the reversal of Eden's "Do not eat." The forbidden fruit becomes the blessed fruit of the vine.

At the Cross, the parable's drama finds its final act. The invited guests have not come; the city has rejected the invitation. Yet the Host will not cancel the feast. He sends His Son outside the city walls, into the highways and hedges of Golgotha, where He gathers the thieves, the sinners, and the nations by the outstretched arms of mercy. The table becomes a tree; the meal becomes sacrifice. When the soldier's spear opens Christ's side, the blood and water that flow are the wine and water of the new banquet. Even in death, the invitation continues. "Compel them to come in," says the Host—and the compulsion is love nailed open.

In that light, every Mass is the continuation of this parable. The liturgy is not a repetition of a story but its sacramental reality unfolding through time. At every altar, the divine servant goes out again, proclaiming, "All is ready." The poor in spirit, the broken in sin, the spiritually lame and blind are gathered once more, not as spectators but as partakers. The Eucharist is both the sign and substance of the Kingdom's feast. To receive it is to enter the story's resolution; to ignore it is to replay the tragedy of refusal. The command to "do this in memory of me" is the Church's lifelong vocation to keep the banquet open until the Master returns.

Patristic writers saw the whole economy of salvation within this meal. Chrysostom called the altar "the table of reconciliation," where enemies are made brothers. Ambrose described it as "the banquet of faith" where the food is the Word itself. Augustine, always the realist of grace, preached that "He feeds us with Himself, that we may live in Him." For him, the parable was not only about mission but about the interior banquet of the soul. "Enter the chamber of your heart," he said, "and you will find the feast prepared." The true miracle is not that the poor are brought in from the streets, but that the human heart itself becomes the dining room of God.

The eschatological horizon of the parable stretches beyond history. The feast of the Lamb described in Revelation is the final fulfilment of the invitation first spoken at that Pharisee's table. "Blessed are those invited to the marriage supper of the Lamb." Every Eucharist is a rehearsal for that eternal banquet. What begins as bread broken in poverty ends as creation transfigured in glory. The poor who once hobbled into the house now reign as kings and priests. The table has become the Kingdom; the Kingdom has become home.

And yet, even in glory, the structure of gift remains. The blessed never stop receiving; the Host never stops giving. Heaven is not static rest but infinite communion—an eternal meal in which every moment deepens the appetite for the next. The parable thus discloses the secret of divine beatitude: God's joy is inexhaustible because His love is unceasingly self-giving. To share in that joy is to be drawn into the rhythm of giving and receiving that constitutes the life of the Trinity itself. The house of the host is the Father's heart, and to dwell there forever is what Scripture calls salvation.

At the human level, this mystery translates into a moral and spiritual law: joy grows by inclusion. Whenever love invites and is refused, sorrow follows; whenever it is accepted, heaven begins. The Great Banquet therefore names both a cosmic and a personal truth. The universe is the scene of God's feast, but the invitation arrives at every human door. Each heart stands at a crossroads between preoccupation and participation. Every time we turn away—from prayer, from sacrament, from neighbour—we repeat the excuses of the first guests. Every time we open our hands to receive, we become the poor brought in from the lanes. The parable leaves no neutrality; it divides the world not into good and bad, but into those who come and those who do not.

To live Eucharistically is to live as one who has accepted the invitation. It means understanding daily life as an extension of the feast—work as collaboration in God's creation, possessions as offerings to be shared, relationships as tables of communion. The Christian who sees the world in this way no longer asks, "How much must I give?" but, "How much room can I make?" The moral life becomes hospitality in action, the imitation of the Host. Every act of mercy, every gesture of forgiveness, is another chair drawn up at the table. The saints are simply those who have learned how to host as they have been hosted.

In the end, the parable of the Great Banquet is the Gospel compressed into a single image: God's invitation to share His joy and humanity's endless evasion of it. Yet even our refusals cannot exhaust His persistence. The doors remain open, the lamps burning, the servants sent. The Kingdom will not remain half-empty. The only tragedy left is to starve at the threshold of abundance. For those who enter, every tear becomes wine, every wound becomes a seat at the table. For those who linger outside, the music of the feast is the sound of mercy still calling their name.

The story ends where it began—in the silence between invitation and response. But its echo continues wherever bread is broken and wine poured. The feast of God waits not in some distant heaven but in every moment offered to love. Each Eucharist is the Host leaning out from eternity, saying again, "Come, for all is now ready."

That is the theology of the Kingdom: grace prepared, grace offered, grace shared until nothing remains outside its reach. The last word of the parable is not judgment but fullness. The house of God will be filled, and the song of the banquet will be the sound of creation finally at rest in its Giver.

### c) Typological and Intertextual Parallels

From Genesis to Revelation, God reveals Himself not as a distant ruler but as a host. Creation itself is the first act of hospitality: the universe arranged like a home prepared for guests. When Jesus speaks of a man who "gave a great banquet and invited many," He isn't improvising a metaphor; He's disclosing the logic of salvation history in its most ancient form. The Kingdom of God is not an empire built by conquest, but a table set by love.

The pattern begins in Eden. Humanity's first breath is drawn in a world already laden with food. Trees heavy with fruit surround the first couple, and the command to eat is given before the command not to eat. God's first word to man is permission, not prohibition. But within this abundance, one tree is withheld—not to test obedience arbitrarily, but to teach the rhythm of gift. To feast is to receive. When Adam and Eve reach for what was not offered, they break more than a rule; they break communion. The first sin is a misused meal—a banquet inverted. Ever since, God's saving work has been a long campaign to reopen the table.

When Israel comes to Sinai, that restoration begins in covenant form. After the thunder and the giving of the Law, Scripture records a brief, luminous scene: "They beheld God, and ate and drank" (Exod 24:11). That verse is the heartbeat of Israel's story. The covenant is not sealed merely by sacrifice but by supper. Eating in God's presence means belonging to His household. Sinai becomes the prototype of every later feast: divine law culminating in divine friendship. In Luke's parable, the master's careful preparation of his feast—his house, his table, his summons—echoes Sinai's same grace. Covenant life is an invitation to dine, not to perform.

As centuries pass, the prophets transform this memory into promise. Isaiah sees the mountain of the Lord turned into a cosmic dining hall: "On this mountain the Lord of hosts will make for all peoples a feast of rich food, a feast of well-aged wines... He will swallow up death forever" (Isa 25:6-8). This is no allegory for national prosperity. It is the vision of salvation itself—the moment when death's famine ends and humanity eats in peace with God once more. When Jesus tells His story of the master's feast, the Galileans listening would have recognised the echo. The "great banquet" is Isaiah's mountain brought down to earth.

Another prophetic voice picks up the same melody in gentler tones. Isaiah 55 opens with a cry that has haunted every liturgy since: "Come, everyone who thirsts, come to the waters; come, buy wine and milk without money and without price." Here the invitation is universal, and the cost is grace. Those who hunger are not told to labour but to come and eat. Luke's host, too, sends his servants not to the wealthy but to the weary, the poor, and the blind. The logic is identical: divine abundance is not earned, only received.

Between the mountain of Isaiah and the streets of Luke lies another thread: Wisdom's banquet. In Proverbs 9, Wisdom is personified as a woman who has "built her house... slaughtered her beasts... mixed her wine... and sent out her maidens to call." Her table is spread; her call rings out, "Come, eat of my bread and drink of the wine I have mixed." To the Hebrew imagination, Wisdom is no mere virtue; she is the radiance of God Himself—the pattern by which all things are ordered. When Jesus, the incarnate Wisdom, describes His master's feast, He is fulfilling Proverbs' promise in living form. He is the voice crying from the high places; He is the house built upon the rock; He is the wine already poured.

The story of David and Mephibosheth adds a human parable of mercy to the pattern. When David finds Jonathan's crippled son, the last remnant of the rival house of Saul, he raises him up and commands, "You shall eat at my table always" (2 Sam 9:7). Mephibosheth, lame and fearful, becomes the adopted son of the king. His daily seat at the royal table is the quiet foreshadowing of Luke's line, "Bring in the poor and the maimed and the blind and the lame." What David did for one outcast, the Son of David will do for all.

The prophets expand this narrative of hospitality and refusal. Isaiah cries, "I called, but you did not answer" (Isa 65:12). Jeremiah laments that from Egypt onward, God sent His servants daily, "but they did not listen or incline their ear" (Jer 7:25–26). These verses form the background music of the parable: every messenger ignored by Israel is one of the master's servants sent again and again. The parable compresses centuries of salvation history into one dramatic moment—an evening meal that reveals the persistence of divine love.

But refusal is never God's last word. Zephaniah foresees the day when the Lord will gather "the lame and the outcast" (3:19). Ezekiel envisions a strange feast in which even the birds of the air are called to eat the flesh of the mighty—a dark inversion that proclaims judgment before renewal (Ezek 39:17–20). Both images stand behind Luke's vision: the lowly raised up, the proud brought down. The hall once filled with kings will now ring with the laughter of beggars.

Even the very detail of "the highways and hedges" hums with biblical resonance. The highways recall Isaiah 40: "Prepare the way of the Lord," the road on which salvation travels. The hedges mark the edges of cultivation, the boundaries between field and wilderness. The servants' mission to those places mirrors the movement of God's word—to the edges, to the forgotten, to those who dwell outside the ordered spaces of religion. When Luke later writes the Acts of the Apostles, this same geography of grace reappears: the gospel moving outward from Jerusalem to Judea, Samaria, and the ends of the earth.

At every turn, the Bible's earlier feasts whisper through Luke's story. The manna in the wilderness taught Israel to depend daily on the Giver; the Passover transformed deliverance into meal; the covenant at Sinai made eating an act of worship; the prophets promised a universal table; Wisdom cried from the rooftops; David welcomed the lame; and now the Messiah gathers them all. Every previous supper was a shadow of this one.

When Jesus finishes His parable with the declaration, "None of those who were invited shall taste my banquet," He is not closing the story; He is summarising history. The generations who refused the prophets find themselves mirrored in the guests who made excuses. Yet even judgment becomes mercy, because every refusal widens the invitation. The table will be filled.

The sweep of Scripture gathers into this parable like converging rivers. Genesis gives the hunger; Exodus the covenant meal; Isaiah the mountain of plenty; Proverbs the Wisdom who calls; David the merciful king; the prophets the relentless invitation. Luke's banquet stands at the confluence of them all. Every previous feast was provisional—Israel tasting grace in advance. In Christ, the Host of all creation has stepped into His own story.

That's why Luke's retelling differs subtly from Matthew's. Matthew's "wedding feast of the king's son" looks forward to judgment; Luke's "great dinner" looks outward to inclusion. They are not contradictions but perspectives. Matthew shows the cost of refusal; Luke shows the persistence of the invitation. Together they reveal the two poles of covenant love: holiness that purifies, and mercy that gathers.

The imagery also reaches forward to the New Testament's final page. In Revelation 19, the angel proclaims, "Blessed are those who are invited to the marriage supper of the Lamb." John's apocalypse is Luke's parable transfigured. The master's hall becomes the heavenly city; the servants' summons becomes the Church's evangelising mission; the poor who enter are the redeemed of every tribe and tongue. The banquet begun in time finds its completion in eternity.

Even the simple phrase "that my house may be filled" echoes earlier covenants. It recalls the ark that could barely hold the gathered creatures, the temple filled with the glory of the Lord, and the promise to Abraham that his descendants would be as countless as the stars. In Luke's theology, fullness is the signature of grace. God does not create to ration; He creates to overflow. The master's insistence that there is still room expresses the entire economy of salvation: the infinity of divine hospitality.

This typological chain also reveals how Luke reads history. Salvation is not a sequence of disconnected events but one unfolding meal. God's table stretches from Eden to the Eschaton, from bread baked by Sarah for the strangers at Mamre to the loaf broken at Emmaus. Each meal expands the pattern of invitation: from one couple to one family, from one nation to all nations. The same Lord who once fed Israel with manna now feeds the world with Himself.

In the end, the parable of the Great Banquet is a mosaic of all these earlier feasts, a single image formed from a thousand glimmering tiles. It speaks with the voice of every covenant: the God who calls, the human heart that hesitates, and the mercy that will not stop calling. The invitation that rang in Eden, at Sinai, in Zion, and from Wisdom's house now sounds in Galilee's air: *Come, for everything is ready.*

Through this lens, the story ceases to be a quaint tale about hospitality and becomes Scripture's great symphony of communion. The same God who spread a garden and built a mountain feast now stands in human flesh, sending out His servants again and again until His house is full. Every verse of the Bible has been leading to this moment—the world's hunger met by the Host who will not dine without us.

### d) Patristic and Theological Synthesis

When the earliest Christians heard Jesus' parable of the Great Banquet, they didn't treat it as a quaint story about good manners. They saw their own lives in it. They were the poor who had been brought in from the streets, the outsiders suddenly seated at the table of God. The banquet wasn't a metaphor to them; it was the mystery they lived every time they gathered for the breaking of the bread.

Augustine loved to remind his congregation that the feast is not only *of Christ* but *is Christ*. "Eat what you see," he preached, "and become what you receive." The Host and the food are one. For Augustine, the parable unfolds the pattern of grace itself: invitation, refusal, persistence, and finally communion. God keeps sending His servants because His love refuses to dine alone.

Chrysostom read the story with pastoral urgency. Preaching in the bustle of Antioch, he warned his hearers that the excuses of the guests are still being made in every age. "One pleads business, another marriage, another field." He had no patience for the polite self-deception that calls distraction devotion. To Chrysostom, the feast is the Mass, and the excuses are the litany of worldly hearts. He told his flock that the poor have already taken the seats we left empty.

Gregory the Great drew the lines of the parable outward to the Gentile world. Israel's refusal, he said, opened the way for "the lame and the blind," the nations who had no claim by lineage but entered by faith. For Gregory, the hall is the Church, and every soul that hears the Gospel is a servant sent to the crossroads. "The highways," he wrote, "are the public ways of the world; the hedges, the hidden paths of contemplation." God's invitation reaches both the marketplace and the monastery.

Ambrose carried the reading even deeper, into the heart of the liturgy. The banquet, he said, is fulfilled in the Eucharist, where the rich and poor kneel side by side. "Christ is our food, Christ is our drink, Christ is our wealth." At that table, social order dissolves; the only rank that matters is hunger. For Ambrose, the miracle of the feast is not merely inclusion but transformation—bread becoming body, strangers becoming family.

Across those voices, the same melody runs: God's generosity outpaces human refusal. The Fathers heard the parable as a miniature of salvation history. From Adam's loss of communion to the Church's daily supper, the divine pattern is consistent—God calls, we hesitate, yet mercy keeps inviting.

They also recognised that every covenant in Scripture is a meal waiting to happen. In the ancient world, a covenant was sealed not by signature but by shared table. To eat together was to become kin. The banquet of Luke 14 is therefore the covenant brought to completion. The mountain meal of Sinai finds its fulfilment in the supper of the Kingdom. The same Lord who once dined with the elders of Israel now stoops to serve fishermen and sinners.

The Fathers often linked this parable with the marriage imagery of the prophets. For them, the feast is the wedding of heaven and earth, and the bread of the altar is the dowry of the Bridegroom. When the guests make excuses, they are turning down a wedding invitation from God Himself. What begins as courtesy becomes tragedy. Yet even that tragedy is redeemed, because the servants keep going out, until the Bride—the Church—is gathered from every nation.

This is the logic of divine love: covenant offered, freedom respected, mercy unrelenting. The Fathers never shy away from the mystery of refusal. They see in it the proof that grace is real. If the invitation could not be declined, it would not be love. Gregory Nazianzen once wrote, "God persuades, He does not compel; He draws, He does not drive." The open door of the banquet hall is both gift and judgment. It reveals who desires communion and who prefers isolation.

Later theologians would give that intuition its classic form. Aquinas explained that God's goodness is "diffusive of itself." Love, by its nature, seeks to be shared. That's why the host in the parable seems almost restless—he cannot stop inviting. For Thomas, creation itself is the first invitation, and redemption the second. Grace is simply God continuing what He began in Genesis: the extension of divine life into human lives. When Jesus says, "that my house may be filled," Aquinas would say this is the voice of Being itself, the infinite goodness that cannot be content with solitude.

## THE GREAT BANQUET (LK 14:15-24)

If the feast is the covenant fulfilled, then the Church is the banquet hall. The Fathers never separated the two. Augustine told his people that to come to the altar is to "come into the house of the Lord." The servants who carry the invitations are the apostles and their successors; the poor and lame are the sinners who find healing within. The Church's very structure—Word proclaimed, table prepared, people gathered—is the architecture of the parable. Every liturgy is a new sending into the highways of the world.

For Hahn, this is where covenant theology becomes visible. The Church is not an institution added later; it's the family born from the meal. The same God who walked with Abraham and fed Israel in the desert now feeds His children with Himself. Each sacrament, each act of mercy, is another course of the same feast. When we evangelise, we're not promoting an ideology; we're carrying invitations. Our mission is hospitality. Evangelisation is the Host's heartbeat.

Yet the parable also carries a sober warning. Every generation risks making new excuses. For the Fathers, the danger wasn't atheism but apathy—the slow erosion of desire. Augustine called it "the noonday devil," that listless spirit that makes us too weary to rejoice. When the host says, "None of those who were invited shall taste my banquet," it's not vengeance; it's realism. We can starve in a kitchen full of bread if we never lift our hands to eat.

Still, the note that triumphs in every patristic homily is hope. There is always another servant being sent, another road to be searched, another soul to be found. The house of God will be full because the heart of God is inexhaustible. That is why the Fathers loved this parable—it told them not only who God is but who they were: beggars turned guests, strangers made sons.

If the Fathers teach us how to hear the parable, the Church teaches us how to live it. The banquet is not only an image of heaven; it's the pattern of history. Every generation of believers takes its place somewhere in the story—some making excuses, some carrying invitations, some stumbling in from the streets with eyes wide in wonder. The parable never ends because the Host never stops calling.

The Eucharist is where the story becomes flesh. At every Mass, the words echo again: "Blessed are those called to the supper of the Lamb." The liturgy is not our weekly obligation; it's the continuation of the Great Banquet. What Jesus described in parable, the Church now enacts in sacrament. The same Lord who once reclined at table in Bethany or Emmaus now reclines upon every altar, offering Himself as both food and fellowship. The Fathers understood this instinctively. For them, the Eucharist was not a symbol pointing backward but a meal reaching forward—a foretaste of the Kingdom that will have no end.

To approach that table is to step into covenant. God's invitation is renewed with every consecration, His persistence embodied in every priest who says, "Behold the Lamb of God." The excuses of the guests are still heard in the world—too busy, too distracted, too self-sufficient—but the servants of the Gospel keep going out. The highways are our cities, the hedges our forgotten places, the poor our daily neighbours. Whenever the Church preaches mercy, builds hospitals, feeds the hungry, or welcomes the stranger, she is obeying that final command of the master: "Compel them to come in, that my house may be filled."

The banquet's moral, as the Fathers saw, is not only about generosity but about identity. God's holiness is hospitality. The mystery of the Trinity itself is an eternal meal of love—Father, Son, and Spirit eternally giving and receiving. Creation is simply that love spilling over, making room for others at the table. Redemption is the restoration of the chairs we knocked over in Eden. The final judgment, then, is not God turning us away; it is the last invitation, accepted or refused.

In the end, the Great Banquet reveals the secret of the Gospel: salvation is not achieved but received. The Host has already prepared the table; the servants have already gone out. What remains is our response. Augustine once said, "The table is set; you are hungry; be thankful." That's the whole of Christian life in one sentence—gratitude answering grace.

Every Mass, every act of mercy, every conversion story is another verse of this same song. The table grows longer, the hall wider, the laughter louder. The Church, standing between promise and fulfilment, keeps echoing the Host's words: "Everything is ready." The Kingdom of God is not a place we reach; it's a feast we join. And the wonder is that the One who prepares it waits for us—because the love that made the world refuses to dine until every seat is filled.

### The Shock and the Turn

It began with a blessing that sounded harmless.

At a Sabbath meal in the house of a leading Pharisee, a guest lifted his cup and said, "Blessed is he who shall eat bread in the Kingdom of God." To everyone at that table, it was the most natural thing to say. They all knew the prophets' promise: when the Messiah came, the righteous of Israel would recline at table with Abraham, Isaac, and Jacob. The banquet of the age to come would vindicate the faithful and exclude the nations. It was a picture of triumph, of covenant privilege confirmed forever.

No one expected that their imagined feast would be turned against them.

Jesus answers the toast with a story. The opening words sound familiar: "A man once gave a great banquet and invited many." Everyone at the table knew where this was heading. God was the host; Israel was the guest list. The Pharisees could almost finish the parable themselves. The only question was which kind of Israelite Jesus would praise—zealous Pharisee, faithful rabbi, or ordinary law-keeper.

But the story turns.

The invitations go out, and the invited refuse. Not rebels or pagans—friends, neighbours, the chosen. Each reply is polite, almost apologetic. One has land to inspect, another oxen to test, another a marriage to attend. The excuses are reasonable, which makes them more painful. The host who had prepared everything finds his hall empty.

At this point, Jesus' listeners would have shifted uncomfortably. In Jewish imagination, the messianic banquet was for the pure, the observant, the deserving. No prophet had ever suggested that Israel herself might decline the summons. The refusal in Jesus' story already sounds ominous:

a covenant people turning away from covenant joy.

Then comes the shock.

The master commands his servant, "Go quickly into the streets and lanes of the city, and bring in the poor and crippled and blind and lame." Every head at the table would have lifted. Those four adjectives carried ritual weight. In the Temple law, the lame and the blind were excluded from priestly service; the unclean could not approach the altar. Yet these are the ones who now fill the hall. Jesus has moved the boundary of holiness from purity to mercy. The unfit have become the invited.

Still, the parable is not finished. The servant reports, "Master, what you commanded has been done, and still there is room." The host answers, "Go out to the highways and hedges, and compel people to come in." At those words, the air would have gone cold. The "highways" lay beyond the city's gates; the "hedges" marked the edges of cultivated land. That was Gentile territory. The order means exactly what it sounds like: take the invitation beyond Israel.

To the men reclining at that table—scribes, lawyers, descendants of Abraham—this was unthinkable. The idea that Gentiles, the uncircumcised nations, might share Israel's eschatological meal was scandal enough. But Jesus goes further: they will not merely share it; they will fill it. The chosen seats left empty by the sons of the covenant will be occupied by strangers.

The parable's polite tone only heightens its force. Jesus never raises His voice. He simply tells the story to its end, letting the conclusion fall like a stone in still water: "None of those who were invited shall taste my banquet." In that sentence, centuries of assumption collapse. Election is no longer guaranteed by ancestry. Covenant membership depends on response. The invitation still belongs to Israel, but its fulfilment now opens to the world.

For the Pharisees, this was more than offensive; it was intolerable. They saw themselves as guardians of holiness, keeping the Torah unsullied amid a compromised nation. Their hope was restoration—Israel purified, Gentiles subdued. Jesus' vision was the opposite: Israel humbled, the nations welcomed. The banquet of God would not be a victory feast for the few but a table where the lost are found.

It's difficult for modern ears to feel the scandal, but to grasp it is to feel the parable's power. Jesus is rewriting Israel's most cherished expectation— the messianic feast from Isaiah 25. "On this mountain," Isaiah said, "the Lord of hosts will make for all peoples a feast of rich food." Generations of interpreters had read "all peoples" as *all Israel*. Jesus reads it literally. The feast is for the nations. What Israel thought exclusive, God meant expansive.

The listeners would have heard another, darker echo too. The refusal of the invited sounds like the prophets' laments: "I called, and you did not answer." In rejecting the host, Israel repeats her history of ignoring God's messengers. The banquet becomes a parable of the prophets and their fate, culminating in the rejection of the Son Himself. The story's path from invitation to exclusion foreshadows the movement from covenant to cross.

The scandal, then, is not that God welcomes sinners or Gentiles—that much the prophets had hinted at—but that He will do so *because* of Israel's refusal. Grace will move outward through judgment. The kingdom will expand through rejection. God's fidelity will be proven precisely by His refusal to let the covenant die with those who spurn it.

For the Pharisees, that meant the unthinkable: their zeal could become their blindness. The very obedience that should have prepared them for the feast might keep them from it. The Law they loved had been given to lead to mercy, and mercy now stands before them in flesh. To decline Jesus' call, even for the sake of holiness, is to decline the banquet itself.

The parable also reverses the common image of purity. In their world, contact with the unclean defiled the clean. In Jesus' story, the opposite happens: the master's generosity sanctifies the impure. Holiness is no longer separation but invitation. God's presence spreads not by isolation but by inclusion. The contagion of grace overcomes the contagion of sin.

For the first-century audience, this was revolutionary theology. The Temple stood at the centre of holiness; the boundaries of purity defined the community of God. Jesus shifts the centre from a place to a person, from law to love. The host of the parable is the image of the Father who sends His Son into the world. The feast begins not in heaven but in Galilee, wherever Christ reclines with sinners and breaks bread with the outcast.

The listeners could sense where this logic led. If the feast belongs to those who accept the invitation, then publicans and prostitutes—people visibly outside the covenant—might enter before them. The Kingdom they longed for would arrive, but it would not look like what they had built their lives around. In that moment, the story ceased to be safe.

The silence that follows such a realisation is heavier than argument. The parable ends without resolution; Jesus leaves it hanging between them like a mirror. The host's final declaration—"None of those who were invited shall taste my banquet"—is less threat than lament. The tragedy of the invited guests is not their loss of privilege but their loss of hunger.

That is what scandalises the Pharisees most: not that the Gentiles will be saved, but that the covenant will be fulfilled without them because they no longer desire it. The sinners and the nations respond first simply because they know their need. The ones who thought themselves righteous are full already.

In the wider arc of Luke's Gospel, this is the turning point. From this meal onward, the story moves toward Jerusalem and rejection. The table fellowship that begins in this house will end at the Last Supper, where another group of chosen friends will hear, "Do this in memory of Me." The invitation will pass through betrayal into resurrection. The hall will be filled, not with the pure, but with the redeemed.

To the men at that Sabbath table, it must have sounded impossible. They, the teachers of Israel, being replaced by beggars and foreigners? Yet that is exactly what history would prove true. Within a generation, the Gospel would cross seas; the Church's first great councils would be filled with Gentile bishops. The words spoken in that small dining room would become the shape of salvation itself.

That was the shock.

That was the turn.

## THE GREAT BANQUET (LK 14:15–24)

### The Revelation in the Son

The Great Banquet is not simply a lesson about hospitality or faith; it is a portrait of the divine life made visible in Christ. Behind the figure of the generous host stands the Father of mercies; behind the servant who bears the invitations, the Son who comes into the world. The hall, radiant and spacious, is creation itself, waiting to be filled with divine life. The parable is therefore not only about grace offered to humanity but about God's own desire — the longing of the Trinity to share Its joy.

From the beginning, God has been preparing this feast. The whole economy of salvation is a single act of hospitality: the Creator making room for the creature. Creation itself is a table set for communion. Every star, every creature, every human soul is invited to share in the infinite generosity that flows from the Father. The Incarnation is the moment when the Host steps into His own house, when the eternal Word who called creation into being enters it as guest and servant.

The servant in the parable who is sent "again and again" mirrors the Son's mission. He is the divine messenger who goes out from the Father to seek the lost. Each stage of the servant's journey traces a movement of the Word: first to Israel, then to the poor within her gates, finally to the nations beyond the hedges. The command "Go out quickly" is the heartbeat of the Gospel. It is the eternal procession of the Son translated into history — God moving outward, love descending into flesh. The repeated sending of the servant is the rhythm of the Incarnation itself: the God who never stops coming.

But there is another layer. In Jesus' ministry the parable becomes autobiography. He is both the teller and the fulfilment of the story. When He eats with tax collectors and sinners, the banquet begins. When He calls the poor, the crippled, the blind, and the lame, He is not offering metaphors but meals. His table fellowship is theology made tangible. Around the bread and wine of ordinary life, the face of the Father is revealed.

Yet the generosity of the Host comes at a cost. The banquet of divine love is prepared not in a palace but on a cross. The Servant sent into the streets is rejected by those first invited; He will be driven outside the city, crucified beyond the walls where the Gentiles dwell. The open door of the parable becomes the torn veil of the Temple; the feast is laid upon the wood of sacrifice. In that hour the story reaches its final turn: the Host becomes the food.

Here lies the deepest revelation. God's answer to rejection is self-offering. When humanity declines His invitation, He prepares a greater one. The crucified Christ is the ultimate banquet—the love of the Father served in the broken body of the Son. Every refusal of grace is gathered into this one act, transfigured into forgiveness. The outstretched arms of Jesus are the arms of the Host welcoming His guests.

At the Last Supper, the parable steps into history. "Take, eat; this is My Body." The words complete the story told in Galilee. The feast once imagined becomes sacrament. The bread and wine that pass from His hands to theirs are the visible form of divine hospitality. What the Father promised through prophets and parables is fulfilled in the humility of bread. The invitation of the ages now bears a human voice.

The Eucharist is therefore the living continuation of the parable. Every Mass is the great banquet renewed: the Master's house being filled until the end of time. The altar is His table; the Church, His hall. The poor, the wounded, the ordinary—all are summoned again and again by the same command: *Come, for all is now ready.* And just as in the parable, the Servant still moves through the streets of the world, compelling souls to enter, urging them to believe they are wanted.

In this light, the parable becomes a vision of the Church's mission. Evangelisation is not recruitment; it is invitation. The Church does not conquer territory; she extends hospitality. Her task is to mirror the Host's persistence—to go out once more, to call again, to search the roads and the hedges until every corner of creation hears the Gospel. The world's conversion is the filling of the house.

But this is not merely human work. The One who sends the servants still moves among them. Christ continues His own mission through His Mystical Body. The invitation that echoes in the preaching of the Church is the very voice of the Son, spoken anew in every age. The servant who "compels them to come in" now speaks through apostles, missionaries, confessors, and martyrs. The urgency of the parable burns in their witness: divine charity made visible through human lives.

The Father's desire, which seems almost reckless in the story, is the eternal generosity of the Trinity overflowing into time. The Son is that generosity incarnate. The Holy Spirit is the fragrance of the banquet, filling the air, drawing the reluctant by the sweetness of grace. Each divine Person participates in the feast: the Father preparing, the Son offering, the Spirit gathering. The parable is therefore not merely moral or ecclesial; it is Trinitarian. It is the life of God projected into the theatre of history.

And still, the mystery deepens. The hall being filled is not only the Church but creation itself transformed. Every soul that responds, every act of faith, every Eucharist celebrated enlarges the feast. Time becomes the process by which the house of God is completed. The final fulfilment of the parable lies not in a distant heaven but in the transfiguration of all things—the universe itself becoming a dwelling for divine love. "That my house may be filled," says the Master, and those words reveal the ultimate purpose of the cosmos: to become the house of God.

In Christ, this purpose is already achieved in principle. The Incarnation is the filling of the house—the infinite entering the finite, the Creator inhabiting His creation. The divine Guest who once walked the roads of Galilee now dwells sacramentally in the Church, mystically in every soul that believes, cosmically in the very fabric of redeemed creation. The Great Banquet is not a metaphor for heaven alone; it is the structure of reality redeemed.

To live the Christian life, then, is to live from that feast. Discipleship is not preparation for a future meal but participation in a present one. Every act of love is an extension of the table. Every word of forgiveness is another guest seated. Every Mass is another measure of the Father's desire realised. The parable is not behind us; it is happening now, every time a sinner is welcomed home and a heart opens to grace.

At the heart of this mystery stands the astonishing humility of God.

The Host who prepares the banquet does not remain enthroned above it; He descends to serve. "The Son of Man came not to be served but to serve," Jesus says, and in those words the parable takes flesh. The divine majesty kneels to wash feet, the Creator stoops to feed His creatures. This inversion is the centre of all Christian revelation: glory revealed in self-emptying love.

The Incarnation is God's own entry into the streets and lanes of the city. The servant seeking the poor and the blind is the Eternal Word entering the poverty and blindness of our condition. Every healing and every table fellowship in the Gospel is a sign of that descent. When Christ touches the leper, He is gathering him from the roadside into the hall. When He forgives the adulteress, He is seating her among the guests of mercy. When He stretches out His hands upon the cross, He is flinging the doors of the banquet wide.

There is a profound irony in this divine hospitality. The Host is excluded from His own house so that others may enter it. Rejected by those first invited, He becomes the outcast who finds the outcasts. Crucified outside the city, He makes His dwelling among the unworthy. From that place of dereliction, the feast begins anew. The Cross is the threshold of the banquet—the point where divine invitation meets human refusal and turns it into grace.

In the light of Easter, the parable's imagery unfolds into cosmic scope. The risen Christ is the Master returned to the hall, the Servant who has completed His circuit through the world. His wounds are the marks of invitation; His Resurrection is the sound of the music beginning. The house is filling, not with the elite of Israel alone but with humanity renewed. The poor are now the blessed, the lame dance, the blind see. The Kingdom's hall stretches beyond history; its walls are the boundaries of creation itself.

Every Eucharist gathers this vast reality into a single moment. When the priest raises the chalice and says, "Blessed are those called to the supper of the Lamb," the parable is fulfilled again. Heaven and earth meet at the table of the Word made flesh. Bread and wine become the very life of the

## THE GREAT BANQUET (LK 14:15–24)

Host, given that His house may be full. The communicant who receives that Body and Blood becomes what he consumes—another dwelling place of divine joy.

In the end, the Great Banquet reveals not a distant paradise but the radiance of Christ Himself filling all things. The hall of the Kingdom is the world transfigured by love, creation returned to communion. The same Lord who once told this story still walks the roads and hedges of our time, seeking those who have not yet believed they are wanted. The invitation endures, spoken through every sacrament and every saint: *Come, for everything is ready.*

### The Word for Our Age

If Jesus told the parable of the Great Banquet in our time, He might set it in a glowing city rather than a village courtyard. The invitations would go out by email, the table would be ready, but the guests would be stuck in traffic, scrolling through updates, half-reading the message that says, *"Dinner is served."* The feast of grace hasn't changed; only our distractions have multiplied. The Kingdom still waits for guests, but the seats remain empty—not from hostility, but from exhaustion.

Our generation has mastered the art of distraction. We live surrounded by abundance—food, entertainment, information—yet starved of meaning. The great spiritual crisis of the modern West is not persecution but preoccupation. We are so busy managing life that we forget to live it. Jesus' parable exposes this gentle tragedy: the refusal not born of hatred but of hurry. No one in the story blasphemes or rebels; they simply have better things to do.

The first guest says he must inspect his new field. We, too, live under the tyranny of productivity. Our worth is measured in output, our days in tasks completed. We cultivate our own little empires of work, reputation, and control. The second guest pleads the care of his oxen—the modern translation might be career, investments, or the endless maintenance of comfort. The third says, "I have married a wife," and stays home. In our age, the idol may be family itself, or the fragile peace of self-care that leaves no room for God. The point is not that these things are bad; it's that they become ultimate. Good gifts replace the Giver.

The house of the Master stands open, yet the seats remain empty. This is our age: filled with blessings but lacking beatitude. We have confused fullness with fulfillment. Our calendars overflow, but our souls are famished. The invitation of the Gospel rings out against a background hum of busyness, and it sounds to many like one more obligation.

Yet the parable also carries immense hope. The Master does not cancel the banquet; he widens it. His response to rejection is not anger but expansion. The command "Go out quickly into the streets and lanes" reveals the relentless mercy of God. In a world that forgets Him, He goes looking again. The mission of the Church in our time is to embody that same urgency—to bring the feast to the forgotten, to the spiritually homeless who no longer believe they're invited.

That means re-learning the art of genuine invitation. Evangelisation today cannot sound like marketing or debate. It must look like love. People return to God when they meet joy they can trust. The servant's task—"compel them to come in"—is not force but fascination: the attraction of holiness that awakens hunger. In a cynical world, credibility is beauty lived with integrity.

The Church must therefore become recognisably joyful again. The Mass, the sacraments, our parish life—these are not duties but foretastes of the feast. When believers live as if Sunday were the centre of the week, others begin to notice. The Eucharist remains the world's quiet miracle: a table set in every generation, where divine hospitality still waits. Each time we receive that Bread, we accept the invitation anew.

But there is a personal side to this story. Each of us carries within our own life the same list of excuses. We mean to pray but check the phone first. We mean to reconcile but postpone the call. We mean to attend the feast but delay our conversion for "after things settle down." The truth is, things never settle down; the feast is always now. Jesus' words are not meant to condemn but to awaken. They remind us that love is urgent, that

## THE GREAT BANQUET (LK 14:15-24)

eternity begins with today's yes.

To live this parable in the twenty-first century is to cultivate holy availability—to leave room for God in our crowded lives. It means scheduling silence as deliberately as meetings, choosing worship over one more weekend task, daring to believe that prayer accomplishes more than control. The banquet still begins in small acts of trust: closing the laptop to sit in adoration, lingering after Mass to speak with someone who is alone, giving an evening to community instead of consumption.

There are modern equivalents of those who dwell "in the highways and hedges." They are the lonely, the addicted, the disillusioned, the digitally lost. They are also the millions who once sat at the table and quietly slipped away, convinced they were no longer welcome. To go out after them is the task of a missionary Church—one that does not wait for the hungry to arrive but goes bearing bread. Every parish that opens its doors in welcome, every believer who listens without judgment, every act of mercy offered without agenda, becomes part of the servant's journey.

And we must remember: the Host is not finished. "Still there is room," He says. Those four words are the heart of Christian hope. They mean that history is not closing but widening, that God's desire outpaces our indifference. No matter how secular the world becomes, there will always be another invitation, another grace, another chance to say yes.

For modern disciples, the banquet is lived out in daily Eucharistic spirituality. To "come to the feast" is to see life itself as communion—to treat every moment as a gift meant to be shared. The Christian's table, workplace, and family become extensions of the altar. When we give time to a friend in crisis, forgive a rival, or serve the poor, we are carrying the Host into the streets. Holiness today will look like hospitality—making space for God and neighbour in the same breath.

We also need to recover the discipline of gratitude. Gratitude keeps the heart poor enough to be filled. It reminds us that grace is not a reward but a meal already prepared. Begin the day with thanksgiving, end it with remembrance. Name blessings aloud. See interruptions as invitations. The life of faith is not sustained by spectacular experiences but by steady awareness: the quiet conviction that, whatever happens, the feast is still being set.

For a Church tempted by self-preservation, this parable is also a warning. Institutions can become like the first invitees—so busy maintaining their property that they forget the purpose of the house. The Church is not a museum for the saved but a home for the hungry. Her beauty exists for mission; her liturgy overflows into service. When she forgets that, she risks the same tragedy as the absent guests: a full treasury and an empty table.

Yet the final word is joy. The banquet will be filled. The divine plan does not fail because of human excuses; it adapts, expands, overflows. The heart of God is larger than our apathy. Even now He sends His servants—parents, priests, missionaries, teachers—out into the world with the same message of mercy. "Come, for everything is ready." That line remains the Gospel's beating heart.

To accept it is to live differently. We begin to measure time not by productivity but by presence, success not by possession but by love. We make choices that keep us free for God: simpler homes, slower schedules, freer hearts. We learn again that the happiest life is the one most given away.

One day the invitation will come for the last time. It will not arrive by email or text but as a whisper at the edge of breath. Then the excuses will end, and the door will open. The banquet we have rehearsed in faith will blaze into sight. Until that moment, every Mass, every act of charity, every quiet yes is practice for eternity.

The feast is not a fantasy waiting beyond death; it begins wherever love is received and shared. The house of God is still being filled, one soul at a time. The only tragedy left is to stay outside when the music has already begun.

### Hearing that Becomes Doing

The story has ended, yet the invitation remains. The hall is lit, the table

## THE GREAT BANQUET (LK 14:15-24)

set, and somewhere beyond the city walls, the servant still walks with the message: *"Come, for everything is ready."* The echo of that call crosses centuries and finds you now. This is not memory; it is presence. The feast is still waiting, and the Host still hopes you will come.

Let the parable linger in your imagination. See the empty chairs, the places set for guests who never arrived. Hear the quiet rustle as the poor and the crippled enter, hesitant, unsure they belong. Watch the Master's face as the room begins to fill—not with the expected, but with the unexpected. That is the expression of God when a sinner finally believes he is wanted.

Now turn the scene inward. The hall is your own heart. Some doors stand open; others are barred by excuses. One corridor may still echo with the words, *"Not now, Lord... perhaps later."* Another may hold the memory of disappointment, the doubt that whispers, *"I was invited once, but not again."* Yet the servant keeps knocking. Grace does not take offense; it keeps returning until you answer.

Pause and listen. Where in your life is God inviting you to come closer? Where have you been too busy to notice? Maybe it's a relationship left unattended, a vocation delayed, a quiet prompting toward prayer ignored amid noise. The Host waits in each of these places. His invitation is not demand but desire: *"I want you with Me."*

When you sense that call, don't rush to justify your absence. Simply whisper, "Here I am." Even a small response opens the way. The first step toward holiness is attention. The feast begins the moment you turn your face toward the door.

Perhaps you fear you've missed your chance—that too many refusals have passed, too many days gone silent. The parable says otherwise. The Master sends his servant again and again. There is always another path back, another place at the table. The heart of God is never full.

Let gratitude rise quietly. You have been sought, not because you are useful, but because you are loved. The One who prepared the banquet is the same One who became bread for you. Each Eucharist is His reminder: *I still want to share My joy with you.* When you receive that Body, you are not an anonymous guest—you are the reason the feast exists.

Take a breath and imagine sitting at that table. The noise of the city fades; the light softens. Christ sits across from you, His eyes gentle, His hands scarred and open. He speaks no words of reproach—only the calm assurance that you belong. Let that truth travel from mind to heart: belonging precedes worthiness. You are invited because He desires communion, not perfection.

Now let the prayer move into daily life. Who around you is still waiting for an invitation? A neighbour unseen, a friend who's drifted from faith, a family member too weary to hope. You can become the servant of the parable—the one who carries the message outward. The Gospel spreads not by argument but by warmth. A single word of welcome, a simple meal shared, a patient conversation may be the doorway through which someone enters the hall.

Discipleship always begins with hospitality. Before you preach, listen. Before you instruct, embrace. The poor and the lame of your world are those who cannot repay you. Love them freely, and you will taste the joy of the Master who rejoices when the house is full.

Tonight, before sleep, you might pray:

*Lord, show me the invitations I have ignored. Teach me to recognise Your voice behind the ordinary. Give me courage to leave what distracts and to come to You.*

Sit for a moment in silence after that prayer. Notice what surfaces—perhaps a face, a memory, a quiet longing. That is where the Spirit is working. Do not analyse; simply bring it to Jesus. Say, "This too, Lord, I bring to the table."

If restlessness lingers, make it physical. Light a candle and watch the flame. Let its steady glow remind you that grace never tires. Or open your hands, palms upward, and breathe slowly. With each exhale, release one excuse. With each inhale, receive mercy. This is what it means to live invited—to let the Holy Spirit turn breathing into belonging.

Tomorrow morning, begin with the same gesture. As you open your eyes, say: *"The feast is today."* Let that sentence shape the hours ahead.

## THE GREAT BANQUET (LK 14:15–24)

Approach your work, your conversations, your meals as extensions of the banquet. Every person you meet is someone Christ longs to seat beside you. Treat them as fellow guests, not rivals.

During the day, keep a small rhythm of remembrance. Before eating, pause to picture the heavenly table. Before sending a message, ask if it carries the fragrance of invitation or exclusion. At evening, thank the Host for the moments you noticed His presence—and for the ones you missed, which He will redeem anyway.

Before you sleep, pray slowly:

**Prayer**
Lord Jesus,
You who left heaven's joy to seek the lost,
enter the rooms of my heart where excuses hide.
Sit at the table of my weariness
and make it Your dwelling.
Teach me to hear Your invitation
in every moment of the day.
Give me grace to go out toward others
with the same mercy that found me.
May my home become a place of welcome,
my words a light in dark streets,
my heart a hall where Your joy can rest.
When my time comes,
let me recognise Your voice—the servant's voice—
saying once more, "Come, for all is ready."
And let me rise without hesitation,
to take my seat beside You forever.
Amen.

Now let the words fade. The music of the feast is already playing somewhere in the distance. The Host waits, smiling, as candles tremble in the quiet air. You are not outside anymore. You have heard, and you have come. Rest there. The banquet has begun.

# 11

# The Wedding Feast / Proper Garment (Mt 22:1–14)

*Jesus spoke to them again in parables, saying:*
"The kingdom of heaven may be compared to a king who gave a wedding banquet for his son. He sent his servants to call those who had been invited to the wedding banquet, but they would not come. Again he sent other servants, saying, 'Tell those who have been invited: Look, I have prepared my dinner, my oxen and my fat calves have been slaughtered, and everything is ready; come to the wedding banquet.' But they made light of it and went away, one to his farm, another to his business, while the rest seized his servants, mistreated them, and killed them. The king was enraged. He sent his troops, destroyed those murderers, and burned their city.

Then he said to his servants, 'The wedding is ready, but those invited were not worthy. Go therefore into the main streets, and invite everyone you find to the wedding banquet.' Those servants went out into the streets and gathered all whom they found, both good and bad, so the wedding hall was filled with guests.

But when the king came in to see the guests, he noticed a man there who was not wearing a wedding robe, and he said to him, 'Friend, how did you get in here without a wedding robe?' And the man was speechless. Then the king said to the attendants, 'Bind him hand and foot, and throw him into the outer darkness, where there will be weeping and gnashing of teeth.'

*For many are called, but few are chosen.*

## The Word Spoken

The morning sun lies hard upon Jerusalem. Its light catches the edges of the great colonnade, running like fire along the white stone. Within the Court of the Gentiles, merchants call over the noise of animals; pilgrims press toward the steps that rise to the inner court. The smell of dust, incense, and sweat hangs in the air.

Jesus stands near Solomon's Portico, surrounded by faces—some eager, some watchful, some hostile. His voice has carried through the courts since dawn. Each story He has told cuts a little deeper. The chief priests and elders have not left; they hover at the fringe, whispering behind their fringed shawls, their lips tight. A line of temple guards waits farther back, uncertain whose command will prevail.

He has just finished the tale of the vineyard—of tenants who beat the servants and killed the son. The crowd's murmur still hasn't died. Everyone understands what the story meant; no one says it aloud. The elders' hands close over their staffs; the disciples glance toward Jesus with unease, aware of the danger in every word. The tension is a string drawn to breaking.

Above them, pigeons wheel and settle on the lintels. The sound of their wings mingles with the low chant of Levites reading from the psalms for the day. A gust of wind carries fragments of the chant down to the crowd: *"This is the gate of the Lord; the righteous shall enter through it."*

Jesus is silent for a moment. He looks toward the upper terrace where the priests stand in their linen robes. Then His gaze moves back to the people at His feet—the labourers with cracked hands, the women holding children, the young men craning to see. Every ear strains toward Him.

He begins again—not loudly, but with that even tone that draws the air out of the noise around Him.

"The kingdom of heaven," He says, "may be compared to a king who gave a marriage feast for his son."

## THE WEDDING FEAST / PROPER GARMENT (MT 22:1–14)

The words settle over the crowd like dust in light. It is a familiar opening—safe, even comforting. A wedding feast means joy, music, and the promise of blessing. People smile; a few nod to one another. But the priests do not smile. They remember the vineyard story and hear the warning underneath the courtesy.

Jesus lets the pause lengthen. A trumpet sounds somewhere deeper in the temple complex, signalling the hour of the morning sacrifice. He waits until its echo fades.

"He sent his servants," He continues, "to call those who had been invited to the feast—but they would not come."

The crowd shifts. Everyone knows what such a refusal means. To ignore a royal summons is to declare rebellion. Jesus' tone remains calm, but each phrase lands with precision, the way a hammer meets a chisel.

"Again he sent other servants, saying, 'Tell those who are invited, behold, I have prepared my dinner, my oxen and my fat calves are killed, and everything is ready; come to the marriage feast.'"

Behind Him, the smoke of the sacrifice begins to rise. The smell of burnt flesh and incense drifts across the courtyard. The words and the scent mingle: a feast prepared, an offering consumed.

"But they made light of it," He says, "and went off—one to his farm, another to his business—while the rest seized his servants, treated them shamefully, and killed them."

Gasps ripple through the outer ranks. A woman draws her shawl over her mouth; a child begins to cry and is hushed. The elders' faces darken. They have heard enough stories about servants killed. They know who the king represents.

"The king was angry," Jesus says quietly, "and he sent his armies and destroyed those murderers and burned their city."

The image cuts through the warm morning air like cold steel. In the distance, the city's outer walls shimmer. Some of the older men remember Babylon, others think of Rome. Everyone feels the heat of prophecy in the simple statement.

He pauses again. A breeze moves across the courtyard, lifting the edges of garments. The guards glance toward the priests; the priests say nothing. Jesus goes on as if He has not noticed.

"Then he said to his servants, 'The wedding is ready, but those invited were not worthy. Go therefore to the thoroughfares, and invite to the marriage feast as many as you find.'"

A thin smile flickers among the poor who have gathered close. They know what it means to be found in the streets. The respectable press their lips together.

"So the servants went out into the roads," He says, "and gathered all whom they found, both bad and good; so the wedding hall was filled with guests."

The courtyard holds its breath. The crowd hears the mercy; the rulers hear the threat.

For a heartbeat the air feels lighter, as if the story has turned toward joy. A wedding hall filled, the poor welcomed, the king's anger satisfied—perhaps the parable is ending in mercy. Then Jesus' voice lowers, steady and grave.

"But when the king came in to look at the guests, he saw there a man who had no wedding garment."

The words hang, almost casual, yet they change everything. The listeners lean forward. Everyone knows that in royal feasts garments are provided at the door—clean robes for those unaccustomed to splendour. To refuse one is defiance in silk. The crowd senses the danger but cannot yet name it.

"He said to him, 'Friend, how did you get in here without a wedding garment?'"

A pause. The pigeons stir again on the ledge above. Somewhere in the outer courts a jar breaks; the sharp crack echoes. No one in the temple moves.

"And he was speechless," Jesus says.

The silence in the story becomes the silence in the court. Even the children's restless shifting stops. It is the silence of a man discovered—one whose mouth can no longer defend what his heart has chosen.

## THE WEDDING FEAST / PROPER GARMENT (MT 22:1–14)

"Then the king said to the attendants, 'Bind him hand and foot, and cast him into the outer darkness; there men will weep and gnash their teeth.'"

The sentence lands like a bell toll. Its weight fills the open air. Those near the front draw back; a few of the priests exchange glances. This is no longer about etiquette; it is judgment spoken through the ordinary.

Jesus does not soften it. His gaze moves from the poor at His feet to the robed officials beyond them, then back to the crowd. His voice is calm, almost tender.

"For many are called," He says, "but few are chosen."

Then He falls silent.

No one answers. The echo of the final phrase slides across the stones, up into the arches, out toward the city. The temple court seems to shrink around them. The elders look to one another, each waiting for another to speak. None does.

The disciples stand motionless. They understand only pieces, yet they feel the danger in the air—the kind of danger that no sword can shield. Beyond the colonnade, the hum of Jerusalem resumes: the calls of sellers, the clatter of pottery, the far-off bray of donkeys on the Mount of Olives. Ordinary life surges back, pretending nothing has changed.

But everything has.

Somewhere in the upper courts a lamb bleats, then the sound of a knife, then the rush of water as blood is washed away. The rhythm of sacrifice continues, unaware that the true sacrifice is already standing in their midst.

Jesus turns toward the exit of the court. The crowd parts for Him without command. His steps are unhurried, measured against the beat of His own words. A few of the poor follow, hoping for one more healing, one more story. The priests remain where they are, murmuring together in low, controlled tones. One of them tears a piece of linen and ties it around his wrist as a reminder to act later. The guards fall in behind at a distance.

At the edge of the portico, sunlight flares through the pillars. The air smells of cedar oil and dust. Jesus steps through the glare and disappears into the outer street, where the city's noise swallows Him.

Behind Him, in the temple's stillness, His words linger: a king, a feast, a son, and a guest cast out for coming unprepared. The meaning lies hidden but alive, like a spark under ash. The rulers feel its heat but cannot yet name the fire. They will remember it when another feast begins in an upper room and a garment of seamless linen lies folded in a tomb.

For now the silence returns. The pigeons settle again; the Levites resume their chant; the city continues its routines. Yet those who heard know that something final has been spoken. The sound of celebration has turned to warning. The music of the wedding has changed key, carrying a note that will not resolve until the end of the week—when another banquet is prepared, and the Bridegroom stands alone.

**The Surface Story**

When Jesus began this parable in the courts of the Temple, His listeners instantly recognised the world He was describing. A royal wedding was the highest expression of joy and loyalty a kingdom could stage. To attend such a feast was to acknowledge one's allegiance to the crown; to refuse was not mere discourtesy but rebellion. In the honour-based culture of first-century Judea, loyalty was woven through invitations and meals. Every table confirmed an alliance. Every empty seat could become a political statement.

A wedding for a king's son was the most public of covenants. It bound generations—the royal line secured through marriage, the subjects reaffirmed through celebration. To be invited was a privilege that conferred standing; to accept was to proclaim fidelity. There was no neutral ground. To decline such a summons after first agreeing to come was to disgrace the host before the eyes of the nation. It called into question a man's honour, his gratitude, even his patriotism.

Royal feasts of that era followed a pattern the crowd knew well. Invitations went out twice. The first established consent: "The king desires your presence." The second arrived when everything was prepared: "The time has come; the hall is ready." To withdraw after the second message was to humiliate the heralds and shame the king himself. It signalled

## THE WEDDING FEAST / PROPER GARMENT (MT 22:1-14)

indifference to his generosity, contempt for his son, and contempt for the bond of peace symbolised by the meal.

The first century was a world sustained by reciprocation. Gifts required gratitude; hospitality demanded response. Banquets were not merely social but sacramental: they enacted the rhythm of giving and return that held society together. When Jesus spoke of servants sent, of invitations refused, His hearers understood the scale of the insult without further explanation. Such behaviour was unthinkable. It tore at the fabric of loyalty that kept order intact.

They also recognised the master's patience as unnatural. No monarch would send a second wave of messengers to ingrates who had already mocked his first. The king in Jesus' story acts with extraordinary restraint—he pleads before he punishes. Yet when his servants are seized and killed, the story snaps back to realism. Every listener knew what followed: reprisal. Ancient kings defended their dignity with armies; their wrath was both justice and deterrent. The burning of the murderers' city would have seemed inevitable, not cruel. In refusing the invitation, they had declared war.

Still, the parable moves beyond vengeance. The king's response is as startling as his anger. He will not allow the feast to remain empty; the hall must be filled. To ancient ears this detail was remarkable. A royal banquet was no casual gathering—it displayed hierarchy itself. Guests of high rank reclined nearest the host, lesser men farther out; the seating itself was a map of honour. For such a feast to be thrown open to the streets was inconceivable. Commoners might watch a procession or glimpse the torches of the palace from afar, but they did not enter its courts.

Jesus' description of servants moving through the city to gather "all whom they found, both bad and good" would have provoked incredulity. The lanes of Jerusalem were narrow, littered with refuse, crowded with traders and beggars. To pass from marble corridor to gutter was to cross the boundaries of purity. Yet the king's servants in the story do exactly that. They sweep the streets clean of strangers and lead them into the royal hall. The picture borders on comic exaggeration—farmers with calloused hands sitting beside courtiers, cripples and labourers feasting beneath chandeliers. But the laughter would have been uneasy. The image violated everything the culture assumed about worthiness.

Banquets in that world were never only about food. They were symbols of covenant and purity. To eat with the unclean was to share their defilement; to admit them to a royal feast was to profane the king's table. Listeners steeped in the laws of Leviticus would have felt the scandal immediately. They would also have heard the echo of Israel's own story: slaves invited to freedom, strangers grafted into covenant, undeserving guests at a divine meal. Yet even so, on the surface of the parable, the shock remains social before it is spiritual. A ruler acting with such reckless generosity would have appeared mad—or possessed by joy too great to care for convention.

Then comes the twist that restores decorum only to overturn it again. When the king enters to survey his guests, he notices a man without a wedding garment. This detail anchored the parable in strict realism. In ancient Near Eastern custom, hosts of stature often provided festival garments at the door, particularly for those unaccustomed to luxury. To refuse one was not poverty but pride. The garment signified respect for the occasion and submission to the host's authority. To enter without it was to mock the feast while partaking of it, to accept the gift while scorning the giver.

Jesus' audience would have understood this perfectly. They had seen such robes distributed at noble weddings, woven of fine linen, dyed with modest colour, simple yet honourable. The absence of the garment was not oversight; it was declaration. In the story, the offender is addressed gently—"Friend, how did you get in here without a wedding garment?"—but his silence condemns him. He has no excuse because none is possible. In a society where honour is public, speechlessness is guilt.

The king's order—"Bind him hand and foot, and cast him into the outer darkness"—is not cruelty so much as consequence. It restores the order the guest has refused to honour. The attendants act not as torturers but as witnesses to propriety. Those who spurn the customs of the feast exclude

## THE WEDDING FEAST / PROPER GARMENT (MT 22:1–14)

themselves. To be thrown into the night beyond the torches is simply to return to the place one has chosen: outside the circle of joy.

To those hearing Jesus that day, the phrase *outer darkness* would have conjured something specific and visible.

Palace banquets blazed with lamps; beyond the thresholds lay the unlit courtyards and the sleeping streets.

Within, music and laughter; without, silence and cold stone.

The contrast between lighted hall and night beyond the door was a moral geography they all knew: honour inside, shame outside.

To be expelled from such radiance was to fall from belonging into obscurity.

It was a judgment more piercing than pain — exclusion from fellowship.

No further explanation was needed.

The entire parable had unfolded according to the social codes of their own lives.

Every hearer could map its logic: invitation, refusal, retaliation, restoration of order.

What startled them was not the justice but the sequence of mercy.

The king endures insult after insult before he acts; he opens his doors to the undeserving before he enforces discipline.

In that patience they sensed something beyond royalty, though they could not yet name it.

At the level of realism, this was still a story of politics and protocol.

A kingdom defines itself by its celebrations; allegiance is proved by attendance.

In a culture where power was personal, to share the ruler's meal was to share his peace.

Hence the double weight of refusal — it wounded the monarch and fractured the state.

Likewise, the man without a garment threatened harmony from within.

His presence desecrated the very table meant to unite.

Every element of the narrative carried this double edge of honour and danger.

The burning of the city, too, fit the world they inhabited.

Rome had crushed towns for lesser acts of defiance; local tetrarchs had done the same on smaller scales.

A feast, in their imagination, could end in fire if dignity demanded it.

The crowd listening to Jesus would have pictured smoke over familiar rooftops, soldiers marching down known streets.

Nothing in the story sounded mythical.

It was the texture of daily life, heightened and arranged like a parable carved out of their own fears.

The mention of servants sent again and again reminded them of the messengers who carried decrees and tax demands through the countryside.

To mistreat such envoys was to strike at the king himself.

In Judea's long memory, every rebellion began with ignored invitations, every exile with unheeded warnings.

So even before theology entered, they could feel the weight of history pressing through the tale: defiance answered by destruction, mercy offered once more to the margins.

The social imagination of the time made feasts miniature kingdoms.

Each host was sovereign of his table; each guest subject to its laws.

Seating reflected hierarchy; garments expressed purity; food was fellowship, not convenience.

At a royal meal, everything became symbol: the bread of allegiance, the wine of gratitude, the garment of honour.

To participate rightly was to affirm the order of the world.

To flout it was to tear that order apart.

This is why the parable's details stung long before anyone sought hidden meaning.

It pictured their society with merciless accuracy, showing its splendor and its fragility.

Yet the tale did not rest on cynicism.

Beneath its realism was a truth even the cautious could admire: a king determined that his joy should be shared.

Despite outrage and betrayal, he will not sit before an empty table.

## THE WEDDING FEAST / PROPER GARMENT (MT 22:1-14)

His banquet must be full, his generosity vindicated in abundance.

For an audience accustomed to careful reciprocity, this extravagance was bewildering.

They might whisper that such a ruler would bankrupt his honour to feed the ungrateful.

But the story's logic insists otherwise — that honour fulfilled itself in inclusion, that glory grew by gift.

To the Pharisees and elders standing near, every phrase carried a mirror.

They could not dismiss it as fantasy; each gesture belonged to their own etiquette.

That was its cunning: realism sharpened until it became revelation.

No allegory was needed to make them uneasy.

They saw their own assumptions acted out and overturned — a hierarchy undone by mercy, a ritual of belonging turned inside out.

By the time Jesus fell silent, the world of the story had merged with the world around them.

They could still smell the incense from the altar and hear the shuffle of sandals on stone.

They might even glance toward the palace of Herod beyond the city wall and imagine torches flaring there for another feast.

The details of the parable fit too neatly into their daily texture to be ignored.

It was realism so precise it became accusation.

At its surface, then, the *Wedding Feast* speaks only of things visible: invitations delivered, garments offered, doors opened and shut.

It is a study in the laws of hospitality that governed every household in Judea.

Yet those very laws already contained tension between obligation and grace.

Jesus simply let that tension play itself out.

The host's patience, the guest's presumption, the final division of light and darkness — each followed the customs of men until those customs collapsed beneath their own weight.

The first hearers would have left the Temple that day thoughtful and disturbed.

They had not been told what to believe, only shown what they already practiced.

The parable held up their order like a mirror: beautiful, brittle, and beginning to crack.

No mystical meaning was needed to wound them.

The realism itself was revelation enough.

**The Hidden Fire**

## a) Text, Translation, and Literary Context
### Greek Text (Matthew 22:1–14):

Καὶ ἀποκριθεὶς ὁ Ἰησοῦς πάλιν εἶπεν ἐν παραβολαῖς αὐτοῖς λέγων·

Ὡμοιώθη ἡ βασιλεία τῶν οὐρανῶν ἀνθρώπῳ βασιλεῖ ὃς ἐποίησεν γάμους τῷ υἱῷ αὐτοῦ.

καὶ ἀπέστειλεν τοὺς δούλους αὐτοῦ καλέσαι τοὺς κεκλημένους εἰς τοὺς γάμους, καὶ οὐκ ἤθελον ἐλθεῖν.

πάλιν ἀπέστειλεν ἄλλους δούλους λέγων· Εἴπατε τοῖς κεκλημένοις· Ἰδοὺ τὸ ἄριστόν μου ἡτοίμακα, οἱ ταῦροί μου καὶ τὰ σιτιστὰ τεθυμένα, καὶ πάντα ἕτοιμα· δεῦτε εἰς τοὺς γάμους.

οἱ δὲ ἀμελήσαντες ἀπῆλθον, ὁ μὲν εἰς τὸν ἴδιον ἀγρόν, ὁ δὲ εἰς τὴν ἐμπορίαν αὐτοῦ·

οἱ δὲ λοιποὶ κρατήσαντες τοὺς δούλους αὐτοῦ ὕβρισαν καὶ ἀπέκτειναν.

ὁ δὲ βασιλεὺς ὠργίσθη, καὶ πέμψας τὰ στρατεύματα αὐτοῦ ἀπώλεσεν τοὺς φονεῖς ἐκείνους καὶ τὴν πόλιν αὐτῶν ἐνέπρησεν.

τότε λέγει τοῖς δούλοις αὐτοῦ· Ὁ μὲν γάμος ἕτοιμός ἐστιν, οἱ δὲ κεκλημένοι οὐκ ἦσαν ἄξιοι·

πορεύεσθε οὖν ἐπὶ τὰς διεξόδους τῶν ὁδῶν, καὶ ὅσους ἐὰν εὕρητε καλέσατε εἰς τοὺς γάμους.

καὶ ἐξελθόντες οἱ δοῦλοι ἐκεῖνοι εἰς τὰς ὁδοὺς συνήγαγον πάντας ὅσους εὗρον, πονηρούς τε καὶ ἀγαθούς· καὶ ἐπλήσθη ὁ νυμφὼν ἀνακειμένων.

Εἰσελθὼν δὲ ὁ βασιλεὺς θεωρῆσαι τοὺς ἀνακειμένους εἶδεν ἐκεῖ ἄνθρωπον

## THE WEDDING FEAST / PROPER GARMENT (MT 22:1-14)

οὐκ ἐνδεδυμένον ἔνδυμα γάμου,

καὶ λέγει αὐτῷ· Φίλε, πῶς εἰσῆλθες ὧδε μὴ ἔχων ἔνδυμα γάμου; ὁ δὲ ἐφιμώθη. τότε εἶπεν ὁ βασιλεὺς τοῖς διακόνοις· Δήσαντες αὐτοῦ πόδας καὶ χεῖρας ἐκβάλετε αὐτὸν εἰς τὸ σκότος τὸ ἐξώτερον· ἐκεῖ ἔσται ὁ κλαυθμὸς καὶ ὁ βρυγμὸς τῶν ὀδόντων.

Πολλοὶ γάρ εἰσιν κλητοί, ὀλίγοι δὲ ἐκλεκτοί.

Matthew's text begins with the formal precision of royal proclamation and ends with the chill of divine verdict. Where Luke spoke of a "certain man," Matthew speaks of a "king." Every word heightens gravity. The Greek verb ὡμοιώθη ("has been likened") places the parable in the passive voice—the divine passive that implies God's authorship. "The kingdom of heaven has been likened..." not by men, but by the Word Himself who is its likeness.

The scene opens not with a table but with a kingdom—the *basileia tōn ouranōn*, Matthew's preferred phrase throughout the Gospel. The possessive plural "of the heavens" roots the story in transcendent order; it is heaven's monarchy, not an earthly one, though told in earthly terms. The subject of the verb is ἄνθρωπος βασιλεύς, literally "a man, a king"—a Hebraic idiom that unites divine and human language. Matthew has the Son of God describe His Father in the ordinary title of kingship: the highest figure of human authority becomes a vessel for divine reality.

The king ἐποίησεν γάμους τῷ υἱῷ αὐτοῦ—"made a wedding for his son." The plural γάμους (gamous) indicates the entire celebration, not merely the ceremony but the days-long feast that followed. The verb ἐποίησεν—the same word used in Genesis for creation—underscores intentionality: the wedding is something fashioned, willed into being. The royal father *makes* the feast the way God *makes* creation: not for utility, but for joy and communion.

The action begins with sending: ἀπέστειλεν τοὺς δούλους αὐτοῦ καλέσαι τοὺς κεκλημένους—"he sent his servants to call those who had been called." Matthew doubles the root καλέω ("to call") so that the sentence reads literally "to call the called." This layering of call upon call captures Israel's vocation: the people already invited through covenant are invited again through Christ. Grammar becomes theology. The repetition of καλέω runs through the passage like a pulse—call, called, invited, chosen—and culminates in the final antithesis between κλητοί (called) and ἐκλεκτοί (chosen).

Yet those first summoned "were unwilling to come" (οὐκ ἤθελον ἐλθεῖν). The verb θέλω expresses will and desire; refusal here is not ignorance but a deliberate act of the will. Matthew's tense—an imperfect with continuing force—suggests obstinate resistance: they kept on not wanting to come. Divine generosity meets human inertia.

The king sends a second group of servants with ampler words: "Behold, my banquet I have prepared; my oxen and my fattened calves are killed, and all things are ready; come to the wedding" (Ἰδοὺ τὸ ἄριστόν μου ἡτοίμακα... πάντα ἕτοιμα· δεῦτε εἰς τοὺς γάμους). The vocabulary overflows with readiness: ἡτοίμακα (I have prepared), ἕτοιμα (ready). It is eschatological language. What has been long promised now stands completed. The possessive "my" repeated thrice—my dinner, my oxen, my fattened cattle—intensifies the pathos of personal investment.

The response is indifference turned violent. ἀμελήσαντες ἀπῆλθον—"they were careless and went away." The verb ἀμελέω means to make light of, to be unconcerned; it describes the spiritual apathy Isaiah ascribes to Israel's hearers: "This people's heart has grown dull." One goes to his field (ἀγρόν), another to his business (ἐμπορία). The words recall Luke's parable of excuses but sharpen them: now indifference escalates into outrage. "The rest seized his servants, mistreated them, and killed them." The verb ὕβρισαν—"they insulted" or "outraged"—implies not only violence but mockery; it is the root of "hubris." In Matthew's diction, arrogance becomes murder.

The king's response is swift and judicial: ὠργίσθη ("he was angered"). The word ὀργή in Scripture denotes not passion but settled righteousness, the wrath of order violated. The king πέμψας τὰ στρατεύματα αὐτοῦ—"sending his armies"—ἀπώλεσεν τοὺς φονεῖς ἐκείνους καὶ τὴν πόλιν αὐτῶν ἐνέπρησεν—"he destroyed those murderers and burned their city." The verb ἐνέπρησεν ("set fire to") burns through history: Matthew's readers, writing after the destruction of Jerusalem in 70 AD, could not hear it without remembering the city in flames. The story's realism becomes prophecy fulfilled.

After judgment, mercy resumes. "Then he said to his servants, The wedding is ready, but those invited were not worthy" (οἱ δὲ κεκλημένοι οὐκ ἦσαν ἄξιοι). The adjective ἄξιοι—worthy—denotes not merit but fittingness. They were invited but out of tune with the invitation. The host's verdict is not on their sin but on their dissonance.

The next command widens the circle: πορεύεσθε οὖν ἐπὶ τὰς διεξόδους τῶν ὁδῶν—"Go therefore to the crossroads of the highways." The compound noun διέξοδοι literally means "outlets" or "crossroads," the meeting places of trade and travel. Here geography becomes theology: salvation moves from the closed city to the open world. The servants are told to "call as many as you find" (ὅσους ἐὰν εὕρητε), without qualification of class or purity. The universal scope is intensified by the participle "going out" (ἐξελθόντες) that begins the next verse.

"They gathered all they found, both bad and good" (πονηρούς τε καὶ ἀγαθούς). Matthew reverses the usual moral order; the bad precede the good, as though grace reaches downward first. The inclusiveness is total: the kingdom's hall is filled not with the elite but with every sort. The result: ἐπλήσθη ὁ νυμφὼν ἀνακειμένων—"the wedding hall was filled with those reclining." The verb ἐπλήσθη (was filled) echoes the purpose clause of Luke's version—"that my house may be filled." Divine fullness is the goal that underwrites divine patience.

Then the scene narrows. "But when the king came in to look upon the guests..." (Εἰσελθὼν δὲ ὁ βασιλεὺς θεωρῆσαι τοὺς ἀνακειμένους). The verb θεωρῆσαι—to behold, inspect, or contemplate—suggests a gaze that judges by seeing. In Matthew's usage it implies discernment: to look and to know. What follows is one of the Gospel's most compressed judgments. The king "saw there a man not wearing a wedding garment" (εἶδεν ἐκεῖ ἄνθρωπον οὐκ ἐνδεδυμένον ἔνδυμα γάμου). The double negative—οὐκ ἐνδεδυμένον—emphasises absence: not clothed in what the feast required. The term ἔνδυμα (enduma) derives from ἐνδύω, "to put on." The noun occurs elsewhere in Matthew (6:25, "what you will put on") but here acquires symbolic edge. A man may be present but unrobed in grace.

The king's address begins with courtesy: Φίλε—"Friend." Matthew reserves this form of address for moments of betrayal (cf. 20:13; 26:50). It is the greeting of wounded love, intimacy turned accusation. The question that follows—πῶς εἰσῆλθες ὧδε μὴ ἔχων ἔνδυμα γάμου;—is both logical and moral: "How did you come in here without a wedding garment?" The particle μὴ assumes the negative: there is no way to justify such entry.

The man's response is silence: ὁ δὲ ἐφιμώθη. The verb literally means "he was muzzled." Used elsewhere for silencing demons and waves (Mark 4:39), it conveys the sudden stilling of unclean speech. The guest stands unmasked, unable to utter pretext or defense. His muteness is the climax of the story: refusal has reached its final form—not words against God, but no words at all.

The king then speaks in the imperatives of justice: Δήσαντες αὐτοῦ πόδας καὶ χεῖρας ἐκβάλετε αὐτὸν εἰς τὸ σκότος τὸ ἐξώτερον· ἐκεῖ ἔσται ὁ κλαυθμὸς καὶ ὁ βρυγμὸς τῶν ὀδόντων.

"Bind his feet and hands, and cast him into the outer darkness; there shall be weeping and gnashing of teeth."

The verbs are sharp and physical: δήσαντες (having bound), ἐκβάλετε (throw out). The phrase σκότος τὸ ἐξώτερον—literally "the darkness, the outer one"—is uniquely Matthean, appearing elsewhere to mark final exclusion (8:12; 25:30). It evokes not annihilation but exile from light, the inverse of communion. What began as invitation now ends as separation, the very opposite of the feast. The vivid participles give the sentence weight, but the real force lies in the shift of mood: the voice that once called now commands. Mercy and judgment converge in the same King.

The parable concludes with a proverb that folds all its themes into a single line: Πολλοὶ γάρ εἰσιν κλητοί, ὀλίγοι δὲ ἐκλεκτοί—"For many are called, but few are chosen." The conjunction γάρ (for) makes the maxim an explanation of everything preceding it. The terms κλητοί (called) and ἐκλεκτοί (chosen) share the same root but diverge in destiny. The grammar itself defines grace: calling is universal, election is responsive. In the

## THE WEDDING FEAST / PROPER GARMENT (MT 22:1-14)

rhythm of these two words Matthew captures the dialectic of divine generosity and human freedom that runs through his Gospel.

Beneath the royal language and violent imagery lies a carefully wrought literary architecture. Matthew arranges the story in seven movements, each marked by verbs of sending and response:

1. **Invitation issued** (ἀπέστειλεν... καλέσαι).
2. **Refusal given** (οὐκ ἤθελον).
3. **Second invitation and detailed preparation** (πάλιν ἀπέστειλεν... πάντα ἕτοιμα).
4. **Violent rejection and judgment** (ὕβρισαν καὶ ἀπέκτειναν... ἐνέπρησεν).
5. **Renewed call to outsiders** (πορεύεσθε οὖν... καλέσατε).
6. **Filling of the hall** (ἐπλήσθη ὁ νυμφών).
7. **Inspection and exclusion of the unrobed guest** (θεωρῆσαι... ἐφιμώθη).

This progression is not merely narrative; it mirrors salvation history. The first servants evoke the prophets, the second wave the apostles; the burning of the city echoes the destruction of Jerusalem; the second invitation prefigures the Church's mission to the Gentiles; the inspection of the guests anticipates final judgment. The pattern—*call, refusal, extension, discernment*—is the rhythm of the Gospel itself.

Matthew's diction amplifies Luke's simplicity into severity. Where Luke used a "certain man," Matthew's "king" introduces majesty and accountability. Where Luke's host expands generosity, Matthew's monarch enforces holiness. The verb ἀπέστειλεν (he sent) occurs three times, each instance heightening tension until it culminates in retribution. Likewise, the repeated ἕτοιμα (ready) carries a liturgical resonance—language of temple and sacrifice now transferred to the Kingdom's feast. The parable thus becomes a miniature of covenant history reframed as liturgy: preparation, consecration, rejection, renewal.

The use of γάμος (wedding) rather than δεῖπνον (banquet) signals a shift from hospitality to nuptial symbolism. In Jewish and prophetic idiom, marriage is covenant: Yahweh the Bridegroom, Israel the bride. The plural γάμοι suggests not a single event but a festal season—the days-long celebration of union. The son's marriage in the parable therefore represents more than joy; it stands for divine communion restored. The king's preparation for the γάμοι mirrors God's preparation of salvation through His Son. The slaughtered oxen and fattened calves evoke the sacrificial language of temple worship, foreshadowing the Lamb slain for the world.

Even at the level of syntax, Matthew writes theology. The alternation of aorist and present tenses creates momentum from event to significance. The past actions—*he sent, they refused, he burned*—move inexorably toward the timeless closing statement: *many are called, few chosen*. The grammar itself widens from history to eternity. What begins as a story about a city's insult ends as an oracle about the human race.

The narrative's turning point, the king's inspection, holds a double function. It affirms inclusion—anyone may come—but demands transformation—no one may remain unchanged. The man without a garment represents not the outsider but the complacent insider. The garment's absence is not ignorance but negligence. Matthew's Greek for "wedding garment," ἔνδυμα γάμου, appears nowhere else in Scripture, making it uniquely symbolic here. The verb ἐνδύω ("to put on") will later become Paul's metaphor for baptismal grace: "Put on Christ." Matthew anticipates that theology by portraying entry without adornment as spiritual nakedness.

Even the brief exchange between king and guest condenses the Gospel's drama. The address φίλε (friend) recalls Judas's greeting in Gethsemane; both moments combine intimacy and exposure. The verb εἰσῆλθες ("you came in") marks voluntary approach—the man entered willingly but wrongly. His speechlessness (ἐφιμώθη) reveals that guilt in the Gospel is not the failure to argue but the inability to love. When the king commands binding and expulsion, it is the external enactment of an interior truth: self-exclusion from grace.

Placed within Matthew's structure, the parable continues a triad of

# THE WEDDING FEAST / PROPER GARMENT (MT 22:1–14)

confrontations that began in chapter 21: the parables of the Two Sons, the Wicked Tenants, and now the Wedding Feast. Each escalates the conflict between Jesus and the Temple authorities. The first exposes hypocrisy ("they say but do not do"), the second exposes murder ("they kill the heir"), and the third exposes presumption ("they attend the feast but reject the garment"). Together they form a trilogy of rejection culminating in the transfer of the Kingdom: "The Kingdom of God will be taken from you and given to a people producing its fruits." The literary continuity makes clear that this is not a new story but the same divine summons met by new refusals.

The imagery of fire and darkness bookends Matthew's vision of judgment throughout the Gospel. Fire purges the false security of the privileged city; darkness envelops the unprepared guest. One symbolizes corporate loss, the other personal accountability. Both together express the completeness of divine justice. The contrast is not between invitation and punishment but between grace received and grace refused.

At the textual level, the parable's symmetry is nearly perfect. Two sendings of servants, two responses, two outcomes; then one inspection and one sentence of closure. Matthew's artistry gives theological rhythm to what could otherwise seem chaotic. Every element of disorder—violence, indifference, presumption—is met by a corresponding act of divine order: invitation, renewal, discernment. The king's actions restore harmony at every turn until the hall stands full and the unworthy are outside.

The closing aphorism—*many are called, few chosen*—therefore reads not as limitation but as revelation. The Kingdom's call is boundless; what narrows it is human response. Matthew's narrative voice, measured and judicial, allows the words to fall like a seal on the scroll of history. The passive ὡμοιώθη from the opening line finds its echo here: what the Kingdom "has been likened to" has now been revealed in its likeness—the divine generosity mirrored in a story of men.

In the end, the passage's literary structure already holds the theology that will unfold in later sections. The king's preparation mirrors creation; the invitations, revelation; the refusals, sin; the second calling, redemption;

the inspection, judgment; the wedding garment, sanctifying grace. Even before allegory, Matthew's syntax performs the movement of salvation. Each verb marks another stage in the rhythm of divine patience—sending, inviting, waiting, burning, filling, discerning. By the final verse, language itself has become liturgy. The story's grammar widens like the open doors of the hall until the reader stands before them, hearing the echo of the same call: "Behold, all things are ready. Come to the wedding."

## b) Theological Interpretation

The parable of the Wedding Feast stands among the most solemn declarations of Jesus' ministry, a story in which the joy of divine communion and the terror of its refusal are shown in one frame. Beneath the realism of invitations and garments unfolds the inner rhythm of salvation history itself. The Kingdom of heaven, likened to a royal marriage, reveals the heart of God as a Father who will not rest until His Son's joy is complete. Every detail—the feast prepared, the messengers sent, the hall filled, the guest cast out—becomes an icon of the divine economy: grace offered, resisted, renewed, and finally discerned.

Matthew positions this parable at a decisive hour. Jesus is teaching in the Temple during the final days before His Passion. He has just told the stories of the Two Sons and the Wicked Tenants—each a verdict on Israel's leaders, each a mirror of covenant history. The Wedding Feast completes that triad, shifting from vineyard to banquet, from labour to love. The shift is significant. The Kingdom is not merely a task to be worked but a joy to be entered. God's reign is not the acquisition of power but the communion of persons. The "king" of the story is no despot maintaining order; he is a father preparing celebration. The "Son" for whom the wedding is made is the messianic Bridegroom foretold by Isaiah and Hosea, the one who will bind God and His people in everlasting fidelity.

From the opening line—"The Kingdom of heaven has been likened to a king who made a wedding for his son"—the nuptial language of Scripture resounds. Israel's prophets had long spoken of covenant as marriage. "I will betroth you to me forever," declared Hosea; "your Maker is your

## THE WEDDING FEAST / PROPER GARMENT (MT 22:1-14)

husband," sang Isaiah. Jesus takes that imagery and places Himself at its centre. The wedding feast is His own mission: the Incarnation as courtship, the Cross as bridal price, the Resurrection as consummation, the Eucharist as abiding union. The Father prepares the feast; the Son becomes both Bridegroom and Banquet; the Spirit is the love that sends out invitations to the ends of the earth. The Trinity itself is refracted through the parable's simple plot.

The first invitations echo Israel's long history of call and response. The servants who carry them are the prophets—sent again and again to summon God's people to fidelity. Their rejection, mocking, and death replay the nation's story from Elijah to Zechariah. Matthew's Greek intensifies the pathos: "They were unwilling to come." The refusal is not ignorance but a hardening of the will. In that obstinacy lies the mystery of freedom. The God who calls will not coerce; He risks refusal in order to preserve love. The Kingdom advances not by domination but by desire.

Yet divine patience is not indifference. The king sends further messengers, speaking more tenderly, describing the meal already prepared—"Behold, my banquet is ready." In that line the reader hears the tone of salvation completed: the oxen and calves are slain, the table set. In biblical idiom, the killing of the fattened calf signals covenant sacrifice; the readiness of the feast prefigures the fullness of redemption. What was promised through the prophets is now accomplished in the person of Christ. To decline this summons is not a matter of manners but of destiny.

The invited guests turn away to their "field" and "business." Here the theology cuts deep. Sin rarely appears as defiance; it appears as distraction. The field and the commerce represent preoccupation with ownership and productivity—the twin idols of self-sufficiency. These men do not hate the king; they simply prefer their projects. In their world, as in ours, indifference is the more lethal rebellion. The refusal of joy is the essence of judgment. For Matthew, this is not a sociological critique but a spiritual diagnosis. The tragedy of the Kingdom is not that the wicked oppose it but that the comfortable ignore it.

When the servants are seized and killed, the story crosses from neglect to violence. Covenant infidelity matures into persecution. The burning of the city is therefore not arbitrary vengeance but theological disclosure. The destruction of Jerusalem, witnessed by Matthew's generation, becomes emblem and consequence of that ancient refusal. The fire that consumes the city is the same fire that purified Isaiah's lips: the holiness of God meeting resistance. Divine wrath is not contradiction of mercy but its shadow—the sorrow of love spurned. As Gregory the Great wrote, "He who is love itself is angry only when love is refused." The parable's catastrophe reveals not cruelty but the moral gravity of grace.

Yet judgment is never God's final word. "The wedding is ready," the king declares, "but those invited were not worthy." Worthiness here means not moral perfection but willingness to receive. The king's response is not to cancel the feast but to expand the guest list. What human insult narrows, divine generosity widens. The invitation goes now to the crossroads—the place of mingled traffic, of strangers and wanderers. The servants are told to "gather all you find, both bad and good." In this widening, Matthew's Gospel moves from Israel to the nations. The crossroads are the Gentile world, the highways of history where grace will run. The Church's missionary vocation is born in this sentence.

At this stage the parable becomes not merely revelation of history but description of the Church herself. The hall filled with "bad and good" is the visible community of believers, the field where wheat and weeds grow together until the harvest. The Kingdom in its present form is inclusive, expansive, open to all; but inclusion is not indifference. Communion demands conversion. The next scene—the king entering to inspect the guests—introduces a new dimension of divine scrutiny. The feast is open, but the feast is holy. Entry is by invitation; permanence is by transformation. The man without the garment stands as the warning written into every liturgy: one may come near and still remain unconverted.

Theologically, this moment shifts the parable from salvation history to eschatology. The king's gaze foreshadows the judgment that will begin "with the household of God." The garment is no mere etiquette; it is

## THE WEDDING FEAST / PROPER GARMENT (MT 22:1–14)

the vesture of sanctifying grace, the robe of righteousness bestowed at baptism and kept through perseverance. In Scripture, to be "clothed" is to participate—to "put on the new man," to "put on Christ." The guest's nakedness is therefore spiritual, not social. He accepts invitation but not transformation. He desires proximity without participation, belonging without conversion. His speechlessness before the king's question— "Friend, how did you come in here without a wedding garment?"—is the silence of a conscience unprepared for love's demands. The judgment that follows is the exposure of hypocrisy: to stand in the hall of mercy yet remain unchanged by it.

The garment motif gathers together the whole theology of grace and freedom in a single image. A robe is both gift and responsibility. It must be received, worn, and kept clean. No one weaves it for himself; yet once given, it must be cherished. In that fabric the tension between divine initiative and human cooperation is perfectly expressed. Grace clothes, but the will must consent to be clothed. The guest's refusal to wear the garment is not ignorance of protocol but a quiet act of rebellion against communion. He wants the feast on his own terms. He accepts the invitation but resists transformation. The outer darkness to which he is cast is the final confirmation of his choice. Hell, in Matthew's idiom, is not God's hatred but the echo of human indifference—the solitude of the soul that will not be robed in love.

Within Matthew's wider Gospel, this scene exposes a recurring danger: the proximity of privilege without participation. The religious leaders who rejected the Son are mirrored in the guest who accepts the invitation yet enters unprepared. Both illustrate the peril of presumption. Election is never a guarantee; it is an invitation to fidelity. The parable thus bridges Israel's history and the Church's present. The first guests symbolise the covenant community that refused; the unrobed guest represents those within the new covenant who remain unchanged. The judgment upon him is a mercy turned inside out—grace refused from within the sanctuary.

For the Fathers, the "wedding garment" became a shorthand for the life of sanctifying grace. Origen saw it as "the purity of works that adorn faith."

Augustine called it *caritas*, love itself—the interior disposition without which all outward participation is void. Gregory the Great interpreted it as humility, the inner fabric that makes every virtue possible. Later tradition would read it as baptismal identity: the white garment received at the font and worn into eternity. Each interpretation converges on one truth—that to be saved is not only to be invited but to be transformed by what one receives. Grace is not a ticket to a table but a garment woven into the soul.

The king's command, "Bind him hand and foot," carries a symbolic reversal. The one who refused the garment is now stripped of freedom. In Scripture, sin always binds what grace would adorn. The man who sought autonomy finds captivity; the light he rejected becomes darkness. Yet even here, Matthew's language bears pathos. The king addresses him as *friend—phile—*before judgment falls. The same word will appear on Jesus' lips when Judas comes with his kiss: "Friend, do what you came to do." Both moments reveal the persistence of divine tenderness even at the edge of separation. God never ceases to address the sinner in the language of friendship, though the response may be silence.

The expulsion of the unrobed guest, harsh as it sounds, serves a deeper revelation of holiness. The Kingdom is inclusive in invitation but exclusive in essence. Mercy draws in all, yet love demands conformity to its own likeness. The feast cannot become disorder; the hall cannot host rebellion. Divine hospitality is not permissiveness. Holiness is the law of heaven— the rhythm by which joy remains joy. To enter without a garment is to introduce discord into harmony; the king's judgment restores music to the feast. The Church Fathers saw here a prophecy of the Last Judgment: the Lord inspecting His own household, separating appearance from reality. "Many are called, few chosen" is not a threat but an unveiling of truth—that salvation is not a matter of numbers but of depth.

The theological weight of that final maxim is immense. The call (*klēsis*) in Scripture is always grace; the choice (*eklogē*) is its fulfilment. God calls all because He wills all to be saved, yet the "few" are those who allow grace to bear fruit. The difference lies not in divine intention but in human response. Augustine heard in these words the echo of both mercy and freedom: *"He who created you without you will not justify you without you."* The Kingdom's inclusiveness is therefore not democratic but divine: it invites universally, yet judges personally.

Every baptised soul stands among the called. The robe is given freely, the feast is opened, the Father desires a full house. The "few" are not a secret handful whom God prefers, but those who keep wearing what they have received—who let the baptismal garment become a way of life. To be called is to receive grace; to be chosen is to persevere in it. Election, in this light, is not exclusion but endurance. God chooses those who keep choosing Him. The call brings us to the door; the life of holiness keeps us at the table. Many receive the robe; fewer guard it, wash it in repentance, and adorn it with charity. The difference is not in what the King offers, but in how deeply His guests allow that gift to shape their lives.

At its centre, the parable is revelation of the nuptial heart of God. The Father prepares a feast for His Son—the eternal plan of salvation is described as a wedding. This is the mystery St. Paul unfolds in Ephesians: "Christ loved the Church and gave Himself up for her, that He might present her to Himself in splendour." The king's insistence that the hall be filled, even with strangers, anticipates the birth of that Church from the nations. The Bridegroom will not dine alone. The burning of the city clears space for a new Jerusalem; the highways become the roads of mission. Divine jealousy, once directed to Israel, now widens to embrace the world.

In the economy of grace, every rejection becomes a door for someone else's redemption. The spurned invitation to the first guests becomes the summons to the Gentiles. God's plan, thwarted in one sphere, flowers in another. This is the scandal of divine patience—that the Lord will allow His messengers to die rather than cancel the feast. The Gospel, seen through this parable, is not a system of reward but a story of relentless love. The king's anger burns only to preserve joy; his justice exists to protect communion. The marriage of the Son will happen, not because the world deserves it, but because the Father wills it. The Kingdom cannot remain half-empty.

That insistence reveals the metaphysical core of the Gospel: creation itself is an invitation to joy. God does not create for utility but for communion. The cosmos exists because the Father desires a Bride for His Son—a humanity capable of sharing divine life. Every covenant in Scripture, from Adam to Christ, is a stage in that courtship. In Eden, the first marriage prefigured the last; in Revelation, the final marriage consummates the first. Between them stands the history of salvation, a drama of proposal and refusal. The parable of the Wedding Feast compresses that drama into a single evening. The hall, the garment, the judgment—all are images of God's unwearied longing for union.

The Eucharistic dimension of the story emerges naturally from this nuptial logic. The "banquet" the king prepares is fulfilled in the sacrament by which the Bridegroom gives Himself to His Bride. "Behold, my banquet is ready," becomes the liturgical invitation, "Blessed are those called to the supper of the Lamb." The Mass is the ongoing wedding feast where heaven and earth meet. Every altar is the king's table; every priest a servant sent with invitation. The bread and wine, once symbols of sustenance, become instruments of espousal. To approach this table unworthily is to reenact the folly of the unrobed guest. St. Paul's warning to the Corinthians—"Whoever eats and drinks without discerning the body eats and drinks judgment on himself"—is the New Testament's commentary on this parable. Participation in the Eucharist demands the garment of grace; reception without repentance is self-condemnation.

The parable therefore interprets the liturgy, and the liturgy interprets the parable. The king's persistent invitation—"Come, for everything is ready"—is the voice that echoes at every Mass. The servants going into the crossroads are the Church's missionaries and ministers, gathering the poor and broken into the Father's house. The hall filled with "bad and good" is the visible communion of the faithful, saints and sinners alike, united not by merit but by mercy. And the king's inspection anticipates the eschatological moment when sacrament becomes sight—when the Bride stands before the Bridegroom, clothed in the "fine linen, bright and pure, which is the righteous deeds of the saints" (Rev 19:8). The Eucharist is thus both foretaste and formation: those who receive worthily are already being fitted for the wedding garment of eternity.

This is why Christian life cannot be reduced to ethics or ritual observance. It is participation in a nuptial mystery—the mutual indwelling of divine and human love. To be Christian is to live as one betrothed, to carry within the soul the joy and reverence proper to a bride awaiting her Bridegroom. Every sacrament, every act of prayer, every moment of mercy is preparation for the wedding. The garment we put on in baptism must be continually washed in repentance and adorned by charity. Holiness is not a dress code but a life woven out of gratitude. The Church's saints are simply those who have kept their garments bright—souls who have allowed grace to alter the very texture of their being until they reflect the splendour of the feast.

The parable also unfolds the mystery of divine justice within mercy. The king's actions, so easily misunderstood as severity, reveal the protective jealousy of perfect love. Love that is holy must also be discerning; it will not let counterfeit affections remain unexposed. The judgment of the unrobed guest is not vengeance but unveiling. In the light of the feast, everything false falls away. The same fire that warms the hall purifies the guests. God's justice is the temperature of His joy. The outer darkness is not a chamber He creates for sinners but the state of those who refuse light. What we call hell is simply love experienced as loss. It is the ache of a heart that will not be converted to the rhythm of gift.

This understanding transforms the parable's tone. It ceases to be a story about punishment and becomes one about the seriousness of joy. Heaven is not an optional extra but the meaning of existence. The universe is designed as a feast, not a factory. The stars and seasons are decorations for the hall; the moral law is the architecture of communion; history itself is the procession toward the table. Sin is therefore absurd—a hunger that refuses food, a guest who will not wear joy. The "outer darkness" begins not after death but whenever a human heart lives closed to grace. Conversely, the feast begins here and now whenever a soul opens to love.

The Church's mission flows from this revelation. She does not merely announce doctrines; she bears invitations. Every homily, every confession, every act of service is the servant's voice crying in the streets: "Come to the wedding." The world's resistance—its mockery, its indifference—is nothing new. It is the same refusal in new dress. Yet the command remains: "Go out again." The king's urgency is the measure of divine compassion. Evangelization is not a strategy but a sharing in God's impatience for joy. The servants who go into the highways do not go alone; the Spirit compels through them, persuading the hesitant, comforting the ashamed, drawing all toward the light of the hall.

At the heart of this divine hospitality stands the Cross. The feast's abundance flows from sacrifice. The oxen and fattened calves "killed" in the parable prefigure the Lamb slain from the foundation of the world. On Calvary, the Bridegroom sets His table with His own body. The wood of the Cross becomes the table of salvation; the nails are the cutlery of mercy. From His pierced side—the open door of the banquet hall—flow blood and water, the wine and water of the Eucharist. The Servant sent to summon the guests is the Son Himself; He goes not with a parchment but with His flesh. His death is the last invitation, written in red across the face of the world: *All is ready.*

From that hour onward, every celebration of the Mass is a continuation of the royal wedding. When the priest lifts the host, heaven and earth meet; the Bridegroom gives Himself anew to His Bride. The Church's task is simply to keep the feast open until the last guest arrives. Her failures—scandal, division, complacency—are the stains on her garment, yet grace remains her cleansing fire. Even her wounds can become windows through which the world glimpses the feast. The saints are the laughter of God echoing through history, proof that the hall is filling.

Eschatologically, the parable points forward to the "marriage supper of the Lamb" in Revelation. There, the themes of invitation, garment, and joy reach completion. The King is the Father enthroned; the Bridegroom, the risen Christ; the Bride, the Church transfigured. The outer darkness has vanished, for every corner of creation now glows with light. What began

## THE WEDDING FEAST / PROPER GARMENT (MT 22:1–14)

as a local feast in a parable becomes cosmic communion. The redeemed wear their garments not as borrowed robes but as their own glorified nature—the humanity of Christ shared with His saints. The table is the universe; the music is the eternal exchange of love within the Trinity. The words "many are called, few chosen" will have become "many were called, and those who came are now one."

For now, we live in the in-between— the feast has begun, yet the wedding is not complete. Each Eucharist is rehearsal for the final feast. Each act of repentance is a laundering of the garment. Each work of mercy is another seat prepared. The Church waits, candle in hand, for the Bridegroom's return, echoing the Spirit's cry, "Come." The urgency of the parable remains alive in the heart of every believer who knows that grace cannot be postponed. To live awake is to live invited.

In the end, the Wedding Feast is not merely a story Jesus told; it is the story He lived. The King's Son enters the world to claim His Bride; He endures rejection, violence, and death; yet the feast goes on. Resurrection morning is the opening of the banquet hall, and Pentecost is the sending of new servants to the crossroads. History itself is the unfolding of that evening. The divine joy will not cease until the last seat is filled. "Many are called, few chosen"—not because God withholds but because man delays. Yet even delay cannot defeat the patience of the Host. The lamps remain lit, the bread warm, the wine poured. In every age, the invitation sounds anew: *Come, for all is ready.*

The theology of this parable, then, is the theology of divine joy—joy that suffers, invites, and persists. The Kingdom is a feast not because it flatters our senses but because it reveals the structure of God's own being: love overflowing into communion. The Father's will is that His Son's wedding be celebrated, that every creature share the happiness of the Trinity. Creation began with "Let there be light" and ends with "Let the house be filled." Between those words stretches the history of redemption, a single meal unfolding through time. Each soul that accepts the invitation becomes another light in the hall, another voice in the song, another reflection of the Host's delight.

Such is the theology that burns beneath the story's surface: the feast is creation, the garment is grace, the judgment is truth, and the King's command is love unending. Every refusal wounds the joy of God, yet none can quench it. The hall will shine, the Bride will be clothed, and the Son will rejoice in the company of the redeemed. The last note of the parable is not warning but music—the eternal laughter of the Father who has found His children home at last.

### c) Typological and Intertextual Parallels

The parable of the Wedding Feast does not emerge in isolation. It is the flowering of a vine that has been growing through all of Scripture, the final movement in the symphony of divine hospitality. From Genesis to Revelation, God reveals Himself not as a distant ruler but as a Father preparing a home, as a King arranging a wedding for His Son. Creation itself is the first table set for His guests. When Jesus speaks of a king who "made a wedding feast for his son," He is not inventing a metaphor but unveiling the design of reality: all of history is a nuptial preparation, all of creation a banquet awaiting its Bridegroom.

The pattern begins in Eden. Humanity's first home is a garden temple, rich with fruit and fragrance. Every tree is given for food except one, and that single exception marks the difference between gift and grasping. God's first command is permission: "You may eat freely." His first prohibition is protection—a reminder that communion depends on trust. To feast rightly is to receive, not to seize. When Adam and Eve reach for what was withheld, they transform abundance into exile. Their nakedness is not only physical but sacramental: they have lost the garment of grace. The first sin is the first desecrated meal. The first act of redemption, therefore, is a clothing—"The Lord God made for them garments of skin and clothed them." From that moment onward, divine mercy takes the form of preparation: God covering His children's shame, teaching them how to dwell again at His table. The wedding garment of Matthew's parable is the final restoration of that first lost robe.

When Israel is born at Sinai, the story of the meal resumes in covenant form. After the thunder and the law, a quiet verse gleams like gold: "They beheld God, and ate and drank." The mountain becomes a table. The covenant is sealed not only by sacrifice but by supper. Eating in the presence of God is the signature of belonging. Every later feast—Passover, Sabbath, peace offering—replays that moment when humanity once again dined with the divine. In the parable, the king's invitation, "Come, for all is ready," is Sinai's echo transformed into eschatological key: the command that once bound Israel now becomes the invitation that gathers the nations.

The prophets transform that covenant memory into future hope. Isaiah stands upon Zion and sees the mountain of the Lord transfigured into a banquet hall: "On this mountain the Lord of hosts will make for all peoples a feast of rich food, of well-aged wines… and He will swallow up death forever." The image of abundance is cosmic; the removal of the shroud of death is the renewal of creation itself. The mountain of Isaiah 25 is the hall of Matthew 22. What was prophecy becomes parable. When the king declares, "My banquet is ready," Isaiah's vision is fulfilled in the Son's presence—the divine feast descending from the mountain into history.

Another strain of the same melody sounds in Isaiah 55: "Come, everyone who thirsts, come to the waters; come, buy wine and milk without money and without price." Here grace is declared as gift, invitation without cost, abundance without price. The prophet's call anticipates the king's insistence that the poor and unworthy be brought in. "Without money and without price" becomes "as many as you find." God's generosity has only one condition: willingness to receive.

But before Isaiah sang, Wisdom had already spread her table. In Proverbs 9 she is described as a woman who "has built her house, hewn her seven pillars, slaughtered her beasts, mixed her wine, and set her table." Her maidens go forth to cry in the streets, "Come, eat of my bread and drink of the wine I have mixed." The Hebrew imagination understood Wisdom as the radiance of God Himself—the divine pattern made visible. When Jesus, the incarnate Wisdom, tells His story of the royal banquet, He fulfils that ancient image. He is the house built upon seven pillars, the wine already poured, the Bread come down from heaven. The maidens sent out from Wisdom's house become the servants of the parable, proclaiming the invitation that has rung through time: "Come, for all is ready."

The Psalms, too, hum beneath this narrative. "You prepare a table before me in the presence of my enemies," sings David, "and my cup overflows." Every Psalmist who trusted God as shepherd or king was tasting that banquet in advance. In Psalm 45, the royal wedding song, the bride stands in garments of gold, the king's heart aflame with love; in Psalm 36, "They feast on the abundance of your house, and you give them drink from the river of your delights." Each image gathers into the single reality Jesus now discloses. The parable's king is the Lord of the Psalms, His Son the Bridegroom of Israel's longing.

The story of David and Mephibosheth gives that longing a human face. The crippled grandson of Saul, living in fear, is summoned by the king he once opposed. David's words echo across centuries: "You shall eat at my table always." The lame and fearful are lifted into the company of princes. David's mercy prefigures the Son of David who will fill His hall with the maimed and the poor. Mephibosheth's daily meal is the miniature of the messianic feast; his seat at the royal table the sign that mercy has triumphed over enmity.

The prophets continue this theme with deepened urgency. Hosea hears the Lord say to faithless Israel, "I will betroth you to me forever." Ezekiel watches the Spirit gather the scattered bones into a living nation and then beholds a terrible reversal—a feast of judgment in which the birds of heaven are invited to eat the flesh of the mighty. Even divine wrath is expressed as a banquet, because communion is the measure of both salvation and judgment. To share the meal is life; to refuse it is death. In Zephaniah, the Lord promises to gather "the lame and the outcast" and make them a people of praise. That prophetic chorus—the lame lifted, the unworthy welcomed—becomes literal in Jesus' parable. The king's command, "Go into the highways and gather all," is not innovation but fulfilment.

Even the imagery of fire that consumes the city has its lineage. In Isaiah 33 the Lord's holiness is described as consuming fire; in Lamentations the

## THE WEDDING FEAST / PROPER GARMENT (MT 22:1-14)

burning of Jerusalem is grief transfigured into purification. The city of man burns so that the city of God may rise. The destruction within the parable is therefore not the end of the story but the purgation that clears the way for joy.

All these threads converge in the prophetic vision of marriage. The nuptial bond between God and His people runs through Scripture like a scarlet thread. In Genesis, Adam's cry at the sight of Eve—"bone of my bones and flesh of my flesh"—is humanity's first act of theology, the recognition of otherness united in communion. In Hosea, that first marriage becomes the image of divine fidelity amid betrayal. In Isaiah and Jeremiah, Zion is the bride adorned for her husband. By the time Jesus tells His story, every Israelite heart knows the symbolism: the coming of the Messiah will be a wedding. The Kingdom will not be conquered; it will be celebrated.

When the king in the parable sends out invitations for his son's marriage, the echo of that long nuptial tradition resounds. The Father is preparing the covenantal wedding between His Son and humanity—the union of divine and human natures in the Incarnation, and of Christ and His Church in redemption. Every earlier covenant was a courtship; every altar was a betrothal gift. Now, in Christ, the wedding itself has begun. The banquet does not merely symbolise the Kingdom; it is the Kingdom enacted—the world's destiny turned into celebration.

Even the *garment* of the parable glows with scriptural resonance. From Eden onward, clothing is never incidental. The first Adam is clothed by God in mercy; the second Adam clothes His people in glory. The priestly vestments of Exodus 28, embroidered with gold and precious stones, prefigure the holiness required to stand before God. Zechariah's vision of the high priest Joshua being stripped of filthy garments and clothed in new robes anticipates the soul's cleansing in grace. Isaiah rejoices, "He has clothed me with the garments of salvation, He has covered me with the robe of righteousness." When the king confronts the unrobed guest, all these images converge: holiness as vesture, grace as adornment, the human person standing before God either clothed in mercy or exposed in self-sufficiency. To "put on the wedding garment" is to participate in that clothing of salvation that runs through the entire canon. St. Paul will later translate the metaphor into doctrine: "As many of you as were baptized into Christ have put on Christ." The garment is baptismal identity made luminous through charity. The man who refuses it relives the tragedy of Eden—naked before God, speechless and alone.

The typological chain does not end in the prophets. It ripens in the Gospels themselves. The first public sign of Jesus' ministry takes place at a wedding in Cana, where water turns to wine—the image of old covenant purification transformed into nuptial joy. John's narrative is not coincidence but fulfilment. The Bridegroom has arrived, and the feast has begun. Every miracle henceforth will be a preparation for the greater wedding: the raising of the dead, the cleansing of lepers, the feeding of multitudes—all foretastes of the day when the Bridegroom will pour out His blood as the new wine of the covenant.

In that light, Matthew's parable stands in dialogue with Luke's *Great Banquet*. The two stories are variations on one melody: Luke's version leans outward toward inclusion, Matthew's downward toward discernment. One celebrates the wideness of mercy, the other warns of the depth of judgment. Both share the same centre: the God who will not feast alone. Together they reveal the two faces of divine love—tender invitation and holy insistence.

Beyond the Synoptic horizon, the imagery unfolds in John's Gospel and the Apocalypse. John the Baptist names himself "the friend of the Bridegroom"; Jesus speaks of Himself as that Bridegroom whose presence turns fasting into festivity. In Revelation 19, the angel proclaims, "Blessed are those invited to the marriage supper of the Lamb." The story that began in a garden closes in a city. The wedding hall becomes the New Jerusalem; the Bride, clothed in fine linen, is the Church transfigured. The river that flowed from Eden now runs through the streets of paradise; the Tree of Life, once guarded, now bears fruit for all nations. The long hunger of creation ends in the sound of music and the light of lamps. History itself resolves into supper.

## THE WEDDING FEAST / PROPER GARMENT (MT 22:1–14)

Every element of Matthew's parable participates in this scriptural tapestry. The king's *sending of servants* recalls the prophets sent to Israel; the *burning of the city* mirrors the judgment of Jerusalem; the *invitation of the outcasts* fulfils Isaiah's promise that all peoples will come to Zion. Even the king's inspection of the guests echoes the prophetic "day of the Lord," when God will search hearts as silver is refined. The wedding feast becomes a microcosm of salvation history: covenant, mission, rejection, purification, inclusion, judgment, and joy—all compressed into the rhythm of a single evening.

The typology also turns inward. The guest list that expands to the highways foreshadows the Church's catholicity—its call to gather from every nation and condition. The hall filled with both "bad and good" reflects the mixed nature of the pilgrim Church: saints and sinners sharing one table until the final discernment. The inspection of the guests prefigures the Last Judgment that begins "with the household of God." The garment itself stands as the synthesis of sacraments: baptism's new clothing, confirmation's anointing, the Eucharist's robe of glory, penance's cleansing. The parable is, in miniature, the map of Christian existence.

Looked at through the long lens of Scripture, the entire Bible reads as the preparation of this feast. The garden is the kitchen of the cosmos; Sinai the first rehearsal dinner; the prophets the heralds delivering invitations; the Incarnation the arrival of the Bridegroom; Calvary the cost of the wedding; the Resurrection the rising of the music; Pentecost the sending of servants into the highways; the Eucharist the weekly foretaste; and the heavenly city the eternal celebration. Every sacrament is a slice of the banquet, every grace a drop of its wine.

Even the language of fullness—"the hall was filled with guests"—has ancient roots. The ark of Noah, overflowing with life, is the first "house filled"; the tabernacle, filled with God's glory, the second; the temple of Solomon, so saturated with cloud that the priests could not stand, the third. Matthew's filled hall is the fourth: the Church, alive with grace, radiant with divine presence. Fullness is the signature of God. He does not create to ration but to overflow. Every moment of salvation history is another vessel being filled.

Finally, the typology of the feast circles back to its origin: the mystery of the Trinity. The Father is the Host whose joy is to give; the Son is the Bridegroom and the Meal; the Spirit is the love that moves outward, the invisible Servant who "compels them to come in." All creation is caught up in this triune motion of generosity. What began in a garden and unfolds through covenant and cross will end as eternal communion—the world transfigured into one great wedding hall, the human race robed and rejoicing.

Thus the parable of the Wedding Feast is Scripture gathered into a single flame. The garden of beginnings, the mountain of covenant, the prophets' cries, the psalms of love, the wisdom of the ages, the Gospel's miracles, and the visions of the end—all burn together in this story. Every feast of the Bible finds its fulfilment here. The same God who once walked with Adam at evening now walks among His guests. The invitation that echoed through prophets and apostles is still sounding, and the table is still being set. The story ends not with absence but with abundance. The house of the Lord will be filled, and the Bridegroom will rejoice over His Bride as the Father rejoices over the Son. What began as a parable closes as a promise: creation itself will become the feast of God.

### d) Patristic and Theological Synthesis

The Fathers never treated the parable of the Wedding Feast as a moral anecdote; they heard in it the sound of their own salvation. To them, this was not a story about other people's refusals but a mirror of grace and response in every age. They saw themselves among the poor and the lame dragged from the streets, suddenly seated where kings had declined to come. The banquet was not metaphor but mystery—the life of the Church itself.

Origen, among the earliest commentators, taught that the wedding feast represented the soul's ascent into union with the Word. The king is the Father, the bridegroom the Son, and the marriage the Incarnation—the divine and human natures joined in one flesh. For him, the guest without

## THE WEDDING FEAST / PROPER GARMENT (MT 22:1–14)

a garment was the one who had entered baptism but not transformation. "He who comes," Origen wrote, "must be clothed with works of light." Faith alone brings one through the door; virtue weaves the robe. The parable, he insisted, reveals the terrifying intimacy of judgment—that one may stand within the Church's walls yet still unprepared for the Bridegroom's gaze.

Chrysostom took the image further into daily life. Preaching in Antioch, he thundered against those who came to the liturgy without conversion: "The hall is full, but how many wear the robe of charity?" For him, the excuses of the first invitees were the same evasions heard in every city—work, possessions, pleasure—while the unrobed guest symbolised the man who attends the sacred banquet yet brings no repentance. The garment, he said, is love expressed in action; without it, "we insult the Bridegroom with our presence." In Chrysostom's voice, theology becomes conscience: the feast is the Eucharist, the king's inspection the self-examination before communion.

Augustine, ever the pastoral psychologist, saw in the same parable the whole rhythm of divine mercy. The king's sending of servants is God's providence moving through history—patriarchs, prophets, apostles, bishops—each carrying the invitation forward. The wedding hall is the Church, spacious enough for every soul, yet divided by desire: some come in humility, others in hypocrisy. The garment, he explained, is *caritas*, the love that alone makes faith alive. "You may enter the hall," he told his people, "but unless you wear love, you are still outside." For Augustine, the unrobed man's silence before the king foreshadowed the final judgment, when no excuse remains except the poverty of a loveless heart.

Gregory the Great, preaching to a Rome weary of invasions and plague, turned the parable outward to mission. Israel's refusal, he said, opened the way for the nations; the servants on the highways are the apostles sent into the world. "The highways," Gregory wrote, "are the broad paths of public life; the hedges, the narrow ways of contemplation." The call of the Gospel thus runs through city and cloister alike. Yet his reading also carried warning: "Let none boast who are gathered in, for many are called but few are chosen." The wedding garment, in Gregory's hands, became perseverance itself—the grace of remaining faithful until the feast is complete.

Ambrose, the bishop of Milan, found in the banquet the deepest secret of Christian equality. "Christ is our food, Christ is our drink, Christ is our garment," he preached. For him, the table of the King was the altar of the Church, where rich and poor, ruler and slave knelt together. In that shared meal he saw not only reconciliation but transformation—bread becoming body, strangers becoming brothers. The wedding hall, he said, is the human soul made capable of God. The Eucharist, therefore, is not merely a reminder of the feast to come; it is its first course, the pledge of glory already begun.

The Eastern Fathers, too, embroidered the image with radiance. Cyril of Alexandria taught that the Incarnate Word Himself is the garment—divinity clothing humanity so that humanity might, in turn, be clothed with God. To be "found without a wedding garment," then, is to reject the grace of deification, to stand before the King in the nakedness of self-reliance. For Cyril, baptism was the moment when this divine robe was first bestowed: "We put off the old man," he wrote, "and put on the new, which is Christ." The robe of light lost in Eden is returned through immersion in the death and resurrection of the Bridegroom.

Gregory Nazianzen, ever subtle in his theology of freedom, cautioned that grace never coerces. "God persuades," he said, "He does not compel; He draws, He does not drive." The parable's open doors reveal the paradox of divine love: a feast prepared for all, yet entered only by consent. The unrobed guest is not thrown out because he was unwelcome, but because he refused to be changed. For Gregory, this is the mystery of human freedom within divine mercy—invitation without compulsion, judgment as the honest consequence of refusal.

The Fathers thus read the parable as both history and prophecy: the history of Israel fulfilled in the calling of the nations, and the prophecy of the Church's life until the end of time. They heard the echo of Sinai's covenant meal, the foretaste of the heavenly marriage supper of the Lamb, and the moral summons of the Eucharist here and now. To them, theology was never separated from worship. To interpret the parable was to enter it.

As the Church's reflection deepened, medieval theologians gave the patristic insights sharper definition. Aquinas saw in the feast the very logic of divine goodness: *bonum diffusivum sui*—goodness diffuses itself. Love, by nature, cannot remain enclosed. The king's restless hospitality is therefore not sentiment but metaphysics. The feast must be filled because Being itself is generous. For Thomas, creation is the first invitation, grace the second, and glory the final course. The wedding garment is sanctifying grace itself, infused charity that gives form to all virtue. Without that interior clothing, even faith and sacrament remain incomplete—one can be at the table yet not of the feast. "Grace," he writes, "is the preparation of the soul for glory." The garment is that preparation made visible.

The scholastics also saw in the parable the architecture of the Church. The invitation extended to "both good and bad" mirrors the Church Militant, mixed until the final judgment. The king's inspection anticipates the purifying vision of Christ at the end of time, when the merely external will be burned away and the true robe revealed. What Augustine intuited as love, Aquinas rendered as participation: the soul's share in divine life. The parable thus becomes a catechism in miniature—creation, vocation, justification, perseverance, glorification—all contained in one evening's story.

The mystical tradition wove the same imagery into its language of union. For the Greek Fathers, the robe is *theosis* itself—humanity clothed in divinity. For the Latin mystics, it is *caritas perfecta*—the heart transformed into flame. Bernard of Clairvaux spoke of the wedding garment as the interior disposition of love by which the soul becomes "one spirit with the Lord." Catherine of Siena, in her dialogues, heard Christ say, "I have wedded you to Myself with the ring of faith, and clothed you with the garment of charity." Across centuries and languages, the garment remains the same: the grace that makes union possible.

This vision reaches its living form in the Church's liturgy. Every baptismal rite begins with clothing: the newly reborn is robed in white and told, "You have become a new creation; see in this garment your dignity." Every priest, before approaching the altar, prays as he dons the chasuble, "O Lord, who said, 'My yoke is easy and My burden light,' grant that I may so bear it as to obtain Your grace." The liturgical garments are not decorative but theological—they signify the clothing of Christ in which the Church ministers and the saints shine. In the Mass, the parable becomes present: the king's feast spread, the Bridegroom offered, the guests gathered, the garment bestowed anew.

The Fathers never allowed the warning at the parable's end to fade into abstraction. "Bind him hand and foot, and cast him out into the outer darkness." This is not cruelty, they said, but consequence. God does not close the door; the unrobed man cannot bear the light. Hell, in their understanding, is not divine rejection but self-exclusion—the tragedy of one who stands before infinite love and says no. The wedding hall remains open; the King remains willing; the garment lies ready. The only barrier left is the hardness of an unconverted heart.

In this light, the parable becomes a mirror of the whole Christian mystery. The Father is the Host whose joy is communion; the Son is both Bridegroom and banquet; the Spirit is the invitation whispering through every age. The Church is the hall that shelters the feast; her ministers are the servants sent down the roads of the world. Each sacrament is an extension of the king's generosity: baptism the first clothing, Eucharist the perpetual meal, penance the washing of soiled garments, anointing the oil that perfumes the Bride before her final meeting with the Bridegroom. Every act of evangelization, every work of mercy, is the same command heard anew: "Go out, compel them to come in."

Aquinas' metaphysical calm and Augustine's burning love meet here in harmony: grace does not abolish freedom; it heals and elevates it. God's invitation remains universal, but the robe must be accepted and worn. In that cooperation—the dance between divine generosity and human consent—the wedding of heaven and earth unfolds. Salvation is not forced attendance but joyful participation. As Gregory Nazianzen said, "The

Kingdom of God is not imposed; it is embraced."

The parable's final resonance is eschatological. In the Apocalypse, John hears the voice of an angel cry, "Blessed are those invited to the marriage supper of the Lamb." The earthly feast has become eternal. The garments of linen are the "righteous deeds of the saints," the hall is the radiant city, the music the praise of the redeemed. The story that began in a royal courtyard ends in the endless Sabbath of God. What was once warning becomes wonder. The Bride has made herself ready, not by her own weaving, but by the grace that clothed her from the beginning.

For the Fathers and theologians alike, this is the heart of the Gospel: salvation as invitation, grace as clothing, communion as destiny. The King has prepared His Son's wedding and refuses to celebrate it alone. Every Mass, every conversion, every act of love is another guest entering, another robe bestowed. The divine hall will not remain half-empty. The feast of the Lamb will be full, and the laughter of the Bridegroom will be the sound of creation at rest.

## The Shock and the Turn

The story begins with joy. A king prepares a wedding feast for his son. In the ancient world, nothing surpassed the grandeur of a royal marriage. It was a celebration of life's continuance, a covenant sealed not by contract but by communion. To the listeners gathered around Jesus, this image would have sounded familiar and comforting. They knew the prophets' promise that the day of the Lord would be like a banquet, when God would vindicate His people and establish His reign. A royal wedding meant triumph, purity, and peace. The righteous would recline in honour; the nations would look on in awe.

No one expected that the story would turn upon them.

Jesus tells it without pause or emphasis, the calm voice of a man setting a snare for the heart. "The kingdom of heaven may be compared to a king who gave a marriage feast for his son, and sent his servants to call those who were invited." The image carries immediate theological weight.

God is the King, Israel the invited. The wedding is the moment of divine union long foretold—the covenant renewed, the nation restored. Everyone listening knew how such a story should end. The faithful would come; the wicked would remain outside. But from the first line, something is wrong.

"The invited would not come."

The refusal is small in its wording but seismic in meaning. These are not rebels, not Gentiles or idolaters. They are those who had already received the first invitation—the covenant people, the ones who had said yes generations earlier. Yet now, when the feast is ready, they decline. The excuses sound reasonable, almost harmless: a field to inspect, business to manage, a marriage to attend. Ordinary responsibilities, each good in itself, but used as shields against the greater good. The story's first shock is its subtlety: salvation refused not through hatred but through habit.

To the religious leaders in Jesus' audience, this would have been unbearable. They saw themselves as the faithful remnant, the ones keeping Israel pure until the promised hour. Yet the parable's logic cuts through their certainty. The King's messengers—the prophets—had long called Israel to repentance, and again and again the people had delayed. Now the Son Himself has come, and still the excuses continue. What began as social courtesy becomes covenantal tragedy.

Then the story darkens. The King sends more servants, but they are seized and killed. The imagery grows violent, and the hearers would know at once what it means. This is the history of the prophets: men sent with mercy, met with hostility. From Elijah to Jeremiah, from Zechariah to John the Baptist, every generation has silenced its heralds. The King's patience gives way to grief. "He sent his troops and destroyed those murderers and burned their city." The words would fall like a stone in the room. To devout Jews living under Rome, the burning of a city could only recall one thing: the destruction of Jerusalem. The feast now stands in the shadow of judgment.

Still, the story moves on. The King is not finished. The feast must go on. "Go therefore to the thoroughfares, and invite to the marriage feast as many as you find." Here the tone shifts again, from fury to grace. The

## THE WEDDING FEAST / PROPER GARMENT (MT 22:1–14)

very anger of God becomes the engine of mercy. What Israel's refusal has closed, divine compassion opens wider. The servants go out, gathering "both bad and good," until the hall is full. The phrase itself is scandal. The word "bad" has no place in a royal wedding. Yet Jesus says it without irony: the unworthy are seated at the table once reserved for the pure. The new community of grace is born not from merit but from invitation.

The listeners would have felt the tension tighten. A feast once theirs has become the feast of strangers. The unclean are reclining where the righteous expected to sit. The parable's politeness makes its force sharper. Jesus never raises His voice; He simply lets the new order unfold until its implications become undeniable.

But then, at the moment when mercy seems to have triumphed completely, the story turns again.

"When the King came in to look at the guests, he saw there a man who had no wedding garment."

No explanation, no introduction. The man is already inside. He has accepted the invitation, entered the hall, taken his place. Yet he stands out as unprepared. The King addresses him directly: "Friend, how did you get in here without a wedding garment?" The question is gentle but absolute. It pierces deeper than command. The guest is silent.

For the first hearers, this was the second shock. After the generous inclusion of the poor and the outcast, now even one of them is condemned. Mercy, it seems, has its own judgment. The garment, in ancient custom, was often provided by the host. To arrive without it was not mere negligence; it was contempt. The guest's silence is the silence of one who cannot pretend ignorance. He has entered the feast without reverence.

Jesus' audience would have recognised themselves again. They who prided themselves on knowing the law had forgotten the heart of worship. The garment becomes a symbol of the interior life—righteousness not as ritual but as response, grace accepted and worn. To be inside the hall is not enough; one must be clothed in the love that the invitation offered.

The King's verdict follows swiftly: "Bind him hand and foot, and cast him into the outer darkness; there men will weep and gnash their teeth."

The phrase, repeated elsewhere in Matthew, evokes the final separation—the soul stripped of communion, excluded from joy. The light of the feast becomes unbearable to one unrobed in grace. The punishment is not arbitrary but revelatory: it exposes what the man already chose. He has entered without transformation, and therefore cannot remain.

The silence that follows this moment is the truest sound in the story. The man's speechlessness before the king is the absence of every excuse, the end of self-justification. Jesus leaves it there—no appeal, no defence, no epilogue. It is one of the few parables that ends without resolution. The listeners are left to sit in that silence, to feel its weight in themselves. The story that began with joy concludes with judgment, and yet the judgment is not cruel. It is clarity. The wedding feast is grace made visible, and grace always reveals the truth of what it touches.

This is the "turn" of the parable. The same invitation that saves also separates. Mercy divides not because God is partial, but because love, once revealed, demands a response. The open door becomes the moment of decision. The garment is nothing other than that response itself—the life formed by faith and love, the yes to the invitation. When it is absent, exclusion follows naturally, as night follows sunset. The king does not rage; he simply enacts what the guest has already chosen. To refuse transformation is to refuse the feast.

For Jesus' audience, this was unbearable news. The idea that one could belong to the covenant community yet still be unfit for the kingdom shattered the security of religious identity. It meant that ancestry, law, and ritual could no longer guarantee communion. What mattered was interior renewal—the garment of grace, not the pedigree of blood. The parable unravels the illusion of collective holiness and replaces it with personal responsibility. God's call is universal, but His feast is intimate: every guest must come dressed in conversion.

Here lies the deeper scandal. The kingdom that Israel had awaited for centuries arrives not as reward but as gift, and that gift can be refused even from within. The chosen may become unchosen; the expected heirs may find themselves outside while strangers take their seats. The parable is not only an indictment of a generation but a warning for the Church herself. It exposes the peril of familiarity—the danger of mistaking proximity to grace for possession of it.

For the Pharisees, who built fences around the law to protect its purity, this was inversion bordering on blasphemy. The holiness they defended was separation from impurity; the holiness Jesus revealed was communion that sanctifies impurity. In their vision, the unclean defile the clean; in His, the clean heals the unclean. The contagion of grace moves outward, overturning the old geometry of religion. The feast is not the reward for those who kept their garments spotless, but the place where the garments are given.

At the same time, Jesus' story refuses sentimental mercy. The man without the garment is not the outcast or the sinner; he is the one who accepts inclusion without conversion. Grace does not erase the need for holiness; it makes it possible. The King's question—"How did you get in here?"—is the echo of every conscience confronted by truth. The garment is the visible sign of invisible transformation, and the absence of that sign reveals the tragedy of hypocrisy: presence without participation, invitation without response.

To those reclining around Him, the implications were devastating. The story's first shock had been mercy—the invitation extended to those outside Israel. The second is accountability—mercy itself demanding change. The wideness of God's welcome does not nullify the seriousness of His love. The same fire that purifies also burns. To enter the hall is not the end of conversion but its beginning. The wedding feast of the Son is not a reception for the complacent but a covenant for the transformed.

In that light, the parable becomes prophecy of what will soon unfold. Jesus is Himself the Bridegroom, and Jerusalem is the city that will reject the invitation. The murder of the servants foreshadows the cross; the burning of the city anticipates the destruction that will follow. Yet the feast continues, spreading outward through the preaching of the apostles, filling the world with guests who were never on the original list. The Church is born in that movement from rejection to redemption, from the closed door of one city to the open gates of every nation.

The moral reversal is complete. The covenant once defined by lineage is now defined by love; the table once reserved for the righteous is now open to the repentant. The new scandal is not exclusion but indifference. Those who imagined themselves chosen find themselves outside, not because they were hated, but because they had stopped hungering. Holiness, Jesus implies, begins with appetite. The feast of God is missed not by those too evil to attend, but by those too satisfied to notice it is happening.

The parable ends as it began, with a sentence that sounds simple until it is heard: "Many are called, but few are chosen." The words do not describe divine favouritism but human freedom. All are summoned to the feast; only those who come clothed in love remain. The shock is that salvation is not automatic. The turn is that judgment is love's final honesty. Heaven is invitation accepted; hell is invitation declined. Between the two lies silence—the silence of the guest before the King, the moment when the garment is revealed for what it is.

That silence still speaks. It is the space in which every soul stands before the truth of its own desire. The feast is ready, the door open, the garments prepared. The only question left is the one the King asks still: *"Friend, how did you come in here?"*

### The Revelation in the Son

In its movement from invitation to self-offering, the story becomes a portrait of the divine life unveiled in Christ. Behind the figure of the generous king stands the Father of mercies; behind the servant who bears the invitations, the Son sent into the world; and behind the radiant hall, creation itself—made to be filled with divine glory. What Jesus speaks of here is not merely human inclusion in grace but the self-manifestation of God. Every element of the parable—king, feast, servant, garment—points to the one in whom all parables find their fulfilment: the Word made flesh.

The Son is the mystery of God's hospitality made visible. From eternity the Father has uttered one Word, and through that Word all things were made. Creation itself is the first invitation—Being overflowing in generosity. When the Word becomes flesh, the Host steps into His own house. The table He prepares is no longer symbolic; it is His very body. The God who once spoke light into existence now stands within that light as Guest and Servant. What He tells in story He lives in truth.

The Incarnation is the wedding of heaven and earth. The king who "prepared a marriage feast for his son" reveals the mystery that the Bridegroom of eternity has come to claim His bride—humanity itself. The union of divine and human natures in the one person of Christ is the marriage at the heart of all creation. The feast is not future alone; it begins the moment God and man are joined in the womb of Mary. "The Word became flesh and dwelt among us," John writes, and in that dwelling the banquet of communion begins. To see Jesus walking the roads of Galilee is to see the king's feast already unfolding—divine life served in human gestures.

Each movement of the servant in the parable traces a moment of that descent. Sent first to the invited, then to the poor, and finally to those beyond the hedges, the servant mirrors the trajectory of the Word: from the covenant of Israel to the nations, from glory into poverty, from heaven into the streets of our exile. The "Go out quickly" of the parable is the eternal procession of the Son translated into time—the divine urgency of love refusing to remain enclosed. The Father sends; the Son obeys; the Spirit breathes life into the obedience. What we call salvation history is simply this: the Trinity stepping outward in search of communion.

Yet the story darkens with rejection. The servant is scorned, the messengers beaten, the invitation spurned. The echo of that refusal resounds through the Gospel. "He came to His own, and His own received Him not." The generosity of God meets the resistance of pride. But here is the turning point: divine hospitality does not withdraw; it deepens. The Son who bears the invitation becomes Himself the invitation's fulfilment. The feast is prepared not in a palace but on a cross. The Host becomes the food. The table of the kingdom is laid upon the wood of sacrifice. Humanity's refusal is answered not by vengeance but by self-gift.

The Cross is the wedding's threshold, the moment when the Bridegroom unites Himself to His bride in the language of total love. The blood poured out is the wine of the new covenant; the pierced body is the bread of life. What was symbol in the parable becomes sacrament in history. The divine feast is served in flesh and blood. In Jesus Christ, the tragedy of refusal is absorbed into the joy of redemption. The outstretched arms of the Crucified are the arms of the Host gathering His guests. Rejected by those first invited, He goes to the highways of human misery, to the thieves beside Him, to the souls who know they have no right to the hall. His final words—"Father, forgive them"—are the invitation uttered once more.

At the Last Supper, the story finds its voice. "Take, eat; this is My Body." The parable becomes liturgy; the feast becomes fact. The bread and wine that pass from His hands to theirs are the visible form of divine generosity. The Bridegroom who was foretold in every covenant now seals that covenant with Himself. The eternal Word gives His flesh as the food of the world. In that moment, the kingdom of God is no longer a future banquet but a present communion. Every altar will henceforth be an extension of that table; every Mass the king's hall filling with new guests.

Evangelisation, seen through this lens, ceases to be conquest and becomes invitation. The Church's mission is not to win arguments but to extend hospitality. The apostles are the servants sent again and again into the world, bearing the same summons: *Come, for all is ready.* Where the Gospel is proclaimed, the Master's house expands. Every baptism is another door opened; every act of mercy, another guest seated. The Church's preaching is the continuation of the servant's voice—the Word Himself speaking through His body. Her mission is Christ's own persistence, the divine charity that will not rest until every place at the table is filled.

Yet the mystery reaches beyond mission to metaphysics. The feast is not simply what God does; it is who God is. The life of the Trinity is itself a banquet—an eternal exchange of self-giving between Father, Son,

## THE WEDDING FEAST / PROPER GARMENT (MT 22:1–14)

and Spirit. The Father is the Host who prepares; the Son is the Word offered and received; the Spirit is the joy that circulates between them, the fragrance filling the house. When Jesus tells this parable, He is revealing His own inner life. The Gospel is not an ethical summons but an unveiling of divine being: love poured out, received, and returned in endless joy.

In Christ, that inner life steps outward into visibility. The Son becomes the transparency of the Father. "He who has seen Me has seen the Father." All that God is, Jesus does; all that the Father wills, the Son enacts in time. The banquet imagery gathers these truths into one table of vision. When Jesus breaks bread, the Creator shares creaturely hunger. When He blesses wine, the Eternal enters time's frailty. The infinite has become intimate. The God who once dwelt behind temple veils now reclines with sinners, revealing that holiness is not remoteness but communion.

This revelation intensifies at Calvary. The Host is cast outside His own house so that every exile might come in. Crucified beyond the city walls, He makes His dwelling among the unworthy. The hill of execution becomes the doorway of the feast. The blood and water that flow from His side are the wine and living water of the new covenant. The wedding of heaven and earth is sealed not by ceremony but by sacrifice. The Bridegroom's gift to His Bride is His very life. The paradox is absolute: divine majesty revealed as service, divine joy expressed through suffering, divine victory shining through wounds.

At Easter, the banquet bursts into song. The risen Christ is the Servant returned to the hall, the Master who has completed His circuit through the world. His glorified body is the table now spread before the Father. The wounds that remain are not scars of failure but invitations still open. When He breathes peace on His disciples, the kingdom begins to fill. Pentecost follows as the fragrance of that feast spreading across creation—the Spirit carrying the invitation into every tongue. The whole of salvation history condenses into a single motion: the Son going forth from the Father and returning with the poor, the blind, and the lame gathered in His arms.

Every Eucharist makes this motion present again. The Mass is not remembrance but re-presentation—the same Host still serving His guests.

The words of the priest, "Blessed are those called to the supper of the Lamb," draw time into eternity. Bread and wine become the flesh and blood of the Crucified and Risen Lord, and in that transformation the cosmos itself begins to be transfigured. The communicant who receives becomes what he consumes: another dwelling place of divine charity. The Church's altar is the axis where heaven touches earth, the banquet of the ages concentrated into a single act of love.

Here the Christological centre shines most clearly. The Son is the bridge between the transcendent and the tangible, the one through whom the invisible God becomes touchable, edible, near. The humanity of Jesus is the table where divinity meets dust. Every gesture of His life—His touch, His words, His silence—is sacramental, revealing the Father's generosity through human form. He is simultaneously Host, Servant, and Feast. In Him, all parables are gathered and fulfilled. The Word that once described the banquet is now the Bread that feeds it.

The Incarnation, then, is not a divine interruption of history but its meaning revealed. Creation was always ordered toward communion; in Christ, that purpose is fulfilled. The hall of the world, once echoing with absence, now resounds with the presence of its Lord. To live in Christ is to live from that table—to measure every joy and sorrow by the rhythm of divine hospitality. The Christian who loves, forgives, or serves continues the same feast, extending its reach across the fields of time. Each act of mercy is the Host bending low once more; each conversion, another chair drawn out for a late guest.

The parable's ending—"that my house may be filled"—thus reveals the very destiny of creation. The cosmos itself is to become Eucharistic, every atom taken up into praise. The King's hall is not somewhere else; it is everything transfigured. In the Resurrection, Christ already fills all things; in the Church, He continues to gather them; in glory, He will make the feast complete. The story of salvation is therefore the story of a meal—prepared in eternity, begun in Bethlehem, served on Calvary, and celebrated without end in heaven.

And at its centre stands the same figure who told it: Jesus of Nazareth, the Son of the Living God. He is the Bridegroom of the feast, the Lamb upon the altar, the Servant who compels the lost to come in, the King who will not dine without His friends. In Him the Father's hospitality takes flesh; in Him the Spirit's joy finds form. The invitation still sounds through every age: not a summons to achievement, but a call to communion.

"Come," says the Word made flesh, "for everything is ready."

## The Word for Our Age

If Jesus told the parable of the Wedding Feast today, He might not begin with a king and a royal palace. He might start with something that feels closer:

A couple sends out invitations months in advance. They choose the date, book the venue, labour over the guest list, pay deposits that make their eyes water. The day comes. The flowers are ready, the tables set, the band tuned. And then the texts begin to arrive.

"So sorry, something's come up."

"Can't make it, work exploded."

"Didn't realise it was *this* Saturday."

A few don't even bother with an excuse. They simply don't show.

If you've ever watched a bride scan a room of half-empty tables, you know something of the ache at the heart of this parable. The difference is that Jesus is not speaking about one couple's wounded feelings, but about the heartbreak of God in the face of human indifference.

Our age is saturated with invitations and starved for commitment. Every day brings a flood of notifications, offers, events, causes, campaigns. We click "going" without going, "interested" without interest. FOMO has become a way of life, yet we still manage to miss what matters most.

Into this haze of half-yeses, Jesus' story cuts with unsettling clarity. A king prepares a wedding feast for his son. The images are thick with meaning: covenant, joy, communion, the union of heaven and earth. This isn't an optional social engagement; it is the centre of reality. But when the summons goes out, the response is chillingly familiar:

"They paid no attention and went off, one to his farm, another to his business."

No atheistic manifesto. No public defiance. Just… other plans.

If the Great Banquet in Luke exposes our temptation to stay away from the feast, Matthew's Wedding Feast goes deeper: it reveals the tragedy of coming without changing. Our world struggles with both. On the one hand, we have the mass exodus from worship—empty pews in lands once shaped by the Gospel, a cultural shrug at the things of God. On the other hand, we have those who still come, still "attend," but without allowing the invitation to reshape their lives.

The first half of the parable speaks to the great forgetting of God. The second half, with its startling image of the guest without a wedding garment, speaks directly to the crisis within the Church herself.

The man without a robe is not the pagan who never heard the call; he is the believer who answered it outwardly but never inwardly. He represents the baptised who no longer live their baptism—the Christians who have received the robe of grace but left it crumpled at the door. These are the lukewarm souls of whom the risen Christ warns in Revelation: "You are neither hot nor cold; because you are lukewarm, I will spit you out of my mouth."

In every generation, there are those who keep the name of Christian but not the life of Christ. They may attend, even serve, yet their hearts remain unconverted. They love the feast's music but not its discipline; they enjoy belonging to the hall, but they resist the transformation the garment signifies. Their faith is sentiment without surrender, affiliation without obedience. In the light of the parable, such half-discipleship is not harmless—it is tragic. To stand in the presence of joy and remain unchanged is the deepest form of refusal.

The unrobed guest is therefore a mirror for all of us. He is the warning against nominal Christianity, the religion of convenience that knows Christ's words but not His will. The garment he lacks is not doctrine or ritual, but a heart reshaped by grace—purified desires, forgiven enemies, chastened appetites, a love that costs something. To be without that garment is to enter the banquet but not the marriage, to come near the fire of God's love yet remain cold.

We live in a time when many like the idea of a God who invites, but not a God who judges; a God who welcomes, but not a God who transforms. The Gospel is often reduced to "come as you are" with the unspoken addendum: "and stay as you are." Jesus' story refuses to accept that half-truth.

When the king's hall is finally filled, the text says it is filled "with both bad and good." The doors have been thrown open wide. The invitation is scandalously inclusive. Yet the king still expects something of his guests. He notices one man without a wedding garment and addresses him as "friend," even as he questions him. The man is speechless. His silence reveals that he has no answer, not because poverty barred him from proper clothing—wedding garments were often provided by the host—but because he has refused what has been freely offered.

For our age, this is a vital correction. The problem is not that God requires too much; it is that we expect Him to require nothing.

Consider how we often treat the sacraments. In many places, baptism, confirmation, or marriage become cultural rites of passage more than encounters with the living God. The white garment placed on a newly baptised child—the sign of a life clothed in Christ—can become a prop for photographs rather than a symbol of destiny. We want the ceremony without the conversion, the feast without the garment.

The parable quietly insists that grace is not a costume we put on for special occasions. The wedding garment is not about outward appearance; it is about the inner life—charity, repentance, the new self born in Christ. It is the life that manifests in obedience, forgiveness, chastity, generosity. To enter the feast without that transformation is to treat God's mercy as decoration instead of medicine.

Our culture conditions us to curate identities like outfits—Instagram filters, personal brands, carefully managed impressions. The Church can be tempted to play along, offering religious "aesthetic" without discipleship. We might dabble in spirituality as one more lifestyle accessory: a retreat here, a candlelit adoration hour there, without ever surrendering the habits that govern our choices.

Yet the King in the parable is not hosting a costume party. He is celebrating the marriage of His Son. The garment He offers is nothing less than the righteousness of Christ Himself. To refuse it is not authenticity; it is tragedy.

The first guests in the story "made light of" the invitation. That phrase could be written over much of our age. We make light of Sunday, light of the Eucharist, light of the call to holiness. We treat mortal sin as a minor misstep, confession as a forgotten option. We speak lightly of heaven and hell—if we speak of them at all. Everything becomes casual, negotiable, subject to preference.

Yet the parable stubbornly resists casualisation. It is full of extremity—burning cities, weeping and gnashing teeth, outer darkness. This language jars modern ears. We prefer God as therapist or life coach, not as King. But Jesus is clear: the stakes are eternal. The feast is not one event among many; it is the meaning of existence. To ignore it is not merely discourteous; it is deadly.

Still, the heart of the story is not threat but yearning. The king's repeated sending of servants reveals a longing that will not die. He does not cancel the feast when the first list refuses. He opens the doors wider. He goes after the ones who never imagined their names could be on the guest list. This is where the parable speaks with fierce hope into our culture of disaffiliation and doubt.

There are countless men and women today who assume the Church's doors are closed to them—because of their past, their wounds, their sins, their questions. They have been divorced, addicted, abandoned; they live with shame they cannot even name. For them, the idea of a "wedding garment" can sound like one more standard they could never meet.

But in the Gospel's logic, the garment is not a barrier but a gift. No one sews it for themselves. It is given at the door. The Church's preaching must therefore hold together two truths that our age constantly tries to separate: everyone is invited, and no one is left unchanged.

The danger in our time is to split the parable in half—either to preach only the open invitation and never the garment, or only the garment and never the invitation. The first leads to cheap grace; the second to crushing legalism. Jesus refuses both. He shows us a King who runs down the roads of the world in search of guests and a King who cares deeply how those guests are clothed.

So what does it mean to live this parable now?

It begins with letting the story read us. Where am I in the narrative? Am I among those who simply "paid no attention," allowing work, entertainment, or comfort to swallow my desire for God? Am I in the hall but without the garment—participating outwardly in the life of the Church while resisting interior conversion? Or am I allowing myself, in all my poverty, to be clothed by grace?

In a hyperconnected age, the refusal may not look like open rebellion. It may look like endless postponement. "I'll go deeper later… once things calm down… once I've sorted my life." Yet life rarely calms down on its own. The feast is always "today." God's invitations are time-sensitive not because He is impatient but because our hearts harden under delay.

To answer those invitations, we need what might be called Eucharistic realism—the conviction that what happens at the altar is the centre of the universe and the centre of my week. If the Wedding Feast is ultimately the marriage supper of the Lamb, then every Mass is a dress rehearsal for eternity. The question is not merely "Did I go?" but "Did I go ready to be changed?"

The renewal of the Church begins not in programs but in hunger. The people who will rebuild faith in our time are those who rediscover their need for God as desperately as a starving man seeks food. Every renewal in history has begun this way—not with strategies, but with saints. The field that once kept men away from the banquet must now become the place where they hear the invitation again. Our workplaces, our homes, our phones, our neighbourhoods: these are the lanes and hedges of the modern world. The servants of the King now move through cubicles and classrooms, through digital spaces and suburban streets, carrying the same message of mercy—*everything is ready.*

To live the parable today means to recover a spirituality of holy simplicity. It is not a call to romantic poverty but to ordered love. The first guests were not punished for owning land or tending oxen or marrying; they were punished for letting those good things become gods. The way forward for us is not rejection of the world but right relationship with it—learning again to treat creation as gift, not as currency. A simple life is not bare; it is uncluttered enough to make room for joy.

That uncluttered life begins with gratitude. Gratitude trains the soul to recognise the feast already set before it. In an age that breeds resentment, thanksgiving reawakens wonder. Try it in small things: naming aloud the mercies of the day, blessing meals without haste, ending the night with the words, "You have prepared good things for me." Gratitude loosens the grip of anxiety; it restores the rhythm of receiving and returning that is the heartbeat of worship.

Silence must follow gratitude. If we are to hear the invitation of God, we must reclaim interior quiet. Noise has become the narcotic of the modern world; it drowns the hunger that would lead us home. To step into stillness is to admit that our own words cannot save us. This is why the saints loved silence—it is not emptiness but expectancy, the hush before the music of the feast. In that space, prayer ceases to be performance and becomes conversation again.

The Church, too, must relearn this rhythm of silence and song. Our parishes cannot out-entertain the culture, nor should they try. What will draw the weary back is not novelty but beauty; not busyness but presence. When liturgy is celebrated with reverence, when preaching flows from prayer, when community life mirrors the warmth of the Gospel, people sense the fragrance of the banquet. Evangelisation becomes not a campaign but an aroma—the scent of Christ in the world.

This is the Church's missionary task: to live hospitality so compelling that even cynics grow curious. In the early centuries, pagans were not converted by arguments alone but by the sight of Christians loving one another. They saw widows cared for, orphans adopted, the dying tended with tenderness. They saw joy among those who had nothing. That same witness remains our best sermon. Each believer becomes a servant carrying invitations simply by the way they live—a kindness offered, a wrong forgiven, a patient act that says without words, "You are wanted."

For the tired believer who wonders where to begin, start small: make Sunday sacred again. Keep it not as restriction but as rebellion against the tyranny of utility. Refuse to let the world measure your worth by productivity. Gather your family for Mass, linger at the table afterward, rest without guilt. The Sabbath is the weekly rehearsal of the banquet. To keep it is to remind yourself that love, not labour, defines the universe.

Modern discipleship also means living as bridge-builders. Many today stand outside the Church not from hatred but from hurt. Some were wounded by hypocrisy, others by misunderstanding. They linger by the hedges, unconvinced that the invitation is truly for them. To reach them requires not slogans but presence—listening more than speaking, accompanying more than advising. The servant's command "compel them to come in" finds its modern echo here: love that persists until the hesitant believe they are welcome.

And still the King repeats, "There is room." Those words should haunt and console us. They mean the Church's work is not finished, that every generation must widen the table again. There is room in the liturgy for new languages and melodies; room in theology for deeper dialogue with science and art; room in our parishes for those who differ, doubt, or limp toward faith. The feast grows by inclusion without dilution, by mercy without compromise.

Ultimately, this parable confronts us with a choice between *comfort* and *communion*. To choose the feast is to relinquish control, to trust that joy lies not in having but in belonging. The life of grace is not the management of sin but the surrender to love. That surrender will always feel risky, like stepping through a doorway not knowing what waits inside. But that is faith: the courage to believe that the Host who calls us is good.

And when our final hour comes, the invitation will arrive one last time—not by message or messenger, but as a whisper known only to the soul. The music of the feast will already be playing. Then all the excuses will fall silent. The world we struggled to control will fade, and the table we ignored will blaze into sight. Those who spent their lives practising gratitude, simplicity, mercy, will recognise the hall immediately. They will know they have been walking toward it all along.

Until that day, every Eucharist, every act of kindness, every breath of prayer is another rehearsal for that moment. The house of God is still being filled, one soul at a time. The only tragedy left is to stand outside when the doors are open. The only failure left is to refuse joy.

### Hearing that Becomes Doing

The story is told, but it is not over. The lamps still glow, and the Host still waits. The servant's footsteps echo through the centuries, down the corridors of your own life, carrying the same words spoken once in Galilee: *Come, for everything is ready.* The parable is not a memory to admire; it is a summons happening now. Somewhere beyond the noise of your day, God is setting the table again, calling you by name.

Let the scene rise in your imagination. See the long table under soft light, the air rich with the scent of bread and wine, places laid for guests who have not yet arrived. Listen for the door creaking open as the poor and the forgotten step inside. Their hesitation is holy—the awe of those who never thought they would be wanted. The Master's face warms as they enter, His joy widening with each soul that believes the invitation was meant for them. Then He looks toward the doorway, where you stand. Perhaps you have lingered there before, uncertain whether there would still be a seat after so many refusals. Yet His eyes are clear and kind. He is not tallying your absences. He is waiting for your yes.

Close your eyes for a moment and notice what stirs within. The same excuses whisper now as in the story: not tonight, not ready, not enough time. There are always fields to tend, tasks to finish, small worlds to manage. But all the while the feast stands prepared, and the Host keeps watch. His invitation was never meant for the perfect. It is meant for the hungry. Let your heart fall quiet. The banquet begins whenever you stop

## THE WEDDING FEAST / PROPER GARMENT (MT 22:1–14)

explaining why you cannot come.

Now imagine that the great hall of the story is your own heart. Some rooms are bright and open; others are dark, shut tight, untouched for years. Christ walks through them with the patience of one who loves what He finds. He does not scold the dust or the silence; He lights a candle in each corner and waits for you to notice. You need not tidy before He enters. Holiness is not the effort to impress Him but the willingness to let Him dwell where He is least expected. Ask where in you He has not yet been invited, and do not be afraid of the answer. Grace does not knock on doors to shame what is inside; it knocks to share a meal.

When you feel that invitation, pause and breathe. God's first language is stillness. The servant's call sounds clearest when the room of the soul falls silent. The field and the oxen, the duties and the distractions, can wait. What matters now is presence. Sit in that quiet and whisper only, *Here I am, Lord.* That small consent is enough to open the door.

Yet the story cannot end in contemplation. The Host who called you also sends you. The parable must take form in the world, or it remains unfinished. Every guest becomes a servant the moment they rise from the table. Begin simply. Make a little space in each day where God can speak without competition. It may be the first five minutes of morning before your hand reaches for the phone, or a brief stillness at the window before work begins. Such pauses are doorways through which grace reenters the ordinary. Keep one day a week for rest and prayer, not as luxury but as protest against the tyranny of utility. The first invitees in the story were too busy building their lives to receive life itself. You do not have to repeat them.

Let gratitude be your discipline. Write down three mercies before you sleep: a kindness received, a beauty noticed, a failure forgiven. Thanksgiving keeps the soul porous; it reminds you that everything has been given. If prayer feels dry, turn it into gesture. Light a candle and let its quiet flame become your reply. Watch how it burns without hurry and gives without measure. Or open your hands in your lap, releasing one excuse with each breath out, receiving mercy with each breath in. The body often prays before the mind can.

Carry the feast outward. Look for the people who linger at the edges of your life—the neighbour you avoid, the colleague you've stopped noticing, the friend who has drifted from faith. Invite them, not with arguments but with warmth. Offer a meal, a listening ear, a patient word. The servant's journey continues every time love crosses a boundary. You need not convert anyone; you need only bear the fragrance of welcome.

Let forgiveness become your hospitality. If someone has hurt you, begin the quiet work of peace. Even if it is only a prayer said through gritted teeth, it is a start. The banquet cannot be full while we hold anyone outside the door. Mercy is the wine of the Kingdom; it must be poured freely or it goes sour.

Live Eucharistically. See every table as an altar, every meal as participation in the feast of God. When you break bread at home, remember the Body broken for you. When you share wine or water, recall the blood poured out so that all may enter. The Eucharist does not end with the dismissal; it continues wherever you carry Christ's love. The more you serve, the more you resemble the Host Himself.

And remember: the house of God is still being filled. There is still room. Those four words are the heart of Christian hope. However far you wander, however late you arrive, a place remains set for you. The invitation endures not because you are faithful but because He is. The music of the feast is already playing beneath the noise of the world, and one day it will rise unmistakably. When that hour comes, all excuses will fall away, and love will recognise its own.

Tonight, before sleep, pray slowly:

*Lord Jesus,*
*You who left heaven's joy to seek the lost,*
*enter the rooms of my heart where excuses hide.*
*Sit at the table of my weariness*
*and make it Your dwelling.*
*Teach me to hear Your invitation*

## THE WEDDING FEAST / PROPER GARMENT (MT 22:1–14)

*in every moment of the day.*
*Give me grace to go out toward others*
*with the same mercy that found me.*
*May my home become a place of welcome,*
*my words a light in dark streets,*
*my heart a hall where Your joy can rest.*
*When my time comes,*
*let me recognise Your voice—the servant's voice—*
*saying once more, "Come, for all is ready."*
*And let me rise without hesitation,*
*to take my seat beside You forever.*

Now let the words fade. Imagine the hall again—the candles trembling, the music rising, the Host smiling as you finally enter. You are no longer outside. You have heard. You have come. Rest there. The banquet has begun.

# 12

# The Ten Virgins (Mt 25:1–13)

*Then the kingdom of heaven shall be compared to ten virgins who took their lamps and went to meet the bridegroom.*

*Five of them were foolish, and five were wise.*

*For when the foolish took their lamps, they took no oil with them; but the wise took flasks of oil with their lamps.*

*As the bridegroom was delayed, they all slumbered and slept.*

*But at midnight there was a cry, "Behold, the bridegroom! Come out to meet him."*

*Then all those virgins rose and trimmed their lamps.*

*And the foolish said to the wise, "Give us some of your oil, for our lamps are going out."*

*But the wise replied, "Perhaps there will not be enough for us and for you; go rather to the dealers and buy for yourselves."*

*And while they went to buy, the bridegroom came, and those who were ready went in with him to the marriage feast; and the door was shut.*

*Afterward the other virgins came also, saying, "Lord, lord, open to us."*

*But he replied, "Truly, I say to you, I do not know you."*

*Watch therefore, for you know neither the day nor the hour.*

**The Word Spoken**

## THE TEN VIRGINS (MT 25:1-13)

It was night on the Mount of Olives. Below them, Jerusalem shimmered in the dark—a valley of oil lamps and murmuring voices. The air was cool and dry, carrying the faint smell of smoke from the evening fires. The disciples sat close to Jesus, their cloaks wrapped tight. They had asked Him what the end would be like, when the world as they knew it would pass away. His answers had left them silent: warnings of deception, wars, lamps gone dark, a master returning when no one expects. The night had deepened around His words.

For a while, no one spoke. Somewhere in the distance, a gate creaked. The sound of a wedding procession drifted faintly through the valley—music, laughter, the rhythmic clap of women keeping time on tambourines. The disciples looked toward it. Tiny sparks of torchlight moved along the road like fireflies. Jesus watched with them. He could see the flash of white garments, the flare of oil lamps against the dark. The wedding was nearing its height, the moment when the groom, escorted by his friends, would go to claim his bride. The air itself seemed to wait.

Jesus turned slightly toward His followers. "Then," He said, His voice steady in the stillness, "the kingdom of heaven will be like ten virgins who took their lamps and went out to meet the bridegroom."

The words hung in the air. They all knew the image; they had seen such processions since childhood. Weddings in their villages always began at night, when the day's heat had faded. The bridegroom would come with his companions to fetch the bride from her father's house, and the young maidens—friends of the bride—would go out to meet him, carrying lamps to light the way. The celebration would move through the streets with music and laughter until it reached the house of the groom. There, behind closed doors, the feast would begin.

Jesus' voice carried the rhythm of the story itself—measured, deliberate, as if each sentence were a step through the dark.

"Five of them were wise, and five were foolish."

The disciples could picture it: ten figures standing under the moon, their lamps flickering in the wind. The wise women checked their flasks of oil, making sure the flames would last through the delay. The foolish smiled, unconcerned. They had brought lamps but no extra oil. The bridegroom was late, as bridegrooms often were, and the night stretched long.

The wedding music faded into the distance. The women waited by the road. Voices turned to yawns, laughter to quiet sighs. The lamps burned lower. Somewhere, an owl called. One by one, they grew drowsy and slept.

Jesus paused. The disciples could hear the shift in His tone, the slow tightening of the story's string.

"But at midnight there was a cry: 'Behold, the bridegroom! Come out to meet him!'"

The valley below seemed to echo it. The city's lamps trembled in the distance like stars. The disciples could almost feel the rush of sudden wakefulness, the scramble of hands reaching for lamps, the smell of smoke as wicks were trimmed. Half the torches flared to life; the others sputtered and died. The foolish maidens turned to their companions, panic in their eyes.

"'Give us some of your oil,' they said, 'for our lamps are going out.'"

The disciples shifted, uneasy. The wise women shook their heads. "'There will not be enough for us and for you; go rather to the dealers and buy for yourselves.'"

It was absurd, of course. No merchants opened at midnight. But desperation does not think clearly. The foolish ran into the darkness, clutching their dying lamps, hoping against reason that someone would answer their knocking.

Jesus' voice fell quiet again.

"While they went to buy, the bridegroom came, and those who were ready went in with him to the marriage feast; and the door was shut."

A cold breeze moved through the olive trees. The disciples felt it as more than wind. The closed door echoed through the night like finality. They knew what that sound meant—the line between inside and out, joy and regret.

"Afterward," Jesus continued, "the other virgins came also, saying, 'Lord, lord, open to us.'"

He did not raise His voice. He didn't need to. The stillness made every word sharp.

"But he replied, 'Truly, I say to you, I do not know you.'"

The disciples looked at Him. The torchlight from nearby pilgrims flickered across His face. He seemed to be looking beyond them, into the horizon where night met the edge of dawn.

"Watch, therefore," He said softly, "for you know neither the day nor the hour."

The words settled like ash, silent and heavy.

Below, the noise of the wedding procession had faded completely. The lamps that had wound through the streets were now hidden behind doors. From where they sat, only a few points of light remained—faint glows in the distance, like small promises against the dark.

Jesus sat motionless. The disciples followed His gaze. Somewhere in the city, a dog barked. Somewhere closer, a lamp sputtered out.

They understood the surface of the story: the waiting, the lamps, the door. But the look on His face told them there was more—something about readiness, about hearts that burn or go dim. They could not yet name it.

The night pressed close around them. Oil lamps flickered at their feet, their little circles of light wavering on the dust. The wind carried the scent of olives and faraway fires. The disciples said nothing, afraid to break the spell of what they had heard. The Teacher's voice had turned a village custom into something eternal.

Beyond the Mount, the city's lights shimmered and dimmed. Somewhere, the bridegroom's house pulsed with music and laughter. But up here, the waiting continued. Jesus' eyes lingered on the horizon. The first faint thread of dawn had not yet touched it.

The disciples would remember that silence for the rest of their lives—the cool air, the weight of the story, the sense that something vast had just been revealed through something ordinary. They did not yet know that He was speaking of Himself, that He was the Bridegroom who would soon be taken, that the delay would be His absence and the door His return. For now, they only sat in the half-light, lamps trembling in their hands, hearts caught between fear and hope.

The last image stayed with them: ten women waiting in the night, the faint smell of smoke in the air, a door closing somewhere out of sight. And in the darkness, a voice—calm, solemn, steady—still speaking: *"Watch, therefore, for you know neither the day nor the hour."*

## The Surface Story

The parable began in the language of weddings, and every listener knew the world it described. Marriage in first-century Judea was never private romance but public covenant. Families arranged it long before the feast. Months, sometimes a full year, separated betrothal from consummation. The bride remained in her father's house while the groom prepared the new dwelling—adding rooms, gathering furniture, storing oil and wine. Only when the father of the groom judged all ready would he send his son to fetch his bride. The hour was rarely announced; anticipation itself was part of the joy.

When Jesus spoke of ten virgins waiting with lamps, His audience pictured a familiar scene. In every village such bridal attendants accompanied the groom's procession at night, their lamps forming a line of moving fire through the dark streets. They were not guests but participants in the ceremony, symbols of honour for the families involved. Each carried a small clay lamp fed by olive oil, its narrow wick needing frequent trimming. To be chosen for this duty was a mark of friendship and esteem; to neglect it was unthinkable.

The custom followed an ordered pattern. When word spread that the groom's father had given his blessing, friends and musicians gathered at the groom's house. Torches were lit; the air filled with shouting and flutes. The procession set out toward the bride's home, winding through lanes already crowded with neighbours eager for spectacle. The bride waited veiled, surrounded by her companions. The moment the groom arrived, the virgins went out to meet him, joining the escort back to the new household where the marriage feast would begin. In the village imagination, that torchlit journey was the passage from promise to fulfillment, from old life to new.

No one doubted that such a scene could stretch deep into the night. A delay in the groom's arrival—whether from bargaining over the dowry or from distance between the houses—was common. The attendants kept their lamps trimmed, refilling the bowls from small flasks of reserve oil. Those who brought no extra supply risked embarrassment if the hour grew late. The village itself expected to be roused by the cry that signaled the procession's approach: "Behold, the bridegroom is coming!" Windows would open, children woken, neighbours stepping outside to watch the blaze of lamps pass by. To miss that moment was to miss the heart of the celebration.

Everything in this custom carried covenant weight. Marriage was not merely alliance between families but image of Israel's bond with God. Prophets had spoken of the Lord as Bridegroom and the nation as His betrothed. The people's faithfulness was measured by their readiness for His coming. When Jesus shaped His parable in this language, He was drawing on centuries of liturgy and poetry. The lighted lamps echoed the perpetual flame of the tabernacle—the golden lampstand in the Tent of Meeting that burned through every night before the Lord (Ex 27:20-21). Every household lamp was, in miniature, a continuation of that holy flame, a sign that covenant life still glowed in Israel's homes.

To run out of oil, then, was more than inconvenience. It meant failure in duty, a breach of honour before families and friends. The shame would linger long after the feast. Weddings were public theatre; honour and memory intertwined. The young women who came unprepared would have felt the weight of ridicule. Their lamps, once bright with expectation, sputtering out in the darkness, became the symbol of negligence all could see. They had been trusted with joy and found wanting.

The others—those who brought extra oil—were not considered clever for its own sake but faithful to custom. Preparedness was respect. Every villager would understand the balance between festivity and seriousness.

A wedding was a covenant renewal of the community itself; disorder in it threatened the harmony of the whole. The groom's household, once the procession arrived, would close its doors when all were inside, both to protect the sanctity of the rite and to mark its completion. Latecomers shouting at a barred gate would have evoked not cruelty but propriety. A feast begun could not be interrupted.

In such realism lay the story's force. Jesus needed no explanation to make His listeners nod in recognition. They could smell the olive oil, feel the dry wind that made flames flicker, see the faces of women waiting in the cold hours before dawn. They had heard those midnight cries themselves and knew the mixture of laughter and fatigue that came with delay. Every detail rang true—the excitement, the drowsiness, the sudden commotion when the torches finally appeared.

Light held sacred meaning for Israel. The psalmist had sung, "Your word is a lamp to my feet and a light to my path." The wisdom writers spoke of the lamp of the righteous shining in darkness, while the wicked stumbled for lack of it. Each household that kindled its evening flame repeated the rhythm of creation itself—darkness divided by divine light. In every festival, from Passover to Tabernacles, lamps marked the boundary between chaos and celebration. When Jesus spoke of lamps at midnight, He touched this deep memory: the conviction that God's presence is known by light, and that to guard it is a form of love.

Waiting too carried sacred weight. Israel's faith was born in waiting—Abraham for the promise, Moses for deliverance, David for the crown. To wait was not passivity but trust. The delay of the bridegroom in the story would have sounded familiar to any listener who knew the patience demanded by covenant life. The wise maidens who kept watch embodied that patience. They honoured the pace of joy. Their readiness was affection measured in time.

The village imagination could picture the whole scene as though it were happening down the next street: the women rousing at the sudden cry, fumbling to light their lamps, the confusion of those who found theirs gone dark, the hurried journey through alleys now alive with flame. They could see the groom's figure approaching, hear the doors closing, sense the stillness afterward. It was a parable woven entirely from the texture of their days. Nothing in it was foreign. It was their own customs speaking back to them.

To those who listened, the story's realism carried its own quiet lesson, though Jesus offered none aloud. They knew that love shown in haste is easy; love that endures waiting is covenantal. Every delay is a chance for fidelity to prove itself. A lamp that burns through the night is more precious than one that flares and fails. In that conviction, every heart that heard Him could find itself: the lover, the servant, the friend who waits in the dark because promise has been given.

The hearers would have felt the ache of that waiting. The night hours in a Galilean courtyard could stretch endlessly—crickets droning, oil lamps hissing, the smell of smoke in the wind. Bridesmaids whispered to keep themselves awake; laughter faded to drowsy murmurs. There was no clock but the stars, no signal but trust. Every sound in the distance stirred anticipation: a dog barking, a shout from the fields, perhaps at last the cry that would break the long suspense. To stay ready through those hours was an act of love disguised as patience.

In their world, readiness itself was virtue. A household that kept its lamp burning when others slept bore quiet witness to fidelity. Ancient rabbis compared Israel to a watchful wife awaiting her husband's return, her lamp never extinguished. The nation's festivals echoed that same posture of expectancy: every Passover table set for Elijah, every Sabbath greeted as a bride. Waiting was not weakness but identity. The people of the covenant were those who waited for God.

The oil the maidens carried had its own dignity. Olive oil was the lifeblood of daily life—used for light, cooking, medicine, and consecration. It anointed kings and priests, marked prophets, sealed covenants. In every household it was stored with care, a symbol of prosperity and divine blessing. To bring a flask of oil to a feast was to bring the substance of peace itself. The careful ones who kept it in reserve showed the discipline of hearts trained by tradition. They knew celebration depends on preparation. The foolish, arriving with empty lamps, represented something more ordinary than rebellion—they showed forgetfulness, the slow fading of attention that every human heart knows.

The midnight cry would have rung through that culture with electric clarity. It was the moment every wedding turned from waiting to wonder. "Behold, the bridegroom!" was more than information—it was announcement of joy fulfilled. The sleepers woke; the wise trimmed their lamps; the procession formed. Those left behind knocking on a closed door would not be pitied so much as pitied for their shame. In a society where honour bound community, missing the moment of celebration was a small tragedy. They had failed not only themselves but their families.

The closed door in such a parable was not cruelty; it was custom. Every feast had its hour, every covenant its boundary. Once the procession entered the groom's house, the threshold became sacred. The door was shut to protect the bride's honour and the sanctity of the union. To arrive afterward, clamouring to be let in, was to misunderstand the order of the occasion. The listeners knew that instinctively. A man who missed the wedding procession did not blame the host; he blamed his own slowness.

For those hearing Jesus in the hills of Galilee, all this was the fabric of ordinary life: light and oil, patience and joy, the rhythm of promise kept through long hours. They did not need theology to feel its beauty. The story's realism spoke its truth. The wise girls with their extra oil were simply faithful people who had learned that love waits. The foolish were the forgetful, the distracted, those who had not thought beyond the first thrill of invitation.

As Jesus fell silent after telling it, the crowd could see the whole picture still: the flickering lamps, the sudden rush of footsteps, the laughter of the wedding hall fading into the night. They might have looked toward their own homes, where lamps glowed through window shutters, and felt the quiet satisfaction of being prepared for whatever joy might come. The lesson was not yet moral or mystical; it was woven into their own experience.

To live in covenant was to live in readiness. Every wedding procession, every burning lamp, every jar of oil kept for the night was a rehearsal of fidelity. Waiting was the measure of affection; endurance the proof of belonging. The parable of the ten virgins, on its surface, was nothing more than a mirror held up to that world—a reminder that love's truest form is patient preparation. The listeners understood that much without needing it said aloud.

So the story ended as it began, in the familiar light of lamps carried through darkness, in the rustle of veils and the soft cry of joy when the bridegroom appeared. It was a scene every villager had known, but in Jesus' telling it glowed with an uncommon tenderness. The feast began behind the closed door, the music rising, the night outside deep and still. Those who heard Him walked away with the sound of it echoing in memory: the mingled warmth of human festivity and divine patience, a love that proves itself by waiting until the dawn.

**The Hidden Fire**

### a) Text, Translation, and Literary Context
**Greek Text (Matthew 25:1-13):**

Τότε ὁμοιωθήσεται ἡ βασιλεία τῶν οὐρανῶν δέκα παρθένοις αἳ λαβοῦσαι τὰς λαμπάδας ἑαυτῶν ἐξῆλθον εἰς ἀπάντησιν τοῦ νυμφίου.

πέντε δὲ ἐξ αὐτῶν ἦσαν μωραὶ καὶ πέντε φρόνιμοι.

αἱ γὰρ μωραὶ λαβοῦσαι τὰς λαμπάδας ἑαυτῶν οὐκ ἔλαβον μεθ' ἑαυτῶν ἔλαιον·

αἱ δὲ φρόνιμοι ἔλαβον ἔλαιον ἐν τοῖς ἀγγείοις μετὰ τῶν λαμπάδων ἑαυτῶν.

χρονίζοντος δὲ τοῦ νυμφίου ἐνύσταξαν πᾶσαι καὶ ἐκάθευδον.

μέσης δὲ νυκτὸς κραυγὴ γέγονεν· Ἰδοὺ ὁ νυμφίος, ἐξέρχεσθε εἰς ἀπάντησιν.

τότε ἠγέρθησαν πᾶσαι αἱ παρθένοι ἐκεῖναι καὶ ἐκόσμησαν τὰς λαμπάδας ἑαυτῶν.

αἱ δὲ μωραὶ ταῖς φρονίμοις εἶπον· Δότε ἡμῖν ἐκ τοῦ ἐλαίου ὑμῶν, ὅτι αἱ λαμπάδες ἡμῶν σβέννυνται.

ἀπεκρίθησαν δὲ αἱ φρόνιμοι λέγουσαι· Μήποτε οὐ μὴ ἀρκέσῃ ἡμῖν καὶ ὑμῖν· πορεύεσθε μᾶλλον πρὸς τοὺς πωλοῦντας καὶ ἀγοράσατε ἑαυταῖς.

ἀπερχομένων δὲ αὐτῶν ἀγοράσαι ἦλθεν ὁ νυμφίος, καὶ αἱ ἕτοιμοι εἰσῆλθον μετ' αὐτοῦ εἰς τοὺς γάμους, καὶ ἐκλείσθη ἡ θύρα.

ὕστερον δὲ ἔρχονται καὶ αἱ λοιπαὶ παρθένοι λέγουσαι· Κύριε, κύριε, ἄνοιξον ἡμῖν.

ὁ δὲ ἀποκριθεὶς εἶπεν· Ἀμὴν λέγω ὑμῖν, οὐκ οἶδα ὑμᾶς.

γρηγορεῖτε οὖν, ὅτι οὐκ οἴδατε τὴν ἡμέραν οὐδὲ τὴν ὥραν.

Matthew begins, as he did with the Wedding Feast, by putting the whole scene under a single heading: "Τότε ὁμοιωθήσεται ἡ βασιλεία τῶν οὐρανῶν…"—"Then the kingdom of heaven will be likened…" The adverb τότε ("then") reaches back into the flow of the eschatological discourse in chapters 24–25. Jesus has been speaking of the end: tribulation, false prophets, the coming of the Son of Man. Now He says, quite literally, "at that time" the kingdom will be made like this. We are not in a timeless moral fable but in the drama of the last things.

The verb ὁμοιωθήσεται is future passive: "will be likened." As in the wedding parable (22:2, ὡμοιώθη), Matthew uses the divine passive. The kingdom has its likeness from God; Jesus, the Word made flesh, is giving us heaven's own comparison. And the likeness is strikingly concrete: "δέκα παρθένοις"—"ten virgins."

The noun παρθένος in biblical Greek carries both the obvious sense of unmarried maiden and the deeper resonances of consecration. Israel herself is called a virgin daughter in the prophets; Paul will later speak of presenting the Church as a "pure virgin" to Christ. But at the textual level, Matthew simply places ten young women on stage, lamps in hand, set "εἰς ἀπάντησιν τοῦ νυμφίου"—"to go out to meet the bridegroom." The prepositional phrase εἰς ἀπάντησιν is a technical term for going out in joyful procession to welcome a dignitary; it will reappear in Paul's description of believers going out "to meet" the Lord at His coming. Even here, the lexical choice quietly prepares for that later hope.

Already in the first verse, light and covenantal joy are woven together. The virgins λαβοῦσαι τὰς λαμπάδας ἑαυτῶν—"having taken their lamps"—go forth. The word λαμπάς evokes a flaming torch more than a delicate oil-lamp: a source of moving light meant for processions at night.

## THE TEN VIRGINS (MT 25:1–13)

In Israel's Scriptures, light is never merely practical. The lamp of God burns in the Tent of Meeting; the psalmist prays, "Your word is a lamp to my feet." Here, though, we are still at the level of narrative: ten girls, ten torches, one bridegroom, and a journey into the dark.

The second verse introduces the contrast that will carry the story: "πέντε δὲ ἐξ αὐτῶν ἦσαν μωραὶ καὶ πέντε φρόνιμοι." Five were μωραί, five φρόνιμοι. Matthew chooses strong adjectives. Μωρός in Greek means more than "silly"; it is the root of our word "moron," denoting one who is dull, thick, lacking sense. It appears earlier on Jesus' lips in the Sermon on the Mount as a word not to be thrown at a brother; here, Jesus uses its feminine form for half the bridal party. Φρόνιμος, by contrast, describes someone prudent, thoughtful, acting from considered judgment. It is the same adjective Matthew uses for the wise man who builds on rock (7:24) and for the faithful servant who manages his master's household (24:45). Already, then, the parable is tied to earlier teaching: wisdom in Matthew is not intellectual brilliance but covenantal attentiveness.

The evangelist pauses to define each group by a single practical decision. "αἱ γὰρ μωραὶ... οὐκ ἔλαβον μεθ' ἑαυτῶν ἔλαιον"—"the foolish, having taken their lamps, did not take oil with themselves." The phrase μεθ' ἑαυτῶν ("with themselves") heightens the irony: they went out, but empty-handed of what mattered. The wise, by contrast, "ἔλαβον ἔλαιον ἐν τοῖς ἀγγείοις μετὰ τῶν λαμπάδων ἑαυτῶν"—"took oil in flasks with their lamps." The doubling—lamps and flasks—repeats the same structure as "call the called" in the earlier parable. Preparation here is not exotic; it is simple surplus, the margin of readiness beyond the minimum.

The noun ἔλαιον ("oil") is one of those charged words in Scripture. It is, on the surface, the fuel that keeps a torch burning. But the very sound of the word would have recalled for Matthew's first readers anointing, healing, gladness. Kings and priests are anointed with oil; the psalmist's cup overflows as oil runs down Aaron's beard. Matthew does not yet interpret it; he simply places it at the centre of the narrative tension. The story will turn on who has oil and who does not.

Verse 5 slows the action with a temporal clause: "χρονίζοντος δὲ τοῦ νυμφίου"—"but as the bridegroom delayed." The participle χρονίζοντος suggests not mere lateness but lingering, time stretching out. This is the same verb used later for the "delayed" master in other judgment sayings. On the narrative surface, any wedding in a village could run late; processions took time; bridesgrooms were not known for punctuality. Yet Matthew's choice of vocabulary already serves his community wrestling with the apparent "delay" of the Parousia. For now, in the text's own world, it simply creates room for drowsiness.

"ἐνύσταξαν πᾶσαι καὶ ἐκάθευδον"—"they all became drowsy and were sleeping." Matthew uses two verbs in sequence. Ἐνυστάζω suggests nodding off, the first heaviness of eyelids; καθεύδω is the more general term "to sleep." The imperfect ἐκάθευδον paints an ongoing state. Notably, πᾶσαι—"all"—succumb. Wise and foolish share the same human frailty. The text does not yet moralize their sleep; it simply notes that, given enough time, even the most vigilant close their eyes.

Then, "μέσης δὲ νυκτὸς κραυγὴ γέγονεν"—"but at midnight a cry happened." The phrase μέσης νυκτός—"middle of the night"—is evocative. It was the Roman world's second or third watch, the time of deepest dark and least activity. In Israel's memory, midnight was the hour of Passover, the time when the Lord passed through Egypt. Here it is the moment when sound breaks stillness. The noun κραυγή is not a gentle call; it is a loud shout, a cry that pierces sleep. Grammatically, γέγονεν (perfect tense) presents it as something that has happened and now stands, its effect continuing: the cry is still echoing.

The content of the shout is short and sharp: "Ἰδοὺ ὁ νυμφίος, ἐξέρχεσθε εἰς ἀπάντησιν"—"Behold, the bridegroom! Come out to meet [him]." Again the verb ἐξέρχεσθε ("go out") and the phrase εἰς ἀπάντησιν bind this scene to the opening and to the broader biblical pattern of going out to welcome the Lord. The narrative rhythm tightens; after the long delay and slow sleep, we get an abrupt imperative.

Verse 7 responds with equal economy: "τότε ἠγέρθησαν πᾶσαι αἱ παρθένοι ἐκεῖναι καὶ ἐκόσμησαν τὰς λαμπάδας ἑαυτῶν." "Then all those virgins rose and trimmed their lamps." The verb ἠγέρθησαν can mean "they got up" from sleep; it is also the verb used throughout the New Testament for "rise" in the sense of resurrection. Matthew enjoys such double resonances; here it works on the narrative level but hums with deeper potential. Ἐκόσμησαν ("they arranged, adorned, set in order") is used of putting things in proper condition; the same root lies behind "cosmos," the ordered world. The virgins now hurriedly "order" their lamps; the time of preparation is over; they must work with what they have.

The crucial dialogue follows. "αἱ δὲ μωραὶ ταῖς φρονίμοις εἶπον· Δότε ἡμῖν ἐκ τοῦ ἐλαίου ὑμῶν, ὅτι αἱ λαμπάδες ἡμῶν σβέννυνται." "The foolish said to the wise, 'Give us from your oil, for our lamps are going out.'" The request is plausible and urgent; the present tense σβέννυνται depicts the flames in the very act of dying. The foolish have lamps—there is no suggestion they were impostors—but they lack continuity of flame. They want transfer, a share in what others have stored.

The reply of the wise is framed in careful Greek: "ἀπεκρίθησαν δὲ αἱ φρόνιμοι λέγουσαι· Μήποτε οὐ μὴ ἀρκέσῃ ἡμῖν καὶ ὑμῖν· πορεύεσθε μᾶλλον πρὸς τοὺς πωλοῦντας καὶ ἀγοράσατε ἑαυταῖς." Literally, "No indeed, lest it should not suffice for us and you; rather, go to the sellers and buy for yourselves." The double negative μήποτε οὐ μή with the subjunctive ἀρκέσῃ is emphatic: they are not being stingy but realistic. The imperative πορεύεσθε ("go") and ἀγοράσατε ("buy") evoke the marketplace, the realm of exchange. At the textual level, Jesus simply has them direct the unprepared to the only logical remedy—obtain what they have neglected to bring.

The turning-point comes in verse 10: "ἀπερχομένων δὲ αὐτῶν ἀγοράσαι ἦλθεν ὁ νυμφίος." "While they were going away to buy, the bridegroom came." The participial phrase ἀπερχομένων... ἀγοράσαι ("as they were going away to buy") gives us motion; the main verb ἦλθεν ("came") falls with quiet inevitability. Matthew loves this simple aorist; it is how he will speak of the Son of Man's coming again and again. "καὶ αἱ ἕτοιμοι εἰσῆλθον μετ' αὐτοῦ εἰς τοὺς γάμους"—"and those who were ready went in with him to the wedding feast." The adjective ἕτοιμος ("ready") has already sounded in earlier parables: all things ready, wedding ready. Here it attaches not to a meal but to persons. Readiness has become a state of soul.

The closing clause of the verse is laconic and devastating: "καὶ ἐκλείσθη ἡ θύρα"—"and the door was shut." The verb ἐκλείσθη is aorist passive: "was closed." Matthew does not say by whom; the subject is the door itself, now no longer open. The narrative leaves us on the inside for a moment: bridegroom present, ready ones within, door firm.

Verse 11 shifts vantage: "ὕστερον δὲ ἔρχονται καὶ αἱ λοιπαὶ παρθένοι λέγουσαι· Κύριε, κύριε, ἄνοιξον ἡμῖν." "Afterwards the other virgins also come, saying, 'Lord, Lord, open to us.'" The adverb ὕστερον ("later") underscores belatedness. The phrase αἱ λοιπαί ("the remaining") marks them now not simply as foolish but as left outside. Their plea "Κύριε, κύριε"—"Lord, Lord"—echoes Jesus' own warning earlier: "Not everyone who says to me, 'Lord, Lord,' will enter the kingdom." The imperative ἄνοιξον ("open") asks for what the previous verse has declared closed.

The answer is short and solemn: "ὁ δὲ ἀποκριθεὶς εἶπεν· Ἀμὴν λέγω ὑμῖν, οὐκ οἶδα ὑμᾶς." "But he, answering, said, 'Truly I say to you, I do not know you.'" The formula Ἀμὴν λέγω ὑμῖν is the seal of authority Jesus uses throughout the Gospel; now it stands in a parable on the bridegroom's lips. The verb οἶδα ("I know") in biblical usage is covenantal: "You only have I known of all the families of the earth," says God to Israel. To say "I do not know you" is to declare not ignorance but lack of relationship. Again, at the textual level, this is simply what the bridegroom says to latecomers. Yet every word carries the weight of Israel's history of knowing and being known by the Lord.

The final verse steps outside the story into direct exhortation: "γρηγορεῖτε οὖν, ὅτι οὐκ οἴδατε τὴν ἡμέραν οὐδὲ τὴν ὥραν." "Watch, therefore, for you do not know the day nor the hour." The imperative γρηγορεῖτε ("stay awake, keep watch") has been ringing through chapter 24; here it gathers up the narrative into command. The motive clause ὅτι οὐκ οἴδατε ("because you do not know") mirrors the bridegroom's own "I do not know you." On one side, the Lord does not "know" the unprepared; on the other, the disciples do not "know" the timing. Mutual knowledge—His of us and ours of His coming—has become the heart of the parable's grammar.

At the level of literary architecture, the passage is remarkably tight.

Matthew arranges it in a balanced sequence:
- Introduction: ten virgins, lamps, going out (v. 1).
- Division: foolish and wise, defined by oil (vv. 2–4).
- Delay and universal sleep (v. 5).
- Midnight cry and rising (vv. 6–7).
- Request for oil, refusal, and proposed remedy (vv. 8–9).
- Arrival of the bridegroom, entry of the ready, closing of the door (v. 10).
- Late appeal and rejection ("I do not know you") (vv. 11–12).
- Moral: watchfulness in ignorance of the hour (v. 13).

The narrative rhythm moves from outward action ("they went out") to inward dispositions ("wise" and "foolish"), from common experience (everyone sleeps) to irreversible separation (door shut). The repetition of key motifs—lamps, oil, going out, coming, knowing—threads the passage into a single fabric. Even before any allegory is drawn, the text itself already burns with a quiet urgency. Something more than a village wedding is at stake. The kingdom of heaven "will be likened" to this: to waiting that reveals wisdom, to light that must be fed, to a door that stands open until, at last, it closes.

## b) Theological Interpretation

The parable of the Ten Virgins is not a sentimental lesson about moral readiness but a theological vision of the covenant in its final stage of fulfillment. It is the bridal mystery of salvation seen through the grammar of waiting. Beneath its calm domestic imagery—lamps, oil, drowsiness, a midnight cry—runs the deep current of the Bible's central drama: God the Bridegroom drawing His bride into the life of divine communion. Everything in this story belongs to the language of covenant love, the nuptial bond between Creator and creation that the prophets described and Christ fulfills. The virgins, the lamps, the oil, the delay, and the closing door are not decorative details but the architecture of salvation history itself.

The ten virgins are the Church in her eschatological posture—called, consecrated, awaiting consummation. The Greek *parthenoi* does not merely mean "young women" but evokes the purity of Israel as "virgin daughter Zion" (Lam 2:13; Amos 5:2). In biblical theology, virginity is not simply physical chastity but covenant integrity: undivided devotion to the Lord who chose her. When Jesus begins, "Then the kingdom of heaven shall be likened to ten virgins," He is speaking not of random attendants but of the people of God invited to share the joy of divine union. The Church, the renewed Israel, is already betrothed to the Bridegroom, yet her perfection lies ahead. Between promise and fulfillment, she lives the vigil of faith.

The number ten itself carries covenant resonance. Ten was the number of completeness—the Ten Words of the Law, the full measure of commandment. Ten virgins thus represent the whole community of the called, the completeness of God's people, both the faithful and the faithless together. Like the mixed field of wheat and weeds, the Church bears both wise and foolish within her until the end. Jesus speaks of them together not to divide prematurely but to warn that external membership in the covenant does not guarantee interior communion. The virgins all belong to the bridal company, all carry lamps, all set out to meet the Bridegroom. Their difference is invisible until the hour of testing.

This duality—five wise (*phronimoi*), five foolish (*morai*)—is not arbitrary arithmetic but moral theology in miniature. Wisdom in Scripture is always covenantal: "The fear of the Lord is the beginning of wisdom" (Prov 9:10). To be *phronimos* is to live in harmony with the divine order, to love rightly what God loves. Folly, by contrast, is not mere stupidity but moral inversion—the failure to align desire with truth. When Paul warns the Ephesians, "Do not be foolish (*mōroi*), but understand what the will of the Lord is," he is describing precisely the distinction that Jesus dramatizes here. The wise are those who have internalized covenant knowledge into habit, whose faith has ripened into prudence; the foolish are those who keep the form of religion but deny its inner power.

The lamps they carry are the visible form of that faith—the outward expression of covenant vocation. The Greek *lampas* refers to a torch fuelled by oil-soaked rags bound to a stick, needing continual replenishment. In Scripture, lamps were not symbols of mere illumination but of participation in divine light. "The spirit of man is the lamp of the Lord," says Proverbs (20:27). The lamp signifies the human soul lit by grace, the visible witness of divine life within. Israel's worship made this explicit: the seven-branched lampstand before the Holy of Holies was to burn "continually" as a sign that the covenant people lived always in God's presence (Ex 27:20–21). The lamps in the virgins' hands therefore signify each believer's life as a sanctuary light—personal, communal, and priestly. To carry a lamp is to bear witness that the world is not abandoned to darkness.

The oil (*elaion*) is the mystery within the mystery. Throughout Scripture, oil signifies consecration and divine indwelling. Kings and priests were anointed with it as the sign of the Spirit's power; prophets spoke of the Messiah as "the anointed one," *ho christos*. Olive oil was poured into wounds to heal, into lamps to burn, into heads to bless. The Church Fathers consistently read the oil of this parable as the interior grace of the Holy Spirit—the uncreated light that feeds the flame of faith. Grace is not external decoration but the very life of God poured into the soul, making the believer capable of divine love. Without that indwelling, the lamp of religion becomes an empty shell: structure without spirit, form without fire.

The wise virgins, then, represent those who live in this state of grace—those who cooperate with the Spirit's work within them. Their vigilance is not anxiety but charity's endurance. They know that love must be sustained; they carry oil because they understand the cost of communion. The foolish are those who presume that faith requires no cultivation, that initial enthusiasm will suffice for a lifetime. They have lamps—perhaps sacraments, knowledge, or outward devotion—but no inward transformation. In covenant language, they possess the sign but not the substance. Their tragedy is not ignorance but negligence: they have received grace in vain.

The parable's next movement—"As the bridegroom was delayed, they all became drowsy and slept"—is the hinge on which the entire theology turns. The delay is not a narrative inconvenience but a revelation of divine pedagogy. In every covenant, God teaches His people through waiting. Abraham waited decades for Isaac, Israel for the Exodus, David for the throne, the exiles for return, the world for the Messiah. Time is the furnace of faith, the crucible in which desire is purified of self-interest. The "delay" of the Bridegroom is thus the training ground of love; it distinguishes passion from perseverance. The wise are those whose charity deepens in the darkness; the foolish are those whose ardour cools when immediate reward fades.

Even the detail that "they all slept" is charged with theological meaning. Sleep here is not sin but mortality. Every believer must enter the sleep of death before the Bridegroom's arrival. The Church, too, passes through nights of apparent silence—ages of persecution, complacency, or confusion. Yet in this slumber the wise are not extinguished. Their lamps, fed by hidden oil, continue to glow. Grace is stronger than forgetfulness. The foolish, lacking that interior reserve, find their flame extinguished; their religion cannot survive the long night because it was never rooted in covenant love.

Then, "at midnight, there was a cry." Midnight in Scripture is the hour of divine reversal. It was at midnight that God delivered Israel from Egypt (Ex 12:29–31); at midnight that Paul and Silas sang hymns in the Philippian jail and saw the doors open (Acts 16:25). The cry is the eschatological trumpet, the voice of the archangel announcing the return of Christ. "Behold, the Bridegroom comes; go out to meet him." The summons is both joyous and fearful, for it reveals each soul as it truly is. In an instant, what was hidden becomes manifest: the wise rise with lamps still burning; the foolish fumble in darkness. The moment of encounter divides appearance from reality.

The foolish virgins' request—"Give us some of your oil, for our lamps are going out"—is a theological impossibility disguised as a plea. They seek to borrow grace. But grace, though communicable in its effects, is incommunicable in its essence. The indwelling of the Spirit cannot be

## THE TEN VIRGINS (MT 25:1–13)

transferred by human generosity. One saint's holiness can inspire another, but it cannot substitute for the other's conversion. The refusal of the wise—"There may not be enough for us and for you"—is not selfishness but realism. It states the metaphysical truth that communion with God must be personal. Charity can overflow; it cannot be outsourced.

The irony of their command—"Go to the dealers and buy for yourselves"—is deliberate. In the logic of the Kingdom, oil cannot be bought or sold; it can only be received freely through long cooperation with grace. The foolish, who have treated faith as a transaction, now attempt to treat salvation as one. They go to "buy" what could have been theirs for free if they had only tended their lamps through the years of waiting. The economy of grace does not operate on last-minute desperation. It is formed by relationship, not by exchange.

While they go off to bargain with time, "the Bridegroom came, and those who were ready went in with him to the marriage feast, and the door was shut." The image of the closed door resonates with covenant history. It recalls Noah's ark, sealed by the Lord before the flood; it anticipates the heavenly Jerusalem, whose gates stand open only to those written in the Lamb's book of life. The door is not arbitrary exclusion but ontological truth: the separation between those united to the Bridegroom by love and those who have remained strangers. Inside the hall is communion—the consummation of the covenant. Outside is self-enclosure, the loneliness of those who have lived only for themselves.

When the foolish return, crying, "Lord, Lord, open to us," they rehearse the words of Matthew 7:21. They invoke the right title, but relationship is missing. The Bridegroom's answer—"Truly, I say to you, I do not know you"—is not rage but revelation. Knowledge in Scripture always implies intimacy: "Adam knew Eve his wife." For God to say, "I do not know you," is to declare that the covenant bond has never been reciprocated. They have known His name but not His heart.

The parable concludes with the command that gathers its whole theology into one imperative: "Watch therefore, for you know neither the day nor the hour." Watchfulness here is not sleepless anxiety but the contemplative attentiveness of love. It is the virtue of the bride who lives by memory and hope, who keeps the lamp of charity trimmed through the long dark until the cry of joy breaks the silence: "Behold, the Bridegroom comes."

The parable of the Ten Virgins becomes luminous only when read through the whole arc of covenant theology—from Israel's bridal election to the Church's Eucharistic vigil. Every symbol in this short scene carries the weight of centuries. The virgins' very identity as *bridesmaids* draws upon the prophetic language of divine betrothal. Hosea had spoken for God: "I will betroth you to me forever… in righteousness and in justice, in steadfast love and in mercy" (Hos 2:19). Israel's history was a marriage, and her unfaithfulness was adultery. Jesus now retells that story, not to condemn but to transfigure it. The Bridegroom delayed is the God of Israel, patient through generations of infidelity, coming at last in the flesh to claim His bride.

The virgins symbolize, therefore, not isolated individuals but the covenant community in its mixed state—the visible Church in history, half-wise, half-foolish, both holy and sinful. They share one vocation: to bear light until the Bridegroom appears. That vocation is priestly and prophetic. Each Christian is anointed—*chrismated*—with oil at baptism and confirmation, receiving the Spirit to be a lamp before the world. The parable is a mirror held up to the baptized: Do we carry within us the oil of living faith, or only the brittle torch of past experience?

The wisdom of the five lies in their recognition that grace must be renewed. Oil, like manna, spoils if hoarded. It must be replenished daily through prayer, sacraments, and works of love. In patristic theology, the lamp symbolized faith's visible profession, and the oil charity. Faith, without charity, can flash bright for a moment yet fail in the long darkness; charity alone feeds the flame of endurance. St. Augustine preached that the foolish virgins "bore lamps but brought no oil—faith they had, but not love." They believed but did not let belief become self-giving. When the Bridegroom delayed, they ran out of themselves.

This interplay of lamp and oil reveals the covenant logic of grace. The lamp is the human response—our cooperation, the vessel of obedience;

## THE TEN VIRGINS (MT 25:1–13)

the oil is divine initiative—grace that saturates and sustains. Salvation is the marriage of the two: God's gift received, tended, and offered back. Without oil, the lamp is lifeless moralism; without a lamp, oil cannot shine. Grace does not eliminate the creature; it elevates and perfects it. In the same way, charity does not abolish works but animates them. The wise virgins represent that harmony—the rhythm of grace and freedom, of divine life dwelling within human fidelity.

The foolish, by contrast, attempt to live the covenant as contract. They possess externals—lamps, rituals, perhaps reputation—but treat these as guarantees rather than invitations. They carry no oil because they expect the feast to occur on their schedule. When the Bridegroom delays, they are scandalized by time. Their lamps go out, not because the fire was weak, but because their hearts were shallow. Jesus is describing the difference between those who love God's presence and those who only love His punctuality.

The delay of the Bridegroom is among the most theologically charged lines in all the Gospels. It names the mystery of divine patience that undergirds salvation history. God is not slow as men count slowness, says Peter, but "patient toward you, not wishing that any should perish." The apparent postponement of Christ's return is not neglect but mercy, allowing the oil of charity to spread from soul to soul, generation to generation. In this delay, time itself becomes sacramental. The wise live each day as a gift of preparation; the foolish treat delay as absence and drift into indifference.

To "sleep," in this light, acquires a double meaning. On one level, it describes human frailty: even the wise grow weary, their vigilance lapsing into rest. On another, it signifies death. Every believer must pass through sleep before the Bridegroom's arrival at the resurrection. The Church Fathers read this line as a prophecy of the interim age: the faithful departed, resting in hope, their lamps still burning in the communion of saints. The foolish, unprepared, die unillumined. The same sleep overtakes both; what differs is whether light survives the night.

The midnight cry—*mesonyktion kraugē*—is the sound of divine intervention, the eschatological shout when eternity pierces time. It is the climax of every prophetic expectation: the trumpet on Sinai, the call of the watchman, the blast that toppled Jericho's walls. The word *kraugē* itself evokes not polite announcement but a voice of power. It is the cry of John the Baptist, "Prepare the way of the Lord," now universalized at the end of days. This voice awakens both groups alike. No one sleeps through the coming of God. But the awakening does not produce equality; it exposes identity.

The foolish virgins' lamps, once bright, sputter and die. Their cry—"Give us your oil"—is the panic of those who have treated holiness as communal insurance rather than personal relationship. Grace cannot be shared the way money can. One cannot borrow another's intimacy with God. At judgment, one cannot lean on a friend's fervour or a parent's prayers; one must stand as oneself, known and loved—or unrecognized. The wise virgins' answer, "There will not be enough for us and for you," is not cruelty but the revelation that salvation is unrepeatable. Each soul must carry its own light.

The moment of the closed door reveals divine justice in its purest form. "Those who were ready went in with him to the marriage feast; and the door was shut." In the covenant pattern, a door always separates holiness from profanation: the blood-marked threshold of Passover, the veil of the Holy of Holies, the gate of Eden barred by flaming sword. Here, the threshold is final—the border between time and eternity. Those within share the Bridegroom's joy; those outside remain in the outer darkness of self-chosen solitude. The shutting of the door is not vindictive exclusion but the solidification of freedom. The foolish have lived as though the feast were optional; they now find that their apathy has become their identity.

When they return crying, "Lord, Lord, open to us," they repeat Israel's ancient plea from Isaiah 26: "Open the gates that the righteous nation may enter." But righteousness, in Jesus' redefinition, is not ritual but relationship. The Bridegroom's reply—"Truly I say to you, I do not know you"—is the unveiled truth of every false religion. To be unknown by God is not to be unloved but to have refused love's knowledge. In biblical idiom, to "know" is to enter communion; God's "I do not know you" is a revelation that intimacy was never reciprocated. The fire of grace had been offered; they never let it in.

The theology of this moment turns from moral to mystical. The Bridegroom's coming is the Parousia, but also every visitation of grace. The Church lives perpetually between the two cries: "Behold, the Bridegroom comes," and "Come, Lord Jesus." Each Mass, each conversion, each act of divine mercy is a foretaste of that final arrival. The wise keep oil because they live liturgically—their lives ordered toward communion. The foolish live episodically, expecting grace to conform to their schedules. When time ends, what remains is not chronology but character: what the soul has become through years of waiting.

To "watch, therefore," is to dwell in covenant attentiveness, the contemplative posture of the Bride. It is not sleepless fear but Eucharistic memory—living every day as vigil, every act as preparation. Watchfulness, for Matthew, is not the fidget of anxiety but the peace of fidelity. The wise virgins are not frantic; they are filled. Their very waiting has become worship.

To grasp the parable's depth, one must see that it describes not only the final judgment but the entire rhythm of the spiritual life—the way grace unfolds within time. The wise virgins' readiness is not the fruit of constant activity but of cultivated interiority. Their lamps burn steadily because their hearts have become altars. They live by a quiet habit of love that can survive silence, obscurity, and delay. This is the heart of covenant wisdom: to remain turned toward the Bridegroom even when His face is unseen.

The *oil* of grace within them is not an abstract virtue; it is participation in the divine life. In patristic language, the oil represents the *charismata* of the Spirit, but also that hidden depth of charity that springs from the indwelling Trinity. Just as olive oil is produced by crushing the fruit, so spiritual oil is pressed from the soul through trial. Waiting, suffering, perseverance—all these crush the heart until love flows pure. The wise virgins' supply is not luck; it is the fruit of long conversion. They have allowed grace to soak into every fiber of their being, so that when darkness falls, their light is not borrowed but born.

The foolish virgins illustrate the opposite dynamic. Their lamps, though once bright, have burned on the fumes of enthusiasm. They resemble the seed sown among rocks—sprouting quickly but withering for lack of depth. Their faith depends on circumstance, not covenant. They have experienced God but have not become His dwelling. When the Bridegroom delays, they experience His absence as abandonment rather than invitation. They want immediacy without intimacy, reward without relationship. Their extinguished lamps reveal what happens when religion remains external: the flame dies because the oil has never reached the heart.

In the Greek phrase *nēnyxen de ho nymphios ēlthen*—"at midnight the Bridegroom came"—Matthew captures the paradox of divine arrival: sudden yet prepared for, terrifying yet tender. The verb *ēlthen* (he came) echoes the Gospel's central refrain: "He who is to come has come." The delay is over, but only those who have learned to wait can rejoice. The others experience the same event as loss. What was mercy now appears as judgment, though nothing in the Bridegroom has changed. His coming reveals what each soul has made of itself.

Theologically, this moment dramatizes the principle that grace perfects nature without bypassing it. The wise virgins' vigilance does not earn the feast; it enables participation. They are ready not because they have predicted the hour but because they have been transformed into those who desire the Bridegroom more than the banquet. Their preparedness is love's maturity. The foolish, conversely, have treated salvation as a calendar event to be anticipated, not a relationship to be deepened. They have prepared for an arrival but not for a union.

The final refusal—"I do not know you"—must be heard in its covenant register. It is the same sentence pronounced over the false prophets who say, "Lord, Lord, did we not prophesy in your name?" (Mt 7:22–23). The tragedy is not ignorance but intimacy denied. In Hebrew thought, knowledge is mutual possession: "You shall know the Lord, and He shall know you." To be unknown by God is to have lived as a stranger to love.

## THE TEN VIRGINS (MT 25:1–13)

The closed door is simply the sealing of that estrangement. Heaven is communion extended eternally; hell is isolation made permanent.

In the grand symphony of Scripture, this parable stands as the counterpoint to the Wedding Feast in Matthew 22. There the problem was refusal to come; here it is unpreparedness when He comes. One rejects invitation; the other neglects preparation. Together they form the full theology of covenant response: *vocation and perseverance.* God calls; man must not only say yes but remain yes. The wise virgins' oil represents that enduring yes—the consent of love kept alive through years of apparent absence.

In the wider narrative of Matthew's Gospel, this parable follows directly after the discourse on vigilance in chapter 24: "Therefore you also must be ready, for the Son of Man is coming at an hour you do not expect." It precedes the parable of the talents, which interprets readiness as stewardship, and the judgment of the nations, which interprets it as mercy. Together, these three parables form a triptych of Christian discipleship: waiting, working, and loving. The Ten Virgins occupy the first panel—the interior life of faith. Before mission or mercy, there must be oil.

From a covenantal perspective, the oil also symbolizes the Spirit as the dowry of the Bridegroom. In ancient Jewish weddings, the groom's gift to the bride was a token of his promise to return and claim her. In the same way, Christ has given the Spirit as pledge of His return. "You were sealed with the promised Holy Spirit, the guarantee of our inheritance" (Eph 1:13–14). The wise virgins are those who guard this dowry faithfully; the foolish squander it. The tragedy of the latter is not moral failure but spiritual amnesia—they forget the love that betrothed them.

Waiting, therefore, becomes a sacrament of love. In the covenant economy, delay is never waste but participation in God's own patience. The Church waits not because God hesitates, but because love wishes to gather all. Every passing century is the heartbeat of divine mercy. To persevere in that waiting is to share in the Bridegroom's own long-suffering joy. The saints embody this theology in flesh: they live as lamps trimmed by charity, spending their lives as slow-burning offerings of faith.

When the Bridegroom finally appears, the wise enter into what they have already lived. The feast is not an abrupt change but the blossoming of what has been cultivated in secret. Heaven, in this light, is simply the soul made fully luminous—the oil of grace ignited into eternal flame. The foolish find themselves outside because they have never lived within. The closed door is not vengeance but veracity: it reveals what is.

The final exhortation, "Watch therefore," is the moral hinge of the entire discourse on the Mount of Olives. Watchfulness (*grēgoreite*) in Greek carries connotations of wakeful prayer, of being spiritually alert while the world sleeps. It is the same word Jesus will use in Gethsemane: "Watch and pray, that you may not enter into temptation." Vigilance is not fear but friendship. The wise virgins are those who have kept Him company through the long night of history.

The parable of the Ten Virgins, then, unfolds as the theology of perseverance, charity, and divine patience woven into one. It teaches that faith must mature into love, love into endurance, endurance into union. It declares that grace, once received, must be guarded as one guards a flame in the wind—shielded by humility, fed by prayer, extended through mercy. And it ends with the haunting joy of hope: the Bridegroom will come, and those whose hearts still burn will enter the feast that has no end.

### c) Typological and Intertextual Parallels

The parable of the Ten Virgins is not a free-floating moral tale about "being prepared." It's the ripened fruit of a whole biblical vocabulary—oil, lamps, fire, virgins, night, and waiting—that's been building from Genesis onward. When Jesus speaks this story into Israel's imagination, He is lighting a match in a room full of stored fuel.

The first great background is Israel's *lamp* before God. In Exodus, after the covenant is sealed, the Lord commands Moses:

"You shall command the people of Israel that they bring you pure beaten olive oil for the lamp, that a light may be kept burning continually." (Ex 27:20; cf. Lev 24:2)

A perpetual lamp in the tent of meeting, fed by pure oil, burning

## THE TEN VIRGINS (MT 25:1–13)

continually before the Lord. That is Israel's vocation in miniature: a people whose life burns in the presence of God, night and day. The menorah becomes the "sacrament" of Israel's faithfulness—light that should never go out.

Now set that beside ten maidens whose job is precisely this: keep lamps burning in the night until the bridegroom comes. Jesus isn't grabbing a random wedding image; He's re-staging the Exodus lamp in eschatological form. The Church is Israel's lamp widened: a people called to keep faith burning until the true Bridegroom arrives.

Oil, in that Exodus text, is already double-symbolic. It's not just fuel for light; it's also the substance of *anointing*. The same "holy anointing oil" is poured on priests and later on kings and prophets (Ex 30:22–33; Lev 8:10–12; 1 Sam 10:1; 16:13). Oil consecrates; oil empowers. To be "anointed" (*māšîaḥ*, Christos) is to be drawn into God's own mission. When Samuel pours oil on David, "the Spirit of the Lord rushed upon David from that day forward" (1 Sam 16:13). Oil and Spirit are bound together.

So when Jesus draws a parable where the *one thing* that distinguishes wise from foolish is the presence or absence of oil, He is not talking about generic good vibes. He is evoking the whole biblical pattern of *Spirit-given, covenantal fidelity*. The wise are those whose lives are actually suffused with the Spirit's grace—who have let themselves be anointed, consecrated, and sustained. The foolish are "un-anointed": they have lamps (external belonging, visible religion) but no oil (inward participation).

This connection becomes even clearer if you bring in Zechariah's vision. The prophet sees a golden lampstand with seven lamps, flanked by two olive trees supplying oil. When he asks what it means, the Lord answers:

"Not by might, nor by power, but by my Spirit, says the Lord of hosts." (Zech 4:6)

Oil flowing into lamps is explicitly interpreted as the Spirit's action sustaining God's people and God's work. That's the spiritual circuitry under Matthew 25. Wise virgins are "Zechariah souls": they know their lamps cannot burn by human strength; they must live from a continual dependence on the Spirit. The foolish are Israel (and the Church) when it forgets Zechariah's line and defaults to self-reliance—lamps without supply.

Lamps themselves carry covenant weight all over the Old Testament. A "lamp" can image:

- God's own guidance: "Your word is a lamp to my feet and a light to my path" (Ps 119:105).
- The king's line: God promises David to keep for him "a lamp in Jerusalem" (1 Kgs 11:36; cf. 2 Sam 21:17).
- The human spirit scrutinizing conscience: "The spirit of man is the lamp of the Lord, searching all his innermost parts" (Prov 20:27).

So lampas, the torch in the virgins' hands, sits exactly at this intersection: it's God's word, the covenant line, and the human spirit all at once—human life meant to shine with borrowed light. A ready lamp is a human being whose inner life (spirit) has been soaked in the word and promises of God, and who therefore actually manifests that light in the night.

Fire intensifies the picture. From the burning bush (Ex 3) to the fire on Sinai (Ex 19:18), to the pillar of fire that leads Israel by night (Ex 13:21–22), to the consuming fire on the altar (Lev 6:12–13), the presence of God in Israel's story is a presence that *burns*. Elijah's sacrifice is accepted by fire (1 Kgs 18:38); Elisha asks for a "double share" of the Spirit as Elijah is taken up in fiery chariot. When tongues of fire descend at Pentecost (Acts 2:3), Luke is not inventing a new symbol; he is saying: all that fire in Israel's history has come to dwell in persons. God's presence has taken the form of an interior flame.

That's what is at stake in the virgins' lamps. The Bridegroom is not merely checking whether they have *equipment*. He is looking for the trace of His own presence—this God who is "a consuming fire" (Deut 4:24; Heb 12:29). To have a lamp with no fire is to have the form of piety without the reality of communion.

But why *virgins*?

In Israel's prophetic imagination, "virgin" is a covenant title. The Lord speaks of "the virgin daughter of Zion" (Is 37:22; Lam 2:13), "the virgin Israel" whom He will restore and adorn with tambourines and dancing (Jer 31:4, 13). Virginity, here, does not mean biological detail so much as *undivided belonging*. Israel is meant to be a people not yet adulterated by idols. "I will betroth you to me forever," God says through Hosea (Hos 2:19), promising to restore a spousal wholeness that sin has shattered.

The ten virgins in Jesus' parable stand in that line. They are "daughter Zion" waiting for her God. They are also, in seed form, the Church: Paul will later say to the Corinthians, "I betrothed you to one husband, to present you as a pure virgin to Christ" (2 Cor 11:2). The virgins' identity is corporate before it is individual. They are the covenant people in the posture of readiness—or not.

Psalm 45, the royal wedding psalm, deepens the typology. The psalm depicts the bride in gilded robes, led to the king, and behind her come "virgin companions, her escort; her companions are brought to you" (Ps 45:14–15). The royal bride (Zion/Church) is not alone; she is surrounded by virgins sharing in her joy. When Jesus sketches a marriage procession with ten virgins accompanying the bridegroom, He is activating Psalm 45: the eschatological King is here, and those who share in His joy are the "virgin companions" who took the bridal vocation seriously.

Even the *number* ten has covenant resonance. Ten words of the Law; ten plagues; ten generations marking key epochs in Genesis—ten is fullness at the human scale. Ten virgins, then, represent the fullness of the covenant community: "all Israel" in miniature, all called to vigilance, all entrusted with lamps. The tragedy is that within this same called people, only some actually carry oil. Many are called, few are truly watchful.

Night and delay add another layer. Israel knows what it is to wait in the dark. The first Passover happens "at midnight" when the destroying angel passes through Egypt (Ex 12:29). The psalms speak of the soul waiting "more than watchmen for the morning" (Ps 130:6), of God seeming to delay while enemies prevail (Hab 1:2; 2:3). The prophets envision a day when "at evening time there shall be light" (Zech 14:7), when God's salvation will break in precisely when hope seems least reasonable.

The parable compresses all of that: "At midnight there was a cry, 'Behold, the bridegroom! Come out to meet him.'" Midnight is the hour of Passover judgment, of exodus, of divine intervention. It's also the hour when lamps are hardest to keep burning, when fatigue is strongest. The wise virgins are new-covenant Israel living Psalm 130—souls that "wait for the Lord" like watchmen who *know* the dawn will come, and have ordered their entire lives around that certainty. The foolish, by contrast, live as if the night were permanent, and so treat vigilance as optional.

All of this converges, finally, in the great marriage imagery of Scripture. From Hosea's wounded husband to Isaiah's promise—"as the bridegroom rejoices over the bride, so shall your God rejoice over you" (Is 62:5)—the prophets insist that history is a love story. When Jesus speaks of Himself as "the Bridegroom," He is claiming to be the very Lord of those texts. The Ten Virgins parable is therefore not about a random Galilean groom. It is YHWH Himself, in the flesh, coming to claim His people—and finding some hearts empty of oil.

The typology sharpens the stakes. Oil, in the biblical story, is the Spirit's gift for kingship, priesthood, prophecy, and light. Lamp is the human vocation to bear that light in the world. Fire is the presence of God Himself, purifying and guiding. Virgins are the covenant people summoned to undivided fidelity. Night is the stretch of history in which God seems absent yet is secretly near. Delay is mercy—time for oil to be sought. Midnight is judgment and deliverance in one moment.

Read that way, the parable becomes a compressed commentary on the whole economy of salvation. God has made His people to be a lamp (Israel, Church); He has poured out His oil (the Spirit); He has promised to come as Bridegroom; He has warned that there will be a stretch of darkness and apparent delay. What remains unresolved—what gives the story its tension—is whether the people will actually live from that oil, keep that lamp, and hold that vigil.

And that's exactly where Matthew wants the reader standing at the end of the story—not thinking about ten anonymous girls long ago, but about the entire covenant people now, lamp in hand, measuring whether the oil they carry is enough to last the night.

### d) Patristic and Theological Synthesis

From the earliest centuries, the Fathers saw in this parable a mirror of the Church's own heart. Its images—virgins, lamps, oil, midnight—were not moral props but revelations of what it means to live between Christ's first and second coming. Beneath its surface lies the whole drama of grace: the light of faith sustained by the oil of charity, burning through the long night until the Bridegroom's return.

Origen, writing in the third century, was among the first to read the virgins as souls who profess faith in Christ but differ in interior disposition. "All take lamps," he writes, "that is, all make profession; but some carry with them oil—the works and dispositions of love—while others are content with the outward vessel." For him, the lamp was doctrine and the oil was the Spirit that animates it. Faith without love is an empty lamp—capable of shining for a time, yet destined to sputter out when tested by delay. Origen's vision already moves beyond moralism into sacramentality: the wise virgins are those whose outer life is fed by an inner participation in divine grace.

Augustine would later distil this insight into a single unforgettable formula: *"The oil is charity."* In his *Sermons on Matthew*, he warns that it is possible to "believe everything, hope everything, confess everything, and yet be nothing, because love is not in you." The lamp of faith can be orthodox and brilliant, but if it is not soaked in love, it cannot endure the long night of waiting. "When the Bridegroom delays," he says, "faith grows tired if love grows cold." For Augustine, the parable unfolds the logic of Paul's own warning—"If I have all faith so as to move mountains, but have not love, I am nothing." The wise virgins are not clever planners but lovers whose affection for God keeps their faith alive through delay.

St. John Chrysostom approaches the story from another angle. Preaching in Antioch, he reminds his hearers that "it was not fornication or theft that shut the foolish out, but mere carelessness." Their failure is ordinary spiritual negligence—what he calls *rhathymia*, the slackness that lets zeal slip away. The oil, he says, is "a life of mercy and almsgiving," the tangible overflow of love into works of compassion. Without such oil, faith becomes sterile. His homily ends with an image both tender and severe: "The flame of mercy is the light by which the Bridegroom knows His own." To neglect the poor is to let that light go out.

In the East, St. Ephrem the Syrian develops the theme in mystical tones. The virgins, he writes, are "souls adorned with virginity of heart," and the oil is "the grace of the Holy Spirit kept in the vessel of the conscience." For Ephrem, the parable is an icon of the entire Christian mystery: baptism kindles the lamp, chrism fills it with oil, and the Eucharist keeps the flame bright until the Lord returns. He imagines Christ knocking at the soul's door like a Bridegroom at midnight: "Blessed are those whose lamps have light, that they may open quickly." Delay is not absence but intimacy stretched to its limit—the Lord testing whether love still burns when sight is gone.

St. Gregory the Great, summarising centuries of reflection, fuses the Greek and Latin strands into a single theology. "The lamp is faith," he writes in his *Homilies on the Gospels*, "and the oil is good works that make faith shine." Yet he adds a deeper note: the oil cannot be shared at the end because virtue is incommunicable; holiness cannot be borrowed at the eleventh hour. The refusal of the wise to lend their oil is not cruelty but metaphysical truth: grace can be offered, not transferred. Each soul must cooperate with the Spirit within its own vessel. Gregory reads the midnight cry as the voice of judgment that reveals what the heart has become. "The foolish, who would not prepare in life, must run in death."

Ambrose and Jerome extend the bridal dimension. For them, the parable belongs to the mystery of the Church as virgin and bride. The ten maidens stand for all believers, called to chastity of heart—an undivided devotion to Christ. Ambrose notes that their lamps burn because "the Word is the flame of faith," and that the oil signifies "the discipline of the virtues that guard love from corruption." Jerome, more austere, warns that virginity of body without oil of mercy is as barren as idolatry. Both insist that vigilance is not fear but desire: to stay awake is to stay in love.

## THE TEN VIRGINS (MT 25:1–13)

The scholastic mind later refined these insights without losing their ardour. St. Thomas Aquinas, reading Augustine and Gregory together, distinguishes between the *form* of faith and its *perfection*. Faith gives light; charity gives life. Without charity, faith's light is a flash in the void. Aquinas also notes that the parable illuminates the theological virtue of *hope*: the wise virgins trust the Bridegroom enough to wait, while the foolish despair of His delay. Hope, then, is the wick that keeps flame joined to oil.

All of this flows back into covenant theology. From Sinai to Calvary, the Lord's people have been betrothed to Him in love, commanded to keep His light before the nations. The parable reveals what that covenant looks like when history stretches on and the Bridegroom tarries. The Church lives in the interval between promise and fulfillment, her faith tested not by persecution but by time. The oil of charity, replenished through the sacraments and works of mercy, is her only safeguard against fatigue. Every Mass is a refill of that lamp: the Eucharistic flame that once rose from the upper room continues to feed her vigilance.

The Fathers also discerned in the closing door a warning to the complacent Church. "They came later, crying, 'Lord, Lord, open to us,'" Gregory laments. "They call Him Lord, but too late." The closed door is not divine cruelty but the fixedness of final choice. Once the Bridegroom enters, time ceases to be merciful. Chrysostom compares it to Noah's ark: the same hand that closed the door to the flood opened it to the faithful. Judgment, for the saints, is simply love made visible.

Yet the note of fear is never the final one. For Augustine, the parable ends not in despair but in invitation. "While there is still time, let us buy oil," he says—by acts of love, by prayer, by humility. The marketplace of mercy remains open as long as the world lasts. Gregory echoes him: "Now is the hour to fill the vessels of our hearts." The delay of the Bridegroom is itself grace, a space for repentance and readiness. Every day of waiting is another chance to love.

The theology that emerges from all these voices is profoundly Trinitarian. The Father is the householder preparing the wedding; the Son is the Bridegroom whose return will consummate the covenant; the Spirit is the oil poured into human hearts, enabling faith to burn. The moral of the parable, then, is not moralism but participation: to live from within the triune exchange of giving and receiving, illumination and love.

In the end, the Church Fathers read the Ten Virgins as a map of salvation history compressed into a single night. Creation was the first lamp lit; Israel's worship kept its flame alive; the Incarnation refilled it with divine oil; the Cross sealed it against the winds of death; and now the Church keeps watch until the dawn of the eternal wedding. The wise are those who understand that waiting is not idleness but worship—that every prayer, every act of mercy, every sacrament is another drop of oil for the great procession.

When the midnight cry comes—whether at the world's end or the hour of one's death—the soul will rise either radiant or empty. The wise will lift their lamps and recognise the light approaching; the foolish will see only darkness of their own making. The parable's last image, the door closed, is not merely threat but truth: love that has become sight excludes all that refused to love. Yet the invitation remains, while time remains: "Watch, for you know neither the day nor the hour." To watch is to love in faith, to keep the oil of the Spirit alive, to live every hour as if the Bridegroom were already at the door. That, for the Fathers, is the meaning of wisdom—the marriage of vigilance and charity that alone can endure the night

## The Shock and the Turn

The shock of the parable is not that five were foolish, but that all were virgins. Jesus was speaking to a people who already saw themselves as the wise, the consecrated, the chosen. To first-century Israel, the image of ten maidens waiting for the bridegroom was a picture of their own story—the nation purified by Torah, waiting for the coming of the Messiah. Their lamps were the law; their oil, the covenant; their waiting, the long night of exile. They believed that when the Bridegroom arrived, His coming would be vindication, not division.

But in Jesus' telling, that confidence shatters. The parable does not oppose Israel to the nations; it divides Israel within herself. Half are ready, half are not. The very people who expected to be welcomed find themselves locked outside. The lesson is devastating: ancestry cannot substitute for holiness, and belonging to the covenant community does not guarantee participation in its fulfilment.

The Jews of Jesus' time believed that descent from Abraham was itself a lamp—that the light of the patriarchs' faith still burned in their children. The prophets had already hinted that such trust was false, but no one had said it with the severity of Jesus. When He declared, "Do not presume to say, 'We have Abraham as our father,'" He was cutting to the root of religious presumption. The parable of the virgins makes that warning visible. The foolish virgins are not outsiders; they are kin to the wise, companions in the same vigil, yet lacking the one thing that matters: the oil of living faith.

That oil is the mystery of the parable's reversal. For generations, Israel had been taught that the lamp itself—external observance, ritual purity, Sabbath, sacrifice—was sufficient. But Jesus speaks of oil hidden within, unseen until the darkness comes. It is not rule or rite, but the inner flame of charity kindled by grace. The wise carry within them what the law could prefigure but not bestow. Their light endures the delay because it burns from a deeper source—the presence of God in the soul.

Delay is itself the scandal of the story. In Jewish expectation, the Bridegroom would come suddenly, triumphantly, sweeping His people into glory. The Messiah's arrival was imagined as the end of waiting, the collapse of night into morning. Yet in Jesus' parable the Bridegroom tarries. The world continues, time lengthens, faith must hold. This is not the apocalyptic victory Israel longed for; it is the discipline of patience, the cross of deferred hope. The delay becomes revelation: the true covenant is not a moment of national exaltation but a lifelong endurance of love.

For the hearers steeped in apocalyptic hope, this was intolerable. They had suffered under foreign rule and dreamed of a day when God would act decisively. But Jesus teaches that God's decisiveness hides itself in delay. The test of fidelity is not crisis but continuance. The foolish virgins fail not because they rebel, but because they grow complacent. They assume that covenant identity will sustain the flame automatically. The wise know otherwise. They watch, they tend, they feed the light even when nothing seems to be happening.

This reversal pierces to the heart of Jewish piety. The people who revered the Temple and the law as the visible guarantees of divine favour are told that visibility counts for nothing. The true temple is interior; the true light burns where no eye can see. The foolish virgins represent the religion of appearance, the external assurance of belonging. The wise embody the hidden life of the Spirit—the remnant whose trust remains alive through silence and delay.

The moment the cry at midnight sounds—"Behold, the Bridegroom comes!"—everything that was presumed is exposed. In Jewish imagination, midnight was the hour of deliverance, recalling the Exodus when God passed through Egypt and liberated His people. In Jesus' parable, that same hour becomes judgment. The cry that once meant freedom now announces separation. Those who thought themselves heirs of the Passover discover that they are Pharaoh's mirror: unprepared, unyielding, outside the covenant they presumed to possess.

The closed door is the final scandal. Israel believed that the covenant door, once opened to Abraham, could never shut against his descendants. Yet Jesus depicts the unthinkable—a door locked from within, a voice saying, "I do not know you." The words overturn centuries of assurance. To be "known" by God had been Israel's proudest claim: "You only have I known of all the families of the earth." Now the same God declares unknowing toward His own. The reversal is not arbitrary wrath but unveiled truth: covenant without communion is self-deception.

In that single phrase, "I do not know you," Jesus exposes the difference between inheritance and intimacy. The foolish virgins possess the symbols of faith but not its substance. They have lamps but no light, history but no heart. They call Him "Lord" yet lack the oil that makes the title personal. In rabbinic tradition, knowledge is always relational—to be known by God is to share His life. The foolish virgins are strangers not because He rejects them, but because they have never entered into that exchange of love which the law was meant to awaken.

The deeper shock is that the Bridegroom Himself—long awaited, long prayed for—becomes the agent of exclusion. Israel expected the Messiah to close the door on Gentiles; instead He closes it on the presumptuous within Israel. Salvation, once defined by lineage, is redefined by love. The parable teaches that divine election is never static. It must be lived. The covenant is not a fortress but a wedding; entry depends on readiness of heart, not records of ancestry.

The cry at midnight still reverberates through every generation of believers. It warns the Church, as once it warned Israel, that grace received can be grace neglected. The virgins are images of the baptized no less than of the chosen people. The same presumption—that proximity to sacred things ensures salvation—haunts every age. Jesus' parable strips it bare. Faith that does not watch will fade. Charity that is not nourished will die. The Bridegroom's delay is mercy, but also test; His arrival, sudden as midnight, reveals what the waiting has made of us.

The shock is thus double: first, that not all within the covenant will enter; second, that the measure of worthiness is not lineage or learning, but love that endures. The turn is from collective privilege to personal fidelity, from external light to interior flame. The wise and the foolish represent not two peoples, but two responses within the one people of God. The dividing line runs not between Israel and the nations, but through every human heart.

In that revelation, the parable becomes prophecy. Israel's story repeats itself in the Church, which too must wait through long delay, tempted by presumption, dulled by routine. The closed door stands as warning: the Bridegroom comes not when we are triumphant but when we have grown tired. The oil of grace cannot be improvised at the last moment. Salvation is the fruit of slow fidelity, love practiced in darkness.

For the first hearers, this was not merely unsettling; it was offensive. The kingdom they imagined as inherited is offered as invitation. The feast they expected to celebrate by right becomes gift given by mercy. Jesus replaces the confidence of descent with the humility of discipleship. To be chosen now means to choose—to keep the flame alive while others sleep.

That is the parable's reversal: salvation is no longer guaranteed by ancestry, temple, or law. It is the reward of love that waits when God seems absent. The wise are those who believe that the delay itself is covenant, that waiting is the Bridegroom's final gift. When the door closes, it will close not in surprise but in revelation. Each soul will find that it already stands where it has long chosen to stand—within the light it has tended, or the darkness it has allowed.

That is the shock. That is the turn.

### The Revelation in the Son

In the parable of the Ten Virgins, Christ does not describe something outside Himself; He discloses His own mystery. Every image in this story—bridegroom, midnight, lamp, oil, and door—is a symbol refracting the light of the Incarnate Word. The Bridegroom who comes is not merely an allegory for divine favour but the revelation of the Son's identity and mission: God made visible, the eternal Logos entering the world's darkness to bring creation to consummation.

The Fathers often said that when Jesus speaks in parables, He is speaking autobiographically in veiled form. The Ten Virgins, then, is Jesus narrating the rhythm of His own life: His hiddenness in the Father, His descent into time, His apparent delay, His death and resurrection, and His final return. What Israel awaited from afar—God's visitation, the coming of the Messiah—Jesus proclaims as present in Himself. *"Behold, the Bridegroom comes."* He is the one long expected, yet arriving in a manner no one foresaw: humility instead of splendour, silence instead of trumpet, wood instead of throne.

The Bridegroom first appears at midnight—the hour of extremity, when the world lies most helpless. In Scripture, midnight is the moment when divine power breaks into human impotence: the liberation from Egypt, the cry of the psalmist, the angel passing through darkness to deliver. That the Son "comes at midnight" reveals His vocation: to enter the deepest shadow of creation, to invade the hour when humanity sleeps in sin and fear. Bethlehem, Gethsemane, Calvary—each is a midnight. The same eternal Word who said, "Let there be light," now utters that command from within the world's night. His very being is illumination; His coming is light expressed as mercy.

The Bridegroom's delay is Christological time—the paradox of a God who is eternal yet willing to wait. In the divine life, the Son eternally proceeds from the Father in perfect simultaneity; yet in history that procession is stretched into patience. The "delay" is not neglect but the kenosis of divine immediacy. The Son who lives in the timeless now consents to inhabit sequence, to grow, to suffer postponement, so that love might ripen freely in His bride. What appears as absence is, in fact, the revelation of divine long-suffering—the eternal Word slowed to the tempo of creaturely response.

The lamps borne by the virgins reveal the mystery of Christ's own humanity. A lamp is a vessel fashioned to contain fire without being consumed. So too the humanity of Jesus: the created nature chosen to bear the uncreated light. In Him, divinity shines through flesh as flame through crystal glass. His body is the lamp of God; His soul the wick through which the fire of the Spirit burns. When He says, *"I am the light of the world,"* He speaks not metaphor but ontology. He is the one in whom matter itself becomes luminous with divinity. The lamp of His humanity allows the inaccessible glory of the Godhead to dwell safely among us, so that we may look upon light and live.

The oil within those lamps discloses another dimension of His mystery. In biblical thought, oil signifies the Spirit—anointing, healing, consecration. In the person of Jesus, that oil is infinite, for "God gives the Spirit without measure." From conception to cross, His entire existence is the vessel of the Spirit's fire. Every word He speaks, every touch, every silence, flows from that inexhaustible anointing. The wise virgins' oil, then, prefigures the plenitude of grace in Him—the divine life always burning, never spent. The foolish virgins, by contrast, image humanity apart from Christ: lamps without oil, nature without grace, form without life.

The cry that awakens the sleeping world—*"Behold, the Bridegroom comes!"*—is the sound of revelation itself. It is the Father's voice announcing the Son's manifestation. At the Jordan, the same proclamation resounds: *"This is my beloved Son."* The Incarnation is the midnight cry made audible. The eternal Word, once hidden in the bosom of the Father, now steps into history, and the world is startled awake. Every miracle, every teaching, every forgiveness is that cry extended through time: the Bridegroom entering His creation.

The moment of arrival—when the virgins rise and trim their lamps—mirrors the resurrection. The trimming of the wick, the cutting away of the charred portion, evokes Christ's own passage through death: the humanity that seemed consumed is purified to shine more brightly. The risen Lord is the Lamp renewed; His wounds are openings through which glory shines. In Him, the divine fire has passed through mortality and emerged unextinguished. The virgins who enter with Him are the redeemed creation itself, re-lit from His light.

The shut door, often feared as symbol of exclusion, also belongs to the Christological mystery. It represents the definitive union of divine and human accomplished in Him. The Incarnation is the closing of the gap between God and world—not a barrier but a sealing of the covenant. When the Word became flesh, the entrance between heaven and earth ceased to be a passage and became a Person. The door is "shut" because in Christ the two realms are joined inseparably: God will never again be without humanity, nor humanity without God. What is outside that union is not rejected by decree but remains untransformed by choice.

Even the dialogue—"Lord, Lord, open to us"—bears the resonance of Christ's own prayer and mission. He is both those knocking and the One who answers. As Son of Man, He pleads for humanity's entrance; as Son of God, He holds the key of David that opens and none can shut. The words *"I do not know you"* uttered by the Bridegroom echo the mystery of judgment, but also the pathos of divine love unreciprocated. The Son, whose knowledge is union, finds absence where communion was offered. It is not lack of awareness but absence of likeness: they are unknown because they have refused to bear His image.

Every feature of the parable, therefore, unfolds a dimension of Christ's person. The Bridegroom—His divine identity; the lamps—His humanity; the oil—His Spirit; the midnight—His descent into death; the cry—His resurrection and proclamation; the door—His glorified unity of heaven and earth. The entire narrative is Christ condensed into story, the eternal Logos translated into human metaphor.

The parable reaches its summit when we perceive that Christ is not merely *within* the story—He *is* the story. The Ten Virgins is the drama of the Word's own mission: divine wisdom entering human history, bearing its own light, encountering both reception and refusal. Jesus is the one who comes, the one awaited, the one shut out, and the one who opens. He is simultaneously the Bridegroom of glory and the Midnight itself through which glory passes.

In His very person, the eternal paradox of God is resolved: light that hides in darkness, majesty clothed in meekness, eternity walking through time. The "delay of the Bridegroom" mirrors the long arc of His earthly mission, which unfolds in three unveilings—Incarnation, Passion, and Parousia. In the first, He comes concealed in humility; in the second, He seems absent in death; in the third, He returns revealed in majesty. The parable's rhythm is the rhythm of His being. Every seeming postponement in salvation history is the self-restraint of divine charity, love waiting until the world is ready to bear its brightness.

The virgins themselves—divided between wise and foolish—embody two responses to the one Christ. Both wait, both sleep, both rise; but only one group carries within them the capacity to receive Him. This mirrors the mystery of Israel's encounter with the Messiah: the nation prepared for centuries to meet its Lord, yet when He came, only those whose hearts were inwardly anointed could recognise Him. The wise virgins are figures of those who perceive divinity through humanity—those who see the lamp and discern the flame within. The foolish are those who behold the same humanity and see nothing beyond. Thus, the dividing line is not between believer and unbeliever, but between those who look upon Christ's flesh and see God, and those who look upon it and see only a man.

The oil, therefore, is not merely moral virtue but participation in the divine nature—the indwelling Spirit that makes recognition possible. The Father eternally begets the Son, and from their shared love proceeds the Spirit: the same Spirit that fills Christ's humanity and overflows into His disciples. To have oil is to share in that procession, to be lit from the same eternal fire. The wise virgins are the humanity in which that Spirit dwells—the portion of creation already divinised by contact with the incarnate Word. The foolish are those who remain external to this circulation of Trinitarian life: lamps designed for light but empty of its source.

When the Bridegroom arrives, the world's concealed order is revealed. His coming does not change reality; it unveils it. The lamps that burn and those that falter simply manifest what has always been true. In Christ's presence, all things are shown for what they are: creation's readiness or resistance to divine communion. This is why the door closes—not in vengeance, but in truth. The union between God and creation has reached its completion in Him; what remains outside is not cast away but stands apart by its own refusal of light. Judgment, in Johannine terms, is simply this: "that the Light has come into the world, and men loved darkness rather than light."

The cry "Behold, the Bridegroom!" resounds through every stage of His mission. It is the angel's announcement to the shepherds, the Baptist's declaration at the Jordan, the proclamation at the empty tomb, the trumpet that will sound at the end of time. Each is the same Word spoken through different veils. The parable thus condenses all revelation into one scene: the hidden God made manifest, the sleeping world divided by its response to light.

Even the final exclusion—"I do not know you"—belongs to Christ's self-revelation. It echoes His own dereliction on the Cross, when He, bearing the sin of the world, enters the loneliness of every soul that has forgotten

God. In that darkness, the Bridegroom experiences the silence of the shut door from the other side. He is locked out so that no sinner need be. When the Father raises Him from death, the door swings open forever. Yet the tragedy remains that some will still choose to stay outside. In that sense, the judgment pronounced by the Bridegroom is not an external decree but the reflection of His own Passion—the pain of love unreturned.

In the Resurrection and Ascension, the parable finds its final meaning. The Bridegroom enters the hall, and human nature enters with Him. The glorified Christ is the feast itself: His divinised humanity the place of union between God and world. When He sits at the right hand of the Father, the lamps of creation are gathered into one unending radiance. What was once symbol—the marriage between heaven and earth—has become ontology. The human and divine are wedded in His person, and that marriage is eternal.

Thus, the parable is not a lesson about vigilance so much as a portrait of the Logos Himself—the One who is always coming, always lighting, always inviting. He is the reason for the delay, the meaning of the midnight, the flame that burns without end. To know Him is to live within that light. The wise virgins are simply those who have begun to shine with His own brightness, bearing within themselves the oil of His Spirit until He returns in glory.

In the end, the Ten Virgins is nothing less than the theology of Christ compressed into story:

the Father's sending of the Son as the coming of the Bridegroom,

the Incarnation as the lamp of His humanity,

the Spirit as the oil of divine life,

the Cross as the midnight of revelation,

the Resurrection as the shout that awakens the world,

and the Parousia as the door at last closed because all things have entered their fulfilment in Him.

He is the beginning and the end of the parable—the storyteller and its substance, the Word who both speaks and is spoken of. When He tells of the Bridegroom, He unveils the inner life of God: the love that leaves eternity to seek its beloved, that enters darkness to ignite it, that delays so that none may be lost, that at last appears and fills all things with light. The Ten Virgins, rightly heard, is not about them—it is about Him. The Bridegroom is Christ the Lord, and His coming is the revelation of what God has always been: light in the night, fidelity in delay, and joy beyond the door.

**The Word for Our Age**

If Jesus were to tell the parable of the Ten Virgins today, it would not be spoken to unbelievers. It would be addressed to those who already call themselves Christian—to the baptised, the churched, the comfortable. The wise and foolish still wait side by side, but their difference has shifted from external appearance to interior fire. In an age when belief has become a badge more than a transformation, the Lord's story pierces our illusions. It tells us that confession without conversion, profession without participation, is a lamp without oil.

Our generation has perfected the art of having faith without flame. We have learned to speak of grace as if it were indulgence, to preach mercy while avoiding repentance. Whole movements now exist within Christianity that have turned the Gospel into slogan: "Just believe," "Just accept Jesus," "It's all done for you." They are not wrong about grace being free—but they have forgotten that what is free still costs everything. The Bridegroom's love does not cancel fidelity; it makes fidelity possible.

The parable warns precisely against this comfortable distortion. All ten virgins believe the Bridegroom will come. All go out to meet Him. All carry lamps. Outwardly they are identical. What divides them is invisible until the darkness falls. So too in the Church: many profess Christ, many bear the outward marks of religion, yet only those whose hearts are converted from within will endure the delay. The foolish are not the atheists or the pagans; they are those who claim intimacy without obedience, grace without discipleship.

This false gospel is the sickness of our age. It whispers that repentance is optional, that holiness is outdated, that the commandments belong to another era. It reduces salvation to a transaction instead of a transformation. "I've accepted Jesus," one says, as though salvation were a contract signed and filed rather than a life joined to His own. But faith divorced from love, belief without obedience, is dead. The oil missing from the foolish virgins' lamps is precisely this—the living presence of grace that animates the soul and bears fruit in charity.

The Church has always taught that faith and works are not rivals but two movements of one heart. Faith receives, love returns; grace fills, obedience overflows. The lamp and the oil belong together. A lamp without oil burns only for a moment, and a soul that believes without loving shines briefly before fading into darkness. The wise virgins are those whose belief has ripened into imitation, whose hearts are filled with the oil of the Spirit, whose daily choices reflect the Bridegroom they await.

In modern times, however, many have traded this interior life for convenience. They attend church when convenient, pray when emotional, repent when desperate. Their lamps gleam occasionally but lack the steady light of perseverance. They call Jesus Lord yet resist His lordship in their habits, their relationships, their moral decisions. They declare that God loves them as they are, and He does—but they refuse to let that love make them new. The parable exposes this counterfeit grace. The Bridegroom's delay is the long night of testing in which real love either deepens or dies.

We see the same pattern in the moral chaos of the age. The commandments are mocked as relics, the Beatitudes dismissed as impractical. Even within Christian circles, it is common to hear that God's will must bend to human feeling, that the Gospel must adapt to culture. Yet in Scripture, obedience is not bondage but intimacy. "If you love Me, keep My commandments." Love proves itself by endurance, not enthusiasm. The foolish virgins loved the idea of the Bridegroom, but not His demands. Their waiting lacked worship; their hope lacked holiness.

The same danger haunts every generation of believers. It is possible to be near Christ sacramentally and far from Him spiritually. It is possible to speak His name while resisting His Spirit. The foolish virgins represent those who mistake proximity for participation—who think being inside the Church is the same as being united to her Lord. They hold the lamp of baptism but neglect the oil of prayer; they receive communion but refuse conversion; they recite creeds but silence conscience. The tragedy is not ignorance but complacency.

In contrast, the wise virgins live the quiet heroism of fidelity. They are not the loud or the famous but the persevering—the mother who prays when no one notices, the man who forgives instead of retaliating, the young disciple who chooses purity over popularity. Their oil is costly because it is daily: drawn from the long obedience of love, replenished through confession, sustained by Eucharist, guarded in prayer. They stumble, but they rise again. Their lamps may flicker, but they do not go out, because they burn with a flame not their own.

The foolish virgins, however, live as if delay means denial. They grow drowsy with the world's distractions, confident that mercy will always be available later. They say, "We will find oil when we need it," forgetting that love cannot be borrowed. When the midnight cry comes—whether at death or judgment or the sudden moment of truth—such hearts discover their poverty too late. The door closes, not because God ceases to be merciful, but because they have ceased to desire mercy. The tragedy of the foolish is not rejection but unreadiness.

This parable is therefore not a warning for the wicked but for the lukewarm. It is addressed to every Christian who mistakes sentiment for surrender. The Church in every age faces the temptation to settle for half-lit lamps—to preach forgiveness without conversion, communion without confession, heaven without the narrow road. But the Gospel cannot be trimmed to fit comfort. The Bridegroom who comes will recognise only those who resemble Him: hearts pierced by love, hands marked by service, faces radiant with perseverance.

What, then, does vigilance look like today? It means living every ordinary day as preparation for eternity. It means confession of sins not as ritual but as restoration of relationship. It means fidelity to the Eucharist, where the Bridegroom feeds His Bride. It means living the moral law not as burden but as the grammar of divine love. It means serving the poor, reconciling with enemies, forgiving the unworthy—because in doing so we refill the oil of our lamps. Vigilance is not anxiety; it is love that refuses to grow cold.

The wise are not those who predict the hour of His coming but those who persevere in His likeness until He comes. Their strength is not self-made virtue but grace cooperating with their freedom. They do not live by perfection but by repentance. Each act of humility draws oil from the inexhaustible heart of Christ.

The greatest deception of our time is the idea that intention is enough—that sincerity can replace sanctity. Yet the Gospel never speaks of those who *meant* to love, only of those who actually did. The wise virgins are not more sincere than the foolish; they are more prepared. They have allowed grace to become habit, prayer to become rhythm, love to become law. The foolish, though perhaps sentimental and well-meaning, have confused emotion with transformation. They proclaim belief in Christ while living as practical atheists—trusting the world for security, pleasure for comfort, and self for salvation.

The lamp they hold is external religion—membership, affiliation, vocabulary. The oil they lack is interior conversion—the fire of divine charity poured into the soul by the Spirit. Without that fire, religion collapses into theatre. Words of praise become noise; creeds become memory verses; "Lord, Lord" becomes lip service. Jesus once said, "Not everyone who says to Me, 'Lord, Lord,' shall enter the kingdom of heaven, but he who does the will of My Father." The parable of the virgins is that teaching told in symbol. It is not the name on the lips that saves, but the light of love that burns within.

To the modern believer, this is a merciful but piercing word. God is not mocked by outward show, nor impressed by shallow slogans of grace. The same Jesus who welcomes sinners demands repentance; the same mercy that embraces the lost commands them to sin no more. Grace is not permission to remain unchanged; it is power to become holy. The oil that sustains the flame of salvation is this grace cooperating with obedience. To say "I believe" but refuse to obey is to carry a lamp with no fire, a promise with no life.

We live in an age of empty lamps—religion reduced to branding, spirituality without sacrifice. The call of the Gospel sounds almost foreign amid our distractions: "Be holy, for I am holy." Yet this is the Bridegroom's only request. Holiness is not moralism; it is communion. To be holy is to belong wholly—to love God without division and neighbour without calculation. Every commandment is simply love's description written in action. The wise virgins understand this. Their oil is not self-righteousness but surrender: lives ordered around the love they await.

Still, the parable's tone is not despairing but hopeful. The door has not yet closed. The Bridegroom still delays—not because He is indifferent, but because He is merciful. His postponement is humanity's chance to awaken, to refill the lamps, to return to the heart of discipleship. Each confession made, each Eucharist received, each act of charity performed is a drop of oil added to the vessel. The Church in our time must rediscover this urgency: faith not as label but as life, not as static belief but as burning love.

For the faithful who persevere, the waiting is not empty but luminous. The longer the night, the clearer the light appears. The wise virgins do not resent the delay; they use it. They live as those already loved, already chosen. Their vigilance is not anxiety but intimacy. To watch for the Bridegroom is to live with the awareness that every moment belongs to Him. Whether He comes at midnight or dawn, they are ready because they have lived already in His light.

This is the invitation for us now. The Church must be recognisable again as the company of those who burn with charity. The world does not need more arguments; it needs more lamps. Our generation will believe again not when we win debates but when we embody joy, when we forgive freely, when our hope outlasts the darkness. The fire of authentic faith is irresistible precisely because it illuminates without consuming. A single saint does more to light the world than a thousand slogans.

The parable ends in silence—the sound of a door closing, a warning without cruelty. It is the silence of opportunity slipping away. Yet even here, the Gospel's note is not vengeance but grief. The Lord desires every lamp to burn, every soul to shine. That is why He tells the story—to awaken the sleeping, to warn the lukewarm, to rekindle the weary. It is not too late to become wise. The oil of mercy is still offered freely, but it must be received while the night endures.

To modern disciples, this means returning to the simplicity of the first Christians: prayer before action, obedience before opinion, love before self. It means turning again to the sacraments, to silence, to Scripture, to the service of the poor. It means examining our hearts each evening and asking, "Is there oil left in my lamp?" The Bridegroom's delay is long, but not endless. The cry will come when least expected. Those who have tended the flame will rise with joy; those who have neglected it will find that no one else can lend them love.

The parable of the Ten Virgins therefore divides not the Church from the world, but the faithful from the merely familiar. It draws a line not through denominations but through hearts. Each of us must decide whether our Christianity is a lamp of custom or a lamp of fire. The Bridegroom's question remains: "Will there be faith on earth when the Son of Man comes?" The answer depends on whether we allow grace to become obedience, and obedience to become love.

For now, the door remains open, and the oil still flows. Christ, the true Light, stands quietly in the darkness, waiting for our return. He does not scold the weary; He refills them. He does not crush the dim flame; He breathes on it until it burns again. The wise are simply those who let Him.

The night grows late, and the cry is nearer than we think. "Behold, the Bridegroom comes." May our lamps be trimmed, our hearts awakened, our lives burning with that love which alone will shine when all else fades. Then, when the door opens and the music begins, we shall enter not as strangers but as those already known, already radiant with the fire of His joy.

## Hearing that Becomes Doing

The story is told, yet it continues to unfold in the quiet hours of every believer's night. The lamps still flicker; the road still stretches toward a Bridegroom who delays, not because He has forgotten, but because He loves too patiently to rush the wedding. Somewhere in that darkness, the sound of His footsteps draws near, and His voice still whispers: *Be ready, for I am coming.* This is not a tale from another age. It is your story, your watch, your waiting.

Close your eyes and enter the scene. The air is cool, the stars bright, the village silent except for the soft crackle of burning wicks. You can smell the oil and the dust, hear the shifting feet of those who wait. Ten lamps gleam, but not all equally. Some glow with steady strength, the oil replenished and the flame at peace. Others sputter, smoke, and fade. The bridesmaids are indistinguishable until the moment of testing, and that moment comes without warning.

Let the parable move inside you. You, too, hold a lamp. The vessel is your heart; the flame is your love; the oil is the grace that keeps both alive. How often has your light burned low—when prayer felt dry, when faith became routine, when hope dulled beneath disappointment? Perhaps you have dozed through long stretches of spiritual twilight, still outwardly faithful but inwardly flickering. Yet the Bridegroom delays for this reason: that your flame might grow steady before He arrives. His patience is not absence; it is mercy stretched through time.

Listen closely. In the distance, a cry rises through the dark: *Behold, the Bridegroom! Go out to meet Him!* The words tremble across the centuries until they reach you. Every Mass, every moment of grace, every sudden awareness of His nearness is that midnight cry. The parable becomes present whenever the Spirit wakes you from complacency and whispers, *Come to Me now, not later.* Delay has always been the enemy of love.

Let that awareness draw you to examine your oil. What fills the vessel of your soul? Is it grace—poured in through prayer, confession, charity—or is it pride, resentment, distraction, self-justification? Oil does not appear by accident; it must be sought, stored, tended. It costs time, attention, humility. To live with oil in your lamp is to live intentionally, choosing

## THE TEN VIRGINS (MT 25:1–13)

presence over preoccupation, faith over fear, mercy over self. The wise virgins in the story are not lucky; they are faithful in small things. Their readiness is the fruit of long, hidden discipline: daily prayer whispered when no one sees, forgiveness given without reward, obedience that feels costly but proves joyful.

For the foolish, the problem is not ignorance but assumption. They once had oil; they believed they had enough. They relied on borrowed light—religion inherited but not lived, grace presumed but never renewed. When the cry comes, they realise too late that no one can lend interior life. The oil of love cannot be shared by command; it must be cultivated by relationship. The tragedy of the foolish virgins is the tragedy of those who confuse appearance with union—who bear the name Christian but live as though salvation were a certificate, not a covenant.

Look honestly at your own heart. Are there places where the flame has gone out? Have you mistaken knowledge of doctrine for intimacy with God, or emotion for transformation? Have you let resentment, lust, or fear siphon away the oil of grace? None of this need end in despair. The Bridegroom is near precisely to refill what you have lost. He carries His own flask of mercy and is not stingy with it. Even a flicker can become a blaze when touched by His breath.

Now let the contemplation turn outward. The waiting for Christ is not passive. The Church keeps watch by loving the world He died to save. Every act of service, every kindness to the poor, every hour spent in prayer is oil added to the communal lamp of the Body of Christ. The Bridegroom wants a luminous Bride—a Church radiant with compassion, chaste in doctrine, awake to the suffering around her. You participate in that radiance every time you forgive, every time you speak truth with gentleness, every time you bless an enemy.

In a world addicted to distraction, keeping watch means reclaiming silence. Turn off the noise for a few moments each day and let the Spirit breathe in the stillness. That is where oil is gathered. In a culture of instant gratification, keeping watch means learning patience—choosing prayer instead of impulse, intercession instead of complaint. In an age that confuses pleasure with meaning, keeping watch means guarding purity, both of body and intention. Vigilance is not fear; it is love that refuses to grow lazy.

You may wonder whether your small flame matters. It does. One lamp can keep another from losing heart. When your neighbour's faith flickers, your steady light becomes their consolation. When yours wanes, another's devotion sustains you. That is why we gather at the altar week after week: many lamps becoming one flame. The Eucharist is the oil press of the Church—the place where crushed hearts are turned into fuel for divine fire. Every time you receive the Body and Blood of Christ, the Bridegroom fills your vessel anew, whispering, *Do not let this light go out.*

The delay of His coming is no reason for apathy; it is the space in which holiness grows. God does not test us by absence but trains us through waiting. Every prayer answered slowly teaches endurance; every silence in the dark becomes the soil of trust. When faith feels dry, remember that oil thickens in stillness. The longer the waiting, the purer the love becomes. The wise virgins are not anxious; they are peaceful, because they know the Bridegroom will come exactly when love is ready.

Let that readiness take flesh in daily habits. Keep a small rule of life: prayer at dawn, examination at dusk, charity whenever possible. Fast from complaint. Practice gratitude until it becomes instinct. Visit the sick. Defend the unborn. Give alms secretly. Forgive before you are asked. These are not random virtues—they are how lamps stay lit. Holiness is simply love sustained through time.

And when the night feels too long, remember that every dawn is a rehearsal for His return. The morning light spilling over the horizon is the first gleam of that eternal day when no lamp will be needed, because the Lamb Himself will be our light. Until then, guard your flame. Let it burn quietly through joy and sorrow, through failure and recovery, until it merges with His.

Now rest in silence for a moment and let the parable become prayer.

> Lord Jesus, Bridegroom of my soul,

## THE TEN VIRGINS (MT 25:1–13)

You have delayed not to abandon me, but to awaken me.
I confess the places where my lamp has grown dim,
where prayer has withered and love grown cold.
Come into the darkness of my heart,
fill me again with the oil of Your Spirit.
Teach me to keep watch not with fear but with desire.
Let my waiting become worship,
my obedience become light for those who stumble.
Give me grace to tend the flame each day—
in the tenderness I show, in the truth I speak,
in the patience I practice when Your silence tests me.
Make me one of the wise who love You quietly,
whose lamps never go out because You keep them burning.
When I fall asleep in weariness, wake me with Your mercy.
When I hear the midnight cry, let my heart leap with joy, not terror.
And when the door opens at last,
let me recognise Your voice and run to You,
carrying only what cannot be lost—the fire of Your love within me.

Remain now for a breath in that stillness. The night is deep, but the stars are many. Somewhere beyond your sight, the Bridegroom walks the path toward you. His delay is almost over. The oil burns quietly; the light holds steady. When He comes, it will not be with thunder, but with the tenderness of one long awaited. And in that moment, all watching will end, and the feast of joy will begin.

# Epilogue

### The Night Between Parables

The stories end, yet they do not finish.

The words spoken beside Galilee still move beneath the surface of the world, glowing like coals beneath ash. Every age has tried to tame them into morals, yet they continue to breathe—unpredictable, untiring, impossible to contain. They speak again each time a heart listens, each time a conscience stirs, each time the old words ignite new obedience.

The Kingdom that began as seed is still germinating. The banquet has been announced but not yet served. The lamps burn through a long vigil whose dawn has not arrived. Between revelation and fulfilment lies this sacred interval—the night of faith. It is not emptiness but expectancy, the silence in which love proves itself faithful. What the world calls delay, heaven calls invitation.

The disciples once left those crowds with more questions than answers. They carried fragments of parables like embers cupped in their hands. Over time, the wind of the Spirit fanned them into flame: the seed became the Church, the field became the world, and the Word kept multiplying. We walk now in that same unfolding. The parables still interpret our days. We are the soil being tested, the lamp being trimmed, the guests still summoned to the table.

Every parable is a lamp set in the dark. Its light is measured not by brilliance but by endurance. Some fade into sentiment; others burn on in hidden lives—the mother forgiving, the priest persevering, the believer praying unseen. The true listener tends that flame in secret, trusting that when dawn comes, the stories will be fulfilled not in commentary but in sight. Their fulfilment will not be read but revealed.

For the Kingdom's final chapter has not yet been written. It waits beyond language, where all metaphors melt into the reality they foretold. There, the seed and the harvest, the sower and the soil, the banquet and the guests, the Bridegroom and the Bride, will be one. The Word who once spoke in riddles will speak plainly, and every story will find its ending in His face.

Until that day, the wind that carried His voice across Galilee still moves. It rustles through Scripture, through the sacraments, through the faithful who keep watch. It calls across the long night: *Do not let the flame go out.* For the Word has not finished speaking, and the fire has not ceased to burn.

## The Kingdom Consummated

The first half of *Hidden Fire* has traced the Kingdom's arrival: seed sown, mercy offered, invitation given, lamps lit against the dark. Yet the story of the Kingdom is not only about revelation; it is also about reckoning. The same love that invites must one day separate. The same light that warms will, at last, expose. The parables that follow speak of that unveiling—of talents trusted and accounted for, of sheep and goats, of workers and wages, of mercy weighing justice.

If these earlier chapters have taught us how to hear, the next will teach us how to answer. The Bridegroom's delay is nearly over; the Master is at the door. The parables of judgment are not threats but promises that holiness will have the final word. In them, the fire hidden in every story bursts into open flame.

Volume II will therefore move from Revelation to Consummation—from the Word scattered through fields to the Word enthroned in glory. It will show how the mercy glimpsed in parable becomes the justice of love fulfilled, and how every seed of obedience sown in this life will bloom in the next.

For now, the night remains. The lamps tremble but do not fail. The wind carries the same voice that once crossed the water:

# HIDDEN FIRE

*"Watch therefore, for you know neither the day nor the hour."*
The dawn is nearer than we think.
The fire is still hidden—but rising.
The Sower still walks His field.
Listen—He is near.

# Appendix A: The Seven-Fold Framework of Interpretation

The parables of Christ do not yield their meaning to haste.

They open, as the Kingdom itself opens, by degrees—seed to sprout, sprout to flame, flame to fruit. To hear them rightly is to walk a path of unfolding revelation, where story becomes symbol, symbol becomes theology, and theology becomes prayer.

The structure used throughout *Hidden Fire* follows this sacred movement in seven stages. It is not a mechanical formula but a liturgical rhythm, mirroring the way divine truth approaches the human heart.

### 1. The Word Spoken — Hearing in the First Century

Every parable began as sound. Before it was Scripture, it was air and voice—the Word breaking into the noise of the world. This first movement restores the scene: the dust, the crowd, the mood, the question that drew the parable forth. The aim is not to retell but to *re-hear*, to stand again on Galilee's shore as the words first fell.

### 2. The Surface Story — The Parable as Event

Revelation enters through realism. Each parable is a credible moment in the life of first-century Israel: sowers and merchants, masters and servants, fathers and sons. To rebuild that world—its economy, customs, and expectations—is to feel the Gospel's first sting. The divine hides in the ordinary until the ordinary breaks.

### 3. The Hidden Fire — Symbolism and Theological Depth

Here the parable's imagery is examined until its inner flame appears. Language, context, and theology converge. This section unfolds in four internal movements:

**a) Text, Translation, and Literary Context:** the precision of words—Greek and Hebrew nuances, syntax, rhythm, placement within the evangelist's narrative.

**b) Theological Interpretation:** the doctrine implicit in image; anthropology, grace, sin, and salvation seen through story.

**c) Typological and Intertextual Parallels:** the Old Testament roots that flower in Christ—the echoes of Genesis, Exodus, Psalms, and Prophets.

**d) Patristic and Theological Synthesis:** the chorus of the Fathers and Doctors, who read these stories as sacraments of meaning.

In this fourfold blaze, exegesis becomes theology on fire.

### 4. The Shock and the Turn — The Scandal of Grace

Every parable contains a rupture—the moment when expectation collapses and grace overturns logic. This is the instant the listener either resists or converts. The parable's sting is its mercy: it wounds presumption to heal perception. Here the reader is meant to feel the reversal that once silenced the crowd.

### 5. The Revelation in the Son — Christological Fulfilment

All parables converge in the Person who told them. Each image—seed, lamp, shepherd, treasure—finds its centre in Christ Himself. The fifth movement unveils how the story is ultimately *about Him*: the Sower who sows His own life, the Samaritan who descends from heaven's road, the Bridegroom who delays until the Cross. The Word reveals the Word.

### 6. The Word for Our Age — Discipleship in the Present Tense

The parables are not archaeological relics but mirrors for the modern soul. In this stage, their ancient light is allowed to fall on contemporary idols—greed, distraction, fear, self-sufficiency. Theology becomes ethics;

grace becomes decision. The same Kingdom once hidden in fields now presses against the heart of every age.

### 7. Hearing that Becomes Doing — Contemplation and Practice

Revelation ends as it began: in encounter. Exegesis must flower into obedience, doctrine into devotion. This final movement gathers understanding into prayer, leading the reader to interior conversion. Knowledge bows before love; study becomes silence. The story that once entered through the ear now lives through the will.

## The Logic of the Seven

These seven stages correspond to the rhythm of salvation itself:

| Revelation Stage | Salvation Parallel |
| --- | --- |
| 1. Word Spoken | Creation—light uttered into being |
| 2. Surface Story | Covenant—God entering history |
| 3. Hidden Fire | Prophecy—truth veiled in image |
| 4. Shock and Turn | Conversion—judgment and mercy meeting |
| 5. Revelation in the Son | Incarnation—the Word made flesh |
| 6. Word for Our Age | Mission—the Gospel alive in time |
| 7. Hearing that Becomes Doing | Sanctification—love perfected in action |

Thus the hermeneutic becomes doxology. The structure is not commentary upon Scripture alone but participation in its movement—from hearing to holiness, from symbol to communion.

*The Word still speaks; the fire still burns. The listener's task is to stay until both become one.*

# Bibliography

### I. Primary and Patristic Sources

Aquinas, Thomas. *Catena Aurea: Commentary on the Four Gospels.* Translated by John Henry Newman. Oxford: John Henry Parker, 1841.

———. *Summa Theologiae.* Translated by the Fathers of the English Dominican Province. London: Burns Oates, 1912.

Athanasius, St. *On the Incarnation.* Translated and edited by John Behr. Yonkers, NY: St Vladimir's Seminary Press, 2011.

Augustine, St. *Confessions.* Translated by Henry Chadwick. Oxford: Oxford University Press, 1998.

———. *Sermons on the New Testament Lessons.* In *Nicene and Post-Nicene Fathers,* First Series, Vol. 6. Edited by Philip Schaff. Buffalo, NY: Christian Literature Publishing Co., 1888.

Basil the Great, St. *Homilies on Wealth and Social Justice.* Translated by C. Paul Sheridan. Crestwood, NY: St Vladimir's Seminary Press, 2012.

Bede the Venerable. *Homilies on the Gospels.* Translated by Lawrence T. Martin and David Hurst. Kalamazoo, MI: Cistercian Publications, 1991.

Chrysostom, St. John. *Homilies on the Gospel of St Matthew.* In *Nicene and Post-Nicene Fathers,* First Series, Vol. 10. Edited by Philip Schaff. Buffalo, NY: Christian Literature Publishing Co., 1888.

Ephrem the Syrian, St. *Hymns on Faith.* Translated by Jeffrey T. Wickes. Washington, DC: Catholic University of America Press, 2015.

Evagrius Ponticus. *Chapters on Prayer.* In *The Philokalia,* Vol. 1. Translated by G. E. H. Palmer, Philip Sherrard, and Kallistos Ware. London: Faber & Faber, 1979.

Gregory the Great, St. *Moralia in Job.* Translated by John Henry Parker.

Oxford: John Henry Parker, 1844.

Gregory of Nyssa, St. *The Life of Moses.* Translated by Abraham J. Malherbe and Everett Ferguson. New York: Paulist Press, 1978.

Irenaeus, St. *Against Heresies.* Translated by Dominic J. Unger. New York: Paulist Press, 1992.

Jerome, St. *Commentary on Matthew.* In *Patrologia Latina,* Vol. 26. Paris: Migne, 1845.

Macarius, Pseudo-. *Spiritual Homilies.* Translated by George A. Maloney. Mahwah, NJ: Paulist Press, 1992.

Maximus the Confessor, St. *Ambigua to John.* Translated by Nicholas Constas. Cambridge, MA: Harvard University Press, 2014.

———. *Four Hundred Texts on Love.* In *The Philokalia,* Vol. 2. London: Faber & Faber, 1981.

Origen, *On First Principles.* Translated by G. W. Butterworth. New York: Harper & Row, 1966.

———. *Commentary on Matthew.* In *Patrologia Graeca,* Vol. 13. Paris: Migne, 1857.

The Holy Bible: *Revised Standard Version – Catholic Edition.* San Francisco: Ignatius Press, 2006.

The Catechism of the Catholic Church. 2nd ed. Vatican City: Libreria Editrice Vaticana, 1997.

The Divine Liturgy of St John Chrysostom (Melkite usage). Newton, MA: Sophia Press, 2009.

The Philokalia: *The Complete Text,* Vols. 1–4. Translated by G. E. H. Palmer, Philip Sherrard, and Kallistos Ware. London: Faber & Faber, 1979–1995.

The Second Vatican Council. *Dei Verbum (Dogmatic Constitution on Divine Revelation).* Vatican City, 1965.

———. *Gaudium et Spes (Pastoral Constitution on the Church in the Modern World).* Vatican City, 1965.

———. *Lumen Gentium (Dogmatic Constitution on the Church).* Vatican City, 1964.

———. *Sacrosanctum Concilium (Constitution on the Sacred Liturgy).*

Vatican City, 1963.

## II. Secondary and Modern Works

Barron, Robert. *The Priority of Christ: Toward a Postliberal Catholicism.* Grand Rapids, MI: Baker Academic, 2007.

Benedict XVI (Joseph Ratzinger). *Jesus of Nazareth: From the Baptism in the Jordan to the Transfiguration.* San Francisco: Ignatius Press, 2007.

———. *Jesus of Nazareth: Holy Week – From the Entrance into Jerusalem to the Resurrection.* San Francisco: Ignatius Press, 2011.

Balthasar, Hans Urs von. *The Glory of the Lord, Vol. I: Seeing the Form.* San Francisco: Ignatius Press, 1982.

———. *Theo-Drama: Theological Dramatic Theory,* Vols. 1–5. San Francisco: Ignatius Press, 1988–1998.

Bailey, Kenneth E. *Jesus Through Middle Eastern Eyes: Cultural Studies in the Gospels.* Downers Grove, IL: IVP Academic, 2008.

Blomberg, Craig L. *Interpreting the Parables.* Downers Grove, IL: IVP Academic, 2012.

Brown, Raymond E. *The Birth of the Messiah.* New York: Doubleday, 1993.

———. *The Death of the Messiah.* 2 vols. New York: Doubleday, 1994.

Cavins, Jeff. *The Activated Disciple: Taking Your Faith to the Next Level.* West Chester, PA: Ascension Press, 2018.

Daniélou, Jean. *The Lord of History.* London: Longmans, Green & Co., 1958.

de Lubac, Henri. *Catholicism: Christ and the Common Destiny of Man.* Translated by Lancelot C. Sheppard and Sister Elizabeth Englund. San Francisco: Ignatius Press, 1988.

———. *Paradoxe et Mystère de l'Église.* Paris: Aubier, 1967.

Gray, Tim. *Mission of the Messiah: On the Gospel of Luke.* Steubenville, OH: Emmaus Road Publishing, 1998.

Hahn, Scott. *A Father Who Keeps His Promises: God's Covenant Love in Scripture.* Cincinnati, OH: St Anthony Messenger Press, 1998.

———. *Kinship by Covenant: A Canonical Approach to the Fulfillment of God's Saving Promises*. New Haven: Yale University Press, 2009.

Jeremias, Joachim. *The Parables of Jesus*. Rev. ed. London: SCM Press, 1963.

———. *Jerusalem in the Time of Jesus*. London: SCM Press, 1969.

Lossky, Vladimir. *The Mystical Theology of the Eastern Church*. Crestwood, NY: St Vladimir's Seminary Press, 1997.

Pitre, Brant. *Jesus and the Jewish Roots of the Eucharist: Unlocking the Secrets of the Last Supper*. New York: Image Books, 2011.

———. *The Case for Jesus: The Biblical and Historical Evidence for Christ*. New York: Image Books, 2016.

Snodgrass, Klyne R. *Stories with Intent: A Comprehensive Guide to the Parables of Jesus*. 2nd ed. Grand Rapids, MI: Eerdmans, 2018.

Sri, Edward. *Into His Likeness: Be Transformed as a Disciple of Christ*. San Francisco: Ignatius Press, 2018.

Wright, N. T. *Jesus and the Victory of God*. London: SPCK, 1996.

———. *Simply Jesus: A New Vision of Who He Was, What He Did, and Why He Matters*. New York: HarperOne, 2011.

John Paul II. *Redemptor Hominis*. Vatican City: Libreria Editrice Vaticana, 1979.

———. *Veritatis Splendor*. Vatican City: Libreria Editrice Vaticana, 1993.

Pope Francis. *Evangelii Gaudium*. Vatican City: Libreria Editrice Vaticana, 2013.

Bonaventure, St. *The Mind's Journey into God*. Translated by Stephen F. Brown. Indianapolis: Hackett Publishing, 1993.

Anselm of Canterbury, St. *Cur Deus Homo*. Translated by Sidney Norton Deane. Chicago: Open Court, 1903.

## III. Reference and Tools

Aland, Kurt, et al., eds. *Novum Testamentum Graece*. 28th ed. Stuttgart: Deutsche Bibelgesellschaft, 2012.

Bauer, Walter, Frederick W. Danker, William F. Arndt, and F. Wilbur

Gingrich. *A Greek–English Lexicon of the New Testament and Other Early Christian Literature (BDAG).* 3rd ed. Chicago: University of Chicago Press, 2000.

Cross, F. L., and E. A. Livingstone, eds. *The Oxford Dictionary of the Christian Church.* 3rd ed. Oxford: Oxford University Press, 2005.

Liddell, Henry G., and Robert Scott. *A Greek–English Lexicon.* 9th ed. Oxford: Clarendon Press, 1996.

Strong, James. *The Exhaustive Concordance of the Bible.* Nashville: Abingdon Press, 1890.

The United States Conference of Catholic Bishops. *Lectionary for Mass.* Washington, DC: USCCB, 1998.

The New Jerome Biblical Commentary. Edited by Raymond E. Brown, Joseph A. Fitzmyer, and Roland E. Murphy. Englewood Cliffs, NJ: Prentice Hall, 1990.

# About the Author

Matthew Sardon is a Catholic author from Melbourne, Australia, whose work is shaped by the depth and breadth of the Church's intellectual and spiritual tradition. Formed through extensive theological study within the University of Divinity and nourished by years immersed in both the Roman and Byzantine rites, he brings to his writing a unified Catholic vision rooted in Scripture, illuminated by the Fathers, and sustained by the Church's liturgical life.

His research and writing centre on biblical theology, patristic anthropology, and the mystery of theosis—how divine grace heals, elevates, and transfigures the human person. He is committed to making the Church's ancient wisdom accessible to the contemporary world, offering clarity and strength where many experience confusion and fragmentation.

Matthew is actively engaged in Catholic ministry, contributing to teaching, catechesis, adult formation, and parish mission. His work as a speaker and presenter reflects the same passion found in his writing: to awaken faith, deepen understanding, and help others encounter the transforming love of God.

**You can connect with me on:**
🌐 https://matthewsardon.com

www.ingramcontent.com/pod-product-compliance
Lightning Source LLC
Chambersburg PA
CBHW060107230426
43661CB00033B/1420/J